D1124500

The Fate of Texas

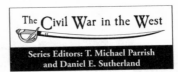

The Civil War in the West

Series Editors: T. Michael Parrish
and Daniel E. Sutherland

The Fate of Texas

The Civil War and the Lone Star State

Edited by Charles D. Grear

The University of Arkansas Press • Fayetteville • 2008

Copyright © 2008 by The University of Arkansas Press

All rights reserved
Manufactured in the United States of America

ISBN-10: 1-55728-883-6
ISBN-13: -978-1-55728-883-7

12   11   10   09   08   5   4   3   2   1

Text design by Ellen Beeler

⊗ The paper used in this publication meets the minimum requirements of the
American National Standard for Permanence of Paper for Printed Library Materials
Z39.48-1984.

Library of Congress Cataloging-in-Publication Data

The fate of Texas : the Civil War and the Lone Star State / edited by Charles D. Grear.
    p. cm.
  Includes bibliographical references and index.
  ISBN-13: 978-1-55728-883-7 (cloth : alk. paper)
  ISBN-10: 1-55728-883-6 (cloth : alk. paper)
  1. Texas—History—Civil War, 1861–1865—Social aspects. 2. War and society—
  Texas. 3. Texas—History—1846–1950. 4. United States—History—Civil War,
  1861–1865—Social aspects. 5. United States—History—Civil War, 1861–1865—
  Influence. I. Grear, Charles D., 1976–
  E580.F37 2008
  973.7'464--dc22
                                                                2008026299

For Chad.
My brother,
my inspiration,
and my hero.

Contents

Illustrations and Maps

Illustrations

Maps

Series Editors' Preface

The Civil War in the West has a single goal: to promote historical writing about the war in the western states and territories. It focuses most particularly on the Trans-Mississippi theater, which consisted of Missouri, Arkansas, Texas, most of Louisiana (west of the Mississippi River), Indian Territory (modern-day Oklahoma), and Arizona Territory (two-fifths of modern-day Arizona and New Mexico), but also encompasses adjacent states, such as Kansas, Tennessee, and Mississippi, that directly influenced the Trans-Mississippi war. It is a wide swath to be sure, but one too often ignored by historians and consequently too little understood and appreciated.

Topically the series embraces all aspects of the wartime story. Military history in its many guises, from the strategies of generals to the daily lives of common soldiers, forms an important part of that story, but so too do the numerous and complex political, economic, social, and diplomatic dimensions of the war. The series also provides a variety of perspectives on these topics. Most importantly, it offers the best in modern scholarship, with thoughtful, challenging monographs. Secondly, it presents new editions of important books that have gone out of print. And thirdly, it premieres expertly edited correspondence, diaries, reminiscences, and other writings by participants in the war.

It is a formidable challenge, but by focusing on some of the least familiar dimensions of the conflict, The Civil War in the West significantly broadens our understanding of the nation's most pivotal and dramatic story.

Charles Grear's edited work, *The Fate of Texas: The Civil War in the Lone Star State,* is a collection of eleven essays written by able and creative scholars that analyzes virtually all levels of society in Texas during the Civil War and features the public memory of the war in the modern era. As Grear states in his introduction, "The greatest strength of this anthology is its scope." Also noteworthy is the fact that all of the essays reflect cutting-edge research and critical understanding from leading historians, and few have been published previously.

This essay collection highlights a level of involvement by Texans in the Civil War that is too often neglected by historians and presents Texas as a decidedly southern, yet in many ways unusual, state seriously committed to and deeply affected by the Confederate war effort in a multitude of crucial ways. All members of Texas society (including governmental leaders, military commanders, soldiers, women, and slaves) experienced the pressures and stresses of war. The contributors to this volume illustrate those stresses by employing a variety of valuable categories of analysis, including politics, military strategy, gender, race, patriotism, class divisions, ethnic identity, emotion and psychology, and post-war reactions to defeat. Far more than previous collections of essays on Civil War Texas—all of which are now badly outdated—this book offers a complex, multidimensional, yet thoroughly accessible set of major contributions to the historiography of the war. *The Fate of Texas* is a much needed and important addition to the Civil War in the West series.

T. Michael Parrish
Daniel E. Sutherland
Series Editors

Acknowledgments

Many people helped me develop this book. Dr. Donald S. Frazier initiated the project, and thanks to an inquisitive phone call I made, he granted me the anthology. Lawrence J. Malley, the director of the University of Arkansas Press, gave of his time (and patience) to make this work possible. Profs. Steven E. Woodworth and Joseph Dawson provided guidance throughout the many stages of the project. Dr. Kenneth W. Howell, my colleague and good friend, encouraged and advised me during our numerous commutes to campus. Dr. Alexander Mendoza, my dear friend and mentor from our days as graduate students, consulted with me over the many issues related to this project. Without the help of the faculty and staff of the History Department at the U.S. Military Academy at West Point, especially Maj. Jason "J. P." Clark, during my three-week stay, I would not have finished this project on time. I owe my deepest gratitude to all my contributors. Their cooperation and dedication to this book made it a joy to work on—more importantly it would not exist without them. Thank you all. I cannot forget my family, my parents, brothers Shawn and Chad, my sister-in-law Cynthia, and niece Kaitlyn, who all supported me throughout this process. I would especially like to thank my wife, Edna, for her patience and my step-daughter Haley for assistance with the maps.

Introduction

In the spring of 1861, alarms calling for war spread across the Lone Star State. "Men of Texas, Look to Your Arms!" exclaimed Ben McCulloch, hero of many of Texas's conflicts, in Corsicana's *Navaro Express*. He concluded his appeal for soldiers using the history and memory of his past struggles for Texas: "Texians! remember your former victories, and prepare to march to others. You won your independence from Mexico, and will again do it from a more tyrannical foe."[1] With this call and many others just like it, numerous young men enlisted in the army, and Texas plunged headfirst into the bloodiest conflict in American history. Texans realized that the fate of their state lay in the results on the battle-field, which created a time of uncertainty. What was Texas's role in the conflict? How would the men fare during the fighting? What would life be like on the home front? Once the conflict concludes, what affect would it have on the veterans and how would it be remembered?

During the American Civil War, Texas faced similar obstacles as the rest of the South but had additional, unique issues. Unlike the rest of the emerging Confederacy, the Lone Star State still had a frontier and a large number of U.S. soldiers within its borders to maintain the relative peace between settlers and American Indians. Although the seat of war was hundreds of miles away on the other side of the Mississippi River, Texans not only participated in those campaigns but still had to defend their frontier homesteads. Being far removed from the balance of the Confederacy, Texans fought farthest from their homes. Three regiments, part of the popularly known Hood's Texas Brigade, served as the shock troops of Gen. Robert E. Lee's Army of Northern Virginia. Numerous other regiments served in the western theater, defending Confederate territory between the Mississippi River and the Appalachian Mountains, the most famous in this region being Terry's Texas Rangers. The state itself was vulnerable on every front, especially along its long coastline and its borders with Louisiana, Arkansas, and the Indian Territory. Although this threat was always present, and the Federals did manage to capture some territory, there was never any prolonged Union occupation in the state. Early in the war, Texans became the only Southerners who attempted to add territory to the Confederacy with the campaign to capture the Arizona and New Mexico Territory (with further ambitions to capture California and northern Mexico). Texans thus fought in more places than men from any other state, both North and South.

With its diverse population, composed mainly of recent migrants from throughout the United States and immigrants from northern and western Europe and Mexico, Texas also experienced internal dissent from Unionists in the north and recently arrived Germans in the Hill Country. Additionally it was the only Southern state that bordered a foreign country, Mexico, which Texans not only relied on for trade but also harbored raiding bandits like Juan Cortina. It was near this border that the last major engagement of the Civil War took place between Union and Confederate Texans at Palmito Ranch. Although the Lone Star State escaped the war relatively untouched, all its people—men, women, children, African Americans, Tejanos, and Germans—were forever changed by the events that transpired. This influenced the way Texans viewed the war and reacted to the consequences of defeat, which we still try to understand today.

This anthology brings together a collection of essays by noted historians on Texas in the Civil War and by junior scholars now contributing to the field. Their research provides a new understanding of the role and reactions of Texas and Texans to the Civil War. The greatest strength of this book is its scope. Contributors provide new perspectives on Texas in the Civil War that historians have generally overlooked or never explored before, ranging from new aspects in military, social, and cultural history to public history and historical memory. These studies present important facets of Texas history that can help us understand better what Texans were thinking and how the state affected the history of the United States.

The first chapter is broad in scope by placing Texas' role in the Civil War in the Confederacy's overall strategy of the conflict, an aspect never examined in its entirety. Joseph G. Dawson III contends that Texas related to Confederate national strategy in four ways: the New Mexico Campaign, the defense of the port of Galveston, frontier and border defense, and the development of a railroad system in the Southwest. Central to this study is Pres. Jefferson Davis's interpretation of the state's role in the overall strategy of the Confederacy and how the status and significance of Texas changed or shifted between 1861 and 1865. Dawson clearly demonstrates that Texas and the Trans-Mississippi as a whole were not just an afterthought to the Confederate government and army but a vital component to the wide-ranging goals of the Southern nation.

The following two chapters take a more intimate look at Texas soldiers. Beginning with Bell I. Wiley's works during the 1940s and 1950s, historians started examining the soldiers' experiences, concerns, and lifestyles. Yet common Texans only began to receive scholarly attention in the 1990s. Richard Lowe's essay examines the nature of the relationship between Texas Confederate soldiers and their wives and children. Were these men the cold, distant, and forbidding authoritarians only minimally involved in the nurturing of their children that some historians have identified as the typical American father of the nineteenth century? Or were they, as other scholars have insisted, warm, supportive, affectionate, and directly involved in the lives of their children? The same general question applies to the soldiers' relationships with their wives. Were these men austere patriarchs who regarded their spouses as domestic servants who also occasionally bore children? Or did they have close, affectionate ties to their wives and accord them respect as partners in family affairs? Through the use of wartime letters and diaries of Texas soldiers from all three theaters of the war, Lowe shatters the preconceived attitudes toward nineteenth-century men.[2]

In his essay Charles D. Grear examines the reasons Texans left the Lone Star State to risk their lives east of the Mississippi River. Why these men fought in the Civil War is a topic historians have attempted to study through many different lenses. Very few people have examined Texans in particular, especially the reasons they fought so far from their home and hearths. Before the secession crisis, waves of migrants from the eastern United States settled within the borders of Texas. But the new arrivals never severed their attachments to their former hometowns and family members in the East. Maintaining these ties allowed these individuals to feel that they had more than one home. When the war started, these attachments heavily influenced Texans in their decision to fight and which unit they would join. The remoteness of the state from the seat of war increased their desire to return east and help defend the towns they were raised in and the extended families they left behind. By analyzing the most famous Texas units, Hood's Texas Brigade and Terry's Texas Rangers, as well as other of the state's commands, Grear uncovers these men's desire to fight east of the Mississippi River.

The Civil War not only affected the lives of those Texans in the army but also those remaining on the home front. The next four chapters examine events and people in the Lone Star State during the war. Although there is considerable research already on many aspects of the home front, these essays reexamine, elaborate, or present a modern approach to older topics. With newly uncovered documents, Richard B. McCaslin reexamines the Great Hanging at Gainesville, the greatest wartime atrocity in American history. Texas militia on October 1, 1862, fanned out through several counties along the Red River, arresting more than two hundred suspected Unionists. In Gainesville, the seat of government for Cooke County, vigilantes executed at least forty-two suspects for conspiring to commit treason and foment an insurrection. Few of the victims had plotted to usurp Confederate authority, and most were innocent of abolitionist sentiments, but their pleas made little difference. Others were lynched in nearby counties as well, but the Great Hanging claimed the most lives, and Gainesville became the community most closely identified with such atrocities in subsequent accounts. This event climaxed years of vigilantism against persons accused of fostering disorder in North Texas. Not only was it the most spectacular of several such occurrences in Civil War Texas, it was also the largest mass hanging in U.S. history and attracted much contemporary notice. An inquiry into the circumstances surrounding the Great Hanging offers useful insights into disaffection in the Confederacy.[3]

The subject of women in Texas during the Civil War has been largely ignored in the past few decades. Angela Boswell uses courthouse documents and private letters to examine the lives of and the Civil War's influence on women in Colorado County. Like other Texans, Colorado County citizens began the Civil War believing that militaristic adventures available only to men would further define gender roles and assumptions. Men would fulfill their duties to "protect" their wives against the encroaching enemy, while women would wait at home and keep the domestic hearth burning. Southern leaders initially relied upon women merely to use their influence at home to encourage men to enlist, to support the war effort, and to contribute to the cause by making flags and clothing. But as the war required more and more men to leave the county, women were forced to take on responsibilities that challenged rather than enhanced gender roles and the assumptions about female abilities and nature. Women took over the duties left on farms and in businesses. Married women found that they had to take care of the financial and public duties of the family. Single women, and war-widowed wives, increasingly took the burdens of public activities upon themselves because they could not find male relatives to do so. Some of these women, alone and acting independently for the first time, made choices that their husbands would not have approved (such as taking new lovers). Others decided that they were willing to make their own choices even after the men returned. Overall, women in Colorado County, whether married or single, entered the public arena in large numbers during the Civil War and acted more independently than ever before.[4]

The analysis of refugeed slaves also has received nominal attention. Dale Baum here provides the first overarching account of this phenomenon in Texas. He presents a statistical analysis, based primarily on lists of 1860, 1861, 1862, 1863, and 1864 "Negroes Taxed," of the best estimate of the number of slaves brought into Texas from other slave states for safekeeping during the war and pinpoints geographically the counties where the highest concentrations of bondsmen were relocated. In a more qualitative manner, he combed through numerous sources, ranging from newspapers to personal correspondence, for all references of slaves being taken to Texas. Additionally Baum provides an estimation about how many slaves and former owners left Texas immediately after the war, based on ratios of "Negroes Taxed in 1864" and blacks registered to vote in 1869, speculating from there about the influence of those who remained on local Reconstruction politics.[5]

In the next chapter Walter D. Kamphoefner reexamines the attitudes of Texas Germans toward the Confederacy and the related issues of slavery and race, taking issue with Terry Jordan's interpretation that these residents were "unremarkable" in their attitudes toward slavery and secession. Kamphoefner brings four types of new evidence to bear: patterns of German (non)slaveholding in relation to their economic status, German voting in the secession referendum of 1861, evidence from German letters written during the Civil War, and German support of the Republican Party during Reconstruction. In all four of these areas, German Texans stood apart from most Anglos in their attitudes and behavior but, from the limited evidence available, showed considerable similarity with many other European immigrants in Texas.[6]

The two subsequent chapters represent the first studies on how the Civil War affected Texas soldiers following Appomattox. Randolph B. Campbell examines this influence on the lives of Texas soldiers after they returned home from war. Did these veterans tend to return to their original homes, receive warm welcomes, and resume ordinary lives? What toll did the physical and psychological scars of war take on these men during the postwar years? Did veterans wield notable political power in the postwar South? Did they come to enjoy a special social status in their home communities? Campbell seeks answers to these important questions by examining Harrison County as a test case.[7]

Carl H. Moneyhon's essay challenges a major part of the standard history of Reconstruction Texas by examining if Texans were more defiant in the postwar years than other Southerners because they had never suffered invasion nor really felt defeat. This view was given currency to a large degree by U.S. Army officers stationed in the Lone Star State after the war, particularly Maj. Gen. David S. Stanley. Moneyhon looks at contemporary letters and diaries to determine the reaction of Texans to the war's end, focusing on both soldiers and civilians. His review is not limited to those who remained in the state during the war but also considers the reactions of those soldiers who fought elsewhere and returned to Texas. By examining the letters of those serving in all three theaters of the war, Moneyhon presents the true reactions of Texans in the later years of the conflict.[8]

The concluding essays consider the resonance of the Civil War on the historical memory of Texans and the war's interpretation in public venues, a topic that recently is receiving national attention and only in the past decade by Texas historians.[9] Alexander Mendoza studies the meanings and conflicting implications of the George Washington Littlefield Memorial on the University of Texas at Austin campus. Even though the fountain and six statues to the purported heroes of the South, which flank the pedestrian pathways leading up to the main building, hold a prominent place in the university's design, the truth of the matter is that most students have no idea how the Jefferson Davis statue and other Confederate monuments made their way to their location on the South Mall. To Littlefield and his supporters, the monuments meant a commemoration of their Confederate history and the South's proper place in the reunified nation. But to a growing number of students and observers during the late twentieth century, the monuments represented a racist past. Mendoza examines clashing visions of cultural history—from public monuments to public celebrations—in order to reveal important changes in how the memory of the Civil War and the Old South have been employed at the university. Setting the conflicts of Civil War memory within a social and cultural landscape, he traces how Texans have chosen to identify themselves and altered the meanings of the Civil War in various eras to fit their contemporary convictions. By providing such insight on the conflicting identities of Texans and their flagship university, this chapter illuminates how a Confederate veteran has influenced the university's historical outlook and shaped its architectural landscape.[10]

The final chapter, written by Julie Holcomb, provides a pioneering interpretation of the Civil War in museums and other public forums in Texas. Through discussions with curators and other public historians who have created memorials, exhibits, and other displays on the Civil War, Holcomb reveals how they have shaped the memory of Texas's role in the conflict. More importantly she shares some personal experiences about presenting Civil War history in a public venue that incorporates the latest research without alienating any group in Texas or American society. The relationship between museums and the general public over the volatile and sometimes personal interpretation of the war is extremely important to all historians, for such public forums are where scholars can influence those who are not attending college and may not be interested in reading history books.

The culmination of these essays displays the wealth and breadth of the history of Texas during the Civil War. Although historians have studied Texas in the Civil War for well over a century, there is still a plethora of topics that deserve greater attention, among them Tejanos in the Civil War, the common Texas soldier's interaction with Confederate Indians, the Texas State Troops, the role of religion among Texans, the controversial Texas Cotton Bureau, and obscure Texas units in the Trans-Mississippi such as Bee's Brigade (to name one). Only through continual research can the true extent of Texas's role in the Civil War be revealed. It is our hope that *The Fate of Texas: The Civil War and the Lone Star State,* the largest collection of original research on Texas in the Civil War to date, will serve as a stimulus for future studies.

Jefferson Davis, president of the
Confederate States of America.
Courtesy Library of Congress, Washington, D.C.

1

Texas, Jefferson Davis, and Confederate National Strategy

Joseph G. Dawson III

Historians have devoted increasing attention to the Confederacy's Trans-Mississippi region.[1] Especially since 1960, they have treated a range of Trans-Mississippi military, political, economic, and social topics. In studies of strategy in the Civil War, however, Texas is not mentioned or only gets passing notice.[2]

Texas held a complex place in Confederate strategy. First, in 1861 Pres. Jefferson Davis decided that the Confederacy ought to expand into the West. His background and strategic outlook played important parts in his decision to initiate a western offensive. Davis authorized that Texas serve as a base for the offensive and selected a general to command the campaign. But all other strategic matters related to the state ranked below the western offensive and national expansion, as far as the president was concerned.

Second, nine of the thirteen Confederate states, including Texas, had a coastline, and Davis's national strategy called for defending the coasts. The Confederacy's list of strategic assets included the port of Galveston, and Texas coastal defense became an issue of contention between the state government and the Davis administration. Galveston was significant economically and politically, but like New Orleans, due to other demands neither the state nor the national government filled the needs for the island's defense. In general, by necessity and choice defending the coast was underfunded and downplayed for Texas and the entire Confederacy.

Third, Confederate leaders relegated most of the frontier and border defense of Texas to the state. Indian attacks and Mexican outlaws crossing the Rio Grande presented no strategic threat to the Confederacy. Likewise, diplomacy and trade relations with Mexico slipped among national priorities, even to the point of leaving some official diplomatic matters to the Trans-Mississippi Department commander or Texas officials. Many Texans concluded that the Confederacy let down its citizens by neglecting the state's borders.

Other factors might have risen to national significance, such as the status of railroads and transporting cattle and cotton, but became regional and state matters after August 1863.

Meeting in the state capital of Austin, a town of around 3,500 people, a special convention announced in favor of secession on February 1, 1861, and Texas soon joined the Confederate States of America (CSA). The Lone Star State offered the possibility of contributing significantly to the new Southern nation. Although it ranked only ninth in population among the first eleven Confederate states, Texas showed great economic potential in cotton and cattle. Vast herds of livestock, deemed capable of feeding large armies, were prospective strategic and logistical assets.[3] Merchants stood ready to ship a bountiful cotton crop from Galveston. Welcoming large, deep-draft, slow ocean-going ships, Galveston's heavy traffic ranked it fifth among ports in the South. Although a railroad connected the port to the town of Houston (population about 4,800), limited railroad mileage in the state and a lack of locomotives, railcars, and materials to lay new tracks restricted sending Texas beef to the East. Galveston and San Antonio, two attractive cities that in 1860 contained around 7,000 and 8,000 people, rivaled the size of Atlanta, Georgia (8,000), and were about the same size or larger than other Southern states' capital cities, including Jackson, Mississippi (4,000); Baton Rouge, Louisiana (5,000); Raleigh, North Carolina (5,000); Columbia, South Carolina (8,000); and Montgomery, Alabama (8,000), the Confederacy's first capital.[4]

In Montgomery on February 18, 1861, Jefferson Davis took the oath as provisional president of the Confederate States of America. The new nation comprised six states, South Carolina, Georgia, Florida, Alabama, Mississippi, and Louisiana, soon joined by Texas. In ringing tones Davis asserted in his inaugural address that the Confederacy was "*moved by no interest or passion to invade the rights of others.*" Contemporary Americans from North, East, South, or West could have interpreted his remarks to mean that, as commander in chief, he did not intend to use an army or navy to force any state to join the new nation.[5] Naturally Davis wanted other states to join the Confederacy, and territories might be annexed as permitted by the provisional constitution.[6]

As in the United States, the Confederacy's president took primary responsibility for formulating national strategy, which always involved political choices. Strategy required decisions to allocate human and economic resources and deploy military forces in order to achieve the nation's political goals. In this case the goal was Confederate independence. In America numerous individuals offered strategic advice to presidents, including cabinet members (particularly the secretary of war), military officers, members of Congress, and state governors.

The president established a defensive strategy for the Confederacy. Critical of this policy, the *Richmond Examiner* lambasted him for a "defensive policy" that "not only cost us [the CSA] men, but it has cost us territory," specifically in western Virginia and Kentucky.[7] Framed not to antagonize other slave states, Davis's strategy may be summarized using phrases that the president himself employed when addressing the Confederate Congress on April 29, 1861: "we seek no conquest" of the Northern states; "all we ask is to be let alone." Stressing this view, biographer William Cooper concludes that Davis harbored no intent either "to capture territory" or "go beyond his borders" in 1861.[8]

Defense ranked high in Confederate strategic thinking, but as Davis looked for ways to capitalize on opportunities he also had to respond to Federal actions. In June, though worried about guarding what he called Virginia's "long and indefensible border," the president wrote to his brother: "Troops are daily arriving [near Richmond] from the South and I hope before long to be able to

The Strategic Location of Texas

Texas
Proposed Confederate Expansion
States Represented in the CSA Congress
Territories Claimed by the CSA

Charles D. Grear
New Braunfels, Texas

change from the defensive to an offensive attitude." He may have meant simply to shift to a local counterattack in Virginia rather than a broader offensive across the South, but such a statement indicated that the president was not thinking only in defensive terms. Of course, part of any adequate defense is developing reserves and supplies to launch counterattacks. Davis conveyed that perspective to Congress on November 18, 1861, stating that Confederate forces had responded "to roll back the tide of invasion from the border," ranging "from the shores of the Chesapeake to the confines of Missouri and Arizona." Part of that response came in September, when Confederate troops marched into Kentucky, a slave state, "a step which was justified not only by the necessities of self-defense on the part of the Confederate States, but also by a desire to aid the people of Kentucky."[9] Davis's initial focus on defense set the right tone.[10]

When the Confederates fired on Fort Sumter in Charleston, South Carolina, on April 12, other slave states, including Virginia, Tennessee, and North Carolina, went through a formal, though unofficial, process to secede. Historians discern that Virginia and Tennessee were crucial to the Confederate cause. Native state of six U.S. presidents, Virginia brought prestige as well as the naval base near Norfolk and the railroads and the huge Tredegar Iron Works of Richmond (prewar population of about 38,000, though it tripled in size) when a special convention voted for secession on April 17. The Confederacy's capital moved to Richmond in May. Tennessee seceded on June 8 and joined the Confederacy on July 22. The Volunteer State provided the lynchpin in the chain of Confederate states and boasted the industrial city of Nashville (30,000 population) and the river port of Memphis (22,000). Thousands of draft animals and bountiful crops filled the Tennessee countryside. North Carolina, wedged between Virginia, Tennessee, and South Carolina, seceded on May 20. It contributed substantial numbers of soldiers to the Southern nation as well as the port of Wilmington. The Confederacy was growing naturally by adding other slave states.[11]

The South and slavery grew together. The Confederacy's continued growth depended not only on adding the rest of the slave states but also western territories. Davis regarded the vast areas from Texas to the Pacific Ocean as a region where expansion was possible. Like most other American presidents before him, situated in a capital city in the East, Davis looked to the West with great interest. For instance, in 1850 he had delivered a lengthy speech in the U.S. Senate contending that slave labor was suitable for both mining and irrigated agriculture in the western territories. Serving as Pres. Franklin Pierce's secretary of war from 1853 to 1856, he had paid close attention to military activities in the West, and an army post had been named for him in West Texas. He also favored a route through the Southwest for a transcontinental railroad to California.[12]

Davis picked up the elements of strategy throughout his life. His views began to evolve from the time of his days at the U.S. Military Academy, where cadets trained to become lieutenants, the army's most junior officers. They appeared to have no need for courses devoted to strategy, but they discussed historical examples of generals and generalship, especially Napoleon Bonaparte. Evaluating West Point's records, historians debate the extent to which the academy's curriculum introduced antebellum cadets to the writings of Antoine Henri Jomini, a Swiss who had served as an officer in Napoleon's armies.[13] Jomini wrote numerous works of military analysis. In the chapter "Strategy" in his key book, *Summary of the Art of War*, Jomini discussed what he called "*the offensive-defensive*," an approach that meant "not to await passively" the enemy's attacks. Instead, a thoughtful leader must be watchful and willing to take counteractions that "may be advantageous in strategy as well as in tactics." Graduating from West Point in 1828, Davis served as a subaltern until 1835 and, holding the rank of colonel from 1846 to 1847, commanded a volunteer infantry regiment during the Mexican War.[14]

In his memoir Davis described his Civil War strategy, calling it the "*offensive-defensive*." Soon after the first battle at Bull Run (July 1861), the president had decided that the Confederate army would act "in *offensive-defensive* or purely defensive operations, as opportunity should offer for the one, or the renewal of [Federal] invasion require the other." Turning to his recollection of Gen. Robert E. Lee's counterattacks against the Union army led by Maj. Gen. George B. McClellan outside Richmond in 1862, Davis wrote that those attacks "inaugurated the offensive-defensive campaign which . . . turned from the capital of the Confederacy a danger so momentous that . . . it is not seen how a policy less daring or less firmly pursued could have saved the capital from capture." Written in French, Jomini's *Summary of the Art of War* was not available in an English edition in America until 1854, but Davis, like other West Point cadets, took courses in French and developed a basic reading knowledge of the language. It is logical to assume that the future Confederate president later picked up the English translation of Jomini, but he did not attribute the concept for his wartime strategy to the Frenchman. It is not clear how much Davis knew of Jomini's writings or if he may have taken to heart the passage about the "offensive defensive," but his use of the same term may be more than coincidence.[15]

Other glimpses into Davis's strategic thinking before 1861 confirm that he had reflected broadly on military matters. Napoleon was an important subject of books, essays, and discussions in antebellum American life, and Davis gave a speech in 1859 briefly indicating that he had thought about the problems or limitations of Napoleon's expanding French empire. In his fourth year holding the War Department portfolio, the Mississippian showed the wide scope of his interests by mentioning the French military in the colony of Algeria, comparing forts on the Black Sea with U.S. coastal fortifications, and explaining that he approved sending U.S. Army officers to observe European armies in the Crimean

War. In 1853 a section of his first annual report as secretary of war had emphasized the vulnerability of the strip of U.S. states and territories on the Pacific, "from its wealth . . . the most inviting and from its remoteness is, of all our possessions, the most exposed to the attack of a foreign enemy." He recommended more forts and arsenals in California, admitted as a state in 1850. Again he mentioned that irrigation in the West "would furnish the means to convert a sterile waste into a fertile region, . . . and add to the power and wealth of the United States, by extending their *settlement in a continuous chain from sea to sea.*" By the time of the secession crisis, colleagues knew that Davis coveted an appointment as a high-ranking general. Instead the Confederacy's founders offered him the presidency.[16]

When Davis adopted an expansionist policy, like the United States had pursued since 1789, Texas provided the best base for any march west into New Mexico.[17] Confederate expansion would be expected to enhance nationalism among its citizens. And the Lone Star State was vital to any Southern strategy related to the West.

No matter their level of nationalistic enthusiasm, most Confederates admitted that their nascent nation possessed only limited resources and manpower, and their leaders had to figure out how to make the best use of available troops and supplies. As an antebellum secretary of war, Davis knew that transporting an army across great distances presented great challenges. Deciding to add an element of offense to his strategy, the president sought to exploit the possibilities of territorial expansion and perceived Northern weakness. The western offensive was his first notable departure from a basic defensive strategy.[18]

Davis ordered a departure from the defensive for multiple reasons. He took steps that he believed would bolster Confederate nationalism and contribute to winning independence. Introducing Southern forces into the western territories could promote Confederate expansion. This in turn could boost morale while encouraging Europeans to support the CSA or at least offer it official diplomatic recognition. Such an offensive would challenge the United States for control of some of the West, perhaps draining away Union resources that might be assigned to other theaters. The offensive would also challenge the Union by expanding slavery into the region.

Although Davis professed that the Confederacy had "no interest . . . to invade the rights of others," in July 1861, less than five months after his inauguration and three months after Confederate cannon fired on Fort Sumter, he met in Richmond with a former U.S. Army major, Henry Hopkins Sibley, to discuss possible military actions in the West. A native of Natchitoches, Louisiana, and a graduate of West Point in 1838, Sibley had been stationed mostly in the Trans-Mississippi during his twenty-two-year career. Approaching the president with a bold strategic idea, Sibley recommended a military *offensive* into New Mexico Territory and asked to lead it. As then configured, New Mexico was a huge expanse stretching from the western boundary of Texas to California. Sometimes called "Arizona," the southern half of New Mexico Territory below the 34th parallel contained vocal Confederate sympathizers seeking to affiliate with the new nation.[19] Sibley had served in the region and described to Davis what he knew about the situation there. Some Federal military units had moved out of the territory, leaving behind only weakened garrisons. New Mexico appeared vulnerable. Southern sympathizers in Arizona already might have acted, assisted by Texans, to claim that area for the Confederacy. Texas formed a crucial part in Sibley's western strategy. Using the state as a base, he intended to raise regiments of volunteers for Confederate service and march to Santa Fe and possibly points west.[20]

Sibley's attractive proposal evidently captivated Davis, but it appears likely that the president had been considering action in the Southwest for several weeks. In April Secretary of War Leroy Pope Walker had presented Davis with a lengthy report on several matters, such as coastal defense in several states, including Texas. Toward the end of this report, Walker linked Texas and the Southwest: "The importance of the question of the *defenses of Texas* is greatly enhanced by *their connection with the future probable annexation of New Mexico and Arizona to this Confederacy.*" Sibley met with Davis in July, but Walker postulated in April: "Recent events render it manifest that the most friendly disposition in those Territories exists toward this Government." The war minister concluded, "[a] vigorous protection of *the frontier of Texas* bordering upon them [New Mexico and Arizona] must contribute to strengthen their confidence in our ability to maintain our own independence and to secure the permanent safety of *all who shall adopt our flag.*" In Montgomery hustle and bustle attended the creation of the Confederacy back in April. In Richmond, as a commander in chief at war, Davis made executive decisions every day in a crisis atmosphere during July. When Sibley sat in the president's office, a large Union army, led by Maj. Gen. Irvin McDowell, menaced the capital, with a major battle fought at Bull Run (Manassas) a few days later.[21]

For Davis, adding New Mexico to the Confederacy created a dilemma. One might think that he would have to forsake his words about not "invading the rights of others," or by implication not invading territory outside the boundaries of states that had seceded and formed the Confederacy. But another notion presented itself. The president found it important that numerous Arizona residents had announced their loyalty to the Confederacy and their desire to have their area become part of the Southern nation. Davis was an honorable Southerner, and he would take offense if accused of violating his word given in public or private, and a president's inaugural address was very public indeed.[22] That Arizonans wanted to join the Confederacy—to "adopt our flag," as Secretary Walker stated—allowed him to condone Confederate troops moving into New Mexico Territory. From the viewpoint of Davis and other Southerners, a military offensive into Arizona thus was not an "invasion."[23]

Banking that Sibley and Secretary Walker had assessed the situation correctly, Davis adopted the idea that a modest force—only a few thousand soldiers —could annex the territory and push the Confederacy to the border of California. Many Americans knew that in the Mexican War, an expedition of around fifteen hundred American soldiers had captured Santa Fe easily and a few hundred had seized California from Mexico in 1846. Given the small size of American armies up to 1861, an expedition of two or three thousand soldiers was not deemed too small to produce significant results.[24] Success of a Confederate offensive into New Mexico held out appealing returns. It could provide land for a southern transcontinental railroad. Southern sympathizers in other western territories might find encouragement to request Confederate support. This included Colorado, containing lead and silver mines, and Nevada, with rich discoveries of silver near Virginia City. Also attractive was Utah Territory, where disgruntled and resentful Mormons might align with the South because the U.S. government had deployed the army to suppress their attempt at religious separatism.[25]

The ultimate prize was the state of California, as Confederate veteran Trevanion Teel asserted after the war. California held multiple attractions, including legendary gold fields, the ports of San Francisco and San Diego, and agricultural land for cotton and other crops. Furthermore, gaining California could mean a bigger bonanza for morale: Davis's nation would reach from the Atlantic Ocean to the Pacific, making the Confederacy a transcontinental power and, as Teel pointed out, yielding more land for slavery's expansion.[26] In 1846 the United States had negotiated with Britain for a portion of Oregon and had accessioned California in 1848 after the Mexican War. Possessing much of the Pacific Coast made the United States a continental nation of great potential. And with the Union breaking up in 1861, Southern leaders wanted to inherit parts of the West.[27]

With several states announcing for secession, the Union seemed fragile, and in his inaugural address in March 1861, Pres. Abraham Lincoln implied that other states could leave as well. Perhaps California and Oregon would form their own republic. From California, Maj. Gen. Edwin Sumner had sent reports informing the U.S. Army Adjutant General's Office about his concern that while most Californians evidenced a "strong Union feeling," as many as "20,000 secession voters [were] in this state." Sumner probably overestimated their numbers, but in mid-1861 on his list of worries, one was the specific threat that Confederate forces moving west from Texas might inspire these western secessionists. In Richmond government authorities had difficulty assessing the strength of Southern support in California's lightly populated southern counties. Regardless, Confederate military forces needed to annex New Mexico to begin expanding the CSA into the western territories.[28]

Operating on their own initiative, Texans rushed into Arizona on behalf of the Confederacy. On August 1, 1861, Lt. Col. John R. Baylor, leading three hundred soldiers of the Second Regiment, Texas Mounted Rifles, found the support he expected and established the Confederate Territory of Arizona. Transplanted from Kentucky to Texas twenty years earlier, Baylor had a reputation as an Indian fighter and newspaper publisher, briefly holding a seat in the Texas legislature. He picked the town of Mesilla, about fifty miles north of El Paso, to serve as Arizona's territorial capital. According to his ambitious proclamation, the territorial boundary ran along the 34th parallel from Texas out to the California border. Baylor stated part of his purpose in a report to a superior officer: Arizona's minerals could be helpful to the CSA, but holding the territory afforded "an outlet to the Pacific, . . . a matter of some importance to our Government." Hearing about Baylor's success, Richmond authorities acted on his proclamation on January 18, 1862, when the Confederate Congress voted to add Arizona Territory to the nation. A month later President Davis proudly informed his fellow countrymen that an official (but nonvoting) delegate represented Arizona in Congress. From his viewpoint, the Confederacy now touched California.[29]

Building upon these tantalizing western prospects held the lure of greatly increasing nationalism in the new nation. Historians continue to debate the strength, depth, and longevity of Confederate nationalism. Drew Gilpin Faust has postulated that "Nationalism is contingent; its creation is a process." Part of that process could involve expanding geographic boundaries. Faust also has made the point that "Confederate nationalism was formed by the limits of the possible."[30] So much seemed possible to Jefferson Davis in the summer of 1861, including the idea of a transcontinental nation. The success of Confederate arms in the West in adding new lands to the nation logically would provide a boost to national pride and patriotism. Yet defeat might disappoint Southerners and undermine, even slightly, their devotion to the new CSA.

To support Colonel Baylor's position, a military expedition would strengthen the hold of the Confederacy on New Mexico and could lead to other gains in the West. It probably would reap diplomatic benefits as well. Capt. Gurden Chapin, a thoughtful U.S. Army officer in Santa Fe, contended that the CSA's territorial growth might increase its chances for European recognition. Thus the

Confederates sought to advance into the West, resulting in armed clashes with Federal forces determined to maintain Union authority in the region.[31]

Adding other Trans-Mississippi states already provided building blocks for the Confederacy's western growth and the potential for increased nationalism. Arkansas had seceded on May 6, 1861, and joined the CSA. Davis anticipated the secession of Missouri, the other slave state west of the Mississippi River. But three Union states bracketed Missouri: Illinois to the east, Iowa to the north, and to the west Kansas, newly admitted to the Union on January 29. Nevertheless, pro-Confederate Missourians pushed ahead with their intent to take their state into the new nation. They were rewarded later, in October 1861, when a rump session of the Missouri legislature claimed to authorize secession. That was enough for the Confederate Congress. In November it officially voted to seat Missouri's senators and congressmen and add another star to the Confederate flag. At that point all or parts of four Confederate states—Texas, Louisiana, Arkansas, and Missouri—were west of the Mississippi River.[32]

East of the river, Confederates arranged to add another state, Kentucky. Luring Kentucky was a matter of both prestige and politics. Davis and Lincoln were both natives of the state. Beside that, in September 1861, writing a letter to a confidant, Lincoln emphasized Kentucky's strategic geographical importance to both sides: "I think that to lose Kentucky is nearly the same as to lose the whole game [the war]. Kentucky gone, we can not hold Missouri, nor, I think, Maryland." The president did not spell out that if the CSA added Kentucky, it would move the Confederacy's northern border to the Ohio River and include the city of Louisville (61,000 population), with the base of the great Louisville and Nashville Railroad and several factories. For weeks after the firing on Fort Sumter, Blue Grass politicians had asserted a policy of "neutrality," but that was a flimsy pretense. Confederate troops crossed into the state in September, and a sizable faction of sympathizers bolted from the legislature. On December 10 that group voted for Kentucky to join the CSA. Again seizing the moment, the Confederate Congress welcomed this opportunity to officially add new senators and representatives along with another star on the national flag. But ultimate control of Kentucky depended on battles fought in the coming months.[33]

Meanwhile, an area north of Texas was open to the Confederacy's influence. Davis had to think about whom to name as the South's special representative to Native American tribes in the Indian Territory. He settled on Albert Pike of Arkansas, an experienced lawyer knowledgeable about Indian affairs. Pike's efforts yielded improved relations with the tribes and hundreds of tribesmen for military service. Nevertheless, some Texas troops patrolled the Red River and operated inside Indian Territory.[34]

Contemplating a map in the winter of 1861–62, the boundaries of the Confederacy had begun to fill in, no longer having a circumscribed appearance.

In March 1861 the nation contained seven states along the Gulf and Atlantic coastlines. By early 1862 a revised map of the nation, as Davis might have seen it, included in the East, Virginia, Tennessee, North Carolina, and Kentucky and in the West, Arkansas, Missouri, Indian Territory, and Arizona Territory.[35] As such Texas would be near the geographical center of the CSA. (By contrast, most modern maps depicting the Confederacy are quite different in appearance, with only a few showing all of the places the Southerners claimed.)[36] Of course, Davis wanted the Arizona offensive to add more territory to the map of the Confederacy.[37]

To continue Confederate expansion, Davis and his adjutant general, Samuel Cooper, needed to determine if Henry Sibley was the right officer to lead the offensive. A forty-five-year-old career officer, Sibley had graduated from West Point in 1838 and won a brevet to major for gallantry in battle during the Mexican War. He had come to Davis's attention during the Mississippian's days as secretary of war as the man who designed a useful field tent for the army— and probably for another reason as well. General Cooper, now the Confederacy's senior army officer, had met Sibley while on an inspection trip to Texas in the 1850s. By then the major had a reputation as a heavy drinker, though the army was replete with officers who drank too much alcohol.[38]

On July 8 a formal letter went out from Cooper naming Sibley commander of the Arizona offensive and investing him with the rank of brigadier general. Cooper confirmed aspects of the Davis-Sibley meeting: "In view of your recent service in New Mexico and knowledge of that country and the people, the president has intrusted you with the important duty of driving the Federal troops from that department." Furthermore, Cooper ordered him to "proceed without delay to Texas, and in concert with Brigadier General Van Dorn organize . . . from Texas troops, two full regiments of cavalry [approximately 2,200 soldiers] and one battery of howitzers [about 100 artillerymen], and other such forces as you may deem necessary." Anticipating success, he expected Sibley to "organize *military government* within the Territory." Regular officers in the prewar army had gained experience in California Territory with the complex issues of military government, a circumstance making them superior to elected or appointed civilian officeholders. Those officers were not available to Davis, and it may have seemed logical that a West Point graduate would perform better at directing a military government than volunteer officers or former Texas Rangers. Sibley later also postulated that he intended to establish "satisfactory relations with the adjacent Mexican States of Chihuahua and Sonora."[39]

Pending success in New Mexico, it was possible for the Sibley expedition to march farther west. On July 8 Cooper instructed that as the campaign developed, Sibley should "be guided by circumstances and your own good judgment." This open-ended phrasing leaves the question of expansion through conquest officially unanswered. Yet five months later Secretary of War Judah Benjamin observed to the president that after Colonel Baylor's Confederates had established Arizona Territory, Sibley's expedition moved to reinforce Baylor, "opening a pathway to the Pacific." Benjamin's allusion is unmistakable: Arizona provided a steppingstone to California. Only a few weeks later, Sibley himself stated that he had ordered troops to Tucson "for the further purpose of opening communications with Southern California, whose people are favorably inclined to our Government."[40]

The president picked Texas for use as a base for a risky expedition pregnant with potential. But it was not a venture that risked considerable resources. Two or three thousand men, their weapons and ammunition, and some wagons and animals made a modest investment that could pay considerable political, patriotic, diplomatic, and military dividends for the CSA. Davis was aware of the basic military principle of "concentration"—not dividing one's forces and carrying out so many operations that all were weakened and few might succeed. Confederates could debate if Sibley's soldiers would have been the decisive margin in battles at Pea Ridge, Arkansas; Shiloh, Tennessee; or New Orleans. Putting aside second-guessing by critics such as Texas senator Williamson Oldham, Davis was right to take a gamble in New Mexico.[41]

Issues of logistics—supplying and moving a military force—did not restrain Davis, Cooper, or Secretary Walker. As strategic planners, they had to balance opportunity, risk, available resources, and potential beneficial results. Any Confederate commander would have had problems forming, supplying, and transporting a western expedition in 1861–62 using only Texas resources.

Assembling troops came first. By August 1861, when Sibley arrived in San Antonio, thousands of Texans already had enlisted in Confederate service and deployed outside the state to Arkansas and Missouri or east of the Mississippi River. With pressures and demands for troops elsewhere, the size of Sibley's force would have to be modest (especially in contrast to the opposing armies in the East, where each side had fielded more than 30,000 soldiers in Virginia). Future developments indicated that Sibley would be on his own rather than expect much in the way of reinforcements—perhaps he hoped to recruit units of pro-Confederate residents from Arizona, Colorado, or even California. How many Federals he would encounter remained uncertain; pro-Union volunteers began enlisting in the West as Confederate forces gathered in Texas.

Adequate supplies for the expedition remained a serious problem.[42] Col. Henry McCulloch, brother of Brig. Gen. Ben McCulloch, the notable Texas Ranger and Confederate commander in Arkansas, complained to Brig. Gen. Paul Hébert that Sibley had "stripped [from Texas] every tent, all the clothing of every kind, and nearly all other quartermaster's stores."[43] Even so, Sibley found it impossible to assemble enough weapons, wagons, rations, horses, mules, and fodder to sustain his offensive. Transporting minimum supplies for his troops, Sibley acknowledged an unavoidable necessity and decided to rely on capturing resources from New Mexico's Federal forts to provision his expedition during and after his campaign. Depending on the enemy for supplies decreased the chances for success.

On the Union side, Lincoln had sworn at his inauguration "to preserve, protect, and defend" the Constitution. He decided to apply the Constitution's terms from ocean to ocean, to all of the states and western territories, including New Mexico.[44] Therefore, the president ordered available military forces, including territorial volunteers, to keep the Union intact. Lincoln gave no indication that he was dissuaded by Davis's assertive strategy or that a Confederate offensive would puncture the Union's will to defend the territories.

To conduct that defense, Lincoln benefited greatly from the steady leadership of Col. Edward R. S. Canby. At forty-four, Canby was a Kentuckian who had graduated from West Point in 1839 and had established a sound record on the frontier, winning two brevets during the Mexican War. In New Mexico he eventually commanded around five thousand soldiers, including U.S. Regulars and volunteers from Colorado and California as well as New Mexico. Gathering these forces, Canby resolutely moved to turn back Sibley's Texans and defeat the Confederate offensive.[45]

Sibley and the Confederates gained the upper hand early in the campaign. On February 21, 1862, the two armies, numbering about 2,600 Confederates and 3,800 Federals, opened the campaign at Val Verde, New Mexico, on the eastern side of the Rio Grande a few miles from Fort Craig, a Union depot filled with valuable supplies. Sibley needed to cross the river, capture the fort, and take its stores for his offensive to succeed. Soldiers and subordinate officers on both sides fought hard, clawing for weaknesses and flanking opportunities. Tom Green, a Texas colonel, saved the day for Sibley by leading a brazen assault that broke the Union line. Canby's troops retreated to the west side of the Rio Grande, giving Sibley the traditional mark of victory by holding the battlefield. But Fort Craig's garrison held firm, refusing to surrender. In one of the campaign's turning points, Sibley showed that he lacked boldness and declined to gamble everything on an all-out assault on the fort. Instead he tallied political points by occupying Albuquerque and Santa Fe, New Mexico's territorial capital. With the campaign thus far favoring the Southerners, Canby could have withered in the face of pressure, abandoned the forts still in Federal hands, and conceded the territory.[46]

Yet despite losing the first engagement, Canby realized that Sibley operated far from his base in Texas and had yet to threaten the largest Federal depot, Fort

Union. Suffering casualties and consuming provisions lessened Confederate chances for victory. In other words, the longer the campaign lasted without Sibley winning or receiving reinforcements or supplies, the greater the strain on his army and logistics. Showing resolve rather than folding after one defeat, maintaining sound field fortifications, and knowing he possessed supplies that Sibley needed gave Canby advantages. He capitalized on them.[47]

Bolstered by the determination of its subordinate officers, Sibley's army pressed on. Almost a month after Confederates occupied Albuquerque, the opposing armies fought the second major battle of the campaign at Glorieta Pass (Apache Canyon), near Santa Fe. In a sequence of engagements over three days in late March, the outcome remained in doubt. The Federals had received reinforcements, notably the flamboyant and controversial Col. John Chivington and nine hundred Colorado volunteers, who had marched through heavy snow and across rough terrain. Sibley dithered in Albuquerque, drunk or ill, depriving his army of central direction, but tactical gains mounted for the hard-pressed Confederates. The Texans again achieved tactical victory on the battlefield, despite their numerical and logistical disadvantages, when an unexpected stroke practically ruined their campaign. Led by Chivington, Federal cavalry located the Confederate supply wagons assembled at Johnson's Ranch away from the main fighting. The Coloradoans burned Sibley's precious wagons and supplies and killed or drove off many of the mules and horses.[48]

The outcome at Glorieta meant a catastrophe for Confederate expansion and denied Davis's goals for the offensive. Morale plummeted among Sibley's soldiers afterward. Within days, rather than receiving the surrender of Canby, his forces, and Union forts, Sibley ordered a retreat to Texas to salvage his own command. The road back to Texas was desperate. Troops lacked food and water for themselves and their horses. Exhausted and hungry, in late April the Confederates staggered into Fort Bliss, near El Paso. The previous January Sibley had harped on his strategic theme: continuing the offensive would have fulfilled the "purpose of opening communications with Southern California, whose people are favorably inclined to our Government." But his campaign had failed, and without recent information from the West Coast, he failed to understand that the strategic situation had changed. Federal forces firmly held California. Making a remarkable overland march, Brig. Gen. James Carleton, leading Union reinforcements from California, forced Sibley to abandon Fort Bliss, continue a debilitating retreat, and give up chances to initiate a second campaign west.[49]

When Sibley retreated to San Antonio in July 1862, President Davis should have removed him from command due to his failed leadership. Showing the shallowness of the pool of Confederate senior officers, Sibley remained in uniform, filling minor assignments. In the months to come, Col. John Baylor continued to use the title "Governor of Arizona," but Federal regiments regained control of New Mexico and reoccupied outposts in West Texas, including the fort named for Davis. In May Sibley reversed his outlook on the West, concluding that New Mexico Territory was "not worth a quarter of the blood and treasure expended on its conquest."[50]

Standard works on the Confederacy vary in their treatment of Davis, Sibley, and Texas in relation to national expansion. Some provide no coverage, others are quite brief, and a few pack insightful analysis into a few pages. Some single-volume histories and textbooks of the Civil War allocate nothing to the Southwest, while others demonstrate cogently the role that Texas played in Confederate strategy and hopes for national expansion. Only specialized works describe and evaluate the New Mexico campaign and its prospects for the South.[51]

On February 22, 1862, the outcome of the western offensive still hung in the balance as Jefferson Davis took a second inaugural oath, following an election for president in which he ran unopposed. His vision for the Confederacy in the West showed imagination, though ordering an offensive into Arizona seemed to contradict what he said in his second inaugural.[52] He pointed with pride to national growth since his first inaugural—"Our Confederacy has grown from six to thirteen states"—though he made no mention of Arizona Territory. Continuing, Davis noted the important implication of acting on the defensive. Knowing that Northerners and Europeans would read copies or summaries of this speech in newspapers, the president stated that he had no intention to lead Confederates on "*a war of conquest*" because "*the Constitution of their Confederacy admits of no coerced association.*" Davis contended that the nation would operate under "the rule of voluntary association" and that Southerners supporting it (during wartime one year after the CSA's founding) remained together for their mutual benefit exactly because it was a voluntary association of states.[53] As had been traditional in the old Union, the Confederacy looked westward for new territories. Rather than prohibiting slavery in the West, the Confederate Congress and the Permanent Confederate Constitution (revised and replacing the provisional constitution) condoned and protected slavery in the Trans-Mississippi. If the CSA had expanded, slavery would have moved west.[54]

Davis had reason to be both sanguine and proud of the past year's developments, but in other ways the Confederacy was on the brink. What direction would the war take in the Western Theater and the Trans-Mississippi? Only a week before his second inaugural, Davis had issued his proclamation recognizing the existence of the Confederate Territory of Arizona. As he spoke on February 22, Sibley's campaign was underway, having won the tactical victory at Val Verde the previous day. It would be more than a month before the New Mexico campaign was resolved, and Davis wished for news confirming his claim to Arizona: a Federal retreat from New Mexico and the march of Confederates elsewhere into the West. At the same time, the president awaited the outcome of other battles. A Confederate army under Maj. Gen. Earl Van Dorn was poised near Pea Ridge in northwestern Arkansas to push Union forces from that state. Davis' favorite general, Albert Sidney Johnston, a Texan, had assembled an army to launch a counterattack against a Union army under Maj. Gen. Ulysses S. Grant as it camped in southern Tennessee near Shiloh Church. Meanwhile a Federal naval squadron had assembled at Ship Island, Mississippi. Ostensibly there to establish a blockade of the Gulf Coast, the squadron actually prepared to attack New Orleans.

When all of these confrontations culminated in favor of the Union, the first four months of 1862 produced a strategic disaster for the Confederacy. Van Dorn was defeated at Pea Ridge (also known as Elkhorn Tavern) on March 7–8, and another Texas general, Ben McCulloch, was killed in action there. Sibley was defeated at Glorieta Pass that same month and began a tortuous retreat to Texas. Johnston was killed at Shiloh, and his army retreated from Tennessee in early April. And the Federal navy captured New Orleans on April 25, with Union army units entering the city on May 1. By necessity in the spring of 1862, Davis's strategic focus shifted east. Virginia and Tennessee became paramount, and he also determined that Vicksburg was a vital defensive bastion on the Mississippi River. Thinking about a counterattack to recapture New Orleans occupied the president for several weeks.[55]

Confederate leaders and Texas governors identified other strategic factors related to the state apart from expanding into New Mexico. Among the most important, Galveston's port needed protection, along with coastal defense from Sabine Pass to Brownsville. Texas governors along with their Southern counterparts bombarded Confederate secretaries of war with advice and demands for protecting their states.[56]

On more than one occasion in 1861, Gov. Edward Clark contended that coastal defense was inadequate to the point of the Texas shoreline being "unprotected and peculiarly vulnerable."[57] Originally from Louisiana, Clark had arrived in Texas before it joined the Union and held various political offices before becoming lieutenant governor under the state's hero, Sam Houston. Houston opposed secession, and a special convention forced him out of office in March. Clark stepped in to fill the rest of Houston's term (ending in November 1861). Supporting the Confederacy, he corresponded with President Davis, the secretary of war, and Confederate military officers. The governor assertively recommended the good idea of taking cannon from inland forts and putting them in shore batteries. Pushing Texans to enlist for Confederate service, Clark sought money, weapons, and soldiers for the state's defense and warned the legislature about deficiencies in coastal fortifications.[58]

About four weeks after Clark became governor, President Lincoln declared a naval blockade of the South's coast from Virginia to the tip of Texas. Clark mentioned the adverse effect of the blockade in his farewell to the legislature in November. During its first months, the blockade was weakest. Lincoln entertained recommendations from military officers for capturing selected points to provide coastal bases for the navy and interdict international trade with the CSA. Coastal outposts fell to Union attacks, including Norfolk, Virginia (April 1861); Hatteras Inlet, North Carolina (August 1861); and Port Royal, South Carolina (November 1861).[59]

While the Confederacy demonstrated consistent problems defending its coasts, Francis Lubbock, a Texas gubernatorial candidate, met with Davis in Richmond in October 1861. A few weeks earlier, in mid-August, Sibley had arrived in San Antonio and started preparing for his offensive, assisted by Governor Clark, also a candidate in the election. Sibley's expedition took priority over other military matters in Texas, which Davis likely made evident to Lubbock, who won the gubernatorial election and took office in November.[60]

Davis found one of his staunchest supporters in Lubbock, who pledged his "fealty & devotion to the cause of the entire South." Having moved to Texas in the 1830s, Lubbock ranched and held public office, including the lieutenant governorship from 1857 to 1859. He worked with Gen. Paul Hébert to improve coastal defenses, especially at Galveston Island, where the general established his headquarters. Some Texans might have been lulled into a false sense of security when the Federal navy made no serious moves against Galveston after blockaders appeared offshore. But after New Orleans fell, it became obvious that the Texas coast was also vulnerable. Hébert thereafter buried himself in specific details and dwelled on his deficiencies in weapons, soldiers, and equipment.[61]

Pressed to set strategic priorities, President Davis and Secretary of War Judah Benjamin in February 1862 decided that strengthening the field armies outranked coastal defense anywhere in the South. Benjamin broadcast notifications to the coastal states. For example, he called for Hébert to strip away many soldiers from the Texas coast and send them to General Van Dorn at Little Rock. Anticipating Hébert's complaint, Benjamin asserted: "No invasion of Texas is deemed probable, but if any occurs its effects must be hazarded, and our entire forces must be thrown toward the Mississippi for the defense of that river and of *the Memphis and Charleston railroad.*" Benjamin also lectured Lubbock: "We must leave the coast exposed." Growing morose, Hébert concluded that the Texas coast was almost indefensible, though he supervised placing cannon in forts and implemented other defensive measures. In October 1862 the Federal navy suddenly demanded the surrender of Galveston. Negotiations permitted the city's Confederate defenders to withdraw unharmed, thereby avoiding a battle. Arranging a minimal defense and reassigning some warships elsewhere, the Federals soon became complacent.[62]

Posted to Texas in November after a checkered record in Virginia, Maj. Gen. John B. Magruder sought to redeem himself by recapturing Galveston. Marshaling every available soldier and outfitting two steamboats with cotton bales as armor, Magruder's enthusiasm ingratiated him with Texans. Launching a predawn attack on January 1, 1863, the Confederates, some led by Tom Green, an officer who had served in Sibley's campaign, swept to victory after a sharp fight. Some vessels and their crews eluded capture, but most of the Union defenders were killed, wounded, or made prisoner.[63]

Soon enough, the blockade resumed, providing an evident danger to small, light blockade runners that entered and left port from time to time. The Galveston stock exchange soon ceased operations, businesses closed, and grass began growing in the city's rarely used streets. The port was technically open until the end of the war, but it obviously was not handling anything near its pre-war volume of trade. The blockade prevented Galveston from contributing significantly to the Trans-Mississippi's economy. A Confederate strategic asset had depreciated in value.[64]

South from Galveston stretched nearly seven hundred vulnerable miles of coastline for Union forces to attack. Governor Lubbock reminded President Davis that Texas had "an immense frontier and sea-coast to look after, both of which are now seriously threatened with invasion." Secretary of War James Seddon replied with a view not shared by the governor: "it must be admitted that Texas can only be effectually and finally defended by the success of the Confederate armies on the great central arenas of conflict" east of the Mississippi River. Meanwhile Confederate officers sometimes used slave labor to build new earthwork fortifications even though they lacked enough cannon for them. Hoping to discourage Union encroachments, gunners painted logs black to look like cannon. These efforts resulted in a thin veneer of protection, which included lookouts and mounted patrols to warn of Federal attack.[65]

The most spectacular Union effort to breach these coastal defenses came in September 1863 during Lubbock's governorship. Sabine Pass, near the border of Texas and Louisiana, appeared lightly defended, and troops landing there would have access to a rail line west to Beaumont, then on to Houston. Maj. Gen. Nathaniel P. Banks drafted a plan to have gunboats support the landing of Union forces near Sabine Pass. Before sending in their troops, senior Union officers decided that the navy had to reduce a modest Confederate earthwork, Fort Griffin, mounting six cannon. There, Confederate officers had required the gunners to take target practice at stakes positioned at set ranges in the waters in front of the fort. Lt. Richard Dowling inspired the defenders. Assisted by daring Confederate gunboats, Dowling's forty-two artillerymen inflicted significant damage to the Federal vessels, prevented Banks from landing his infantry in strength, and captured 400 Union prisoners. President Davis, the Confederate Congress, and Texas politicians all praised Dowling, an Irish immigrant and saloonkeeper with no significant military experience.[66]

Thereafter Union soldiers set up camps or occupied outposts along the Texas coast, including Brownsville and Matagorda Island in November 1863. To keep the Federals from using the short-haul rail line from Indianola to Victoria, Confederates intentionally damaged its rails and locomotives. Rather than reinforcing such modest successes and coordinating a push deeper inland at the same time, these forces withdrew and joined Banks, who launched an offensive along the Red River in 1864. His objective was capturing Shreveport, headquarters of Lt. Gen. Edmund Kirby Smith, commander of the Confederate Trans-Mississippi Department. From Shreveport, the logical next steps would lead west to Marshall, Texas, and into the interior. But the Union offensive ended in failure in April before reaching Shreveport. In the spring of 1865, about eight hundred Federals made a surprise intrusion near Brownsville, bringing on the last battle of the Civil War, a Confederate victory at Palmito Ranch, May 12–13.[67]

Frontier defense remained of great importance to Texans throughout the war. From the beginning of the conflict, West Texas settlers and ranchers voiced concern over Indian attacks. Following the withdrawal of U.S. Army units in 1861, this frontier lay open to Indian raids as well as a Federal invasion from New Mexico. The Confederate government and the Texas state government disputed responsibility for defending the nation's and the state's western border.[68]

Texas and the CSA also had a lengthy boundary with Mexico. This border held some promise for commerce that might benefit the blockaded Confederacy as well as bring profits to local residents. But bandits and Indian raiders along the Mexican border had created problems in antebellum years and remained a threat following secession. Underwriting costly defensive measures in the region could offset income or benefits of trade and collection of taxes. Raising military units, paying soldiers, garrisoning forts, and patrolling the Texas borders created points of contention for the rest of the war between the state and the government in Richmond.

Frontier defense, funded by the Texas legislature and using state troops, remained a political priority for wartime governors. They tried to persuade the Confederate government to provide partial or complete financial support for replacing U.S. Army units at posts guarding against Indian attacks or Mexican intrusions. In a letter to Secretary of War Walker, Texas senator Williamson Oldham also emphasized that "the defense of the frontier belongs properly to the General [CSA] Government." Receiving limited Confederate funding for units on frontier service, state leaders realized after a few months that if Texans wanted their boundaries defended, they would have to do most of it themselves. Following up on the heels of the Sibley expedition, Union troops gained footholds in West Texas at Fort Bliss and Fort Davis, causing Governor Lubbock to fret that a general invasion was coming. (Such an action might have been worthwhile in the spring of 1864 had Union troops in Texas coordinated with Banks's forces during the Red River campaign; instead the Union exercised economy of force and stood firm in Texas.) Nevertheless, despite realizing that the western boundary of Texas also equaled the western boundary of the Confederacy, Richmond authorities put most national resources into the war east of the Mississippi River, though authorizing modest operations in Arkansas and Missouri.[69]

Meanwhile Texas governors, including Pendleton Murrah, who had won election in August 1863, devoted scarce state supplies and troops to the frontiers to placate citizens' concerns, especially their sincere worries over Indian raids. Soldiers enlisting in state frontier regiments suffered criticism for supposedly avoiding service in the famous units fighting for the Confederate cause in Louisiana, Tennessee, and Virginia. But these men consoled themselves in the fact that they contributed directly to the state's defense.[70] Governor Murrah, in contrast to Clark and Lubbock, professed public attachment to the Confederacy but found fault with President Davis and his policies. Murrah hailed from Alabama and received an exceptional education, graduating from Brown University in Rhode Island before returning south. He set up a law practice in his native state but moved to Texas around 1850, quickly getting into politics by running for the legislature, winning on his second try in 1857. When Lubbock opted out of running for reelection, Murrah seized his chance.[71]

During his term, Murrah found that Confederate leaders already had decided the major factors of national strategy regarding coastal and frontier defense, but the Confederacy's commercial and diplomatic relationships across the international border with Mexico never produced the benefits some expected. Trying to revitalize the French empire in the Americas, Emperor Napoleon III used French soldiers to enthrone Maximilian, an Austrian archduke, in Mexico City. Fumbling Confederate diplomats mishandled Maximilian's precarious regime while contentious Southern policies soured contacts with Mexican Liberals. Confederate dealings with Mexico ranged from modest to disappointing to barren.[72]

Never airtight, the Union blockade curtailed the South's overseas cotton trade, and looking for alternatives to shipping out of Galveston, Texans used wagons to transport heavy cotton for sale in Mexico. Ships took the cotton from

Mexico across the Gulf and eventually to waiting markets in Europe or the North. This outgoing trade from Texas into Mexico brought profits to some merchants and produced some benefits for the CSA.[73]

General Smith explained to Governor Murrah how the Trans-Mississippi Department benefited from the cotton trade to Mexico. By supervising much of the cotton trade, Smith obtained vital money and military supplies to keep his department operating, but Murrah, just as desperate to find money for the state's treasury, wanted to have Texas cotton agents control as much of the trade as possible. This difference set the governor at loggerheads with the general. Although not as obstructionist or as harshly critical of Confederate policies and leaders as Govs. Joseph Brown of Georgia or Zebulon Vance of North Carolina, Murrah positioned himself among the strongest proponents of states' rights in the Confederacy.[74]

Selling cotton to get military supplies and munitions from Mexico and across the Rio Grande was one thing, but transporting those goods from Texas to the Cis-Mississippi was another matter. The great distance to the rest of the Confederacy, the lack of railroads Texas and Louisiana and bridges across major rivers, and the general difficulties of overland transportation hindered the delivery of supplies to the East, particularly after the fall of New Orleans. The situation grew worse after July 1863 with the capitulation of both Vicksburg and Port Hudson, Louisiana.[75]

In an effort to coordinate Confederate and state goals, in August 1863 General Smith held a conference with Murrah and the other Trans-Mississippi governors or their representatives. Vested with extra authority from President Davis and Secretary of War Seddon, the general increasingly made decisions on his own after July 1863. The isolation of Smith's command became evident in the coming months, despite Seddon's contention that "communication with the Trans-Mississippi, while rendered somewhat more precarious and insecure, is found by no means cut off, or even seriously threatened." In contrast, the department's civilian leaders acknowledged that the "fall of our strongholds" on the Mississippi River resulted in "interrupting communication between the two sections of the Confederacy."[76]

At the conclusion of a second conference between Smith and the western governors, the principals issued inflated reports touting the capabilities of each state and urging Southern patriots to rally to the Confederate cause. They called upon tradition, heritage, and hyperbole, asserting that "[w]estern skill and valor will prepare a San Jacinto defeat for every invading army that pollutes the soil of this department." The governors claimed to "look forward confidently to the day when these *thirteen Confederate States* will in peace and safety occupy their rightful position among the great powers of the earth."[77]

Railroads, another strategic asset, grew in importance during the Civil War. In 1861 Texas rail lines languished in the early stages of development. Companies operated less than five hundred miles of track in the state.

Most of the rail lines operated in southeastern Texas and along the coast. A short-haul line connected Indianola and Victoria near Corpus Christi. The most important tracks looked like a spider web spun around Houston. One with promise stretched east to the town of Orange, near the Louisiana border. Another reached west to Hempstead, toward the capital of Austin. A third track went south to Galveston's port. Along the coast a separate line ran from Sabine Pass to Beaumont. All lines in East Texas provided attractive access into the interior for invading Federals. Nevertheless, neither entrepreneurs nor state agencies had taken the financial risk to construct a bridge across the Sabine River from Orange toward New Orleans and Baton Rouge. And the Mississippi River presented a greater challenge than the Sabine. The wide, fast-flowing river defied the engineering technology of the day. As Sen. Williamson Oldham lamented to Governor Clark, "We have no railroads connecting us with [the other CSA states]."[78]

Lacking all kinds of materials to construct railroads in 1861, Southerners had unappealing choices to make. The Confederacy needed to improve existing rail lines *and* build new ones, including in the Southwest. President Davis identified the missing rail link from Danville, Virginia, to Greensboro, North Carolina, as a priority. Congress acted slowly to close that gap, but a majority eventually voted for the needed appropriations. When completed in 1862, it facilitated transportation between Virginia and the rest of the CSA.[79]

Meanwhile the Texas legislature took modest steps in regard to railroads. It approved charters for new rail companies but provided no state financing. Indeed, by 1865 Texans operated fewer miles of track than in 1861.[80]

Back in Richmond, numerous matters begged for attention in Congress, and farsighted legislators advocated providing assistance to complete the rail line from New Orleans to Houston. Running near Louisiana's Gulf coast, the tracks went from Algiers, near New Orleans, to Brashear City (modern Morgan City). The next stops in Louisiana were proposed for New Iberia, Vermilionville (modern Lafayette), and on toward the Sabine River. Before the war the thriving market of New Orleans had been easily accessible from Galveston by ship, thus proving another element delaying rail construction in the region. After Federal ships began patrolling the Gulf of Mexico and blockaders appeared off Galveston, New Orleans still acted as a magnet drawing Southern dreams of developing southwestern railroads.[81]

But suddenly New Orleans lost its attraction. In the spring of 1862, a Federal naval squadron captured the city. Ironically just five days earlier the

Confederate Congress had approved $1.5 million to help rail construction from Brashear City to the Texas border. For good measure, three months later a Federal expedition assaulted Baton Rouge. These actions ended the possibility of completing railroad connections west from either of those cities to the Sabine River.[82]

Once the Federals possessed New Orleans, the Confederates needed to turn their attention northward to completing a rail line across northern Louisiana to connect Texas with the eastern Confederacy. Businessmen had invested in a short-haul line in the northeastern corner of Texas. It shipped goods from Marshall to just across the Louisiana border at Swanson's Landing on Caddo Lake. A more promising line developed when workers extended tracks from Marshall eastward to the town of Greenwood, Louisiana, only fifteen miles from Shreveport. From there to Monroe, a major gap of one hundred miles lay undeveloped. Monroe benefited from a track connecting it with Desoto, on the Mississippi River opposite Vicksburg.[83]

Given the Confederacy's needs to improve east-west communications, completing the line from Monroe west to Shreveport was a necessity. But this was a project too big to be left to private, local, and state efforts. The states of Texas and Louisiana needed to cooperate with the national government, and the Texas legislature was remiss for not taking some direct action on its own. Completing these connections would have been helpful, even if engineers were unable to build a bridge over the powerful Mississippi River.[84]

The Union's capture of New Orleans caused significant repercussions for the entire Southwest. Never easy to begin with, Confederate communications from the Trans-Mississippi to the East grew more difficult. By the late summer of 1863, for several reasons, Texas was unable to contribute much strategically to the Confederacy. The state now no longer served as a base for westward expansion. The Union blockade crippled routine trade from its major port at Galveston, only partly made up by commerce across the Rio Grande. No railroads connected the state to the East. Union military power, combined with geography, resulted in the strategic isolation of Texas for the last two years of the Civil War.[85]

Lt. James R. Loughridge, Fourth Texas
Infantry, Hood's Texas Brigade.
Courtesy James Rogers Loughridge
Family Papers, Pearce Civil War Collection,
Navarro College, Corsicana, Tex

2

Warriors, Husbands, and Fathers

Confederate Soldiers and Their Families

Richard Lowe

In traditional combat histories written during the first century after the American Civil War, the relationships of soldiers and their families were not examined in any detail. Who won battles and wars, and why and how they won them—these were the foremost questions in conventional historical accounts, and few readers asked for more. In the last few decades, however, increasing numbers of writers have broadened their perspectives to examine the ways in which war and society intersect. How does society shape war, and how does war shape society? This double-edged question opens countless new windows into the Civil War: discord on the home front, morale in the army, divisions of class and race, urban development, environmental effects, gender relationships, trade patterns, wartime migration—the possibilities seem limitless.

This "new military history" is not as new as it is often portrayed by its practitioners. As early as 1912 the president of the American Historical Association, one Theodore Roosevelt, called for a broader definition of military history. More than six decades ago, in 1943, a young scholar named Bell Wiley published one of the very best examples of new military history—a book that still influences the writing of Civil War history—*The Life of Johnny Reb,* a close look at the character and behavior of common Confederate soldiers. Nevertheless, only in recent decades have these new questions about the war attracted sustained attention by large numbers of historians.[1]

One topic that has intrigued researchers interested in family and gender relations is the interaction between married men who went off to war and their wives and children on the home front. Some writers of family history have found that nineteenth-century American husbands were generally remote and cold, distant from their mates. They were overbearing patriarchs, insensitive to the emotional needs of their wives, who had to sustain themselves without the sentimental or tender support of a husband. Other scholars have detected a very different type of husband in Confederate gray: affectionate, loving, and sensitive to his family's needs.[2]

Where did the Texas soldier place in this range? Did he gambol off to war with little thought of the hardships his family might encounter in his absence? Did he regard wife and children primarily as traditional trappings to full manhood? Or was the typical untamed Texan really, at heart, a sentimental and caring husband who longed for a wife's loving embrace and a child's playful cuddle? Hundreds of letters from soldiers in three of the state's most storied Civil War units—Hood's Texas Brigade, Terry's Texas Rangers, and Walker's Texas Division —definitely place the Texans in the second category. Some haughty patriarchs may have mingled among the other troops, but they left little evidence of their presence in their letters home to Texas.

The pain of separation from loved ones struck some men even before they reached their first destinations after leaving Texas. William E. Stoker, a farmer from the Coffeeville community of Upshur County in northeastern Texas, wrote his wife shortly after marching off to Arkansas that he was already aching for home: "Betty, I cant express my feelings when I think of you and Priscilla [his young daughter]. My heart leaps, but at the same time being so fare off and cant come home and see you it almost makes my heart break." Stoker kept his wife's letters, but when he looked at them in moments alone, he admitted, "I cant keep from weeping about you, feeling so loley [lonely] bye your self." To make matters worse, he had to face the possibility that he would never see her again: "I want to see you so bad, I am nearley ded but I dont know wether I will eveer be blessed with the pleasure of seeing you any more or not. . . . If I ever get the chance to come [home], I am a comeing like a feather in the wind."[3]

Edward Ross, a member of the Eighth Texas Cavalry (also known as Terry's Texas Rangers), missed his wife and children in Milam County in central Texas as soon as he crossed the state line on his way to the war. "There is but one thing that trulbles me and that is leaveing you and the children[.] if I could see you and the children this morning how happy I would bee." His longing for family affection continued when his regiment reached its destination in Kentucky. On a quiet Sunday night, he had time to daydream about home. "I can imagine, while I am writing this lovely Sabbath evening, that I see you and Sarah Jane, Davey, Wiley, Margaret, all down at friend Ned's and that you are about now, calling them up to start home and perhaps trying [to] get John Pettis or William to go with you all. Such thoughts is passing through my mind." Details of daily life that seemed mundane until he left home now called up intense emotions: "It seems to me that if I could see you and the children, that I would be willing to die." Two weeks later Ross was still fixated on his wife and children, writing that he "dramped [dreamed] last night that I was at home with you and the children and the injoyment that it was to me in my amagination is unexspressible but when I awoke up it was a sad dissiapointment." In fact, he continued, "there ant a hour in the day that pases over my head but what I am thinking of you and the children."[4]

Pvt. Samuel Farrow of the Nineteenth Infantry (Walker's Texas Division) likewise felt the first pangs of loneliness shortly after leaving his home in Panola County in northeastern Texas. "I wish I was with you this evening and would like very much to eat supper at home with you," he wrote while still in Texas. "Josephine when you write to me write what is going on and how the Folks is generally throug the neighborhood generally." Two weeks later Farrow continued on the same theme and repeated Stoker's fear that he might never see his wife again: "Men never know what Pleasure a home [is] until he is compelled to leave his wife and children. . . . But if I never see you anymore you must remember your ever loving husband." Arthur T. Rainey of the First Texas Infantry, bound for Virginia in the early months of the war, was homesick almost as soon as he parted with his wife. Rainey addressed a letter to "My Sweetest Little Wife" from Shreveport, Louisiana, just barely across the Texas state line: "Oh, how often I think of my little wife and child."[5]

A captain in Farrow's regiment demonstrated that early longings for home were not limited to the enlisted men. "I know I am hard but I cant read your letters with out shedding Tears," H. A. Wallace wrote to his wife in Rusk County. A sergeant in the Seventeenth Infantry fought the same demons. John Holcombe wrote his wife, Mandy, "if I could erace the thauts of home from my mind I could make myself contented but the thauts of home makes me spend many disagreeable hours & if it was not for the cause of freedom stimulating me I could not stand it." When he received his first letter from home, Holcombe was overcome with emotion, even in front of his fellow soldiers: "I never was so proud in my life though I could not suppress my tears to of saved my life. some of my friends asked me if any of my family was dead. when I told them they were all well & doing well they laughed at me but it was not funny to me." Like many of his comrades, Holcombe gained a new appreciation for family life as a result of his absence. "If I ever git home I expect to be a better husband and farther than I ever was," he assured his wife.[6]

Religious belief in an afterlife, in which God's children would be reunited with loved ones, sustained many of the soldiers who contemplated death and separation from earthly families. Frank Batchelor, a sergeant in Terry's Texas Rangers—a man not normally given to religious outpourings—nevertheless found solace (after the death of a family member) in the promise of heaven: "how sweet the consolation which comes to us through the promises of our Redeemer. If we remain faithful to our high calling we shall rejoin the glorified body of our brother. . . . O how sweet the thought that after the busy cares of this mortal life we shall be permitted to join our dear George 'in the green fields of Eden,' and dwell together, without care or sorrow, with the chosen of God, forever!" William L. Edwards of Hood's Texas Brigade, having fought in the Battle of Fair Oaks (also known as Seven Pines) near Richmond early in 1862, not surprisingly pondered the whole subject of death in a letter to his wife. "Oh, Roxie if the good Lord spares me to get back I shall lead a more devoted life to him [than] I ever have before[.] pray earnestly that we may live to meet again on earth but if we do not, oh; may we meet in heaven." Protestant Christian teachings about a happy and peaceful afterlife comforted many Texas Confederates who feared that earthly reunions with their wives might never occur.[7]

Contrary to their portrayal as cold, distant overlords—men who would never express their affection for their wives around a campfire with other soldiers—these Texans openly proclaimed their feelings about their families. A surgeon in the Twenty-Second Infantry wrote that "we have a fine time talking about our Mary's. There are six married men in my mess & four have wives named Mary." A soldier in the Sixteenth Cavalry "told the boys I thought I would marry you again when my three years are served out as three years absence intitles a woman to a divorce." William Stoker, the farmer from Upshur County, felt it necessary to declare his love of family to his comrades. When some of them urged him to lead them home, without permission from their superiors, Stoker refused. "I told them no, I loved my rib [wife] as well, & would do as much as any boddy to see them [his family] on honerable terms," but he would not leave the ranks without consent.[8]

Young men far from home thought about all sorts of attractions they had left behind. Their almost total separation from women for months at a time inevitably stimulated their imaginations and memories of their wives. Their letters rarely mentioned their sexual longings—such thoughts were generally kept private by nineteenth-century men—but at times the Texans' urges were expressed in indirect language. Sergeant Batchelor admitted, "My heart beats wildly at the thought of holding my Julia again to my aching breast & my letters seem so tame in comparison with my boundless affection that I'm often tempted to tear them up but I cannot put on paper the full depth of a love which absorbs my entire nature." The sergeant sighed in another letter that "pleasant visions of happy days with my little pet wife steal over my dreams." Capt. Harvey Wallace of the Nineteenth Infantry doubtless brought a smile to his wife's lips when he wrote: "I spend many an hour thinking about you on my bed. It would be a great pleasure to sleep with you on my arm one night." In another letter he complained about the cold tents in camp: "oh what a pleasure it would be to me to hug you up to my bosom these cold nights."[9]

Some soldiers felt it necessary to assure their wives that, unlike some of their comrades, they remained faithful to their wedding vows. Private Stoker of the Eighteenth Infantry was disgusted by the women of Arkansas and some of his fellow Texans. "Betty, I must tell you something about the women in arkingsaw. As we came along, I can say there is but verry few vertious ones along the road we travailed. There husbands had gone to the ware and they [the wives] have for saken them. The men [in Stoker's regiment] would go way on be fore & some would stay behind and go [to] their houses and get all around them and such talk you never hea[r]d among straingers." In fact, Stoker continued, "there was so many [soldiers who] would croud up on the women that it was enough to scare them to do any thing[,] but such as that was just as lots of them wanted. I can speak for my self—I hav ben jus as virtious as I could be but, all of the boys cant say it."[10]

Theophilus Perry, a lawyer from Harrison County in northeastern Texas, likewise assured his own wife that, despite all the temptations surrounding him, he would remain faithful. "I have always been lucky so far as the girls are concerned," he wrote in February 1863, but "I shall behave properly towards the Ladies & the lasses." Perry showed a certain flair in explaining away his attraction for the women who visited the army. "Every Pretty woman will but serve to transport me in sweet fancy in to the presence of her, that makes the sun to shine & the skies to look Blue over my head. And my Dear so long as I cultivate the society of the girls, just for the purpose of thinking about you, I shall be within the bounds of Taste & Duty."[11]

Capt. Elijah Petty of the Seventeenth Texas Infantry, like Perry, attempted to tease his wife about the whole situation. In one letter to his home in Bastrop, he recounted a dream in which, upon his return from the war, his wife had refused to kiss him and accused him of having kissed the easily available women of Arkansas. "Now, was'nt that funny[?] but the funniest thing of all will be that

I intend to kiss some of them before I do leave for it shall never be said that I left Arkansas where kissing is so cheap and did'nt take any stock at all[.] but you know this is all a joke and if a man cant joke his own wife who can he joke." A few weeks later, probably in response to a sharp scolding from his unamused mate, Petty tried to set her mind at rest. "My Dear Wife let me assure you that I shall never be guilty of any thing that if known would tinge the cheek of her I love best and of my dear little children. No Never Never. This is enough on the Arkansas girl question."[12]

Whether Stoker, Perry, and Petty held to their vows cannot be known, but many of the Texas soldiers found the women of Arkansas and Louisiana irresistible. Captain Wallace saw the signs all around him: "I am surrounded by wickedness where men are alone and none of the sacred influences of women to constrain them. they become perfectly Reckless. here there is Thousands of us men some times never see a woman in weeks." Private Stoker, worried that soldiers still in Texas might have similar ideas about his own wife, could rest easy, remembering that he had left her armed with a Mexican *pistola.* "There is some men mean enough to do any thing. They go too or three miles off of the road to pester the women [whose] husbands has gone to ware. . . . if any boddy pesters you, just to take your pistole and blow their trotters from under them." Mr. and Mrs. Stoker were not a couple to be trifled with.[13]

Faithful or not, Texas soldiers worried about their wives. Could they raise the children without the presence of a father? Could they handle the farm or shop in the absence of the normal breadwinner? In general, the soldiers thought there was no substitute for a man when it came to running the farm or business. Granville Gage of the First Infantry (Hood's Texas Brigade) could only hope that one of his male relatives would guide Gage's wife. "I hardly know what kind of advice to give you for the best. I hope & trust that uncle James helps you when ever help is necessary[.] I have confidence to believe that he wil not see you suffer, if he can help it." Although he could not be home in Cass County to run his farm, Lt. Orange C. Connor of the Nineteenth Infantry (Walker's Texas Division) assured his wife that other adult males were available to help her. "I am not able to tell you what to do but I know [your father] will advise you well."[14]

Despite their concerns, the Texas soldiers generally gave way to necessity, accepted their situations, and placed their faith in the intelligence and competence of their wives. Sergeant Holcombe of Bastrop County was typical of many soldiers in advising his wife on crops and animals: "write how you are gitting on generaly & how mutch land you have broke up. I think it would be best to plant but little cotton but probaly you had better plant a few acres to buy sutch things as you will be forced to have next fall. you must bear in mind that you will have to pay your tax again soon & will have to have some gold or silver. you had better git it and lay it by and have it ready. I would allso like to know [how] your corn is holding out, how your shoats looks & if you have any more pigs & how many and especialy how our children are gitting on."15

Captain Petty of the Seventeenth Texas, an attorney before the war, counseled his wife about farm animals too, but his advice leaned more toward the business side of the wartime economy. "I think your hog trade was magnificent provided you don't loose them all. They will have to be watched and taken good care of or they will all run wild or some body will get them and in either case they will be lost to you. You had better buy you about 25 or 30 bushels of Sweet potatoes. You can bury them and use that old hay in covering them up so as to keep the frost off—You had better buy about 100 lbs of salt for if the feds get Corpus Christi salt will be an object [of scarcity]. . . . You had better buy 100 lbs of sugar—the feds may get that sugar country in Texas and sugar will be scarce and high."16

Some husbands were pleasantly surprised by their mates' common sense and business acumen. "I am proud to learn that you are so provident that you manage the affairs of a family so well," Captain Petty wrote to his wife, "and I hope that by the time I return home you will be such an adept in these matters that I will have no trouble of the sort on my hands[,] that you will do it all." His proposals, Petty assured her, were merely advisory: "I only suggest—I am not now the head of the family and don't pretend to dictate." Surgeon Becton of Hopkins County, a man with traditional ideas about women in general, was fully confident in his own wife's ability to handle the family's affairs: "you have managed my business in every particular to my entire satisfaction. You have exhibited more judgement & business qualification tha[n] most women possess." In the minds of the Texans, farming and business were normally best left to men, but many of them were proud of their wives for standing up to necessity in an emergency.17

Family communications to and from the soldiers were normally civil and often tender. Occasionally, however, some letters only intensified the anxiety that was chronic among some men far from home. Words of loneliness by wives were particularly troublesome for the Texans. Private Farrow of Panola County, already given to fits of despair, must have sunk even lower when he read some of his wife's letters. "Sam you dont no how bad I feel," she wrote shortly after he left home. To drive the point home, she signed her letter, "Your wife until death." Volney Ellis of Lavaca County in south central Texas admitted that he had been brought low by a recent missive from home: "I must confess that my heart sinks with sadness, my dear Mary, when I peruse your last letter, burthened as it is with sorrow." James R. Loughridge, far away in Virginia with

Hood's Texas Brigade, received one letter that set him to worrying about his wife's reaction to his absence. "Borrow some ancient work to read that will give you an idea of the Roman and early Grecian chareter [character], found among the matrons of the early days of those Republics," he advised her. "Oh! I want you to nerve your whole soul, for what ever may come."[18]

Such letters were not at all uncommon. Few men had more to contend with than Lieutenant Perry of Harrison County. His wife, Harriet, complained regularly about his absence, and she never hesitated to scold him from afar. Less than two months after he left his home in Marshall in the summer of 1862, she wrote, "Oh me—when will it end & let my husband come back to me." In the next few weeks, she signed her letters, "At home All alone" and "At Home Alone." Pregnant and unhappy, she continued her protests in December. "I don't think it possible for me to go on any longer, for I am almost *entirely* helpless, it is all I can do to get in & out of the bed. I do hope & pray I never shall be in this condition again, death is nearly preferable. You don't know how I feel & never can. . . . I don't think any *man* can." If Perry was not wobbly yet, she finished him off with a broadside of defeatism: "I don't feel confident of our success by any means. I think the South is nearly exhausted." Ten days later, more gloom: "I am dying to see you, but I will not write my feelings, for I will only make you unhappy & will do no good. There is no pleasure in life to me, having to live separated from you as I do. I don't care to live."[19]

Mrs. Perry began to fear that her husband was happier in the army than he was at home with her. He seemed not to notice her tribulations. When he did not acknowledge receipt of some packages she had sent him, she reprimanded him stridently. "If you do not [acknowledge the packages] I shall feel *slighted & unappreciated*. . . . I can't bear to be treated with indifference & especially by you. I set too much value on *my labor* to let it go without being appreciated." Reports that her husband was thriving in his new profession of arms elicited more subtle scolding. "All the accounts I have of you my darling are that you are an incessent talker & the bussiest man in Camp & *very cheerful & happy.* Now, husband you must devote some of your 'talking time' to writing your wife." The war did not suit Mrs. Perry at all.[20]

Some women, unlike Harriet Perry, took pride in their ability to overcome hardship and separation. At least their husbands were proud of their wives' stoicism. Edward Cade of the Twenty-Eighth Cavalry instructed his pregnant wife that she must not complain that he was not there to help her through her ordeal: "In the trial of your confinement you must show yourself a *soldiers* wife." Five weeks later, after delivering a healthy son, Allie Cade assured her husband that she had met his expectations: "The ladies all say they never saw greater forbearance. You may say you have got a *soldier* wife." Surgeon Becton of Hopkins

County boasted that his wife's letters "have the ring of the pure metal. A friend read me his wife's letter a short time ago. I was tired long before she closed. 'Oh do come home darling. Oh for one hour with you. I would come to you if I could &c &c.' Now isn't that childish? Thank God you have more sense than that." Two months later Becton complimented his sturdy companion again: "I am truly glad my dear Mary that you appreciate my contentedness—for nothing would make me more unhappy than to receive 'whining, homesick epistles' from you. . . . You talk like a woman of sense & not like a sixteen year old girl."[21]

Mary Becton was at least as tough as her husband. No crying about loneliness or hints about desertion entered her letters. "My own dear Edwin my feelings in respect to your being a soldier are just yours precisely. I have thought just as you said often but never expressed it before that I would not have you at home if I could[,] dearly as I love you. I had rather you were just where you are than lying round at house [as a deserter] and then it [the shame of desertion] would not only be visited on you but on your children." And if he died on duty, so be it. Honor before comfort. "Nothing would do me more good than to know of your standing firm and doing your duty even if you died. let you die at your post." In a completely unnecessary reassurance, she promised, "I do not intend to be a draw-back to you if I can help it with my whining."[22]

Most surviving letters from Hood's Texas Brigade, Terry's Texas Rangers, and Walker's Texas Division were written to or by wives, so spousal relationships are a leading theme in these records. Almost as numerous, though, were discussions of children. Similar to the view of nineteenth-century American husbands as cold and distant patriarchs is the related notion that they were also forbidding "enforcers of discipline and arbiters of family morals," men who left child-rearing to women and expressed little affection or tenderness toward their children. If their private thoughts expressed in letters home are any indication, that theory is as wrongheaded as the first. The rough-handed Texas farmers and stock raisers and town-based lawyers and merchants frequently, almost constantly, expressed affection and tenderness toward their children.[23]

Soldiers often requested that their wives "kiss the children for me." Lieutenant Loughridge of Navarro County ended one letter, "I now send many kisses to you & my sweet babes." He and his children soon sent their love back and forth in graphic form by drawing a circle with numerous dots inside, each dot representing a kiss. John S. Bryan of Collin County, a man who had worked in the rough gold-mining camps of California and now soldiered in the equally rough military camps of Arkansas, asked his wife to "kiss my boy for me. tell him of how I would love to see him and you." Captain Petty instructed his daughter to "kiss all the little rats [his children] for me and tell them to think of

Pa who thinks of them very much." Even colonels were not immune. Richard Waterhouse, commander of the Nineteenth Infantry, asked his wife to "kiss my little boyes for me." Expressions like these are too numerous to count.[24]

The Texans did more than add a line or two about kissing their children to the ends of letters. Some of their missives were truly tender. Pat Martin of the Twenty-Eighth Cavalry celebrated his young son's progress at home. "Bless the sweet little boy. I feel so rejoiced to hear of his proficiency in singing and counting and Papa will send him a ballad of 'Nellie Grey' and he must learn to sing it all and if Papa comes home in January he will assist his little [boy] to sing it." Adopting language that he would have used in speaking to his son, Martin asked his mother-in-law to "tell Jimmie that Papa will come home this winter to see his boy, if he can get off, and then he wants to find a big fat boy and a good boy and then Papa wants to sleep with him on a bed." Lieutenant Loughridge of the Fourth Infantry also resorted to speech patterns he might have used at home: "Ella, Pa's sweet little child! Pas good little babe[.] Pa dreamed of you & Sissa last night, and Ma. Pa is going to send you some pretties. . . . Pa has bought you a little red Album book, with nice pictures in it and Pa has bought a red Album book for Sissa Mary. Pa got your nice little letter with the kisses you & Sissa sent to Pa."[25]

Sergeant Holcombe of the Seventeenth Infantry showed keen interest in his children's upbringing and education. "Marthy Pa will be verry proud to hear you and Lina read for him when he comes home," he wrote. "God bless your little souls." The sergeant could barely wait to return to his children: "tell the children I often think of how mutch I used to pride in making their little swings [and] playhouses and go haw [berry] hunting & to go abraud with them & tell them if I ever git home again I will never tire in trying to add to their pleasure." D. E. Young of the same regiment likewise looked forward to the day when he could enjoy his wife and children: "I hope that Pease Will Soon com and We Will get home and then We can eat drink and Be Merry With our litle Children." Arthur Rainey of the First Texas asked his wife to "Kiss Arthur and Herbert for me and tell them that father loves his little soldier boys and that they must learn their books and be good boys until I come home again. an then kiss the little spoiler, pet child Lula, and tell her that father is always thinking about her and is going to bring her some pretty things when he comes home." Private Stoker of Upshur County mentioned his five-year-old daughter, Priscilla, in virtually all his letters. In the fall of 1862, he did the best he could to talk to her, at least indirectly: "Get Priscilla to say some thing and write it. You wrote that she was as smart & as pretty as ever." Hoping for some clever reaction, he wrote, "Betty, Shew Priscilla my ampletipe [ambrotype] and write what she says about it."[26] Texans may have had rough reputations in the rest of the country, but many of them were affectionate and loving fathers in their homes.

Their tender feelings for their families, not surprisingly, were accompanied by apprehension too. What they feared most—other than the possibility that they would never see their wives and children again—was that their young children would forget them while they were away. A steady stream of letters pleaded with wives to remind the children of their father, to show them a portrait. Other messages asked whether the children "have forgot me yet." Tacitus Clay, far away in Virginia with the Fifth Texas Infantry, begged his wife, "Kiss our babies for me and tell them not to forget their father." Another soldier in Hood's Brigade, Arthur T. Rainey, made the same request to his own wife. Lt. E. Steele of the Twelfth Infantry expressed this fear almost as soon as he left home, even before he left Texas. "You must not let Manny forget me," he pleaded in February 1862. A month later, "tell all the children to learn fast and not forget me." Lt. Edward Cade of Smith County also worried while still within easy traveling distance of home in June 1862: "Kiss Henry—Dont let him forget his papa." Ten days later, "Dont let Henry forget papa."[27]

Private Farrow of Panola County worried along with other young fathers. "I am very anxios to see you and my sweet children. Please do not let them forget me in my absence," he pleaded. Private Stoker could not bear the thought that his beloved Priscilla might drift away from him: "Write if Priscilla has forgot me or not." Five months later the possibility still gnawed at him. "I want to see you so bad I am nearley ded & the thoughts of Priscilas forgetting me, hurts me." Only a few weeks away from his home in Bastrop County, Sergeant Holcombe repeated the same theme. "Has the children quit talking of me?" he asked pitifully. "Has John & Charley forgotton me[?] kiss them for me."[28]

Images of wives and children swirled through the minds of the Texans during their long nights so far from home. The pleasant memories of warm embraces, intimate conversations, and laughing children mixed with pangs of loneliness, worries about the farm, alarm that their children might forget them, and dread that they would never see their homes again. Whatever their longings and anxieties, Texas soldiers frequently and sometimes openly declared their affection for their mates, and they dreamed and daydreamed of kissing, cuddling, and playing with their children. If haughty patriarchs walked among them, most Texas soldiers doubtless found them strange creatures indeed.

Col. Adam Rankin Johnson, Tenth
Kentucky Partisan Rangers.
Courtesy William C. Davis

3

"If We Should Succeed in Driving the Enemy Back Out of My Native State"

*Why Texans Fought East of the
Mississippi River during the Civil War*

Charles D. Grear

For well over a century, historians have examined the reasons why Southern men joined the Confederate military. Most scholars have concluded that the defense of hearth and home was a primary factor pushing soldiers to the front. None of them, however, have clearly defined or examined the complex nature of this motivation. "Home and hearth" is essentially a collection of attachments that people develop throughout their lifetime. Attachments involve issues that concerned the soldiers the most, including families, both immediate, extended, and friends; localities, where they were born, their current homestead, and places where they lived for a time or had significant experiences; and a way of life, ranging from occupations and hobbies to slavery and social status. All of these devotions had a direct influence on the decision of Southern men to leave their homes and families and endure hardships and chance death for the Confederacy. Attachments affected soldiers from every state, but Texans demonstrate most clearly the complexity and extent of this motivation since they originally came from many places and served in all theaters of the war.[1]

Approximately a quarter of all units raised in Texas fought east of the Mississippi River. Most of these soldiers had their origins in one way or the other from that region since many had recently moved west, leaving their extended families behind. One of the strongest motivations for Texans to fight in the East was the desire to protect cherished localities, including the hometowns, family members, and friends they years before had left behind. Since a majority of Texans were migrants from the East, many of them had more than one homestead, and most still had a "home" in their native state, metaphorically and sometimes physically. These were the dwellings where they had grown up and the areas where their parents had raised them. In some cases parents and extended kin still inhabited the old homestead east of the Mississippi, forming a continuing, loving connection with the Texas soldier. These men thus had to make a decision as to which location they most wanted to protect, Texas or their eastern hometowns. At the beginning of the war, A. T. Rainey, a soldier in the First Texas Infantry, expressed what many thought: "No one here believes that Texas will be invaded."[2] So for such men, their former states back east were under a more immediate threat by the Union army. These attachments influenced Texans to leave their immediate families in the Lone Star State to fight east of the Mississippi in defense of their old hometowns and kin presently threatened by Yankee guns. While men in many Texas units answered the call to enlist in distant theaters, for brevity this essay will examine Hood's Texas Brigade and Terry's Texas Rangers, the most famous units east of the Mississippi, as well as lesser known Texans such as those in the Grapevine Volunteers and

Col. Richard Montgomery Gano,
Seventh Kentucky Cavalry.
*Courtesy Confederate Research
Center, Hill College,
Hillsboro, Texas*

individuals such as Charles Trueheart and Adam Rankin Johnson who went as far as enlisting in regiments from their former states.

Attachments were not an isolated influence that solely affected Texans; it motivated many soldiers throughout the South. Two fine examples of this motivation includes the "Red River Company" of the Fourteenth Tennessee Infantry and the Sixth Kentucky Infantry. Attachments affected the men of the Fourteenth Tennessee when they lost their hometowns to the enemy early in the war after the fall of Fort Donelson. When they reorganized in 1862, the men reexamined the reasons why they wanted to remain together as a fighting unit, finally producing a contract among themselves entitled "'Red River' Company Agreement." In this document they outlined their motivation to remain in the Confederate army and continue "to stand together and drive that enemy from our Childhood homes—from the home of our Fathers and Mothers." These men welded a strong desire to "remain united and joined as a band of brothers, honorable representatives of the Old Red River Neighborhood" to "make an effort in behalf of our Red River homes that will be donned with honor and credit to us through all ages." They wanted to take back their hometowns, the only place in the nation for which they held an emotional bond. Similarly William E. Minor, a private in the Sixth Kentucky, wrote of his motivations to fight in a letter to *The Weekly Courier* early in the war: "[T]he North don't understand our spirit. They mistake for what we are fighting. They had as well try to quench the fire of life—as to try to subjugate those who are satisfied they are fighting for their mothers, fathers, sisters, kindred, and the tender ones of their hearts." While the influence of attachments extends to men from throughout the South, it is the most pronounced in Texans since they had more than one home and had to decide which one to defend.[3]

There is also psychological justification for Southerners and Texans to defend their extended family. According to Roy R. Grinker and John P. Speigel in their study of the psychological influences on men in combat, the motivation to fight in a war began

with the individual's past history and especially with his capacity to form identifications with other groups of people and to feel loyal to them. This process, as with any identification, is based on strong love and affection and begins very early in life. . . . The earliest identification made by an individual is with members of his family circle, and is at first confined to those that provide love and care, the parents, and especially the mother. Later the feeling of identity spreads to include both parents and then brothers and sisters and other members of the family. During childhood, the range of identification becomes constantly broader as the horizon of social contacts expands. Eventually, the school, then the community and finally the nation itself are included.[4]

Families are the first and most important influence on how people identify themselves. It is only logical to think that family members will continue to be a very important part of a person's life. For Southerners, the ties proved even stronger.

These bonds remained strong because Southern families tended to migrate and settle together. Close family ties, though very similar to those throughout the South, helped create one of the greatest differences between Texas and what would become the rest of the Confederacy. Southerners moved to the Lone Star State for such reasons as soil depletion and financial hardships. In some cases planters took over yeoman farmers' property and forced them to go someplace where land was cheap. When Southerners migrated and settled in Texas, they wrote back to the family they left behind, encouraging them to move to Texas. This influx created a population boom for the state. From 1850 to 1860, the population of Texas increased 184 percent, from 212,592 to 604,215. Southern migrants tended to settle in areas that resembled the region they left because they already possessed the skills to farm that type of land and possessed the proper tools to be successful. Consequently, people from one state would concentrate in one area of Texas, those from another, elsewhere. A pattern developed in which people from Tennessee settled in the black waxy prairie, Louisianans in the counties bordering the Gulf of Mexico, Georgians in the plantation districts of northeastern Texas, Alabamans in the inland counties east of the Tennesseans, Mississippians in western south-central Texas, and Kentuckians in North Texas. Within these regions, families and friends settled together.[5]

This antebellum migration dramatically altered the composition of the state's population, making it far different than the rest of the South. By 1860 the population of Texas reached 604,215. Only a quarter of these people (153, 043) could call Texas their birthplace, while a third (192,109) were Southern born. A very small fraction of Texans, 4 percent (21,712) came from the North, and a little over 7 percent (43,422) were foreign born. Of the foreigners, half were Germans, a quarter Mexicans, and the last quarter consisted of Irish, French, English, and a mix of people from eastern Europe. Slaves (182,921) composed the final third of the state's population. No other state in the South had such a large number of migrants with very few natives within its borders.[6]

Since Texas was recently populated with people from other parts of the United States, its citizens identified almost as much with their former homes as with their new home. Yet those who had lived there the longest established a strong attachment to Texas and the locality where they lived. How long a man had resided in the state determined his motivation for fighting in the Civil War, and more important, where he wanted to fight. Migration had a direct influence on their decision and created a special situation for Texas at the onset of the war.[7]

To raise military units to fight east of the Mississippi River, the Confederate government advertised in newspapers. During this period, very few copies of distant newspapers reached Texas, but other newspapers copied the advertisements and reprinted them in other states. Over time these reached the Lone Star State. An example of this call for troops appeared in Marshall's *Texas Republican* on June 22, 1861: "The Last *Richmond [Virginia] Enquirer* contains an editorial article eulogizing Texas for the promptness, patriotism, courage and humanity displayed by our people during the present struggle and stating that one or two regiments from this State are much needed and will be received."[8] The advertisement proved effective. "The Marshall Guards," later to be known as Company E, First Texas Infantry, were soon on their way to Virginia. Men who responded to this call would form part of the most famous of all Texas units, John Bell Hood's Texas Brigade.[9]

The brigade was composed of the First, Fourth, and Fifth Texas Infantry along with the Eighteenth Georgia Infantry and the Third Arkansas Infantry. The companies that constituted the Texas regiments came from distinct areas of the Lone Star State. Most of the men who served in the First Texas came from East Texas, while those serving in the Fourth and Fifth Texas Infantry came mainly from central Texas, with a smaller number from East Texas. Among the Texans of Hood's Brigade, approximately half of them called Southern states east of the Mississippi River their birthplace and childhood home. Compared to Texans who enlisted in regiments serving in the Trans-Mississippi, which had a similar percentage of men from the region, Hood's men had lived in Texas for three fewer years on average. A smaller percentage of the men serving in Virginia, more than 7 percent, had moved to Texas before or during their fifth birthday compared to 12 percent of those who remained behind to defend the Lone Star State. These men remembered their old homes and consequently had a stronger attachment to the Cis-Mississippi than those serving west of the river. Their connection to the East combined with living in Texas for a shorter period of time, thus having fewer opportunities to develop an attachment to their locality, contributed to their desire to fight in that theater of the war.[10]

Texans returned to the East to protect their former hometowns, places to which they had a local attachment. This reveals itself through the personal histories of the men of the Hood's Brigade.

During the war, Capt. George T. Todd was a company commander in the First Texas Infantry. Born in 1839 in Matthews County, Virginia, Todd migrated to Texas as a child in the early 1840s but did not sever his ties to his native state. When he came of age, he chose to attend college at Hampton Academy in Virginia, just across Chesapeake Bay from where he grew up, for his first three years, then transferred to and in 1860 graduated from the University of Virginia, rejuvenating his attachment to the state. That same year he returned to Texas, where he studied law and was admitted to the bar. The combination of being born in Virginia and spending his college years there influenced Todd's decision to leave his immediate family behind in Texas to defend the Old Dominion.[11]

Other Texans had strong connections to Virginia too. Asa Roberts of the Fourth Texas Infantry, born at his grandfather's house in Madison County, Virginia, did not move to Texas until 1858. When the war began he went back to Virginia to defend his old hometown and his grandfather, who nursed Roberts back to health when he was stricken with typhoid fever during his service. Along with Todd and Roberts, other Virginia Texans included Frederick S. Bass, commander of Company E, First Texas Infantry and later colonel of the regiment, a graduate of the Virginia Military Institute; William H. Hamman, Fourth Texas, who graduated from the University of Virginia before moving to Texas in early 1858; James D. Roberdeau, Fifth Texas Infantry, who was born and raised in Fairfax County, Virginia, before moving to Texas in 1858; and John Robert Keeling, whose family's roots in the Old Dominion extended back two hundred years before the war.[12]

Not all of the soldiers of Hood's Brigade came from Virginia; a significant number came from other states in the Cis-Mississippi. One of these men was Edward D. Ryan, captain of Company E, Fourth Texas Infantry. Born in Alabama in 1837 and raised there, Ryan migrated to Texas in the late 1850s. Twenty-four years old when the war began, he left his new state to defend the one he left behind. At that time the best place to prevent Northern soldiers from invading Alabama was to fight them in Virginia. Another officer with a similar situation was R. M. Powell. Born in Montgomery, Alabama, Powell migrated to Texas in 1849. He enlisted to fight in Virginia as a soldier in Company D, Fifth Texas Infantry at the onset of the war, later commanding the regiment. Edward Richardson Crockett signed up to fight in Virginia with Company F, Fourth Texas. Born in Decatur, Alabama, in 1834, Crockett moved to Texas in 1853. His eastern roots influenced him to seek service in Virginia. Similarly two Alabama-born brothers, Robert and Billy Gaston, moved to Tyler in 1849 but enlisted in the Virginia-bound First Texas Infantry. The men believed that by confronting the enemy in Virginia, they could keep them away from their native state.[13]

Nobody demonstrated their desire to enlist early in the war to protect their home many states away more than Jerome Robertson. Robertson was born in

Christian County, Kentucky, where he lived most of his life, eventually becoming a doctor. In 1836 he left with his wife for Texas, where they settled near Washington on the Brazos. Between the years 1838 and 1844, he served on average two military campaigns a year against Native Americans and Mexican invaders. When the Texas Congress called for a secession convention, he represented Washington County and voted in favor of disunion. When the call came for Texans to enlist to fight in Virginia, he joined the "Texas Aids," which later became Company I, Fifth Texas Infantry. As the war progressed Robertson became commander of Hood's Texas Brigade and served in that capacity longer than anybody else.[14]

Yet many who were born and raised in Texas also fought in Virginia. These men differed from the others in several ways, the most obvious being their age. Since Texas was a recently settled region, most native citizens were youths. Youthful ambitions played a role, especially for these Texans, in the recruitment of men to fight east of the Mississippi. The thoughts of a young man with the opportunity to experience adventure came from the pen of David Cary Nance, who wrote: "But like all boys in Early life, I loved adventure, so that when the first call came for volunteer troops I was crazy to go yes, crazy, for that is the only way to describe a boys sentiment when he is anxious to go to war." Youthful excitement was common during the Civil War, and many of the men who fought east of the Mississippi described their comrades' youth and enthusiasm to reach the front lines. Once promises of war reached the ears of young Texans, they flocked to the recruiters because they were afraid that the war would be over before they could participate in combat. A. T. Rainey, a soldier in the First Texas Infantry, expressed this belief when he wrote: "The current opinion is that the war will be a very short one." Many Texans expressed this fear, including John W. Stevens, who fought in Virginia with Hood's Texas Brigade and wrote, "if we did not hurry up, the fight would be over or declared off before we could get there." With all their enthusiasm, the young men needed a place to fight. After the firing on Fort Sumter and the secession of the Upper South states, Northern Virginia immediately became the most important battleground. A testament to the youthfulness of native Texans is found in Felix Huston Robertson, the only Texan born in the state to become a general officer, the youngest in the war.[15]

These young Texans did not fight in the East for honor alone. They also sought to defend their home, the Lone Star State, by fighting in Virginia. John Marquis Smither epitomizes this notion. Born in Walker County, Texas, in 1845, Smither enlisted in Company D, Fifth Texas Infantry at the age of sixteen. His motivation to fight is found in a letter he wrote to his mother from Virginia on February 27, 1862, "that although fighting in Virginia I was striving to maintain the honor and in defense of 'Texas my native land; my home.'"[16] Although he had few ties to Virginia or the East Coast, Smither still believed that the fighting there was important to the future of his state and hometown. He is representative of the young men who had no direct connection to the East but instead enlisted in the early months of the war because they thought that it was better to fight the enemy in Virginia than to engage them in Texas.[17]

Family ties also influenced the actions of these young Texans once they arrived in the East. Many visited their extended families. Although born in Alabama, William H. Lewis had relatives in Virginia. To his mother he wrote: "One of our Virginia cousins came over to see me a week or so ago. His name is Murrie S. Anderson a son of cousin Lucy Anderson of Ablemarle Co. Va. . . . His mother has been very kind to me indeed I have never had the pleasure of paying her a visit—but intend to do so the first opportunity."[18] James T. Hunter, Fourth Texas Infantry, had similar desires. He wrote to a friend, "I was very anxious to have gotten a short furlough to visit my friends in Buckingham and Appomattox Counties this winter."[19] Others, such as C. S. Worsham, visited their childhood homes. Worsham wrote to his mother, "I am right here at my old home."[20] The proximity of family, friends, and childhood homes to the war zone influenced many Texans to leave the Lone Star State to defend these attachments. Visiting their kin reinforced their desire to fight in the region.

Rufus King Felder provides another example of this influence. At the age of fifteen, Felder moved to Texas from South Carolina in 1855 with his cousin Miers, leaving behind a large number of family members. When the war started, both Felder and Meirs enlisted in Company E, Fifth Texas Infantry, originally known as the "Dixie Blues." While they fought for the Confederacy and for Texas, the two had a more immediate desire to defend their extended family back East. Felder wrote letters late in the war to his family in Texas revealing his connection to his kin and describing an opportunity he took to visit relatives and friends at Orangeburg, South Carolina, while en route to Chickamauga, Georgia, from Virginia: "Things had changed so much in the family it did not seem natural, Cousins John and Sam are no more and cousins Eugene and Adella have moved off, and Ed is in the service. I did not see any of the family except cousin Lon."[21] Another letter written by Felder further reveals his concern for his eastern relations. On February 23, 1865, he wrote his sister: "Yes, my dear sister, the insolent foe have dared to march through the very heart of South Carolina & I have no doubt committed depridations on the property, if not on the persons of our dear, but unfortunate relatives. God grant that they may have been spared and that the scenes of our childhood of our noble ancestors not desecrated by the ——— of our brutal enemy."[22]

Not all of the Texans who enlisted early in the war fought in Virginia. Another famous Lone Star regiment, the Eighth Texas Cavalry (more commonly called Terry's Texas Rangers after its first colonel, Benjamin Franklin Terry), fought between the Mississippi River and the Appalachian Mountains. Although the men enlisted under the promise of fighting in Virginia, they were transferred later to Kentucky by Gen. Albert Sidney Johnston, the highest ranking Texan in the Confederate army at that time. These horsemen experienced the same motivation to defend their attachments as the infantrymen in Hood's Brigade.

The organization of Terry's Texas Rangers began at the conclusion of the First Battle of Manassas, when Thomas Saltus Lubbock, brother of future Texas governor Francis Richard Lubbock, along with Benjamin F. Terry and John A. Wharton, arrived in Virginia and asked if Confederate forces there needed some cavalry from Texas. All three men had ties to places east of the Mississippi River—Lubbock, born in Charleston, South Carolina; Wharton, born in Nashville, Tennessee; and Benjamin Terry, born in Russellville, Kentucky—and thereby desired to meet the enemy before the Yankees neared their former homesteads.[23] The eastern connections of these three men certainly influenced the formation and history of the regiment.

All three were optimistic about receiving permission from Jefferson Davis and "the Secretary of War to raise a regiment of mounted rangers for service in Virginia."[24] With such authorization, they returned to Texas to recruit their unit. One of their newspaper advertisements in the *Dallas Herald* of May 8, 1861, appeared under the loud title, "Texas Guerillas HO! To the Rescue!" It "call[ed] for volunteers to form an independent company to go to Virginia, to aid and assist in the great drama that is about to come off in that State." Similar advertisements appeared in other papers across the state.[25]

Once Lubbock, Wharton, and Terry raised enough men to form a regiment, they marched toward Virginia. But their dreams of getting into the war in Virginia ended quickly when they arrived in New Orleans. There the men heard the news that they were no longer going east but instead north to Bowling Green, Kentucky, to join General Johnston's command (at the general's request). This upset many of the men who had dreams of fighting in Virginia. In his diary James Knox Polk Blackburn expressed his disappointment about not going to the Old Dominion. "This change of destination," he wrote, "brought deep disappointment and displeasure to everyone, as their hearts had been set on going to Virginia."[26] Another soldier agreed with Blackburn's dismay in a letter to his mother: "We received orders last knight by Telegraph to go to Kentucky instead of Virginia We will leave here in the morning for Nasvile Tenesee where we will be mounted There is som dissatisfaction among some of the Companyes as to the change of our servise from Virginia to that of Kentucky."[27]

Although the Rangers may have been upset about losing the opportunity to fight in Virginia, they would have their chance to prove themselves sooner than they thought. And at the same time, other motivations quickly emerged. Unlike

Lubbock and Wharton, most of these Texans, including their commander, came from the states in the Western Theater. In comparison to Hood's Brigade and Texans serving in the Trans-Mississippi, 10 percent more men came from the Cis-Mississippi (a total for the regiment of almost 60 percent). Additionally they had spent less time in Texas, a year less on average than Hood's men and four less than those serving west of the Mississippi River. The difference was more pronounced in Terry's Texas Rangers because it was raised after Hood's Texas Brigade, the recruitment of which had provided the opportunity for those not solely looking for adventure but with stronger ties to the East.[28]

But other men in the regiment, besides the initial leaders, had connections to the eastern side of the Mississippi River. The man who led the regiment for the longest period of time, after the departure of Terry, Lubbock, and Wharton, was Thomas Harrison. Harrison, initially a major in the regiment, earned a promotion to colonel in late 1862. Born in Ruhama, Jefferson County, Alabama, in 1823, he moved with his parents to Monroe County, Mississippi, where he grew up. By 1843 he had moved to Brazoria County, Texas, though for only a brief time before moving back to Mississippi. After serving in the Mexican War, Harrison returned to Texas and was living in Waco when the Civil War broke out. Although born in Alabama, his strongest connection was with Mississippi, and by serving in Terry's Texas Rangers, he could be satisfied that he was protecting both localities by blocking the Union advance through Kentucky, the most direct threat to the two states at that time.[29]

Like those who joined Hood's Brigade, the men of Terry's Texas Rangers fought to defend family, friends, and hometowns left behind when they migrated to Texas. Ephraim Shelby Dodd was born and raised in Richmond, Kentucky, and did not move to Texas until late 1860. While in Kentucky, Dodd, one of the newest Texans, "went over to Cousin Mec's to take dinner." Aside from visiting family members, he also went back to his old hometown to visit friends, writing: "I went down to our old stamping ground to-day. I stopped to see Miss Eugenie Holt; had just returned from visit to Marietta and was looking very pretty." He then continued to see several more people from his hometown. Some of these people and places include, once again, extended family members such as when Dodd "[w]ent to Grandpaps . . . and got breakfast."[30] Such reports demonstrate the strong influence that local attachments had on these Texans.

The greatest indication of migrant Texans' continuing attachments to their original locations is that some simply joined units from other states. This sometimes happened on a large scale, as with the Grapevine Volunteers, a squadron from Tarrant County that traveled to Kentucky to enlist en masse in a regiment belonging to that state, or individually, as with Charles Trueheart and Adam Rankin Johnson. Their experiences illustrate this phenomenon.

The commander of the Grapevine Volunteers was Capt. Richard Montgomery Gano. His antebellum life played a significant role in the origins of the Grapevine Volunteers. Gano was born in Bourbon County, Kentucky, on June 17, 1830, to Elder John Allen Gano and Mary Catherine (Conn) Gano. Educated there and in Virginia, he graduated from medical school and soon moved to Louisiana, where he practiced medicine for several years. In March 1853, two years after moving to Baton Rouge, he married Martha J. Welch. By 1857 he and his wife moved to Grapevine (Tarrant County), Texas.[31]

In early May Gano began to organize two companies, which would later form a squadron of cavalry. On June 28 this squadron officially entered state service as the Grapevine Volunteers, named for the location where they mustered.[32]

A unique aspect of the Grapevine Volunteers is that a majority of its men had recently moved to Texas. As new residents, they felt the strong pull of previous local loyalties, intensified by kinship ties. In other words, the motivation for these men to leave Texas to fight east of the Mississippi was a combination of where they grew up and the family bonds that existed throughout the South before the war. Only 1 percent of squadron members had been born in Texas, 1 percent came from foreign countries, and 5 percent came from free states. The rest of the men, 93 percent, had come from elsewhere in the South; specifically, 26 percent were from the Lower South, and 67 percent from the Upper South. This was a significant factor for the men when they decided which military unit to join, for most wanted to enlist for someone who could promise that they would have the opportunity to join the western army and defend their extended families in the region from the Mississippi to the Appalachians.[33]

By early March 1862, Gano received orders from General Johnston, an acquaintance, that the Grapevine Volunteers be mustered into the Confederate army. Gano and his men were to meet Johnston at Bowling Green, Kentucky and serve as scouts for his headquarters. In the process of transferring his men enlisted national service, Gano advertised in the *Dallas Herald* on January 28, 1862, to fill the openings in their ranks created by men receiving transfers to other units or who had to return home because of illness: "Doctors J. M. Huffman and R. M. Gano, have authority to muster into Confederate service, two companies as a cavalry squadron, to be marched by Little Rock, to Memphis, and thence by cars to Bowling Green, Ky." Besides making a call for men, this advertisement makes a specific call for those who wanted to serve in Kentucky.[34]

For months, Gano wrote to the Confederate secretary of war asking to be given the opportunity to receive a permanent assignment in Kentucky. He expressed these desires clearly in two letters written while en route to Johnston's command. Gano tried to get his men attached to the command they desired by arguing that, by having "been reared in Bourbon Co[unty] and partially educated at Harrodsburg and having married the daughter of Dr. Thomas Welch of

Craborchard, . . . I have a knowledge of the country that would aid us greatly in the service of my beloved country. If we should succeed in driving the enemy back out of my native state." The captain was not above the use of flattery either: "We hope to vie with Captain [John] [Hunt] Morgan's Squadron for honors and laurels. We expect a place in your command, and do not let us be disappointed. . . . I shall never get over it if we are placed anywhere else. I used that as an argument in raising the squadron and the consequences was your warmest admirers flocked to us and we must not be disappointed. All we want is that place."[35]

Gano emphasized the desire of the men to defend a specific region of the Confederacy, the Upper South—especially Kentucky and Tennessee—the area where most of his soldiers had been born and where their extended families lived. In another letter he repeated the theme: "I am well acquainted with all central Kentucky and upper Tennessee. . . . We can under Genl B[reckenridge] who knows well the section of country I am acquainted with, render to our country efficient service."[36] Gano and his men got their wish and received orders to join John Hunt Morgan's command. These Texans would fight under Morgan for almost two years, participating in almost every fight as the nucleus of the Seventh Kentucky Cavalry.[37]

While the Grapevine Volunteers enlisted as a unit to fight in Kentucky, other Texans enlisted as individuals in the regiments of other states. One of these was Charles Trueheart. Born in Virginia, Trueheart moved to Texas with his family as a child. At the outbreak of the war, he was studying medicine at the University of Virginia and "felt it my duty to take up arms in defence of this the state of my birth." At first he enlisted in a company formed by students at his university but eventually transferred to the Rockbridge Artillery because "[a] large num[ber of my] college mates belong to it. . . . So I [have] a number of friends and relatives to [keep me] company." Another influence on his decision to defend Virginia was his extended family. Throughout the war he constantly visited with his relatives and reported to his family in Texas that "all of our kith and kin there abouts were as well as usual." Even though he spent most of his life in Texas, Trueheart had a profound attachment to Virginia because it was the state of his birth, the place where he was attending college, and the home of his extended family. He even claimed, "If there is one thing that I am proud of, it is being a Virginian, and a Texan!"[38]

The most notable Texan to enlist in another state's regiment was Adam Rankin "Stovepipe" Johnson. Born in 1834 and raised in Henderson, Kentucky, Johnson moved to Burnet County, Texas, in 1854 at the age of twenty. In Texas he surveyed the frontier and worked on the Overland Mail Route but found no success in either. When the Civil War began, Johnson had few material possessions in Texas and sought to do as his friends "Helm and Barnet," who had "returned to their native States." His neighbors pleaded with him to stay because he had just married a sixteen-year-old Texan, but that was not enough to hold Johnson in the state. He decided to protect his native Kentucky and, more important, the town of Henderson in western Kentucky on the border with Indiana, where his parents still lived. He made arrangements for the safety of his wife and then left for the Blue Grass State.[39]

According to Johnson, once in Kentucky, "I determined first to pay a visit to my father and mother, in Henderson," which "was occupied by Northern troops."[40] Alarmed by the Federal occupation of the town, he sought to join a Confederate command that would promise to stay in western Kentucky so he could protect his old hometown and nearby family. The first commander he met who made this promise was Brig. Gen. Nathan Bedford Forrest. After an elaborate conversation with the general, Johnson told him, "I wish to go to Henderson, Kentucky." Forrest responded, "I want to go there, too, and we will go together." Forrest kept his promise, and soon thereafter the unit scouted the area just south of Henderson, where all except Johnson fought their first engagement.[41]

The Texan missed the fight in Sacramento because "Forrest's horses were in such a condition that he could not undertake the expedition to Henderson without a rest of two days, and being too impatient to see my parents to brook such a delay, I set out in a buggy with one of my old schoolmates who lived there." Impatience cost Johnson his opportunity to fight Northern soldiers, but it did not matter to him because his main priority was to visit his family and assure himself that they were safe, though behind Yankee lines. He eluded the Federals and "entered Henderson without interruption, and . . . was soon in the arms of. . . both my mother and sister." Besides seeing his sister and mother, Johnson visited with old schoolmates and his brothers, who all enlisted in the Union army. His homecoming was bittersweet because he knew that he could do nothing at that moment to rid his beloved hometown of the enemy's forces, though it fueled his desire to do what he could.[42]

General Johnston cut the Texan's visit short when he ordered Forrest "to hold his command in readiness to move to Fort Donelson." Johnson's reaction was typical of a man who had a deep-seated desire to protect his hometown and family. "I was greatly disappointed," he wrote, "for I had anticipated capturing the blue-coats or driving them out of my native town." Although he did not want to obey the order, he left his hometown to fight in the battles at Fort Donelson and accompanied Forrest when he made his escape from the encroaching Federal force.[43]

He remained with Forrest as a scout until another threat arose against Henderson. "As soon as Martin, Owen and I heard of the arrival of the Federal provost guard, about eighty men, in Henderson, we determined to attack it." Johnson and his two companions attacked groups of Northern soldiers but quickly retreated to a nearby family friend's farm to hide from any Yankee retaliation. Realizing that they could not rid Henderson of the Yankee presence, the men remained outside of town.[44]

Johnson continued to be acutely sensitive to any perceived threat to his hometown and family, fearing for the safety of both. In an extraordinary response to the Federal threat, Johnson did the unimaginable: raise a Confederate unit behind enemy lines to protect western Kentucky. Initially he attracted enough men to create a battalion dubbed "The Breckenridge Guards," but eventually he raised enough for a regiment that became the Tenth Kentucky Partisan Rangers. This Texan not only crossed the Mississippi River to defend his hometown but also organized a full regiment of Kentuckians. While raising the unit, he made an attempt to draw more Texans to Kentucky through an advertisement in *The State Gazette,* dated December 10, 1862, to "raise another company of Texas Rangers to serve in Tennessee or Kentucky under the celebrated A. R. Johnson of Burnet County, Texas, now commanding a brigade of Kentucky cavalry."[45]

Johnson was an extreme representation of Texans crossing the Mississippi to defend their old hometowns and kin. Time and again he returned to western Kentucky to drive the Yankees out of the region and ensure the safety of his parents and sister. When Johnson received orders from his superiors to leave the area, he would find ways to keep his men in western Kentucky. Then attached to Gen. Braxton Bragg's army, Johnson sought to leave that command and join another unit in order to stay near his hometown. Bragg ordered his units out of the area to the dismay of Johnson. The Texan quickly contacted "General [John Hunt] Morgan, who offered me the command of one of his two brigades, I united my force with his upon the understanding that General Morgan would divide his battery with me and allow me to return to my old department of Western Kentucky."[46] In addition, whenever he could not find a local solution to remain in western Kentucky, Johnson was not afraid to look to the seat of the Confederate government. "I continued to be anxious to get back to my department of western Kentucky, and as soon as we got far enough into Tennessee to send letters to Richmond I wrote Hon. Henry Burnett and Colonel William Preston Johnson, two Kentucky friends, and presented to them urgent reasons for my return to this special territory."[47] Only after the war ended and "having confidence in the great resources of Texas," Johnson wrote, "I am determined to return to my home in that state."[48] Not all Texans were as adamant about a specific location as Johnson was, but the influence was still present.

Texans' desire to fight in the eastern theaters of the Civil War stemmed from a combination of many motivations. A powerful one was their attachments to people and places in those regions. Since many Texans had family members, friends, and their origins on the other side of the river who appeared more vulnerable to the Union army, many enlisted in the Confederate army to defend these attachments. This motivation is more pronounced in Texans than men in other Southern states such as Georgia or South Carolina. Most other Southerners did not have any real desire to travel hundreds of miles to fight in the Trans-Mississippi because they had only one hometown, which was east of the Mississippi. Texans such as those who fought in Hood's Texas Brigade, Terry's Texas Rangers, and the Grapevine Volunteers, however, had many different locations they wanted to defend, and therefore where they chose to fight depended on the attachments in their lives and the strength of the connection they had. Texans who enlisted to fight east of the Mississippi did not make their decision lightly—they had a strong desire to protect the families, friends, and hometowns they had left behind.

This fanciful engraving of the hanging tree at Gainesville is
based upon an account by Frederick Sumner. In fact,
while the victims were all hanged from the same elm,
they were executed singly or in pairs.
Originally published in *Frank Leslie's Illustrated
Weekly Newspaper,* February 20, 1864.

4

The Price of Liberty

The Great Hanging at Gainesville

Richard B. McCaslin

The deadliest lynching in U.S. history occurred in Texas during the Civil War. Militia mustered under Confederate authority in Cooke County arrested more than 150 men in October 1862. Vigilantes in Gainesville, the county seat, hanged 40 men. A few more were executed in other counties, but Gainesville became most closely linked to the "Great Hanging." The news traveled widely, but hopes for justice were stymied by wartime endorsement of the event by state officials and postwar efforts by national and local leaders for reconciliation. Ironically, a concern for order and security motivated participants on both sides, frustrating many who sought redress afterward.[1]

Cooke County lies in the watersheds of the Trinity and Red rivers in North Texas. Early settlement proceeded slowly, and like much of the antebellum frontier, the region was plagued with vigilantism. Settler David J. Eddleman recalled that a "rope and some convenient tree" were often used "to dispatch business."[2] It was not until 1849, a year after Cooke County was created, that commissioners asked Daniel Montague to locate a seat for the government. Controversy postponed a decision until August 1850, when locals acted to end the debate. A referendum was scheduled, but while some were visiting a tract, Chief Justice Robert Wheelock waved a jug of whisky and asked all who wanted the seat on the Elm Fork to follow him. Most did, and the commissioners accepted their choice. Several had served under Gen. Edmund P. Gaines against the Seminoles, so the town became Gainesville, though it was not incorporated as such until 1873.

The establishment of the Butterfield Overland Mail route transformed Gainesville. The stagecoaches entered Texas across the Red River, then stopped in Sherman and Diamond's Station in Grayson County before rolling to Gainesville. Settlers followed in droves. The population of Cooke County in 1850 was 220; by 1860 it was 3,760. An army officer in 1854 found Gainesville to be a "collection of five or six log cabins, dignified with the name of a town." In 1859 a visitor saw fifty or sixty houses, "most of them neat edifices and none shabby." The census in 1860 listed 280 people in the town, which the *Texas Almanac* asserted was "perhaps one of the most pleasant . . . in North Texas."[3] The flood of immigrants created deep divisions that mirrored those in the state as a whole. By 1860, nonslaveowners from the Upper South remained a majority, as they had been from the start, but a slaveowner minority, mostly from the Lower South, occupied the best lands and dominated the local economy. Nonslaveowners settled in the Eastern Cross Timbers on the line between Cooke and Grayson counties. Those in the southeastern corner of Cooke County, known as "sandlappers," built a school and church on land donated by Rama Dye. Montague and other slaveowners resided on Fish Creek, which flowed into the Red River. More slaveowners clustered on the river at Sivell's Bend and Delaware Bend, where James G. Bourland, a former state senator, built his home.

As elsewhere, economic prominence became political dominance for Cooke County slaveowners. In 1861 the chief justice, sheriff, and three of the four county commissioners owned slaves. Local slaveholders also led volunteers against Indians. Bourland added to his two decades of service by commanding a company of volunteers in 1858, and his brother did the same in Grayson County. Their targets were not always Indians, though. Four whites accused of raids in Jack County, carved from Cooke County in 1856, were acquitted by a court but hanged by vigilantes. Bourland's brother killed two slaves in an uprising allegedly inspired by abolitionists. Also, his son-in-law, slaveholder Samuel C. Doss, chaired a Gainesville vigilante meeting that exiled an accused abolitionist.

Unfortunately for those concerned with order and security, more abolitionists came, including some ministers of the Northern Methodist Episcopal Church who continued to work in areas claimed by southern preachers. Unrest in Kansas and John Brown's raid in 1859 increased tensions. Tempers flared when fires erupted in the summer of 1860, damaging Dallas, Denton, Pilot Point, and Gainesville. Some insisted that high temperatures had ignited newly introduced phosphorous matches in local stores, but many believed abolitionists started the fires. John Marshall of Austin's *Texas State Gazette* printed a note from Charles R. Pryor of the *Dallas Herald,* who declared that the fires were evidence of a "deep laid scheme of villainy to devastate the whole of Northern Texas."[4]

Many fled North Texas after the fires, but vigilantes still found several victims. William H. Crawford, an accused abolitionist, was lynched at Fort Worth. Methodist elder Anthony Bewley was chased to Missouri, returned to North Texas, and hanged in a grim event that was applauded by many editors. Nearly a hundred slaves were arrested in Dallas; three were lynched, while the others were whipped. Emotions were inflamed by rumors of abolitionist activity that increased with each retelling; Pryor's list included poisoning, assassination, kidnapping, rape, and arson. Despite reassurances from Gov. Sam Houston, patrols formed after the "Texas Troubles," as these events became known, to watch for abolitionists, including in Gainesville.

Such vitriol infected Texas politics as the Democratic Party became militant in its defense of slavery. Despite efforts to forge a consensus, however, voters in Cooke County consistently cast a higher percentage of their ballots against the Democrats than the rest of the state. Concern for order and security, and a lack of compelling economic ties to slavery, led them to reject calls for disunion. This alarmed those who endorsed the Democrats, and the election of Abraham Lincoln as president pushed them to organize for secession. John R. Diamond held a rally at Diamond's Station for this purpose on November 23, 1860. His brother James J. Diamond, a delegate to the national Democratic convention in 1860, chaired a steering committee. Most of the men who attended owned slaves. All but four signed a petition declaring that secession was necessary and demanding that Houston call a convention.

Later James J. Diamond, the brother of John R. Diamond, also served on the steering committee for a Gainesville meeting chaired by Bourland on December 15. Prominent slaveowners again dominated the debate, but the result was less harmonious. Diamond and Bourland pushed for secession but were opposed by a group led by U.S. marshal William C. Young, who owned more slaves than anyone else in Cooke County. Ironically, Young had fought alongside Bourland against Indians, and Bourland had been lieutenant colonel of a regiment commanded by Young during the Mexican War. Young was supported by District Attorney William T. G. Weaver and Chief Justice Ralph G. Piper. Despite the angry opposition of Young and his allies, Diamond and Bourland prevailed, and most voted for a secession convention.

Houston opposed secession, but radicals posted dates for the election of convention delegates in newspapers. This strategy succeeded as three-fourths of Texas counties sent representatives, most of whom endorsed secession. James J. Diamond allegedly won in Cooke County, though the returns cannot be found. In protest editor E. Junius Foster of the *Sherman Patriot* printed a proposal to separate the Red River counties from Texas, ally with nations in the Indian Territory, and petition for admission as a state. Marshall responded in the *Texas State Gazette:* "Every honest man should trample under foot this mischievous development . . . and treat its authors as public enemies."[5]

Hoping the legislature would not authorize the secession convention, Houston called a special session in January 1861. When lawmakers did endorse the convention, Rep. Robert H. Taylor of Fannin County in North Texas asked, "In this new *Cotton Confederacy what will become of my section, the wheat growers and stock raisers?*" He answered his own question: "I fear they will hang, burn, confiscate property and exile any one who may be in the way of their designs." Marshall in turn denounced Unionists, declaring that "we cannot tolerate in our midst the presence of an internal hostile element." His solution for them was simple: they "should be strangled by the hangman's knot."[6]

James W. Throckmorton of North Texas opposed secession as a legislator and delegate to the convention, but only seven voted with him against disunion. When the convention scheduled a referendum on disunion, in keeping with a legislative mandate, Throckmorton and William A. Ellet of Cooke County were among the legislators who protested against secession at a rally in Austin. In Cooke County James J. Diamond and Bourland campaigned for disunion, but Abraham McNeese and John M. Crisp spoke against them. Violence again surfaced as secessionists carrying shotguns watched the polls in adjacent Grayson County. Texans returned a majority of more than three to one in favor of secession, but Cooke County cast 61 percent of its votes against disunion.

As North Texans feared, secession brought civil war. Many in Cooke County joined a Confederate regiment raised by Young in April 1861. Three-fourths of his troops opposed secession, and Throckmorton became his lieutenant colonel, but they enlisted to defend their families from Indians. They occupied posts in the Indian Territory, but their number dwindled after it became clear that the regiment would be sent east. When Young's unit, despite his protest, became the Eleventh Texas Cavalry and was ordered beyond the Mississippi River, more than two-thirds of his men left the service. Among them were Young; his son James D. Young; James J. Diamond, who replaced Throckmorton; William C. Twitty, Montague's son-in-law; and former sheriff Alexander Boutwell.

Some who left the Eleventh Texas Cavalry refused to serve again, joining a growing number of North Texans suspected of disloyalty by Confederate officials. Others enlisted in local defense units created in response to the concern for security throughout Texas. The first were home guards. At Gainesville the Cooke County Home Guard Cavalry mustered in June. These were superseded by a statewide system of militia brigades, reorganized from the old militia by the legislature. Bourland declined to command the district that included Cooke County. Upon his advice the title of brigadier general of state troops went to William R. Hudson, a slaveowner from Cooke County. Hudson recruited about a thousand men into three battalions, one of which was commanded by Twitty.

Hudson originally worried that he could not find enough men. Recruiting became easier after the Confederacy began drafting troops, but another problem arose. As Hugh F. Young, commander of the Grayson County militia and a former major in the Eleventh Texas Cavalry, remarked, "Our families, our property, our all is now comparatively in the care and keeping of strangers."[7] Many people left the region after Texas joined the Confederacy. These refugees, who were often accused of being abolitionists, were replaced by suspicious newcomers from outside of Texas. Conflict began as the Confederate government tried not only to draft these men but also to sequester the property of enemies, collect taxes, and impress goods. Periodic combing of militia musters by officials created much resentment, while tax collectors such as Jeremiah E. Hughes in Gainesville became as despised as the impressment details and receivers of sequestered property. Fears were enhanced by the arrival of more slaves from areas threatened by Federal raids. Many turned again to proven leaders, especially slaveowners who had earlier defended order and security, and methods such as vigilantism to cope with dissenters in and out of the militia.

Vigilantism had actually persisted as the war escalated. Following the lead of other counties, Cooke County commissioners appointed new patrollers: Boutwell, Hudson, slaveowner James M. Peery, and Deputy Sheriff James B. Davenport Jr., the son of a slaveowner. This group did little to stop vigilantes. After two murderers of a Gainesville barkeeper were lynched, a girl wrote, "Just why they were hanged, no one seemed to know or care."[8] A rash of cotton gin fires in North Texas in early 1862 prompted Charles DeMorse, editor of the *Clarksville Standard,* to declare that a "speedy hanging" should be provided for "vile miscreants" who supported the Union. Downstate Austin's *Texas Almanac-Extra* and the *San Antonio Herald* demanded action from Brig. Gen. Paul O. Hébert, commander of the Department of Texas. To quell unrest and enforce conscription, the general imposed martial law. Hugh F. Young then asked if he could "try an individual by Court martial for uttering treasonable sentiments," and both he and Hudson enlisted "Police Guards" for their districts.[9] Partisan rangers also mustered to chase dissenters. In North Texas John L. Randolph commanded a partisan battalion, in which one company was led by Capt. James D. Young.

Perhaps the most effective foes of dissenters were provost marshals. Although they primarily were enrolling officers, they could arrest anyone that appeared to threaten order and security. Their authority was analogous to that of a civilian grand jury: if evidence of guilt was found, then a prisoner would be tried by a military court. These were to be conducted in accordance with the rules for civil courts, but the emphasis was on efficiency, not a strict compliance with the law. After Hudson was appointed to command upon Bourland's nomination, he recommended that the latter serve as provost marshal for his area. Bourland proved to be a fearsome foe to dissenters, who found him to be deadly in his zeal to maintain order and provide security.

Bourland learned that the draft had led to the creation of a secret organization in Cooke County. Samuel McNutt, a New York carpenter, allegedly penned a petition against conscription that was signed by more than thirty men and sent to the Confederate Congress. Newton J. Chance, an emigrant from Kansas who had left the army due to disabilities, copied McNutt's list for Bourland, who had McNutt exiled. Obediah B. Atkinson, a lieutenant in the Cooke County Home Guard Cavalry who retained his rank when he joined Hudson's militia, replaced McNutt and enlisted about two hundred men into the "Peace Party." Thomas Barrett, a Disciples of Christ minister, encountered a group discussing conscription. When one, perhaps Atkinson, said he would organize resistance to the draft, Barrett declared that these were dangerous words. The man, who must have realized that such bravado in front of a stranger was foolish, said that he would abandon the idea.

Atkinson did not quit, and his efforts contributed to unrest in Cooke County. Rumors circulated that a large "clan" had links to Unionists in Kansas who planned to invade Texas. Asked to do something, Bourland arrested a "Mr. Hillier" and ordered him to enlist, after which vigilantes hanged Hillier's wife for making Unionist remarks to the provost marshal. Bourland's role in this was unclear, but he did not punish the vigilantes. In turn, when he arrested two men who tried to escort a Unionist and her two daughters to the North, an angry mob surrounded the Gainesville jail. Stymied, Bourland let the two men join James D. Young's company, which encouraged the dissenters. In August 1862 the Federals advanced in the Indian Territory. Hudson assembled his militia for a campaign but canceled this when the enemy retired. Many did not respond to his muster, and some said that others intended to desert or mutiny. Such angry defiance encouraged more to refuse openly to support the Confederacy.

Bourland's opportunity for a counterattack came when one of Hudson's militiamen met Ephraim Chiles, who offered to initiate him into the Peace Party. Bourland asked the man to learn more. The resulting report on Chiles and his brother Henry intrigued the members of a small investigating committee organized by Bourland. This group included his fellow Masons Hudson, Twitty, Peery, and James J. Diamond as well as Charles L. Roff, a slaveowner who commanded a company for Hudson. The first spy declared that the two brothers were involved in nothing important, but Bourland's committee sent Chance to meet Henry. The latter apparently spoke freely about the Peace Party, and Chance informed Bourland that Chiles and his group were planning an uprising to support a Federal invasion of Texas.

Bourland's committee—expanded by the addition of Montague and Doss as well as Peery's father, William—decided to act. These slaveowners uniformly supported Bourland, and they sent a plea to Austin for help. Gov. Francis R. Lubbock forwarded their request and those of others such as William C. Young to Hébert, but the general could not send troops. Instead he temporarily accepted Hudson's militia into Confederate service. At the same time, Lubbock conveyed his approval to Hudson and Bourland for their planned operation against the dissenters. With authority from Hébert and approval from Lubbock, and thus with the clear support of his superiors in the state and Confederate governments, Bourland acted decisively. Twitty had directed the earlier militia muster to which many had not responded; now he ordered those in the ranks to surround the shirkers' homes. They were to arrest all those implicated by Chance and anyone who had not answered the muster.[10]

The arrests began in a driving rain at daybreak on October 1. The militia by noon had about seventy prisoners corralled in a vacant store on the Gainesville square. A few such as Atkinson escaped, but some who tried to flee or resist were shot; a slave recalled helping bury Hiram W. Kilborn, a Canadian-born school trustee, election supervisor, and Baptist lay minister. Because the prisoners remained calm, witnesses assumed that they expected to be rescued. Their guards were three companies of Hudson's militia, including Roff's men, sworn into Confederate service by James J. Diamond and commanded by Twitty, who took orders from Bourland. The presence of these troops, plus an unknown number of zealous volunteers, did dissuade at least two groups, one of which was another company of Hudson's militia, from attacking the town. Tragically fifteen of those who decided against a rescue attempt were later arrested and hanged.

Confederate reinforcements quickly arrived in Gainesville. The first was a Grayson County company of Hugh F. Young's militia led by Capt. John Russell, formerly of the Eleventh Texas Cavalry. Lubbock wrote to Col. Douglas H. Cooper, in command of the Indian Territory, asking him to send troops. In response two partisan-ranger companies arrived under Capts. Abner M. Marshall and John K. Bumpass. Capt. Nick Wilson led Company B, Twenty-Ninth Texas Cavalry, whose colonel was DeMorse, into Gainesville on October 7. With this assistance Bourland continued his arrests until he had about 150 prisoners.

A vigilante tribunal quickly organized to try the prisoners. Chance and Boutwell held a rally on October 1, mustering support for Bourland before a town meeting. Barrett and others opposed violence, but most seemed to support the idea of hanging at least some of the prisoners. William C. Young was elected to chair the meeting. He chose five men to select a dozen others to serve as a jury to decide all cases. The five were Davenport, who had become sheriff; District Clerk Aaron Hill, a Southern Methodist elder; William Peery; Chief Justice Piper; and slaveowner James B. Stone. They in turn selected jurors not for "strong southern or secessionist predilections, or enmity toward Union men" but for "moderation, intelligence, and virtue." Their selections were endorsed in a referendum, giving the sanction of democracy to the "Citizen's Court."[11]

The twelve jurors—Barrett, Doss, John W. Hamill, Hughes, James Jones, Reason Jones, Wiley Jones, J. Pope Long, Montague, Benjamin Scanland, William J. Simpson, and Thomas Wright—were prosperous community leaders. Among the seven who owned slaves, Montague and Wiley Jones were county commissioners and would be elected to the legislature. Another, Barrett, was a minister, while Hamill, a nonslaveowner, was a Southern Methodist minister who opposed abolitionism. They were all too old for the draft, and none had been in the army, but Simpson was in Hugh F. Young's militia. Their decision to convict on a majority vote boded ill for the prisoners. Not all of the jurors were "ultra," but three were "very bitter against the accused" and others had suspicions. Most of the accused men never owned slaves, which made some think that they were abolitionists.[12] Also, most of them were eligible for the draft but did not enlist, thus they were shirkers.

Resolutions adopted at the town meeting authorized the Citizen's Court to convict and execute defendants. Piper swore in the court and those who testified. The prisoners could employ legal counsel (though apparently none did), issue subpoenas, and cross-examine all witnesses. Piper became a clerk for the court along with James M. Peery, and they worked with Hill, militia captain Cincinnatus Potter, and James E. Sheegog, a slaveowner and former county commissioner, to question witnesses and record testimony. William W. Bourland, the provost marshal's son and a veteran of the Eleventh Texas Cavalry, acted as a constable. With Montague as foreman, the trials began on October 2. William C. Young served as prosecutor, and through his efforts the jurors acquitted most who came before them. Only seven were condemned for disloyalty and organizing the Peace Party: Henry and Ephraim Chiles, Henry S. Field, M. D. Harper, Leander W. P. "Jacob" Lock, William W. Morris, and Edward D. Hampton. All were hanged within seven days. Slave Bob Scott drove a wagon from under each after Boutwell put a rope around their necks, suspending them in pairs from an elm on Pecan Creek.

The condemnation of seven men horrified Barrett. When he proposed surrendering the guilty prisoners to proper authorities, other jurors tried to have him expelled. He exploded after the sentencing of an eighth man to be hanged, denouncing his fellow jurors. Long rose to leave with him, but the others convinced them to stay by agreeing to convict only on a two-thirds vote. The change provided clemency and reversed the eighth man's conviction. The Citizen's Court then worked quickly to acquit the other suspects to foil angry mobs, who twice had tried to lynch prisoners. By Saturday, October 11, the jurors had reviewed all of the defendants, but they decided to hold the remainder for safekeeping. An informant leaked the news, and two men came into the courtroom and demanded twenty prisoners. Piper gave a list to one of the pair, who chose fourteen names. Shaken, the jurors decided to wait one week before freeing the others.

The fourteen selected on October 11 were a diverse group. C. F. and George W. Anderson, Rama Dye, and William W. Wernell had been implicated during earlier trials. Three others had plotted to attack Gainesville on October 1: Benjamin C. Barnes, Henry Cockrum, and James A. Powers, who was Atkinson's brother-in-law. McNeese opposed secession but was a captain in Hudson's militia. William R. Rhodes had left a frontier-defense company, perhaps deserting, while Samuel Carmichael refused to muster and spoke against the Confederacy. Nathaniel M. Clark also opposed disunion, but the rest—Thomas O. Baker, C. A. Jones, and Elliot M. Scott—had done little to distinguish themselves. Boutwell hanged them in two groups, three on a chilly Sunday, October 12, and the rest on Monday, which proved to be little warmer.

An uneasy peace settled over Cooke County after the Citizen's Court adjourned but was shattered by the murder of Col. William C. Young on October 16. Young was ambushed as he led a posse along a tributary of the Red River in pursuit of unknown men who had killed a local hunter. The news inflamed emotions. When the jurors reassembled on October 18, several moderates were absent. Their places were taken by Chance, who also replaced Montague as foreman, and slaveowner William W. Howeth, brother of the man who had shot Foster. Montague and others who advocated retribution welcomed the newcomers. A third new juror, James McPherson, was in fact a member of the Peace Party, which he must have hidden. Without Young's moderate influence, the Citizen's Court retried and condemned nineteen prisoners who had been acquitted earlier. Protests from Barrett and McPherson prompted Bourland to arrest the latter, but he was soon released.

The nineteen were hanged on October 19 under the supervision of James D. Young, the son of the slain colonel. Like the victims on October 12 and 13, many had been implicated in earlier trials. Nine conspired to rescue their friends on the night of October 1: William B. Anderson, Barnibus Burch, Arphax R. Dawson, Hudson J. Esman, Curd Goss, William W. Johnson, David M. Leffel, John W. Morris, and Gilbert Smith. Another, John M. Crisp, tried to earn clemency by offering information about others, but his proposals were rejected by the jurors. A similar appeal from Eli M. Thomas was spurned as well, while Alexander D. Scott stoically accepted his amended verdict. Richard N. Martin delivered an angry speech under the hanging tree, denouncing his brother-in-law, William Boyles, for luring him into the group. Boyles was never caught, but he was murdered in nearby Collinsville. The rest—Richard J. Anderson, John B. Miller, John A. Morris, M. W. Morris, William B. Taylor, and James A. Ward— were apparently selected only for their membership in the Peace Party.

These killings brought the total number of victims in the Great Hanging, as the event became known, to forty-two, including Drs. James T. Foster and Thomas B. Floyd, who were shot as they tried to run. Scott carried all of the bodies to an empty building on the town square. A few families claimed the remains of relatives—some of them mutilated by hogs that pushed through a hole in the back wall—but most were left for the county to bury. Slaves were detailed to build rude coffins. Frank Foreman tore down an empty house for lumber, then when that was exhausted, wrapped the remaining bodies in blankets and buried them in shallow graves along Pecan Creek. Rain washed some corpses from the ground, while hogs uncovered others and fed upon them. A young girl saw a large hog drag her stepfather's arm down a Gainesville street.

The testimony of the condemned men illustrated the irony of the Great Hanging. Some in the Peace Party professed a commitment to the Union, but they were a minority, as were those who planned uprisings. The majority simply sought to protect their families on a violent frontier. Most had become convinced that the Confederacy could not survive and trusted the party to provide security by cooperative action. Ironically, the concern for order and security among neighbors who supported the Confederacy led to a grim backlash that killed many innocent men. Most of the men who were freed soon fled, but some were drafted to fight for a cause they did not support. The violence did not end in Cooke County as Bourland asked for arrests elsewhere based upon testimony before the Citizen's Court. He sent names to John W. Hale, commander of Hudson's militia at Decatur. A commission of two dozen men, led by Southern Methodist minister James R. Bellamy, convened in a store that served as Hale's headquarters. They condemned five men: Ira Burdick, John M. Conn, Jim McKinn, Henry R. Maple, and a man known only as Ward. Sheriff Robert G. Cates hanged them from wagons on October 18. Several were arrested in Denton County, but all were set free. Sixteen were tried by a commission of two dozen men in Sherman, but they were spared by the intervention of Judge

Robert W. Waddell and Throckmorton, who had resigned from the Sixth Texas Cavalry and returned to Collin County. Throckmorton and Waddell convinced the commission to transfer their prisoners to the Confederate district court at Tyler, which set their bail at a paltry $200. Most posted bond and scattered; only two returned for a trial, and they were acquitted. One of the two, Clement Wood, quietly went home, but the other, Richard Lively, berated his accusers in newspapers and was killed after the war by pro-Confederate guerrillas.

The dismissal of charges by the Confederate district court was seconded by Waddell in his state court. A former Kentucky legislator, Waddell was a staunch Confederate but opposed vigilantism. His chance to curb the violence came when Joel F. DeLemeron was brought before him on November 7. The grand jury that indicted DeLemeron for helping refugees flee from Cooke County included Citizen's Court members Wiley Jones, Stone, and Montague. The evidence was strong that DeLemeron not only assisted people to escape but also proposed an attack on Gainesville. The jury convicted him, but Waddell refused to sentence him to death. DeLemeron went to the state prison, whence he was released after the war.

Military authorities tardily followed the civilian example to end the killing. On October 4 John Randolph asked Bourland if any of his men had been implicated by the Citizen's Court. He added that it would be his "greatest pleasure to arrest them, and if necessary assist you in hanging them."[13] Days later Bourland rode into Sherman with more than two dozen prisoners from his partisan battalion. He presided over a court-martial that condemned three of the company led by James D. Young, who hanged them at his late father's home. Randolph allegedly presided over the hangings of others accused of belonging to the Peace Party, which prompted many of his troops to desert. Like the vigilante tribunals, the court-martial ran its course, and Randolph sent a handful of men to the Confederate district court.

James D. Young did not stop with the execution of three men from his company. He tracked Daniel Welch, a deserter who had allegedly killed Colonel Young, to the Indian Territory, took him to the Young homestead, and hanged him in front of his late father's slaves. He then burned the body on the site of the killing. His next victim was Foster, the editor in Sherman who had published several editorials on the hangings, including one applauding the murder of William Young. Three horsemen—James Young, Chance, and an accomplice—accosted Foster at his office. Young demanded that Foster recant his statement about his father. When the newspaperman refused, a rider pointed a double-barreled shotgun at him and pulled both triggers. Young continued until superiors demanded that he resign, which he did after penning one last diatribe against Unionists.

News of the Great Hanging spread throughout the Confederacy. Charles DeMorse of the *Clarksville Standard* and Robert W. Loughery of Marshall's *Texas Republican* printed a letter from Throckmorton, who dismissed the victims as "refugees and suspected persons." South Texas editors proved more ready to believe in a Union conspiracy. Edward H. Cushing of the *Houston Telegraph* wrote his account from official reports and condoned the lynchings. Willard Richardson of the *Galveston News*, I. R. Worrall of Austin's *Texas State Gazette*, and David Richardson of the *Texas Almanac Extra* printed eyewitness accounts and added their own approval. Ironically, the *San Antonio Herald*, which had opposed secession, published the most vitriolic support of the hangings. Because Galveston was the primary source for Texas news, Willard Richardson's opinions reappeared in Southern newspapers. Most agreed with Little Rock's *True Democrat* that "[b]y the fortunate discovery of this scheme Texas has been enabled to purge herself of traitors."[14]

Confronted with the news, the Davis administration largely ignored the affair, while Texas officials condoned it. The president had already removed Hébert on October 10 for his imposition of martial law. The Great Hanging belied Hébert's argument that prisoners had been given the legal support normally expected in a civil trial, but nothing more was done. Texas adjutant general Jeremiah Y. Dashiell admonished Hudson that "extreme measures" had to be based upon "undoubted evidence," but Colonel Young's murder ended his reservations. Dashiell wrote to Hudson again that while the vigilante actions were "deplorable," the "strictest measures of the sternest justice" had to be imposed on any "traitors that pollute the soil of our State."[15] Lubbock and Hébert had already conveyed their approval of Bourland and Hudson's plans. When the former called a special session of the legislature in February 1863, he again endorsed Hudson's actions. Hale represented Cooke County, and he and his comrades paid Hudson's expenses. Davis did not protest, and Lubbock later became his advisor on the Trans-Mississippi.

Dissent along the forks did not end with the Great Hanging; tragically it was Bourland who was entrusted with suppression. Militiamen who participated in the Great Hanging were mustered into regular service as a regiment commanded by Bourland. His task was to patrol North Texas, which he did with a zeal that brought protests from military associates and civilians alike. Two of his superiors, Brig. Gens. Smith P. Bankhead and Henry E. McCulloch, had experience suppressing dissent in Central Texas but found the work in northern counties to be almost unbearable. Bankhead got a transfer from what he called "this God-forsaken country," but his successor as the commander of the Northern Sub-District, McCulloch, stayed through the end of the war. He had others, such as John R. Baylor and William C. Quantrill, removed from command or chased from Texas, but he supported Bourland in his operations. After all

McCulloch believed an "energetic, fighting, hanging man" was the best way to combat dissent.[16]

The end of the Civil War encouraged Texas dissenters to believe that redress would come. Prominent refugee Andrew J. Hamilton had spoken often about atrocities against Unionists in Texas, and the former congressman was appointed as the military governor of Texas by Abraham Lincoln. Hamilton's accusations were reinforced by grim reports of the Great Hanging in Northern newspapers. The result was popular support for a Texas invasion and a series of proposals, none of which succeeded. Federals landed at Galveston in June 1865, but diplomatic concerns prompted a transfer of most of the troops to the Rio Grande. None could be spared for remote regions such as North Texas, where Bourland ironically was chosen by Union officers to dispense paroles for Confederates.

Hamilton, who became provisional governor of Texas in the summer of 1865, promised justice but made crucial mistakes in selecting leaders to advise him. For North Texas he relied upon Throckmorton, unaware that he believed order and security should be trusted to men who had supported the Confederacy. Among those appointed was Weaver, who had become a Confederate officer after opposing secession, as the judge for the district that included Cooke County. Allegedly when Bourland, James D. Young, and the jurors of the Citizen's Court were indicted on November 11, 1865, Weaver deliberately issued flawed writs. He denied this, but they were not served until a week after he adjourned, permitting many of the accused to escape. Residents of Cooke County asked Hamilton to remove several officials, which he did but kept Weaver. Petitioners also requested Federal troops to enforce the law, and Maj. Gen. George A. Custer sent two companies. They arrested some who evaded Weaver's court, but county officials allowed many to escape again.

Vengeance for wartime atrocities became the topic of angry debates during the constitutional convention in February 1866. The assembly was dominated by ex-Confederates, prominent among whom were Throckmorton and Bumpass, who had commanded a company at Gainesville in October 1862. Also present from Cooke County was James M. Lindsay, whom some said had participated in the Great Hanging. Throckmorton led the push for conciliation, and the delegates adopted Ordinance No. 11, which prohibited the prosecution of anyone for acts done under Confederate authority. A furious minority recalled the Great Hanging, condemning Hudson by name, while Hamilton denounced the bill for legalizing murder and theft throughout Texas.

If Hamilton had plans for retribution, they were undone by Throckmorton's triumph in the election of 1866. Throckmorton defeated Elisha M. Pease, a former governor and noted Unionist, for the governor's seat, while other conservatives dominated the legislature. Violence against wartime dissenters and blacks surged; seventeen murders occurred in Cooke County alone during the first two months of 1867. State courts did little to end the onslaught. Weaver presided over the acquittals of six jurors from the Citizen's Court: Doss, Reason and Wiley Jones, Scanland, Simpson, and Wright. Some claimed that bribes were paid, but more likely a jury to convict them could not be mustered from among residents who had supported the Confederacy. In this they were encouraged both by Ordinance No. 11 and Pres. Andrew Johnson's amnesty proclamation, issued in May 1865.

The violence in North Texas contributed to the Republican revolt against Johnson's reconstruction policies. In March 1867 Congress passed the Reconstruction Acts, which placed Texas in a military district commanded by Maj. Gen. Philip H. Sheridan. The general received reports that Throckmorton refused to protect Unionists and freedmen as well as false accusations about the governor's involvement in the Great Hanging. Throckmorton wrote to James J. Diamond, who had become the editor of the *Houston Dispatch,* and asked him to publish a denial, but the damage was done. Sheridan removed the governor and many other officials from power, replacing them with men more amenable to reform.

Sheridan's removals renewed hope for justice on the forks. One of the new appointees was Atkinson, while Chief Justice John E. Wheeler, who was arrested but freed during the Great Hanging, was allowed to stay in office. Weaver was replaced with Hardin Hart by Pease, Throckmorton's successor as governor, in December 1867. Hart, a Unionist whose brother Martin had been hanged by Confederates, mounted a last attack on those who had participated in the Great Hanging. Barrett and Long, each of whom had fled the state but returned, were tried in December 1868. Defended by Throckmorton and Weaver, both were acquitted by a Cooke County jury. Hart also tried Bourland, who had a pardon from Johnson, but the result was the same.

Among the key witnesses at Bourland's trial in December 1868 was James Jones, who moved to the Indian Territory in 1865 after threatening to shoot Boutwell. In return for testifying against Bourland, Jones was given immunity for the Great Hanging and for an indictment in November 1863 for an unrelated murder. Jones also testified against James D. Young, who remained at large until 1871, after Hart had stepped down. On December 20 of that year, a jury acquitted Young for the murder of Foster. When his wartime accomplice, Chance, was finally arraigned in 1885, Young confessed in court that he killed Foster. Because Young had been acquitted earlier, both men went free.

The acquittal of Chance ended the trials of those involved in the Citizen's Court. Nine jurors had been acquitted by a legal jury. Hughes, like Bourland, had a presidential pardon, but unlike the latter he was not tried and charges were dropped. James Jones received immunity, but oddly no records remain of dispositions for Hamill, Howeth, McPherson, and Montague. Howeth stayed in Gainesville, but both Hamill and McPherson may have followed Montague into exile. The latter lived in Mexico until 1876, when he returned to his daughter's Cooke County home, where she lived with her husband, Twitty; McPherson died within a few months. Montague need not have stayed away so long. No Cooke County jury would convict him because most had supported his efforts and those of others to protect order and security. They would not betray either local leaders or those at the state level who had authorized their actions. To do so was to risk the disruption of legal retribution and the personal turmoil of admitting that they had been wrong. Confronted with an uncomfortable choice, they chose to endorse what had been done, not to raise questions whose answers could be quite disturbing. In years to come most would focus on trying to forget.

Caroline Shropshire and her infant son, Charles, of
Columbus, Texas, an image probably taken during the
Civil War, perhaps to send to her husband, John, who
obtained the rank of major in a Confederate cavalry unit.
Courtesy Nesbit Memorial Library, Columbus, Texas

5

The Civil War and the Lives of Texas Women

Angela Boswell

The majority of women in Texas never had to deal with the upheaval of Union troops fighting in, marching through, or occupying their homes and farms as did women elsewhere in the South. Much historical literature has documented the profound effect the presence or threat of warring armies had on women's lives, roles, and expectations. Yet this study of women in one interior county of Texas shows that the Civil War generally, and not the presence of Union troops specifically, altered the roles and the expectations of Southern women. The courthouse documents of Colorado County, Texas, offer insight into the increasing participation of women of all classes in public affairs during the war. Women more actively probated the estates of their husbands; sued and were sued; participated in business transactions; ran farms, plantations, and businesses; and even filed for divorce. Women's public participation in courts corresponded with greater participation in other public matters and reflected not just necessity but also a subtle, though significant, shift in society's expectations of women.[1]

Located about seventy miles west of present-day Houston, Colorado County was more than a hundred miles from the nearest occupation by Union troops at any point during the war. The county was one of the first created under the Republic of Texas in 1836. The majority of residents hailed from other Southern states and thus brought their attitudes with them, though a large minority of German-speaking immigrants and their descendants also lived within the county. This county sat on the very western edge of the South's cotton-producing, slave-holding society, and its agricultural and economic strength was cotton. Colorado County produced more cotton than any other Texas county in 1850 and the fourth-largest cotton crop in the state in 1859. As its residents counted upon cotton as their primary cash crop, they depended upon slave labor to make it profitable. Because the overall economy of the county depended so heavily upon cotton and slaves, it is not surprising to find that the editors of the county's primary newspaper, the *Colorado Citizen,* defended slavery and castigated those who would question the institution. Thus the residents of Colorado County were very Southern in their outlook, which included the Southern ideals of womanhood that had taken firm root before the Civil War.[2]

After the election of Abraham Lincoln, Colorado County supported immediate disunion in the election of secession convention delegates and on the secession referendum. Convention candidates, those who voted for them, and the editors of the newspaper that endorsed them were, of course, all men. Yet men rallied women's support from the very beginning as crucial to the Confederacy. According to the *Colorado Citizen,* "That cause can never perish which is sustained by the smiles and approval of our noble Southern women!" The newspaper consistently applauded the "powerful influence" of women at home, in the market, and with their decision-making husbands. Its editors delighted in a story about a delegate from Williamson County, Texas, who had voted against secession but asked permission to change his vote after he went home and "his wife wouldn't let him in at the front door!"[3]

"Ladies" responded to the earnest requests of the *Citizen* to use their powerful influence to promote all things Southern and formed at least two organizations to support the war effort. The Ladies Military Association raised funds "for the purpose of equipping a company of volunteers from Colorado County, for the war." A second group of women made and presented a flag to the departing Company A, Fifth Regiment Texas Mounted Volunteers. Other women earned or raised money for clothing and supplies for the men. R. V. Cook, in supplying Captain Upton's company, "found the ladies everywhere filled with ardor and zeal and the cause of their country. None were unwilling to contribute."[4]

When their support for the troops did not suffice to enlist all the young, able-bodied men in the county, women used other powers of influence. At least one woman resorted to shame. Writing under the penname "Helen," she suggested that "all the young men that won't go to the wars, ought to put on hoops and long gowns." The article said that if these men thought they might "stay at home and marry while the choice young men are gone to the wars, . . . they are much mistaken! A man that won't protect his country won't protect his wife." In a private letter John Shropshire asked his wife, Caroline, to "tell Georgia that if she had the pluck of our ancient mothers that she would hen peck Ben like the ———— if he did not leave soon for the wars."[5]

In its first year or so, the war served to define gender roles further. Helen bemoaned that her sphere would not allow her to "go to the wars" since that public honor was reserved for men only. Women "supported" or "influenced," while men protected and warred. Male heads of household left to protect their positions in Southern society from the threats made to it by Union forces. Females knitted and sewed flags to enable men to pursue their honor on the battlefield. Women stoically sacrificed their men and boys to the fight, not complaining about their impending absence but instead encouraging them to enlist and defend Southern society, including women's place in it.[6]

Men might have left their homes to fulfill their masculine roles in the war, but they had no plans to abdicate their places as heads of households. They had often left their homes temporarily before the war, leaving overseers, male kin, or others to look after their household affairs or to assist their wives in these matters. Expecting a short conflict, Southern men believed that their military duties would not interfere with their domestic duties. In the first years of the war, husbands and fathers continued to direct activities at home. For instance, Capt. John Shropshire, in letters in 1861 and early 1862, sent instructions to his wife about business with the expectation that she would forward them to her father. In January 1862 Caroline was to "ask the Dr to have some cotton baled . . . and have it sold." John also included in his letter details of accounts that he held, debts that he owed, and those he wished to have paid first. He expected her to relay this information to her father because, as John wrote, "I rely upon him entirely and feel satisfied that he will act entirely for the best."[7]

The Civil War, however, was no short affair. As the fighting dragged on for years, the men of Colorado County faced obstacles to their expectations of maintaining male authority over their households and over the community. Embroiled in battles or even surviving the boredom of camps where regiments saw little or no action, soldiers and officers faced new and different challenges that consumed their energies. Far removed from their farms, plantations, and businesses—which were facing new challenges brought about because of the war—they comprehended less and less the difficulties there and less often had salient advice to give. Later in the war, soldiers east of the Mississippi River had to rely upon their wives' judgments entirely since all communication was limited after the Union victory at Vicksburg and letters could not be delivered to or from home.[8]

Union blockades disrupted the cotton trade, decreasing profits and livelihoods dependent upon the crop. The demands of the armies for food, clothing, and manufactured goods drove up civilian prices and led to scarcities. The flood of Confederate paper money caused inflation and confusion. With the men away from home, food and cotton production fell, leading some families subject to hunger and general privation. Of course, many families felt the devastation of losing male family members in the Texas units that suffered heavy casualties.[9]

The length of the war also required many more men to leave the county, increasing the number of women left behind to manage the household. The patriotic zeal of the county's men and women led to the formation of at least four volunteer companies during the war. These companies enlisted a total of 424 men, an equivalent of 35 percent of the county's adult male population. By April 1862 the Confederate Congress had enacted a conscription law, which demanded the enlistment of more men between the ages of eighteen and thirty-five, later expanded to include ages seventeen through fifty. While some of the wealthy were able to hire substitutes, at least some of those substitutes were from Colorado County. The less wealthy could not afford the high price of a substitute and were drafted. In addition to those who joined the county companies, evidence shows that many more enlisted in other regiments, though it is impossible to know precisely how many men left to fight for the Confederacy. In addition, at least a few German men from Colorado County fought for the Union army. By 1863, according to one resident, "almost all the men in the county were drafted to the military service."[10]

Those remaining often determined that the shortage of men in the county meant that certain public activities could not continue. By the end of 1861, the *Colorado Citizen* editors had all joined the army, leaving the county without a newspaper. With the large number of men enrolled and unavailable to answer suits as well as the legislative enactment of stay laws suspending the collection of debts, the district judge canceled district court completely for the duration of the war.[11] Although some activities could be neglected, most daily activities could not be suspended until the men returned to resume their public and head-of-household duties. Food and cotton crops still had to be raised and sold to support families as well as to support the Confederacy. Other legal matters, such as probating the estates of the men who died in and during the war, could not wait. Although the men who remained guided both business and law in the county, women increasingly had to become actors in these public matters.[12]

Of all the changes wrought in gender expectations during the war, the most notable was the increase of married women's active participation in financial transactions. The antebellum laws of coverture had declared married women's business actions invalid without their husbands' express permission and signatures. Yet husbands increasingly relied upon their wives, rather than other men, to take charge of the family plantations and businesses. As a result merchants and other men in the county abandoned their usual reluctance to conduct business with women.[13]

Although it is uncertain if Helen Le Tulle's husband, Victor, joined the army, he was absent during 1862 and 1863. During his absence, she "acted in the capacity of agent for Le Tulle and Co.," her husband's business. When James Darby called on her with the intention of repaying a note Le Tulle and Company held against him, she "examined the claims left with me by Le Tulle and Co. and failed to find any note." She then "received . . . Confederate notes from James A. Darby and receipted to him for it." When her husband came home, Helen gave him the money and the accounts, and although the company no longer held the note, she reported that never "did her husband express any sorrow at my having received the money from Mr. Darby."[14]

Although she was a married woman, unable in normal circumstances to conduct her own business, much less that of her husband, Helen acted as her husband's agent in this and presumably other financial transactions during his absence. Darby showed no reluctance at conducting business with this married woman and in fact, insisted upon paying her money despite her hesitancy to take it. Victor did not regret or challenge Helen's actions, nor did anyone challenge her ability to act as her husband's agent during a court case that finally went to trial in 1868. The case against James Darby centered not on Helen's marital status, but on the fact that Le Tulle and Company had previously traded the note to another party.[15]

Victor Le Tulle never recorded any legal document giving his wife express permission to conduct his business or her own. He assumed that amid war Helen, though a married woman under the confines of coverture, naturally should serve as his agent. Other husbands, however, did attempt to leave legal documents giving their wives power to conduct business. Fanny Darden had spent her antebellum years protected from public activities, even in the seven antebellum district-court cases that disputed her separate property. William Darden had, as expected by society and law, acted as manager of Fanny's estate, handling the legal and financial aspects of protecting her property. She had never even been required to sign a document in its defense or appear in court. By the time William entered the Confederate army as a substitute in mid-1862, the social proscription against wives conducting business in Colorado County had already been eased. Rather than try to run his and her business from the battlefield or turn matters over to another man who might subsequently leave for the war, William intended for Fanny to make the necessary decisions for their household. He recorded a power of attorney at the county courthouse appointing W. S. Delaney as his agent "in order to enable my wife Mrs. Fanny A. Darden . . . the better to manage and transact business during my absence in the wars." William intended for Fanny to make her own decisions, with Delaney instructed to sign his name "to any and all instruments of writing which my wife may think or deem necessary."[16]

At least one other husband attempted to enable his wife legally to take care of the family's financial matters. Michael McLemore registered a power of attorney in 1863. In this document duly recorded in the Colorado County clerk's office, McLemore appointed his wife, Mary, "to be my true and lawful attorney in fact to act for me and in my name, place and stead as agent to sell and convey any lands, houses and lots in the Town of Columbus or else where, or any negro slaves now belonging to either of us individually or owned by us as community property in as full and complete a manner as the same could be done if I were personally present and joined with her in making said conveyance."[17]

Mary McLemore had already begun conducting business in her own name before her husband left this power of attorney. In January 1862 she had sold the family's piano to W. B. Dewees. The power of attorney made it easier for Mary to conduct business of all kinds, but she did not use it for a major land transaction until nearly two years later. On March 20, 1865, she sold a plot of land for $1,200 to A. J. Folts. Ironically, even though she signed both her own and her husband's names, the county clerk conducted the married woman's separate examination to assure that her husband had not coerced her to sign the deed.[18]

While William Darden and Michael McLemore had the foresight to ensure that their wives had unquestionable legal ability to act upon their own financial decisions, few other husbands did so. Some, however, still expected their wives to make such decisions and expected that the community would accept them. While wives did transact business, when land titles were in question, some had to resort to legal maneuvering to assuage the fears of purchasers that they alone could not effectively convey titles. When Martha Pankey wished to sell 160 acres of land to Robert Stafford in 1864, she enlisted John Hope to sign the deed on behalf of her husband, Joseph. After the war Robert Stafford instituted a friendly (and uncontested) case in district court to clear the title of any doubt.[19]

If married women found ways of selling land without their husbands' express permission, they also entered into sundry other transactions that were not as legally regulated. As with Helen Le Tulle, another merchant and farmer, Samuel J. Redgate, left his wife, Mary, in "control" of his goods and merchandise. Mrs. Frances S. Chesley ran a hotel in 1865, signing leases and contracts without her husband. Numerous other married women carried on the business of farms and plantations, contracting with merchants for supplies, though the law allowed them to contract only for "family necessaries."[20]

Merchants and other businesspeople in Colorado County accepted the premise that married women acted as agents for husbands away at war. Such assumptions were widely held, and the exceptions made to laws during the war were upheld later in the Reconstruction era. The notes that Helen Le Tulle signed on behalf of her husband's company were accepted as valid by the courts, judges, and attorneys. The accounts, debts, and promissory notes signed by married women without their husbands also remained legally valid whenever they became aspects of litigation. No litigant during or after the war questioned the legality of a married woman's business transaction made during the conflict. As the law was reinterpreted to allow women more responsibility and agency, social prescriptions fell away.

Colorado County women, married and single, left few wills (fourteen) between 1837 and 1873, and the drafting of wills by women did not necessarily increase during the Civil War. Only two women wrote wills dated during the war, and only one of those was probated during the conflict. Eliza Grace's will, however, was unique in that for the first time, a married woman took the opportunity provided by statute to leave her separate estate to someone other than her husband.[21]

During the Civil War, Eliza took advantage of a right that had been allowed to married women since 1837 but never claimed. Shortly before she died in 1862, Eliza chose to bequeath all of her separate property to her children and none to her husband, Thomas. The greater likelihood of her husband's death due to the war probably prompted Eliza to consider her children's best interests in case of the death of both parents. Her husband most likely consented to the provisions of the will before her death, or she believed he would after her death. She requested that he hold the property in trust for her minor children until they came of age, paying 10 percent interest on the proceeds to her children. The war years produced this unique instance in which a married woman chose to leave her property to someone other than her husband, though his acceptance of the situation was probably crucial in Eliza's decision. Between 1837 and 1873, no other married woman in Colorado County made this kind of financial decision about how her property should be divided after her death.[22]

Married women were not the only ones to exhibit increased agency in public during the war. Most notably, the percentage of women taking active roles in probating the estates of deceased family members greatly increased. The percentage of widows acting as sole executors or administrators of their husbands' estates in fact was double that of the antebellum years. Of the twenty-four estates of married men probated during the Civil War, only 33 percent of the widows declined to administer, compared to nearly 59 percent during the antebellum years. The most obvious reason for this was the shortage of men left in the county to conduct such business. The administration of estates in probate court, like the raising of food and cash crops, could not wait for men to return to resume their public responsibilities. Women, therefore, stepped into those male roles.

Seven widows during the war found men, usually relatives, to administer their deceased husbands' estates. But twelve women took on the task for themselves, and two others coadministered estates with a male relative. In one of these latter cases, the widow eventually took over the case. In the other Elvy Ann Carson took an active role, appearing in court and signing petitions and documents herself.[23] It is not possible to determine with any certainty whether the widows who chose to administer had the option of allowing male relatives to do so in their stead. In several cases there clearly were no grown sons to take responsibility.[24] Wealth seemed to be the greatest determinant in whether or not a widow would administer an estate herself. Half of the eight who acted as neither executor nor administrator had deceased husbands whose estates were valued in the top quarter of the population. All but one estate was valued in the top half or higher. The two widows who coadministered with male relatives dealt with estates in the top tenth of the population in terms of wealth. Those who served as sole executors or administrators, however, administered less valuable estates. Of those fourteen estates, the value of ten can be determined. Four fell in the bottom half of the population in terms of wealth, while only one fell in the top quarter and none in the top tenth. (Table 1 shows the number of widows administering and declining administration of estates as broken into categories of wealth.)

The choice by widows not to administer the wealthiest estates contrasted starkly with the antebellum practices. Before the war, widows were more likely to administer or at least coadminister a high-valued estate themselves. But conscription laws favored exemptions for the wealthy by automatically excluding those who owned twenty or more slaves and by allowing the hiring of substitutes. Older families were often wealthier, and some husbands, though not necessarily all, in this wealth bracket were too old to fight in the army or be conscripted. As more men from wealthy families, for a variety of reasons, stayed home during the war than did those less wealthy, women within the wealthiest population bracket were more likely to have male relatives help them run their farms, plantations, and businesses than others. Therefore, those male relatives were available to take up administration of estates as well. Those less wealthy were more likely to have male relatives, especially sons, participating in the war and were already in the position of taking care of the family's business. When their husbands died, they continued the businesses, even if great difficulties were involved. Maria Dungan complained to the district court after the war that she was unable to enforce a lease because she was "old and female" and the lessor declared "his intention of maintaining the property with the strong hand." Yet she continued the administration, neither remarrying nor turning it over to another male relative even after the war.[25]

Regardless of class, age, or ability, widows chose to rely on male relatives or their own efforts when it came to the administration of estates. This also contrasted starkly with the antebellum years, when half of the estates leaving wid-

TABLE 1

Widows and Their Deceased Husbands' Estates, by Wealth

Quarter of Wealth*	3	2	1		Total
				top 10%	
Administrator or Executor	4	5	1	0	10
Coadministrator	0	0	0	2	2
Declined Administration	1	3	2	2	8
Total	5	8	3	4	20

*No estates were valued in the bottom quarter of wealth. The value of four estates of those widows who administered cannot be determined.

Sources: Probate Records, County Clerk of Colorado County; Schedule 1 (Free Inhabitants), Colorado County, Texas, Eighth Census of the United States (1860).

ows had unrelated male administrators or executors. Women now began to take a more active role in their families' financial affairs. As more husbands left their wives to conduct business for them in their absence, the social prohibitions against women taking an active public role eased, making it not only possible but likely that women would exhibit more agency in the courtrooms.[26]

As the number of single women in the county increased, so did their activity in the public sphere. Those whose husbands had died in or during the war, as well as a few young, unmarried women, often did not have the option to marry or remarry. Some, such as Helen of the *Colorado Citizen* editorial, perhaps really did choose not to marry men who would not protect their country. But by 1862 the war had required so many men to leave for military service that fewer women could find single men to marry. The number of marriages in 1861 reached an all-time high at fifty-two. The next year the number dropped to less than half that, with only twenty-one marriages taking place. In 1863 and 1864 the number of marriages barely increased to thirty and twenty-seven respectively.[27]

As a result single and widowed women, often already accustomed to taking care of their family business, increasingly entered into business transactions. Mary Toland and Louisa Odom signed promissory notes to merchants for goods and farming supplies. Sarah E. Kuykendall, Elizabeth McAshan, and Julia Currie all loaned money or traded for notes during the war. Most frequently in order to make money, single and married women alike rented out their slaves, sometimes taking promissory notes for payment. The estates of deceased women also indicated an increased amount of financial activity. Sarah Mason's estate showed that not only had she contracted debts during the war, but she had also lent money to merchants.[28]

Leonora Miller, barely twenty-one years old in 1864 and never married, became intricately involved in business dealings. William Harbert owed her

$250 and had no money to pay. Instead of cash he offered her cotton, which at the time was not easily turned into currency because of Union blockades. Leonora accepted the cotton and hired John Taylor to use her wagon to take the load to Brownsville to be sold.[29]

Elderly widow Elizabeth Turner saw her sons leave for war and thereafter entered into an agreement with Benjamin Ingram to jointly farm a portion of her land and split the proceeds. She furnished five of her slaves, "sufficient teams and farming tools," and food for the slaves and animals as well as the land. Ingram furnished two slaves, teams, and farming supplies as well and agreed to oversee raising cotton, corn, and potatoes personally. The agreement did not work out as smoothly as planned. In addition to other problems, Ingram was drafted into the army at the height of cotton-picking season. "Being unable to have a man to take charge of the farm in his absence," the cotton rotted in the field.[30]

Turner had other lands under cultivation at the time of her agreement with Ingram. She decided that it would be in her best interest to remove her slaves to other projects than to allow them to work under only "such general supervision" as two male neighbors could provide. Women throughout the South had to make such decisions regarding their slaves. Some undertook this job vigorously, though with great difficulties. Without the physical threat of a white male nearby to make slaves work and with the hope of impending freedom in the air, women faced extraordinary difficulties forcing slaves to labor. Some chose to rent or sell their slaves rather than deal with overseeing and disciplining them when no white men could help. Yet many women, even after nearly all the men in the county were drafted, continued to supervise slaves as well as possible under the circumstances.[31]

Even poorer women who had no slaves continued to raise some crops without the assistance of their husbands or sons. Raising crops, entering contracts, making financial decisions, and relying on the few remaining men less and less, women increasingly took on male roles. Yet the hardships of war were more than some could manage. Removing the male members of the household, no matter how financially savvy the remaining women, created poverty for families who relied upon men for labor in the fields. Deprived of their male heads of household, destitute women (as well as elite women) turned to the government that had deprived them of their providers, asking either to release their men from service or to fill their place in providing at least minimal survival.[32]

Colorado County certainly did not face the extent of need or provide the same level of support as urban and war-torn areas of the South did. Even so, beginning in 1862 the county court commissioned a census of families of soldiers needing support. In January 1863 some seventy families, almost exclusively married women and their dependents, received support from the county in amounts ranging from ten to forty dollars. Nearly every month thereafter "widows, parents, and children" on a list were provided with a small sustenance to curb starvation.[33]

As women took on unaccustomed male roles, and as the war loosened the restrictions placed on women to remain domestic, pure, pious, and submissive, tensions increased between husbands and wives. Many of these stresses related directly to the nature of war. War eased the normal restraints of courtship. Many young women, accepting the belief that women's goal was marriage, feared that the decreasing supply of men might doom them to spinsterhood. Some young couples married hastily in the excitement of war before the men went off to combat only to find later that they had made a mistake.[34]

Even couples who married before the threat of war was imminent faced strains. Martha Ivey at the age of thirteen had married Stephen Conner in 1860. When he joined the army, she lived with his mother, who "treated [her] with much unkindness." She appealed to her new husband to provide her with a new home, but "he disregarded her appeal." Stephen's absence surely complicated the possible success of this young marriage. In addition to the bonds of matrimony being tested by his mother's cruel treatment, Martha apparently had fallen in love with another man. After the war Stephen countersued and won a divorce when he produced a document proving that Martha committed not only adultery but also bigamy by marrying another man.[35]

George Metz also returned from two years in the army to find that his significantly younger wife had "formed a guilty and adulterous intimacy." Sarah "manifested no affection or welcome" to George when he came home, and shortly after that he discovered the reason.[36] Mike Scherer had lived in the Metz household to raise crops and tend the homestead after George joined the army. Scherer, however, took on more than just the business role of the husband in George's absence: Sarah had become "so notorious for illicit conduct between the said Sarah and Scherer that the ladies of the neighborhood dropped her. They neither visited her nor encouraged her to visit them on account of her familiarity with said Mike Scherer and her indecent conduct towards the said Scherer unbecoming a married woman."[37]

Even after George's return home, Scherer refused to leave the house. He allegedly claimed "that he was bound to have communication with her, that there was 'a cord of love'(!) between him and the said Sarah which could not be severed until death." Before the war George and Sarah Metz had been upstanding members of their community. He had served as an elder in the Lutheran Church, while she had been received in the company of some of the community's most elite ladies. Scherer's reputation before the war is unknown, however, his brother served as minister of the same congregation to which Metz had been elected elder. The young Sarah, who otherwise would have remained under the constant and watchful eye of her older husband, found an opportunity in the war to form an illicit relationship with a man closer to her age and apparently more to her liking.[38]

Although E. H. Blum was not a soldier, the war caused him to leave his home in 1861–62 to conduct business in Mexico. According to his petition, his wife, "Emma taking advantage of his absence did . . . commit adultery with one John Duffy." Husbands had sued wives for adultery before the war, but the extended absences of husbands led to an increase in such cases. Many wives, left to make their own decisions, exercised not only financial independence but also independence of affections. Other wives, unaccustomed to the difficulties of providing for themselves and their families (which only increased because of wartime shortages), turned to other men when their husbands left their duties as heads of household.[39]

Marriages that had been clearly unhappy before the war were strained further by the demands of the time. H. A. Tatum complained that his wife, Jane, had treated him cruelly before the war. After he returned from military duty, she "was incapable of returning his affection or of performing any of the duties of an affectionate wife." In his 1864 petition Tatum stressed his loyalty and his male duty to protect his community: "he entered in the military service of our country and remained with our army in Virginia until he was broken down in health and discharged from the service." Jane, though, "instead of contributing to the comfort and wants" of a patriotic and returning soldier, "was constantly leaving him alone, and engaging in frivolous amusements with noisy company."[40]

Jane Tatum countersued, producing reams of evidence that H. A. Tatum had been cruel and abusive even before the war. Like Martha Conner and Sarah Metz, she was significantly younger than her husband. At the time of the marriage, Jane "was quite young, much younger . . . so that [she] naturally looked up to [him] and instead of meeting with that reciprocity of affection which is due from one conjugal consort to the other, said advance and manifestations of affection were always repelled with sneers, or rebuffed with sarcasm, and often accompanied with oaths." Jane had separated from her husband before he joined the army. But on his return in 1863, he promised to reform his habits, so she agreed to return to him "in consideration of [his] just having returned from the war." She, like her husband, stressed her loyalty by forgiving the patriotic soldier. But his service in the army, according to Jane, had merely increased his habits of drunkenness and cruelty, and she soon wanted a divorce.[41]

Ellen Lacy's husband too had been cruel, drunken, and abusive since their marriage in 1858. While serving in the army, Beverly Lacy would come home on furlough "reeling drunk, and wholly inebriated . . . cursing and abusing" her. When he returned to their home after the war, Ellen made her first attempt to end their marriage through divorce.[42]

Although no divorce cases could be heard during the war, two men and four women submitted petitions for divorce anyway between April 1861 and April 1865. The first four who filed, after years of not having their cases heard, consented to dismissal when court resumed in 1866. Some who filed their petitions before the war did not have a hearing before 1861 so they could not extricate themselves from their marriages, and at least two dismissed their cases after waiting years for a hearing. Only two cases filed during the war were continued to a final hearing when the district court resumed functioning, and several more cases were filed after the war, though the separation and difficulties between the spouses had occurred during the war years.[43]

While wartime traumas undoubtedly were not the only causes of difficulty between these couples, the absence of men did exacerbate marital problems. Women worried about their husbands' fidelity far away from home. Men worried about their wives at home. Some young women left alone for the first time did find new lovers by choice; others turned to other men out of desperation. Some older women discovered that they would rather live without their husbands, in peace as in wartime, than continue in unhappy and abusive marriages.[44]

Colorado County citizens began the Civil War believing that militaristic adventures available only to men would further define gender roles and assumptions. Men would fulfill their duties to "protect" their wives against the encroaching enemy, while women would wait at home and keep the domestic hearth burning. These Southerners initially relied upon women merely to use their influence at home to encourage men to enlist, to support the war efforts, and to contribute domestically by making flags and clothing. But as the war required more and more men to leave the county, women were forced to make contributions that challenged, rather than enhanced, gender roles and assumptions about women's abilities and nature.[45]

Women had to take over the duties left on farms and in businesses. Married women who before the war had relied exclusively on their husbands to take care of the financial and public duties of the family stepped into these formerly male roles. Single and newly widowed women, instead of looking to men in the county to protect them from public activities, increasingly took the burdens upon themselves because they could not find male relatives to do so. Some of these women, alone and acting independently for the first time, made choices that their husbands would not have approved, such as taking new lovers. Others decided that they were willing to make their own choices even when the men returned. Overall, women in Colorado County, whether married or single, entered the public arena in large numbers during the Civil War and acted more independently of the men in their lives than ever before. This greater independence and assertiveness throughout the South has often been attributed to the stress of nearby battles, but Colorado County, far from the battlefields, changed as a result of the war itself, accepting women's greater participation in many aspects of society.

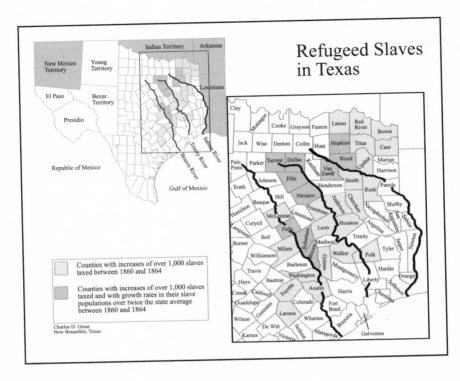

Refugeed slaves in Texas.
Courtesy Charles D. Grear

6

Slaves Taken to Texas for Safekeeping during the Civil War

Dale Baum

The victory of Ulysses S. Grant's soldiers at Shiloh in the spring of 1862 and the subsequent surrender of New Orleans, along with the ensuing movement of the U.S. Navy up the Mississippi River, dramatically increased the flow of Confederate refugees into Texas. Among them were many slaveholders, especially from Louisiana, Arkansas, and Mississippi, who were determined to take their slaves with them for protection from Union forces occupying or threatening areas close to their homes and plantations. Although the exact number of slaves "refugeed" (a coined variant by contemporaries of the word "refuge") into Texas during the Civil War cannot be precisely determined, their movement into the state enlarged the population in the "black belts," or bottomlands, along the Sabine, Trinity, and Brazos rivers.

Relying heavily on local tax records and federal census data, presented here is: (1) an identification of the Texas counties where refugeed slaves were disproportionately relocated; (2) a description of a segment of refugee slaveholders with considerable slave property and speculation about their welcome and adjustment to their new residences; and (3) a new estimate of the number of slaves transported into the state for safekeeping and a rough calculation of the percentage who remained in the state after their emancipation—all of which provide a better understanding of the nature and effects of wartime refugeeing. County increases in both the absolute numbers of slaves and their slave growth rates must be taken into account in order to pinpoint where refugeeing had its greatest consequences within the state. Although causing no severe problems for slavery in Texas, it nevertheless triggered grievances stemming from tensions between wealthy planters and plain folks. More refugee slaveholders than previously acknowledged most likely decided at the time they fled their antebellum homes to permanently pull up their roots. The bondsmen they transported into Texas from other slave states could have without difficulty reached more than 50,000, and of this number about 60 percent probably remained in the state during the immediate postwar years.

Once the first Confederate shots hit Fort Sumter, many slaveholders in the Upper South and Border States, especially those concerned about the future security of their investment in slave property, considered moving farther south, particularly all the way to Texas. The recollections of former slave Van Moore aptly describe their motivation: "[T]hey said the Yankees would never get that far, and they wouldn't have to free the slaves if they came way over here." As the last frontier of American slavery, Texas was similar to other states of the Lower South but was different because it was the only slave state with an international boundary and a history of having briefly been an independent slaveholding republic. In the wake of Abraham Lincoln's election to the presidency, many zealous proslavery "Texians" had talked about unfurling once again the "glorious flag of the Lone Star." After the fall of Vicksburg isolated Texas from the eastern Confederacy and the Richmond government, "Texas firsters," who bordered on putting local concerns ahead of Confederate priorities, were willing to consider either declaring independence with existing slave codes firmly in place or opening separate negotiations for returning to the Union on the basis of a gradual and counterfeit emancipation.[1]

Expectations that Texas would elude the ramifications of Lincoln's Emancipation Proclamation died hard. After the fall of Atlanta in 1864, only the most stalwart of heart sustained any hope for the Southern cause, but most Texas Confederates did not feel defeated. Proximity to Mexico had allowed the marketing of cotton via Matamoros and the nearby port of Bagdad, where ships could come and go without fear of the Union blockade. The majority of the state's slaves had remained undisturbed by advancing or occupying Union troops and had few chances to run off behind Federal lines or join the Northern cause. All in all, Texas had avoided being a major arena of military operations, its economy (in contrast to other Southern states) had not been as disrupted by the war, and the refugeed slaves had helped increase the amount of land under cultivation for growing cotton. In the fall of 1863, Gov. Francis R. Lubbock had proclaimed that the state had plenty of work to keep the thousands of newly arrived slaves "beneficially and constantly employed." Even the ominous decline of the South's military fortunes by spring of 1865 failed to destroy a widespread confidence in slavery's survival. Not even after Robert E. Lee's surrender at Appomattox did all Texans believe that slavery was doomed. Not, that is, until occupation of the state by U.S. soldiers, who finally arrived in Galveston on June 19, 1865—a date forever celebrated as "Juneteenth" by former Texas slaves—when the buying, selling, and hiring of slaves legally ended.[2]

The most definitive study of the "peculiar institution" in the Lone Star State calculates that the total number of refugeed slaves could have reached without doubt 32,000—a figure based on the number of bondsmen rendered in every county for taxation in the years 1860, 1862, and 1864, for which the corresponding numbers of slaves were 160,526; 186,884; and 240,099. Collection of annual ad valorem taxes on slave property was a main source of revenue for antebellum and wartime Texas governments. To what extent a lack of enthusiasm by refugee slaveholders for paying taxes to their new temporary county governments might have led to an underreporting of their slaves to local tax assessor-collectors is impossible to know. Nevertheless, had the rate of increase in "Negroes Taxed" between 1860 and 1862 remained the same between 1862 and 1864, then the state would have had approximately 32,000 fewer bondsmen in 1864 than actually were recorded. The estimate marks the low end of the parameter for the actual number of refugeed slaves. Additional information and assumptions suggest that slaveholders fleeing other states to protect their slave property brought many more than 32,000 slaves to Texas during the war years.[3]

One can argue that the 11.1 percent increase in slaves rendered for taxation from 1858 (144,463) to 1860 (160,526) more accurately represents the late antebellum trend in the rate of increase in slaves taxed—a trend that in all probability would have continued had the Republicans lost the 1860 presidential election. The 16.5 percent increase between 1860 and 1862, which generated the 32,000 estimate, was inflated (by way of contrast to the 1858–60 increase) by the secession crisis trigged by Lincoln's victory and, far more importantly, by the numbers of bondsmen reported for tax purposes by Missouri refugees residing in Texas by January 1, 1862.[4]

In the spring of 1861, pro-Unionist forces in Missouri seized the St. Louis arsenal and captured nearby Camp Jackson—events that threw the state into civil war when pro-Confederates retaliated with attacks destroying roads, bridges, and property. Rampages of secessionist guerrillas and Unionist freebooters soon turned areas of the state into "a no-man's land of hit-and-run raids, arson, ambush, and murder." One month before the First Battle of Bull Run, a group of fleeing Missouri slaveholders bringing with them nearly ninety slaves was reported encamped a few miles from Dallas. Additional newspaper accounts confirmed that the roads behind the group were "lined with emigrants" transporting "an immense number of valuable negroes" and predicted that "thousands" more refugees would arrive before the year's end. By autumn seeing the streets of Dallas "thronged with emigrants from Missouri" was no longer a novelty. The newcomers allegedly cursed Jayhawkers and Unionists "with an unction and relish" that rendered speechless even the most zealous local Confederates.[5]

The early Missouri evacuations demand a reformulation of the conventional estimate of the total number of slaves refugeed. In point of fact, Texas had about 42,000 more slaves taxed in 1864 than it would have had if the rates of increase between 1860 and 1862 and then again between 1862 and 1864 had mirrored the late antebellum 1858–60 pace. Moreover the customary tendency of county tax assessors to excuse slaveowners from paying taxes on incapacitated, elderly, and newborn slaves must be factored into the estimation procedure. Numbers of slaves reported to assessors were invariably less than reported to federal census takers. The 1860 U.S. census enumerated the Texas slave population at 182,566, but county tax rolls list assessments on only 160,526 slaves. In other words, the number of slaves taxed by local officials was 12.1 percent less than the number counted by federal enumerators. If assessors in 1864 had levied taxes on slaves at the same rates at which they taxed them in 1860, then the estimated enslaved population in 1864 would have totaled 273,066 (87.9 percent of 273,066 equals the reported 240,099 "negroes taxed" in 1864). Assuming that refugee slaveholders received comparable tax forgiveness on their unproductive slaves, then the 42,000 figure embodies a number closer to 47,800.[6]

Because fugitive slaves were typically forgiven by tax assessors, the sharp rise in the number of wartime runaways also must be taken into account. As one former Texas slave recalled, "[h]undreds of slaves" escaped to Mexico, where "you could be free" because nobody there cared "what color you was, black, white, yellow, or blue." Another remembered how "de white folks rid [rode] de Mexican side [of] dat river all de time, but plenty of slaves git through anyway." Slaves accompanying wagon trains laded with cotton bales for Brownsville frequently "strayed off" when in close proximity of the Mexican border. Such occurrences caused the *Houston Telegraph* to warn planters against conveying with them even "their trusty negroes" on business to Matamoros, which the newspaper described as "overrunning with these trusty, now insolent negroes."[7]

Also absent on tax rolls during the wartime years were slaves taken to the

Texas frontier by Confederate-allied Indians, particularly the slaveholding Creeks, Choctaws, and Chickasaws who fled their homes in Indian Territory (modern Oklahoma) to avoid internecine fighting with pro-Union Indians. Threats from marauding and hostile Indians caused evacuation of many white settlements on the western frontier, specifically the sparsely settled parts attached for administrative purposes to Young (Fort Belknap) and Bexar (San Antonio) counties and labeled as "Young Territory" and "Bexar [Land] District" on Civil War–era maps. Nevertheless, after the fall of Vicksburg, a few East Texas slaveholders temporarily moved to the edge of the frontier in their determination to put their slaves far beyond the possible range of emancipation and, as an unintended result, beyond the reach of the tax assessor-collectors at Fort Belknap and San Antonio.[8]

Finally, and perhaps most importantly, the spring of 1864 witnessed a surge in the number of slaves brought into the state by planters fleeing Maj. Gen. Nathaniel P. Banks's Red River campaign. By the beginning of April, refugees from the areas around Alexandria in central Louisiana had poured into the northwestern city of Shreveport, the temporary Confederate state capital and gateway to Texas. Refugeed slaves arriving in Texas in 1864 due to military events in Louisiana were not subjected to taxation until the first day of the *next* year—the year in which emancipation caused the lists of slaves taxed to be incomplete or nonexistent. Moreover, many slaves continued to arrive in early 1865 on the eve of the Third Marshall Conference in Harrison County, where Trans-Mississippi military and political leaders drafted an unworkable plan of surrender. In attendance was Louisiana governor Thomas Overton Moore, who had relocated to Houston County along the Trinity River—an area that newspaper reports described as "thronged with Louisiana refugees." Nor did slaves transported into the state during the final months of the war originate from only Louisiana. Elvira Boles recalled being refugeed to Texas all the way from Mississippi in 1865 by her owner, constantly "a dodgin' in and out, runnin' from de Yankees."[9]

If an unusually high number of nonrefugeed Texas slaves were left off the tax rolls during the war because they escaped to Mexico or were taken for safekeeping to the "unorganized" parts of the state's western frontier, then their drag on the growth rate of slaves taxed must be offset by a proportional boost in any estimation of refugeed slaves. One must also account for nontaxed slaves accompanying Confederate Indians who temporarily relocated to extreme western areas of the state. Similarly, any estimation procedure has to take into consideration the slaves mainly from Louisiana, though also from Arkansas and other Southern states, who were not present in Texas on the first day of 1864 but subsequently were residing in the state by the beginning of 1865 or at the time of the Juneteenth proclamation. The end result would conservatively add at least 3,000 or 4,000 slaves to the 47,800 estimate. The total number of slaves transported into Texas by slaveholders hoping to shield their "species of property" from emancipation by advancing Union forces could thus have easily reached 51,000. Finally, although both white and black refugees experienced higher-than-normal death rates due to the numerous hardships they endured, the slaves suffered more than their masters. Because nobody bothered to count the slaves who died alongside the roads from starvation, exhaustion, and sickness, the 51,000 figure could conceivably be adjusted even higher.[10]

Unsystematic use of tax-roll data can fail to put into proper context the relative effect from one place to another of refugeed slaves. For example, Grimes County witnessed its slave population expand between 1860 and 1864 by more than 2,000—a number that undoubtedly included many refugeed slaves (see table 1). Yet it is misleading to claim that "an influx of planter refugees" seeking greater security for their slaves "had swollen the local slave population" by 1864 to such an extent that the "demographic impact" of wartime refugeeing was made "conspicuous" by 1870, when the federal census revealed that blacks composed "virtually 60 percent of the county's population." In point of fact, on the eve of the war, slaves in Grimes County outnumbered whites, and by 1864 their rate of increase lagged *below* the rate of increase in slaves throughout the entire state. To pinpoint more accurately where the highest rates of refugeeing occurred and where the relative effect of raw numbers of new slaves was considerably greater, only those counties that between 1860 and 1864 experienced increases on their tax rolls of more than 1,000 "Negroes Taxed" and growth rates in their slave populations over *twice* the state average are discussed here.[11]

Of the ten counties with over double the average wartime growth rates in slaves and having actual increases of more than 1,000 slaves, only Hopkins County does not border on the Sabine, Trinity, or Brazos rivers (see map 1). Otherwise, Wood and Van Zandt counties are located on the upper part of the Sabine River; Tarrant (Fort Worth), Dallas (Dallas), Ellis, and Navarro counties are situated along the Trinity River; and Falls, Robertson, and Brazos counties are located along the Brazos River. Three regions thus emerge as the temporary residencies of many slaveholding refugees whose bondsmen composed comparatively high percentages of the wartime increases in the respective county slave populations: (1) the adjacent counties on the central part of the Brazos River southeast of Waco and northwest of Navasota, ranging from Falls to the north and Brazos to the south, with Robertson sandwiched between; (2) the contiguous counties along the upper Trinity River, bounded on the north by Tarrant

TABLE 1

Increases in Slaves Taxed between 1860 and 1864

A. Texas counties with increases of more than 1,000
"Negroes Taxed" between 1860 and 1864

County	Increase in Slaves Taxed between 1860 and 1864	Slaves Taxed in 1860	Slaves Taxed in 1864
Smith	2,849	4,363	7,212
Falls	2,661	1,569	4,230
Freestone	2,616	2,997	5,613
Rusk	2,466	5,398	7,864
Robertson	2,437	1,955	4,392
Cherokee	2,286	2,706	4,992
Anderson	2,275	3,154	5,429
Upsher	2,260	3,611	5,871
Navarro	2,189	1,724	3,913
Grimes	2,155	4,850	7,005
Red River	2,082	2,573	4,655
Washington	2,047	6,616	8,663
Houston	1,864	2,446	4,310
Polk	1,842	3,639	5,481
Lamar	1,706	2,424	4,230
McLennan	1,702	2,105	3,807
Cass	1,674	3,515	5,189
Bowie	1,664	2,474	4,138
Dallas	1,559	923	2,482
Titus	1,540	2,040	3,580
Walker	1,509	3,766	5,275
Austin	1,503	3,199	4,702
Fayette	1,311	3,190	4,501
Brazos	1,278	735	2,013
Leon	1,231	2,225	3,456
Hopkins	1,183	918	2,101
Van Zandt	1,170	291	1,461
Wood	1,161	923	2,084
Ellis	1,078	1,008	2,086
Lavaca	1,059	1,654	2,713
Tarrant	1,042	730	1,772
Milam	1,011	1,136	2,147
In all Texas Counties	79,573	160,526	240,099

TABLE 1 (CONTINUED)

B. Texas counties with above the state-average percentage increases in "Negroes Taxed" and with increases of more than 1,000 slaves between 1860 and 1864

County	Percentage Increase in Negroes Taxed	Increase in Slaves Taxed between 1860 and 1864
Van Zandt	402%	1,170
Brazos	174%	1,278
Falls	170%	2,661
Dallas	169%	1,559
Tarrant	143%	1,042
Hopkins	129%	1,183
Navarro	127%	2,189
Wood	126%	1,161
Robertson	125%	2,437
Ellis	107%	1,078
Freestone	87%	2,616
Cherokee	84%	2,286
Red River	81%	2,082
McLennan	81%	1,403
Houston	76%	1,864
Lamar	75%	1,388
Titus	75%	1,540
Anderson	72%	2,275
Bowie	67%	1,664
Smith	65%	2,849
Lavaca	64%	1,006
Upsher	63%	2,260
Leon	55%	1,232
Polk	51%	1,842
In all Texas Counties	50%	79,573

Source: For the number of slaves or "Negroes Taxed," see Records of the Comptroller of Public Accounts, Ad Valorem Tax Division, County Real and Personal Property Tax Rolls, 1860, 1864, Texas State Library and Archives, Austin, microfilm.

and Dallas and to the south by Ellis and Navarro; and (3) the counties of Wood and Van Zandt, which border each other on the extreme upper end of the Sabine River, in combination with neighboring Hopkins to the northeast of the river's headwaters.

Before Union forces captured New Orleans, Houston had become "the major refugee center" along the Texas Gulf Coast. Long before Galvestonians fleeing a Union attack on their island city arrived in the fall of 1862, Houston newspapers asserted that adequate numbers of refugees existed "to whip any Yankee force" attacking their city. Initial news of massive numbers of slaves being transported into the state, however, began in the final months of the year. In December reports appeared of "the roads leading from Louisiana" being "filled with wagons coming into Texas." The refugees, traveling more often than not in large wagon caravans and with "their families and negroes and all the effects they have left," had purportedly often abandoned "their crops in the field" in their haste to flee from Yankee soldiers. If only inches of newspaper columns are counted, then the largest coverage of what was called "the exodus to Texas" occurred predictably in 1863.[12]

"And still they come! Line after line! Caravan after Caravan, crowd the roads and chokes the ferries." Such were the lead sentences written by Col. Caleb Goldsmith Forshey, an engineering fortification expert and eyewitness to the flow of refugees into Texas via Louisiana after the fall of Vicksburg. Personal stories followed statements about the heartbreaking sight of many wealthy planters reduced to despair, but descriptions containing references to their slaves were often more revealing: "[W]hite and black are sharing alike their shelterless emigration. . . . . Such wan visages—such dirty and patched habiliments, such crippled mules and rawboned horses; such crazy carts and rickety wagons." Passing through an encampment in an unrelenting drizzling rain, Forshey later wrote: "Groups of the genuine descendants of Ham . . . were standing sullen and motionless, around little smoking camp fires; trying to dry, while the rain mocked their efforts. Mothers wrapped their children in rags, and held them close. . . . Carts, wagons, drays, carryalls and every species of vehicle, some covered, and others crammed full, but open, were taking in the rain. Clothes that had been rinsed in the Sabine [River] waters . . . were satyrically [*sic*] hanging out to dry; while 'the rain rained on.'" More problematical was Forshey's assertion that even the slave who had run off behind Yankee lines to a "houseless camp to starve and die in," but who had been recaptured, reprimanded, and refugeed to Texas, "still yearns to his old Louisiana home."[13]

Newspaper accounts understandably exaggerated the number of slaves being refugeed to Texas. By 1863 the conventional wisdom was that the state's slave population would double as a result of the war. In the following year Maj. Gen. John B. Magruder claimed his sources put the number of people relocated just from Arkansas and Missouri at 150,000. Perhaps more accurate were reports that a disproportionate number of enslaved arrivals were females because the men had "escaped to the enemy of their own accord." Yet for many bondsmen on the roads to Texas, nighttime lockups in shackles and chains had been unnecessary. As former slave Smith Austin, who along with a hundred other slaves in his convoy arrived in Texas from Tennessee at the beginning of the war, recalled years later: "Us was too scared in the strange country. . . . Us just marched behind the wagons like soldiers."[14]

Also in 1863 for the first time the flood of refugees sparked a variety of concerns. After the outbreak of the war, the state legislature had anticipated potential problems with slaves by criminalizing actions by slaveholders leaving their bondsmen unattended without "free white" supervision or permitting any slave to pretend to own or be in charge of land or other slaves. Yet most Confederate Texans believed that refugeed slaves, if unsupervised or uncared for by their masters or in the absence of any available employment, could always be "placed at work upon the formidable line of fortifications" located along the western bank of the lower Sabine River. When impressments of slaves became a military necessity by early 1863, many refugees fleeing to Texas complained that immediately after they had crossed the Sabine, there suddenly appeared Confederate agents who commandeered "one-third to one-half of their slaves to work on fortifications" or perform other tasks for the army. By the fall of 1863, Lt. Gen. Edmund Kirby Smith, in command of the Trans-Mississippi West—a virtually independent area severed from the Richmond government—ordered "persons changing their homes" or "refugees with their property" be allowed to at least get settled in Texas before expropriating their property and slaves for defense. Although throughout the war Texan hospitality in protecting, aiding, and comforting the refugees stemmed from "interest, Christian duty, and patriotism," complaints against the refugees inevitably arose.[15]

In the late summer of 1863, the editor of *The Tyler Reporter* (Smith County), while not disapproving of the many slaves being brought into the state for greater protection, objected that "they are sometimes permitted to do pretty much as they please." Singled out for criticism was "one [of] Dr. Blackman's negroes," who "committed thefts on a large scale, and when informed of it, [Blackman] made light of the matter." In a rare pronouncement by local authorities in January 1864, the Hunt County Commissioners' Court ordered an agent for a refugee slaveholder to "either set your negroes to work or take them from our County or the Court will proceed to hire them at public out cry." Otherwise, the records of the proceedings of the commissioners' courts in counties affected most by refugeed slaves are remarkably silent about the newcomers causing any threats to law and order.[16]

Although refugeeing, as the foremost scholar of the period concludes, "caused no serious disruption of slavery in Texas," it nevertheless exacerbated economic class tensions within white society. For Texas soldiers fighting skirmishes with invading Yankees in northwestern Mississippi in the summer of 1863, the sight of "cowardly" and "able bodied" slaveholders fleeing with their property rather than staying and putting up a fight fueled the notion of, in the words of John G. McNemar, "a rich man war and a poor man fight." Encamped with his cavalry brigade about forty miles south of Memphis, Tennessee, he wrote home to his wife: "These Mississippians have run off their negro men, women and children into Alabama and Georgia to eat the bread and meat from soldiers wives and children that is off in service of their county defending these same rich mens property and I expect they have or will fill up Texas with negros the same way to eat the bread and meat from the soldier wives and children." McNemar held such slaveholders, who he numbered in the thousands, in more contempt than deserters from his own ranks: "I thank God that the Federals have stolen as many negros in Miss[issippi] as they have. If the Yankee cannot humble these rich mens pride it is pretty hard to humble."[17]

A cursory look at wartime indictments handed down by Texas grand juries against planters known to have large numbers of refugeed slaves residing on their lands suggests that slaveholders who were indifferent or disloyal to the Confederate cause elicited the most serious complaints. A magnet for anti-secessionist slaveholder refugees was the rich alluvial bottomlands of the Brazos River in the southwestern corner of Robertson County—a county with over twice the growth rate of slaves during the war years and with the second-highest increase in the number of slaves on its tax rolls (see table 1). Here resided a group of wealthy prewar Unionist planters who became reluctant Confederates, including most prominently former state senator Charles Lewis and his wife's brothers and cousins who made up the extended Hearne family. In their midst lived Telemachus ("Telephus") Johnson, a cantankerous planter who on the eve of the war had owned forty-nine slaves. Although Johnson served in the Texas Home Guard, he was allegedly the only man in Robertson County who throughout the war withheld "any and all support, aid, or comfort to the Rebellion." As a consequence county officials subjected him to "more abuse and persecution" than any other person in the county.[18]

Moving into Johnson's neighborhood in 1863 was Louisiana refugee Robert C. Myers, who also was an unapologetic "union sympathizer." By early 1864

Myers had moved his twenty-one slaves onto Johnson's plantation. Subsequently, during the Robertson County District Court's spring term, a grand jury indicted Johnson with the criminal offense of putting his bondsmen in charge of lands detached from his home residence. Johnson's "extraordinary shrewdness and unflinching nerve," combined with his status as a large slaveholder, allegedly saved him from extralegal retaliation. His being on good terms with the Hearne and Lewis families and their overseers also shielded him, for they refused to appear at the courthouse as witnesses against him. Johnson died of natural causes in the 1880s, and his wife buried him "seated at a poker table with a whiskey bottle in one hand and a six-shooter in the other." But Myers, while serving in 1871 as a scalawag radical Republican officeholder in neighboring Brazos County, was assassinated by a Democratic Party rival.[19]

Although payments of wartime taxes on slaves provide no direct evidence of slaveholder motivation, the tax rolls when combined with census data can be used to identify individuals who were unquestionably refugee slaveowners. Because many nineteenth-century county tax rolls or abstract books were unfortunately either lost or destroyed after they were microfilmed in the mid-twentieth century, blurry or indecipherable writing in microfilm editions often cannot be double-checked with the originals. The meticulous transcription by genealogists of the Brazos County tax rolls for the years 1863 through 1866, when combined with comparable U.S. census data for 1860 and 1870, is extraordinarily helpful in delving into the county's wartime history. Brazos County's nearly three-fold increase in the number of its bondsmen taxed between 1860 and 1864 was surpassed by only Van Zandt County (see table 1). Brazos County had approximately 1,105 more slaves taxed in 1864 than it would have had if the rate of increase in slaves rendered for taxation had maintained the statewide 1858–60 antebellum rate of increase. Between 1860 and 1864 the county also had a 59 percent increase in persons paying taxes on slaves, or seventy-two more individuals, including agents and executors of estates.[20]

Slaveholders not residing in Brazos County before the war, but who subsequently paid taxes there in 1863 or 1864 on at least 10 or more slaves but not on any land, meet the criterion for being almost certainly medium or large slaveholders seeking greater protection for slave property. Sixteen masters or agents of slaveholders fitting this description paid wartime taxes on 390 slaves (see table 2). Of their slaves transported into the county, the largest single group was those from other Texas counties, followed in descending order by slaves from Louisiana, Arkansas, Mississippi, and Alabama.

TABLE 2

Refugeeing Slaveholders in Brazos County

A. Refugees paying taxes on ten or more slaves, but owning no real estate, in Brazos County in 1863 or 1864

Name	Age and Occupation, 1860	Number of Slaves	Residence, 1860	Civil War Military Service
Daniel E. Batte	20-year-old minor with a "guardian"	28 slaves	Harrison County, TX	"Private," 5th Regt., TX Inf. (Hood's Brigade)
William A. Bell	50 year-old "farmer"	18 slaves	Union County, AR	"Captain," AR Home Guard
Louis B. Benefield	43-year-old "merchant"	14 slaves	Avoyelles Parish, LA	None
Thomas Boone	46-year-old "physician"	20 slaves	Carroll County, MS	None
James B. Durant	28-year-old "planter"	35 slaves	Brazoria County, TX	"1st Sergeant," Co. K, 9th Regt., TX Inf. (Nichols's Inf.) [6 mos. 1861–62]
Joel Evans	41-year-old "merchant"	48 slaves	Clay County, MS	None
William H. Farner	47-year-old "physician"	20 slaves	Caddo Parish, LA	"Assistant Surgeon," 4th Regt., 4th TX Cav. (Sibley's Brigade)
Malcolm Gandy	30-year-old "farm hand"	45 slaves	Lavaca County, TX	"Private," 26th Regt., Debray's TX Cav. (Davis's Mounted Btn.)
A. C. L. Hill	41-year-old "merchant"; "planter"*	11 slaves	Union County, AR	"Private," AR Home Guard
Richard W. Lovett	41-year-old "farmer"	26 slaves	Union County, AR	Capt. Jesse Batt's Co., Brazos County Minute Men
Thomas F. Lovett	38-year-old "farmer"	10 slaves	Union County, AR	AR Home Guard
William C. Lovett	30-year-old "farmer"	14 slaves	Union County, AR	"Corporal," Co. F, 19th Regt., AR Inf. (Dockery's)
Thomas M. Neal	63-year-old "farmer"	21 slaves	Rapides Parish, LA	None

TABLE 2 (CONTINUED)

Name	Age and Occupation, 1860	Number of Slaves	Residence, 1860	Civil War Military Service
Willis C. Pollard	53-year-old "farmer"	25 slaves	Caddo Parish, LA	None
Watson Reed	53-year-old "farmer"	16 slaves	Claiborne Parish, LA	None
James M. Turner	23-year-old "farmer"	39 slaves	Lowndes County, AL	[Multiple listings, C.S. Army]
All of above:		390 slaves		

B. Refugees paying taxes on eight or nine slaves but owning no real estate, Brazos County, 1863 or 1864

Name	Age and Occupation, 1860	Number of Slaves	Residence, 1860	Civil War Military Service
Andrew J. Allen	36-year-old "farmer"	9 slaves	Anderson County, TX	"Private," Co. K, 11th Regt., TX Inf. (Roberts's)
John Burrows	56-years old**	8 slaves	St. Mary's Parish, LA	None
John Collins	48-year-old "merchant"	9 slaves	Henderson County, TX	None
K. David Stevens	36-year old "farmer"	9 slaves	Union County, AR	"Private," Co. G, 18th Regt., TX Cav. (Darnell's)
All of above:		35 slaves		

*A. C. L. Hill, Union County, Arkansas, is described as a "merchant" in Champagnolle in the 1850 census, but in 1860 his occupation is listed as "planter."

**John Burrows, owning 18 slaves in St. Mary's Parish, Louisiana, is listed only in the 1860 slave schedules.

Note: The number of slaves rendered for taxation by each slaveholder listed above includes payments made as an "agent" for another, as an "executor" of a decedent's estate, or for oneself in joint ownership with another. The number does not include paying merely "for" or "per" someone else. Nor does it include paying as a legal "guardian" for someone no longer a minor, as in the case of Daniel E. Batte, who was away serving in the Confederate army. Misspellings of names, an unfortunately frequent occurrence in the original manuscript censuses or tax rolls, have been left unchanged.[21]

The large percentage of slaves temporarily relocated to Brazos County from other Texas counties was a result of planters moving their slaves farther away from anticipated or actual Federal invasions. Texas counties alongside the lower Sabine River bordering Louisiana or along the Gulf of Mexico experienced little growth in their slave populations during the war (see map 1). Declines in slave populations occurred in a string of counties on the Texas coast from Copano Bay to Matagorda Bay, along with briefly Union-occupied Galveston County farther north. From Lavaca County close to Matagorda Bay, Malcolm and Alfred Gandy refugeed a combined fifty-one slaves to Brazos County. On the eve of the war, Malcolm had no slaves, but his father owned six, and Alfred, their relative living immediately next door, owned five. The joint prewar value of personal property owned by these two households equaled less than one-third of the wartime value declared for their slaves in Brazos County—details suggesting, but not proving, that Malcolm, who had been a clerk in his father's mercantile store in Alabama before the family moved to Texas in 1853, was perhaps an agent for other slaveholders or himself a slave trader. At the end of the war, Malcolm returned home to Lavaca County.[22]

From the same Gulf Coast area, James B. Durant, a member of a wealthy planter family from Brazoria County, in the spring of 1862 relocated his family and thirty-five slaves to Brazos County. After the war his baby daughter died in the 1867 yellow fever epidemic—a misfortune that was followed in 1869 by the deaths of his wife and the family's only surviving child. Durant himself died in 1875 while a defendant in civil litigation in the Brazos County District Court. Under similar circumstances, from Harrison County on the Texas-Louisiana border, Daniel E. Batte and his older brother transported twenty-eight slaves into Brazos County, where their relatives, the prominent Moseley slaveholding family, owned thousands of acres of prime cotton land in the Brazos bottoms. In 1864 the combined total value of personal property declared for tax purposes by the Batte brothers, including their slaves, promissory notes, and Confederate cash and notes, was $92,225—a remarkably high amount of taxable property exceeded by the tax declarations of only three other local families. In 1868 both brothers declared bankruptcy. For the remainder of their lives, they lived in Brazos County and were buried there in the early 1890s.[23]

In terms of numbers of slaves taken to Brazos County from other Confederate states, Louisiana, closely followed by Arkansas, ranked the highest (see table 2). The groupings of slaves inventoried from Louisiana were from at least four different parishes: from Claiborne Parish on the Arkansas state line appeared Watson Reed with sixteen slaves; from Rapides Parish along the Red River, another large antebellum planter, Thomas M. Neal, transported twenty-one slaves; from Avoyelles Parish along the Mississippi River came Louis B.

Benefield, a merchant refugeeing fourteen slaves; and from Caddo Parish (Shreveport) arrived Willis C. Pollard with twenty-five slaves and Dr. William H. Farner with twenty slaves. Why Farner, a paroled Confederate army surgeon who had abandoned his wife and family in Iowa to fight for the Southern cause, decided to refugee slaves for safekeeping to Brazos County will never be known, but once there he remarried. (His new and extremely young Texas wife, however, remained invisible to his Midwestern relatives in their later-day historical sketches of his life.) Prior to 1863 Farner, who had lived during the antebellum years exclusively in the North, had never owned slaves, and Benefield, on the eve of the war, had owned only one—circumstances suggesting that they were acting for others or were themselves speculating in slaves. Although Pollard owned only four slaves in 1860, he (like the Batte brothers) was related to the Moseley family. Only Pollard and Neal cannot be subsequently traced in easily available records. Otherwise Farner, Benefield, and Reed remained in Brazos County or its close vicinity during the postwar period. In 1869 military authorities removed Benefield from the Brazos County Commissioners Court, whereas Farner achieved an unsavory reputation as the area's first Freedmen's Bureau agent and subsequently as a radical Republican newspaper editor.[24]

The refugeed slaves from Arkansas itemized in table 2 came from plantations located along the Ouachita River in eastern Union County near the Louisiana border. They were brought in 1863 to Brazos County in a large caravan composed of at least seven slaveholding households with no less than ninety-six slaves. Business partners William A. Bell and A. C. L. Hill led the migration. Bell, who had once served in the Alabama state legislature, quietly lived out the remainder of his life in Bryan, the county seat of Brazos County, as a widower with his daughter's family. Like Bell, Hill also remained in Bryan, where he declared bankruptcy in 1868 but subsequently became a successful cotton buyer, a prominent local Democratic politician, and an owner of a large cottonseed-oil factory. Hill also remained in Brazos County until his death. Less is known about the other Arkansas refugees who accompanied Bell and Hill, such as the three Lovett brothers. The Lovetts came with a total of forty-five slaves and were joined by their sisters' family, who brought with them eighteen slaves. Richard Lovett lived out the remainder of his life in Brazos County, whereas his younger brothers, Thomas and William, moved to neighboring Robertson County.[25]

No Confederate refugee brought more slaves into Brazos County than Joel Evans, a large planter and prominent merchant from West Point, Mississippi. The declared value of his forty-eight slaves, cotton bonds, Confederate cash, and other personal property exceeded $47,000 in 1864. But the following year, upon his death in Brazos County, the taxable properties in his estate had dwindled to only a couple of wagons and some horses and oxen valued at $710. Also from

Mississippi, Dr. Thomas Boone and his family from Carroll County arrived with twelve slaves. Accompanying them was Sarah Knox, a minor child who had been living in the Boone household in 1860. Serving as Sarah's agent, Dr. Boone paid the taxes on her eight refugeed slaves. Sarah's kinship to the well-known Knox family of Brazos County accounted for the Boones' choice of destination. Edward C. Knox, who owned a large Brazos County cotton plantation, subsequently paid the taxes on the slaves owned by Boone. At the war's end Sarah left for Arkansas to live with her mother, but Boone remained in Brazos County as a practicing physician.[26]

From farther east—Lowndes County, Alabama—came James M. Turner, a young and unmarried slaveholder, with thirty-nine slaves, or eleven more than the twenty-eight he had owned in 1860. After the war he moved to Crockett Bluff, Arkansas. Otherwise, little is known about his brief stay in Brazos County, except that he personally appeared to pay his taxes in 1864 and 1865 only to witness the total value of his property, devoid of slaves and Confederate money, plummet at the end of the war from $32,825 to $1,295—a devastating 96 percent decline in his net worth.[27]

At the end of the war, all refugeeing Brazos County slaveholders suffered declines in fortune when their financial holdings in human chattels and Confederate money, bonds, and IOUs became worthless. At least two of them, Batte and Hill, filed for bankruptcy. While this crippling financial result of the war seems in hindsight to have been foreseeable, for contemporaries of the era this outcome was less certain. Many Confederates had believed that in the event of their defeat and subsequent occupation by Union troops, their landed property would be insecure and at least in as much danger as their slave property. Although those who shared this belief were to a huge extent wrong, many, if not a majority, of their Confederate counterparts failed to realize that land ownership would be far safer than virtually most any other form of investment. Few slaveholders during the war had the prescience to buy up all the land they possibly could with the use of all their Confederate money and the proceeds from the sale or exchange of all their slaves. Such opportunities were not lacking. In 1862 in Brazos County, the following offering price would have been equal to a couple of good adolescent field hands: "640 acres unimproved land, heavily timbered, within three quarters of a mile from the Central road, at two dollars per acre." The seller was willing to "take young Negroes, Confederate notes, state notes, [or] payable one half cash, the balance when [the South defeated] the damned Yankee ruffians!"[28]

Somewhat unexpected, however, is the finding that among the fourteen largest refugeeing slaveholders who can be found subsequently in federal censuses or other records, only one, Malcolm Gandy, returned to his antebellum residence in Lavaca County. In addition, if one considers the four individuals composing the upper layer of small refugeeing slaveholders paying taxes on eight or nine slaves but owning no land in Brazos County in 1863 and 1864, they also share a high probability of not returning to their antebellum residences. K. David Stevens, while away in the Confederate army, had his taxes on his nine refugeed slaves paid for him by the Lovett brothers, who were his brothers-in-law. After the war Stevens bought a town lot in Bryan and registered to vote in Brazos County. John Burrows from St. Mary's Parish, Louisiana, who had refugeed eight slaves and had owned considerable Confederate notes and bonds, died in Brazos County at age seventy in late 1863. Andrew J. Allen, who early in the war brought his nine slaves from Anderson County in East Texas, served in the Confederate army, then at the war's end moved to DeWitt County in South Texas. Only merchant John Collins, who had brought nine slaves to Brazos County, returned to his antebellum home in Athens, Texas.[29]

All in all, among the top twenty refugeeing slaveholders in Brazos County, only two Texans, Collins and Gandy, from Lavaca and Henderson counties respectively, can be found after the war living in their prewar residences. None of the masters or slave drivers from states other than Texas can be traced back to their antebellum homes or to where their journeys as refugees originated. The overwhelming majority of them remained, for whatever reasons, after the war in the central Brazos River valley. These somewhat surprising circumstances do not vitiate their initial intentions for "only a brief stay in Texas" or, in the cases of Allen, Batte, and Durant, a temporary safe location within their own state, but rather they suggest that far more refugeeing masters than previously suspected had decided to permanently abandon their antebellum residences when they made their decisions to flee. They also admittedly might have reassessed any plans to return to their former homes in light of the Confederate defeat.[30]

Despite suspicions that among the refugee slaveholders were "too many [who wanted] others to do their fighting," none of the largest of those relocating in Brazos County evaded the Confederate conscription acts. Their average age at the outbreak of the war in 1861 was just over forty-one years. Only Thomas Lovett's liability to the draft in 1863 at age forty-one raises the question of his possible avoidance of conscription because of an infirmity, an occupational exemption, or use of the unpopular slave-overseer exemption, or "20-Negro Law," but there is no evidence that he did. Otherwise the overall collective record of their military service was exemplary: Farner at age forty-eight had volunteered as a surgeon in the Fourth Texas Cavalry; Bell at age fifty-one had been a captain in the Arkansas Home Guard; and Batte, Durant, Gandy, and the youngest Lovett brother, most likely along with Turner, had all served in the Confederate army (see table 2).[31]

How many of the 425 bondsmen brought into Brazos County stayed in Texas after the war can never be known, but obviously many of them also remained in the central Brazos valley during the immediate postwar years. Although the ex-slaves had the choice to adopt whatever family name they themselves desired at the time of their registration to vote under the Congressional Reconstruction Acts, it is of some interest that only the surnames "Benefield" and "Farner," who most likely were slave traders or agents for other slaveholders, are missing in Brazos County or in adjoining counties from the names of freedmen either registered to vote from 1867 to 1869 or enumerated in the 1870 federal census.[32]

When the news of an impending "surrender," the most dreaded word in the vocabulary of ardent Confederates, reached Robertson County, refugee slaveholder Judge John T. Mills, for whom Mills County was later named, decided to move his family back to its antebellum home in Harrison County. His stepson years later recalled the "weeks of packing" and the late-afternoon start to a previously announced camping site where his family's "outfit" spent its last night in the Brazos River bottoms. Planters came, "bringing wagon loads of prepared food, including barbecue, and everything good to eat and everybody . . . both black and white had all they could drink and then some." This "first night out" was followed the next day by the beginning of the long journey to Marshall. Although not all the departures by refugees were marked by similar extravagant sendoffs, the recollections by Mills's stepson about the family's seventy-one refugeed slaves were more representative: "We left a good many of the negroes in the Bottom, hired out, and after the surrender some came 'home,' but a number did not, and I have never seen one of them since."[33]

More anecdotal evidence predictably can be found about refugeed ex-slaves who stayed rather than left. In the spring of 1865, when prominent Robertson County planter William "Bill" Anderson purchased slaves at bargain prices from masters in Louisiana anxious to sell them, he learned of the Confederate surrender while encamped on the road returning to Texas with his cargo of human chattels. "De next morning," as Wash Wilson recalled, "Marse Bill [told us] Boys you's free as I is." Nonetheless Wilson and his freed, albeit still not officially emancipated, counterparts, having taken a liking to their new owner, decided to remain with him permanently. As Wilson explained, "All de seven familie Marse Bill done buy in Louisiana stayed round him and he family till dey all dead." Yet many refugeed slaves left Texas after the end of the war. While some departed to merely test their new freedom on the roads or return to their antebellum "homes," far more left to look for family members from whom they had been separated or to hurry to marry the partners they had been prevented from marrying under slavery.[34]

The massive amount of documentation contained in the Freedmen's Bureau records in the National Archives indicates that of all the forces unleashed by Reconstruction, nothing was more powerful than the former slaves trying to reunify families that had been broken up during their enslavement. Inherent in any movement of slaves such as refugeeing was the separation of fathers, mothers, and children, along with extended family friends and sweethearts. After the war bureau agents spent considerable time trying to help Texas blacks find missing relatives by writing letters to agents outside of the state and printing circulars for postings. The ex-slaves themselves, through their newly established newspapers and churches, frequently took the initiative. Sally Harvey, for one, placed a notice in the freedpeople's *Methodist New Orleans Advocate* in the spring of 1867 concerning her son James, who had been refugeed by his master from Morehouse Parish, Louisiana, to Ellis County, Texas, in 1862 and then later taken by his master's wife to Brazos County: "Any information may be sent to his mother, care of Rev. J. R. Fenner, Monroe, La." The success rate of black family reunifications cannot be tallied, nor will the number of freedpeople who left the state to either search for or be reunited with relatives and loved ones ever be known.[35]

Teetering conjecture upon supposition is risky, but there would have been about 20,000 fewer blacks than expected in Texas by 1869 if one assumes the following: (1) under the Congressional Reconstruction Acts the fullest possible registration of black voters (56,810) occurred by 1869; (2) underenumeration problems with the 1870 federal census make it unsuitable for estimating the state's black population in 1869, though it is reasonable to assume that as enumerated in the 1870 census, the percentage of adult black males to the entire black population (20.3 percent) was the same percentage in 1869; and (3) the estimated growth rate in the entire black population between 1864 and 1869 during the turbulent postwar years of readjustment occurred at one-third of the more vibrant 1858 to 1860 growth rate in slaves taxed. Accordingly it is estimated here that there is a chance that about 40 percent of the slaves taken to Texas for safekeeping subsequently left the state, or conversely, about 31,000 former refugeed slaves from other ex-Confederate states still remained in the Lone Star State at the outset of the brief years of Republican Party ascendancy.[36]

The wartime influx of refugeed slaves attracted the considerable attention of local Texas bondsmen and brought them firsthand knowledge about invading Yankee troops that stirred their hopes for what the future might bring. Moreover, by communicating through neighborhood grapevines stories of their masters' diminished roles in flight as patriarchal authorities, the refugeed slaves might have influenced in measurable ways the course of grassroots Reconstruction. The fact that Brazos County in 1868 was the scene of the so-called Millican

Race Riot, the worst statewide incident of Ku Klux Klan violence against the freedpeople, does not prove that black political assertiveness was associated with areas having excessive concentrations of refugeed slaves made less slavish by their wartime experiences. But in explaining statistically the variation from one county to another in the levels of violence against ex-slaves from reports by Freedmen's Bureau agents, or for that matter in the rates of black registration and voting recorded in federal military records, wartime growth rates in county slave populations, when controlling for a host of other explanatory background variables, would provide a fruitful path for further research on the ramifications of slave refugeeing.

Writing the story of the transportation of tens of thousands of slaves to Texas during the Civil War years will also require uncovering more traditional primary materials not within easy reach, such as documents buried in the files of courthouse records. The task will entail the acknowledgment that their trials and tribulations on the roads into the state and their experiences in the networks of fellow slaves in the bottomlands of the Brazos, Trinity, and Sabine rivers were inextricably linked to their masters, their masters' agents, or others who hired them—all of whose lives in turn were interwoven by the debasement of slavery and its impending demise. Regardless of whether refugeed slaves left or stayed in Texas after the war, they shared an additional long metaphorical walk into freedom—a journey on which they suffered terribly but at least carried with them a new set of dreams for a better life for their children.

Monument to Comal County Civil War
Soldiers in New Braunfels, Texas.
Courtesy Charles D. Grear

7

New Perspectives on Texas Germans and the Confederacy

Walter D. Kamphoefner

Texas, which was home to 20,000 of the 70,000 Germans residing in the eleven Confederate states, was the only place where the German element was large enough to play an appreciable role in politics and war.[1] Just what role these Texans played, however, still remains under dispute. In the popular press various characterizations of Germans have portrayed them as everything from "fire-breathing secessionists" to "virtually all Unionists."[2] The range of scholarly opinion is nearly as broad. Older accounts often reflect the characterization of antebellum traveler Frederick Law Olmstead, portraying Germans as largely abolitionist in sentiment. Recent scholarship has cautioned against generalizing from a few radical "Forty-Eighters" to the bulk of ordinary German immigrants. But perhaps this scholarship has gone too far in attempting to place Texas Germans into the mainstream of the Lone Star State.

One of the most influential of these revisionists, geographer Terry Jordan, has pointed out important distinctions between East and West Texas Germans as far as attitudes toward slavery and the Civil War are concerned. Eastern settlements were older, their immigrants more acculturated to American values, and

Treue der Union Monument in Comfort, Texas. *Courtesy Walter D. Kamphoefner*

their local economy well suited for plantation agriculture and slavery. The Hill Country west of Austin, by contrast, was more recently settled. With its semi-arid ranching economy, it had very few slaveholders, Anglo or German. A frontier region, it was exposed to dangers of Indian attacks should Federal military protection be withdrawn—a consideration that also promoted Unionism among Hill Country Anglos. In a more recent work, Jordan outlines four "myths, or stereotypes," regarding Texas Germans: they "(1) did not own slaves, (2) favored the abolitionist cause, (3) were morally opposed to slavery, and (4) harbored Unionist sentiments," all of which he claims were "inaccurate" when applied to "many or most" ordinary Texas Germans. While Jordan is certainly correct in disputing that Germans were fully united on any of these issues, he goes too far in his revisions and exaggerates the degree to which Germans agreed with Anglo Texans on issues such as slavery, race, secession, and Civil War.[3] Neither he nor anyone else has dug deeply into the local press for precinct-level voting returns or other evidence of German attitudes toward the Confederacy, nor has anyone closely examined patterns of German slaveholding in relation to overall property holdings.

One must beware of geographical determinism in explaining the regional differences among Texas Germans in slave ownership or support for secession. Although geographic conditions in the Hill Country may have discouraged slavery, Jordan's own work shows that in three counties where 11 percent of the Anglo families owned slaves, not a single German did. According to Jordan, lack of capital was the main factor restricting slaveholdings among Germans in eastern Texas. Yet a recent study has documented some sixty Germans in the older settlements in Austin, Fayette, and Colorado counties who did own slaves between 1840 and 1865. Still, despite the strong presence of Germans in these counties, they made up less than 5 percent of local slaveowners (see table 1). Moreover, at every level of wealth, a higher proportion of Anglos than Germans owned slaves. For example, among persons worth from $3,000 to $6,000, more than 50 percent of the Anglos but barely 2 percent of the Germans were slaveowners. People of the servant-keeping class in Germany, especially those from the East Elbian nobility, were especially prone to slaveholding. But even among the wealthy worth over $15,000, only 50 percent of the Germans owned slaves in contrast to 92 percent of the American born. Moreover, the size of the slaveholdings were smaller among Germans, who made up 4 percent of the slaveowners but possessed only 2 percent of the slaves in the area. Granted, slaveholding was a voluntary act among Germans unless they married into an Anglo family, whereas many old-stock Americans in Texas inherited slaves rather than purchasing them outright. But contrasts of this magnitude could hardly have arisen without a conscious choice by many or most Germans against human property.

TABLE 1

Slaveownership, Ethnicity, and Wealth Levels in Fayette County, Texas, 1860

Total Property Value in $1,000	Germans			Slaves owned by Germans		Anglos			Slaves owned by Anglos	
	TOTAL	SLAVEOWNERS				TOTAL	SLAVEOWNERS			
	N	N	percent	N	per owner	N	N	percent	N	per owner
0–2.999	688	2	0.3	18	9	690	56	8.1	172	3.1
3–5.999	47	1	2.1	2	2	151	80	5.3	228	2.9
6–8.999	19	5	26	17	3.4	100	61	61	242	4
9–11.999	11	5	45	28	5.6	50	35	70	210	6
12–14.999	2	1	50	4	4	38	34	90	292	8.6
15–147	6	3	50	6	2	154	141	92	2,341	16.6
Total	753	17	2.3	75	4.4	1,183	407	34	3,485	8.3

Source: Adapted with additional calculations from Cornelia Küffner, "Texas-Germans' Attitudes toward Slavery: Biedermeier Sentiments and Class Consciousness in Austin, Colorado, and Fayette Counties" (M.A. thesis, University of Houston, 1994), table 2.

(Indeed Jordan's own figures show a higher incidence of landownership among Texas Germans than among their Anglo neighbors, further evidence that it was not mere poverty that prevented them from owning slaves.) So geography was important, but ethnicity and culture were more important.[4]

Several pieces of evidence suggest that domestic service was a primary reason Germans held slaves. The small number per owner would point in that direction. So would the fact that several German slaveowners were outspoken Unionists and emancipationists.[5] People of the servant-keeping class in Germany were faced with a dilemma in the South: native whites, no matter how poor, thought domestic work was beneath them, fit only for slaves or other blacks. Immigrant women usually filled the gap only temporarily; given the unbalanced ethnic sex ratio, they were much in demand as marriage partners. Being true to antislavery principles often meant forcing one's wife to do without domestic help entirely. Whatever the explanation, it was more than just lack of capital that kept the incidence and size of German slaveholdings low.

The secession referendum of February 23, 1861, provides another measure of Texas German attitudes. In this context it is important to remember that German and Anglo Unionists were not the natural allies one might suppose. Many of the latter had earlier expressed their nationalism in the form of nativism, especially during the Know-Nothing movement of the mid-1850s. Thus Germans were faced with a devil's choice between an alliance with Southern fire-eaters or with political opponents of the foreign born.[6]

Across Texas, secession won by a landslide, with less than a quarter of the voters opposing. In an appeal to ethnic voters, the declaration of secession had been printed not only in 10,000 English copies but also 2,000 each in Spanish and German. But the German copies largely found unsympathetic readers. Two German frontier counties, Gillespie and Mason, led the state with a 96 percent margin against secession (table 2). Some largely Anglo counties in this region also turned in majorities against secession, but wherever precinct-level returns are available, they show the German communities of a county to be most hostile. In Kerr County the German community around Comfort (soon to become Kendall County) voted nearly two-thirds against secession, actually a surprisingly small margin considering its subsequent resistance to the Confederate cause. But the Anglo half of this frontier county went ten to one for secession.[7] Bexar County, with the largest number of Germans in the state, witnessed a narrow secessionist victory, but the city of San Antonio turned in a razor-thin margin for the Union. There too Germans proved to be the most consistent Unionists (though they obviously had some Hispanic and also Anglo help), and even after the election, German city councilmen resisted for several months demands to turn over seized federal arms to the secessionist state.[8]

TABLE 2

County and Precinct Returns from the Texas Secession Election, February 23, 1861

County	Precinct	Ethnicity[a]	Votes For	Votes Against	% Against
Western Counties					
Bexar[b]		28%	827	709	46%
	San Antonio				
	Pct. 1	Hispanic	227	146	39%
	Pct. 2	Hispanic	72	160	69%
	Pct. 3	German	124	186	60%
	rest of county	mixed	292	147	33%
Blanco		20%	108	170	61%
Comal	(New Braunfels)	88%	239	86	26%
Gillespie	(Fredericksburg)	87%	16	398	96%
Kerr[c]			76	57	43%
	Pct. 2 (Comfort)	60%	34	53	64%
	rest of county	11%	42	4	9%
Mason		55%	2	75	97%
Medina[d]	(Castroville)	43%	140	207	60%
Eastern Counties					
Austin[e]		45%	825	212	20%
	Cat Spring	German	8	99	93%
	Industry	German	86	2	2%
	New Ulm	German	36	30	45%
	Shelby	German	16	51	76%
	SUBTOTAL	German	146	182	55%
	rest of county	Anglo	679	30	4%

TABLE 2 (CONTINUED)

County	Precinct	Ethnicity[a]	Votes For	Votes Against	% Against
Bastrop[f]		25%	335	352	51%
	Rabb's Creek	German/Wend	1	56	98%
	Bastrop	mixed	158	183	54%
	rest of county	Anglo	176	113	39%
Colorado[g]		35%	584	330	36%
	Frelsburg	German	22	154	88%
	Mentz/Bernardo	German	10	41	80%
	Weimar	German	7	37	84%
	SUBTOTAL	German	39	232	86%
	Columbus	mixed	201	93	32%
	rest of county	Anglo	344	6	2%
Fayette		37%	580	628	52%
State of Texas		7%	46,153	14,747	24%

[a]Percentages based on calculations from the 1870 census, multiplying percentage of foreign parentage among whites by percentage of Germans among foreign-born voters. County-level vote data taken from Joe E. Timmons, "The Referendum in Texas on the Ordinance of Secession," *East Texas Historical Society Journal* 11 (1973): 12–28.

[b]Bexar County figures from Lawrence P. Knight, "Becoming a City and Becoming American: San Antonio, Texas, 1848–1861" (Ph.D. diss., Texas A&M University, 1997), 267–70.

[c]Bob Bennett states that Precinct 1 was practically the area that became Kendall County in 1862, thus the exact figures for ethnicity from the 1870 census. Bennett, *Kerr County, Texas, 1856–1956* (San Antonio: Naylor, 1956), 136.

[d]These figures do not include French Texans, who in Medina County were primarily German-speaking Alsatians; their inclusion would have raised the German proportion to about two-thirds.

[e]Figures for Austin County as published in *Bellville Countryman,* February, 27 1861.

[f]Bastrop County information from Bill Moore, *Bastrop County, 1691-1900* (Wichita Falls, Tex.: Nortex, 1977), 77–78.

[g]Colorado County figures from L. R. Weyand and H. Wade, *An Early History of Fayette County* (LaGrange, Tex., 1936), 244–45.

Even older German settlements farther east show little evidence of enthusiasm for secession. The 64 percent support level in Colorado County, for example, masks an internal polarization. Three German precincts (named after immigrant founder Wilhelm Frels and the hometowns of Weimar and Mainz) voted 86 percent against secession, while five Anglo precincts cast all but six votes in favor; only the county seat, with its mixed population, fell near the average. Despite religious differences, Wendish Lutherans and German Methodists in Bastrop County were nearly unanimous in their opposition to secession. Although there were also some Anglo Unionists, it was the Germans who tipped the scales to give the county a majority against secession. Similarly in Fayette County (where precinct returns are unavailable), some Anglos must have contributed to the 52 percent majority against secession. But a local paper with the telling name *State Rights Democrat* blamed the "sauer-kraut *dirt-eaters*" who were anything but fire-eaters. It pilloried Texas Revolution veteran "Benedict Arnold [F. W.] Grassmeyer" for deceiving "the honest Germans of Fayette County" in the election and for his abolitionist sympathies and friendliness toward free blacks.[9]

Only in Austin County did close to a majority of Germans vote for Southern independence, still a rather lukewarm result compared to the 96 percent level in six Anglo precincts. One of the state's oldest German settlements, Industry, voted almost unanimously for secession, for which a prominent German slave-holder had "worked manfully." (Its two opposition voters were allegedly Anglos.) This initially seems to confirm Jordan's assertion that over time Germans became increasingly acculturated to the Southern way of life. Before jumping to conclusions, however, one should note that the neighboring settlement of Cat Spring, which also predated Texas independence, took a diametrically opposite position, weighing in at 92 percent against secession.[10]

One local German leader also had a profound influence in heavily German Comal County, the only western county that voted strongly in favor of secession. More than anything, this stand reflected trust in the advice of the venerable Ferdinand Lindheimer and his *Neu Braunsfelser Zeitung*. What was the basis for editor Lindheimer's position, enthusiasm for slavery and the Confederacy? Although he himself probably became a hesitant supporter of secession, he seldom attempted to sell his constituents on the merits of the secessionist case, stressing instead the nativist antecedents of many Unionists and the reprisals Germans might suffer should they be perceived as opposing it: "When in Texas, do as the Texans do. Anything else is suicide and brings tragedy to all our Texas-Germans."[11]

In general, the factor of intimidation must be kept in mind when examining Texas German behavior in the winter of disunion. Wherever Germans fell below a certain threshold, perhaps 15 percent of a county's voters, they hardly dared take a stand against secession. Notwithstanding some scattered Germans in the plantation counties of Brazoria and Fort Bend just west of Houston, only two voters in a thousand dared oppose secession. Perhaps not coincidentally, a vigilance committee was monitoring citizen behavior there from the fall of 1860 onward. Urban Germans were more acculturated to Southern society and more subject to intimidation; both factors worked against Unionist voting. Although Galveston was nearly one-third German and home to Unionist editor Ferdinand Flake, with a low turnout it voted 96 percent in favor of secession. Mob violence had destroyed one of Flake's presses the previous month and sent an unmistakable message to Unionists.[12]

Jordan called New Braunfels a "secessionist hotbed," but it was one of the few places in Texas where Confederate sympathizers were subject to intimidation. Editor Lindheimer's pragmatism was not universally appreciated. In June 1863 he noted, "Remarkable is the hatred, which many people here now exhibit against the original secessionists." Even ninety years later the centennial issue of his paper admitted, "Because of its strong southern tendencies during the war the *Neu Braunfelser Zeitung* attracted the bitter enmity of the loyally Unionist part of the German population in West Texas and especially in Comal County, which made the further existence of the paper nearly impossible." So incensed were some residents that they threw the press and type into the Comal River— but Lindheimer fished it out of the clear water so that the paper did not miss an issue. His windows were also stoned in twice, and his dogs poisoned with strychnine. Throughout the war his paper manifested a pronouncedly defensive tone in matters involving the Confederacy.[13]

Even with the support given by the local German press, the secession cause received slightly less support at the polls in New Braunfels than in Texas as a whole. The only homogeneous German county or precinct where support for secession exceeded the statewide average was the settlement of Industry. With respect to Unionism, Jordan states that Texas Germans were split, "just as Anglo-Americans were." Both groups were indeed split, but there the similarity ends. With Anglos there was at least a three-to-one majority for secession, while Germans produced at least a slim majority for the Union, and a disproportionate number of stay-at-home voters as well.[14]

Willingness to serve in the Union or Confederate military provides yet another measure of the attitudes of Texas Germans. Published muster rolls of the First and Second Texas Cavalry (U.S.) reveal the presence of disproportionate numbers of Germans. Persons of German stock made up about 7 percent of the state's population but more than 13 percent of its Union troops, despite the fact that they were recruited largely in the Brownsville area, far from centers of

German settlement.[15] At the outbreak of the Civil War, Texas Germans faced an unenviable choice—to go or to stay. Flight from the Confederacy was theoretically possible, but the experiences of those who tried it probably gave pause to many others. It took a strong dose of ideological conviction, especially if it involved abandoning hard-earned property—farms that had been laboriously hacked out of the post oaks, for example—and leaving wife and children to an uncertain fate or exposing them to even greater dangers in Mexico. Consequently Texas Germans in the Union army were obviously outnumbered by German Confederates. There is strong evidence, however, that many of the latter served reluctantly. Although Confederate conscription was instituted earlier and enforced more stringently than the Union draft, Germans in the North were overrepresented in the Union army relative to their share of military-aged males. While systematic studies of Confederate recruitment are lacking, there is little doubt that the German presence in Rebel ranks was even smaller than their meager presence in the Southern population.[16] Among the underlying factors at work were both aversion to slavery and devotion to the Union.

For example, there were three German companies in Waul's Legion, two largely from Austin County. But they were not formed until the Confederacy had instituted conscription; the first Austin County company, mustered in on October 20, 1861, was virtually devoid of Germans. When service appeared inevitable, Germans enlisted in order to serve with comrades and under officers they knew and trusted more than from dedication to the Confederate cause. Even one of the sergeants, Wilhelm Hander, proves in his diary entries to be at odds with the basis of Southern civilization: "Several plantations . . . made a pleasant scene but certainly not inviting when one thinks of the Negro whips that are so often used." German captain Robert Voigt wrote home in February 1863, "the Germans in general, and especially the ones here in [another] company, most of whom are our neighbors, behave at various times in a manner that makes one ashamed." His company was on detached service at the fall of Vicksburg, and instead of being paroled, the men ended up in Union prisons. There a number of Germans "took the oath" to the Union, including Voigt himself in February 1865.[17]

Sometimes their descendants may have tried to retrofit Germans into the Texas mainstream. In the beautiful little cemetery of Bethlehem Lutheran Church in Round Top, the gravestone of Carl Bauer notes his Confederate unit and the fact that his letters had been acquired by the state archives. But rather than an enthusiastic Rebel, Bauer's letters, almost from beginning to end, reflect a tone of pious resignation (Traugott, "trust in God," was his middle name) mixed with war weariness. Already in December 1862 Bauer noted: "War enthusiasm is cooling. Many of our men do not believe that the South can win."

The next April he reported from Louisiana: "half of our men volunteered to go on the ship Alexandria, there to try to add luster and fame to their name on the water. As I was not in a mood for great military laurels, I decided to stay on land." After hearing of the fall of Vicksburg, he wrote: "We are all tired to death of war. I believe our beloved South is whipped." This one word, "beloved," is the nearest indication of support for the cause to be found in the dozens of his letters home.[18]

According to Terry Jordan, "many or most" Texas Germans became "inaccurately" stereotyped as Unionist because of a single incident, the 1862 shootout on the Nueces involving Hill Country refugees from the Confederacy attempting to escape to Union lines via Mexico, commemorated by the Treue der Union monument in Comfort. But here too regional contrasts of Texas Germans can be exaggerated. It was not only Gillespie or Kendall counties in the Hill Country but also the eastern counties of Austin, Fayette, and Colorado that were placed under martial law in January 1863 because of German draft resistance. A list of thirty-two draft resistors from Austin County includes only four with Anglo names. A resistance meeting held over the 1863 New Year's holidays at the central location of Roeder's Mill (present-day Shelby) in northwest Austin County attracted 400 to 600 Germans from five counties.[19] Whether typical of Texas Germans or not, the Unionists of the Hill Country were extremely atypical of Southerners in general: The only monument to Unionists erected by local residents on the soil of the former Confederacy is Comfort's Treue der Union memorial.[20]

Victoria and DeWitt counties, inland from Corpus Christi near the coast, produced only a 15 percent opposition on the secession vote despite a German population share probably twice that high. They also contributed nearly two full companies to the Sixth Texas Infantry. But here too a closer examination reveals contrasts between Germans and other Texans. In January 1863, when the regiment was captured at Arkansas Post, 152 of its men, mostly Germans and Poles, took an oath of allegiance to the United States. Capt. C. P. Nauheim resigned his commission because his nearly all-German Company I had virtually disappeared. The rest of the regiment was exchanged and served to the bitter end in the Army of Tennessee.[21] The standard work on "galvanized Yankees," rebel captives who volunteered for Union service, professes to find no ethnic distinctions setting these men apart, though only because the author failed to look closely enough.

The contrasts between German and Anglo Texans persisted into the Reconstruction era and sometimes beyond.[22] Whatever their position during the war, New Braunfels residents took a distinctively un-Southern view of the occupying U.S. troops in its aftermath—had Maj. Gen. Philip Sheridan made his headquarters there, he might have preferred Texas to hell after all. When one Anglo Yankee from the Fifty-Ninth Illinois Infantry said goodbye in December 1865, he noted in his diary: "Some of them shed tears almost. I never felt so bad at leaving any place as that[,] except home in 1861. Farewell Braunfels." Two days later he recorded, "presents from New Braunfels friends received." His was not an isolated case—at least two other Anglo members of his regiment married local girls and settled permanently in the community. Less than three months after Lee's surrender, New Braunfels had celebrated the Fourth of July in what sounded like a huge sigh of relief: the Stars and Stripes was unfurled from the highest hill, a marching band led a well-attended parade throughout the town, and a number of dances rounded out the evening and lasted into the next day.[23]

The political attitudes of Texas Germans in the aftermath of war likewise set them apart from the bulk of their Anglo counterparts. There is very little of a political nature in the minutes of the Cat Spring Agricultural Society, located in Austin County at one of the earliest German settlements. But the meeting of April 1866 found the members preparing a report to be published in papers back in Europe, among other things warning prospective immigrants not to sign labor contracts with former slaveholders. The month's minutes conclude: "It was deemed necessary that the Union men of [Austin] county make preparations . . . to organize and hold a convention for the purpose of putting up or accepting a ticket" for the next election.[24]

Forty-Eighter Edward Degener, who lost two sons at the Nueces Massacre, represented the San Antonio area as a Republican in the first Texas congressional delegation during Reconstruction. Even in areas farther east, where it required considerable cooperation with blacks, Germans were among the strongest white supporters of the Republican Party. When the legislature took up public education in August 1870, one reads of lawmakers with the German names of Prissick, Schlickum, Schlottmann, Schutze, Zapp, and Zoeller lining up with the two black House members in an effort to table an amendment requiring racial separation in schools. The measure came within one vote of being tabled; if there had been no blacks or Germans in the legislature, it would not have even been close.[25]

Two adjacent eastern counties, Colorado and Washington, remained under Republican control well beyond Reconstruction and into the 1880s, in both instances largely the result of black-German coalitions. In the postwar era the first time Colorado County went Democratic in a gubernatorial or presidential race was 1888, and it elected its first Democratic county judge only in 1890. Lower-level Republican officeholders included a number of blacks and Germans, and even the Germans who were Democrats tended to be of the moderate sort.[26]

Washington County, with close to a black majority and a sizeable German minority in its population, was represented in the first reconstruction Texas legislature by a black, Matt Gaines in the Senate, and an immigrant (and Confederate veteran), William Schlottmann in the House, both "radical" Republicans. Support for this coalition in the local German press is reflected in the comment of its rabidly antiblack and anti-Republican rival, the *Brenham Banner*, in a January 14, 1876, column: "What does the *Volksbote* think of [the] idea of consolidating" the "German vote of this county with negro-radico swindlers" when six prominent Germans "come forward and identify themself with the democracy in opposition to free negro domination." Apparently this did not signal a wholesale shift in German allegiance. Washington County remained under Republican control until 1884, supported by the bulk of the blacks, about half of the Germans, and a few white Anglos, often of Unionist background. As long as this coalition held, blacks served as deputy sheriffs and on grand and petit juries, giving them a relatively fair shake in the local justice system. A Democratic takeover in 1884 could only be accomplished through violence and intimidation against blacks, and an attempted Republican comeback in the extremely close election of 1886 was foiled when Democrats stole three Republican ballot boxes, lynched three black Republicans, and ran three of their prominent white allies out of the county. At least one of the last was German: Carl Schutze, who had been the Radical Republican candidate for county attorney in 1876.[27]

In June 1888 Schutze wrote from his California exile to a Texas friend: "it's totally different for me here than back there. Here it is no crime to be a Republican and they don't sling mud at you for it. . . . The Republican Party in Washington County is done for once and for all; the mobsters have complete control and everything will probably be quiet and still." In an August letter he went into more detail:

I fear that in this election the mob will put on the same show that we experienced two years ago. Violence and intimidation will be their main weapons again, with which they intimidate the Negroes and if need be control the ballot boxes. What does the mob need to worry about the consequences? The officials [i.e., of the county] are all the main instigators and leaders of the murderous gang. . . . I can imagine that these are just the rascals who are doing their best to play themselves up as the friends of the Germans and to stir up the Germans against the Negroes, just as they stir up the Negroes against the Germans. . . . You feel entirely different out here than in Texas. . . . Besides, here you live among respectable people and don't have to deal with rowdies and murderers.[28]

If anything, the Germans farther west in Texas stood apart even more from their Anglo neighbors in political and racial attitudes. Beginning in 1920, Harry Wurzbach served for over a decade representing the San Antonio–Seguin area in the U.S. House, the only Republican congressman from Texas during this era and the first of his party to be reelected.[29] New Braunfels, with only a 2 percent black population due to its low rate of slaveholding a century earlier, integrated its schools immediately in 1954 when ordered to do so by the Supreme Court.[31] The fact that even ten years later less then 6 percent of black Texans were attending integrated schools shows just how unusual this was. Gillespie, the most heavily German county in the Hill Country, remained an undeviating Republican stronghold. Except for the depths of the Great Depression in 1932, the first time it went Democratic in the twentieth century was for local boy Lyndon Johnson in 1964.[31]

There was nothing primordial about German ethnicity that immunized against slavery. For example, the largest slaveholder and leading secessionist in Kerr County was Dr. Charles Ganahl, born in Georgia, son of an Austrian immigrant and a Charleston belle. Although he had studied medicine in Germany and France, the doctor identified fully with the planter society from which his mother came and into which he also married.[32] In general, opposition to the peculiar institution derived largely from an egalitarian republicanism of the European enlightenment, an ideology that penetrated more deeply into the immigrant rank and file than most scholars have realized.[33]

Still one cannot assert that Texas Germans were unique in their coolness toward the Confederate cause. In practically every county they found at least a few Anglo allies, and their reservations toward slavery and secession were shared by most other Continental Europeans in the state. One sees very similar patterns with Czechs, Poles, Wends, the Alsatians around Castroville, and probably most Scandinavians in Texas: only a small, atypical, well-assimilated elite, often at the fringes of the ethnic communities, embraced slavery and unreservedly supported the Confederacy.[34] Farther down on the social scale, where most immigrants were concentrated, attitudes ranged from indifference to hostility. Some were able to evade the draft, gain exemption as teamsters, or restrict their service to local militias; others served reluctantly as Confederate soldiers.[35] Even before the war Czechs as well as Germans were harassed for their association with "abolitionist" foreign-language newspapers.[36] In Bastrop County Germans combined with Wends to vote down the ordinance of secession. Not only Germans but also Poles from Victoria and Karnes County went over to the Union cause together after being taken prisoner.[37] The First Texas Cavalry (U.S.) included a scattering of Wends, Poles, Czechs, and Alsatians among the hundreds of Germans.[38] In Austin County Germans and Czechs had constituted the bulk of the deserter lists during the war and in 1865 joined in a Fourth of July celebration affirming Union victory.[39] During Reconstruction, Poles in Karnes County were harassed by ex-Confederates just as Germans were elsewhere.[40] But Germans were far and above the largest European immigrant group in Texas, probably outnumbering all others put together. Their high level of literacy and strong concentrations in a number of counties made them much more of a political factor.[41]

So while Terry Jordan has provided a needed corrective to Texas German ancestor worship, overturning the legend that his forefathers were overwhelmingly Unionist and abolitionist, he goes too far in his characterizing of Texas Germans as "unremarkable" in their race attitudes, and he underestimates the degree to which Germans stood apart from their fellow Texans on the issues of the Civil War.[42] Moreover, by not following the story beyond 1865, Jordan overlooks Texas German Republicanism during Reconstruction and sometimes persisting into the twentieth century, which clearly had its roots in the bitter experiences of the Civil War era.

Josiah Perry Alford, Seventh Texas Infantry. Alford
served with the regiment until the Battle of
Chickamauga, where on September 18, 1863, he
suffered a wound in his left leg and endured an
amputation on the battlefield. After the war he
served as county clerk for Harrison County.
*Courtesy Collections of the Harrison County
Historical Museum, Marshall, Texas*

8

After the Surrender

The Postwar Experiences of Confederate Veterans in Harrison County, Texas

Randolph B. Campbell

For more than a century, the Civil War and the soldiers who fought it have been the subjects of an unending flood of books and articles. Interest in the soldiers, however, generally ends with Lee's surrender in 1865. As historian Maris Vinovskis observed in 1989, "Almost nothing has been written about the postwar experiences of Civil War veterans."[1] Vinovskis's statement is less accurate now—thanks especially to studies by Gaines Foster, Gerald Linderman, Eric Dean Jr., and Larry Logue—but this recent scholarship, rather than closing the subject, has highlighted issues that call for further investigation.[2] Did veterans tend to return to their original homes, receive warm welcomes, and resume ordinary lives? What toll did the physical and psychological scars of war take on veterans during the postwar years? Did veterans wield notable political power in the postwar South? Did they come to enjoy special social status in their home communities? Answers to these important questions concerning the postwar experiences of Confederate veterans can be discovered by examining Harrison County, Texas, as a test case.

Harrison County, which is located in northeastern Texas on the Louisiana border, was among the most "southern" of the state's counties during the antebellum years. Natives of the South headed more than 90 percent of its households in 1860, and 61 percent of those households owned at least one of the county's 8,784 slaves, the largest population of bondsmen living in any Texas county at that time. Harrison's 1859 cotton crop was 21,440 bales, the second-largest grown in any Texas county. When the secession crisis began in November 1860, the slaveholding, cotton-producing citizens of Harrison County were among the first Texans to call for a convention to consider leaving the Union, and on February 23, 1861, its citizens endorsed disunion by the overwhelming vote of 866 to 44.[3]

Secession, of course, soon led to war. When word of the firing on Fort Sumter reached Marshall, the county seat of Harrison, on April 17, the town resounded with cannon fire and patriotic speeches. And within two years the county's population of military-age white men provided many or most of the soldiers for thirteen companies that entered Confederate service—a company having about one hundred men and officers.[4] A brief sketch of the wartime service of each company is necessary to appreciate what these soldiers faced during four years of conflict and how their wartime experiences affected them as veterans in the postwar years.

The first company raised in Harrison County was called the W. P. Lane Rangers in honor of Marshall resident Walter P. Lane, a noted veteran of the Texas Revolution and the Mexican War. Members of the company proceeded to the San Antonio area, where they became Company F, Second Texas Cavalry, commanded by Col. John S. "Rip" Ford. Their job was to protect the frontier against hostile Indians and garrison abandoned posts along the road from San Antonio to El Paso. At the end of a year, most of the Lane Rangers reenlisted, returned to Marshall, and were sent as an independent company to Arkansas Post (Fort Hindman) near the mouth of the Arkansas River. When Arkansas Post fell to Union forces early in 1863, many of the Rangers wound up as prisoners of war at Camp Butler, Illinois. After being exchanged later that year at City Point, Virginia, the company's men were placed under the command of Gen. Braxton Bragg in Tennessee. Most were dissatisfied there, however, and soon after the Battle of Chickamauga simply left for the Trans-Mississippi, where they joined a cavalry unit commanded by Lt. Col. Charles L. Morgan. Morgan's Cavalry was attached to Parsons's Cavalry Brigade and participated in the Red River campaign in 1864, though not in the major battles at Mansfield and Pleasant Hill. The remnants of the Lane Rangers apparently missed all of the fighting in 1864–65 because they served as guards at Camp Ford, the prisoner-of-war facility near Tyler.[5]

The second company formed in Harrison County was called the Marshall Guards. Its men elected Frederick S. Bass, a graduate of Virginia Military Institute and president of Marshall University, as captain and left for Richmond, Virginia, in May 1861. They became Company E, First Texas Infantry, which later joined the Fourth and Fifth Texas and Eighteenth Georgia Infantry regiments to form Hood's Texas Brigade, one of the most famous units in the Confederate army. The Guards arrived in Virginia too late for the First Battle of Manassas in July 1861, but as part of Hood's Brigade they fought in thirty-eight battles and skirmishes, including Antietam, Gettysburg, Chickamauga, and the Wilderness, and took incredible casualties along the way. Captain Bass suffered at least three wounds during the war but rose to become colonel in command of the First Texas Infantry. He surrendered the regiment at Appomattox in April 1865.[6]

The third 1861 unit from Harrison County was formed by men from the eastern half of the county, who adopted the name "Texas Hunters" and became Company A, Third Texas Cavalry. Their captain was Thomas W. Winston, a thirty-two-year-old planter, and their first colonel was Elkanah Greer, a Harrison County resident who had served with Jefferson Davis's famed regiment, the Mississippi Rifles, during the Mexican War. The Texas Hunters saw their first action in the Arkansas-Missouri border area at the battles of Wilson's Creek in 1861, where they took the first casualties suffered by Harrison County soldiers during the war, and Pea Ridge in 1862. In the spring of 1862, the Hunters crossed the Mississippi and fought in the effort to hold northern Mississippi after the Battle of Shiloh. In 1863 they became part of Ross's Texas Brigade (commanded by Lawrence Sullivan "Sul" Ross) and served in both the Atlanta and Tennessee campaigns in 1864.[7]

The fourth and fifth Harrison County units raised in 1861—the Bass Grays and the Texas Invincibles—became Companies D and H of the Seventh Texas Infantry, commanded by Col. John Gregg. Assigned to Gen. Albert Sidney Johnston's army in western Kentucky, these two companies were trapped at Fort Donelson on the Cumberland River in February 1862 and forced to surrender. The soldiers became prisoners of war at the notorious Camp Douglas in Illinois, but those who survived the experience were exchanged within a year. Then they fought in the defense of Vicksburg, suffering terrible casualties in a "skirmish" at Raymond, Mississippi, and surrendering again when Vicksburg fell. This time they were immediately exchanged and wound up fighting at Chickamauga in September 1863 and in the Atlanta and Tennessee campaigns in 1864.[8]

Thus Harrison County provided a large part of the men for five companies that joined the Confederate army in the first year of the conflict. The defeats at Pea Ridge and Fort Donelson made it clear that the war would not be over in a hurry, and that fact, coupled with the passage of the Confederacy's first conscription act in April 1862, encouraged even more men to volunteer during the second year. Originally the draft applied to men aged eighteen to thirty-five, but the upper age limit was raised to forty-five later in 1862, then the subject ages were extended to seventeen to fifty in February 1864. It is impossible to say how many men volunteered willingly when they saw that their services were needed to win the war and how many volunteered under the threat of being drafted. Being conscripted generally was considered a disgrace—"There will be no conscripts in Texas," wrote editor R. M. Loughery of the *Marshall Texas Republican.* In any case, whether willingly volunteering or being pressured, Harrison County men came forward in such numbers beginning early in 1862 that they provided many of the recruits for eight more companies.[9]

The first two companies raised in 1862—the sixth and seventh overall—were the Clough Rangers and Hendricks's Company. They became Companies E and K of the Seventeenth Texas Cavalry, commanded by Col. George F. Moore. A "dismounted" cavalry unit after July 1862, the Seventeenth surrendered at Arkansas Post in early 1863, after which the men spent time as prisoners of war, were exchanged, and fought as part of Granbury's Texas Brigade at Chickamauga and in the Atlanta and Tennessee campaigns.[10]

The third 1862 company was the Harrison County Lancers, commanded by Capt. Phil Brown. They became Company F, Twenty-Eighth Texas Cavalry and as part of Maj. Gen. John Walker's Texas Division fought in the Trans-Mississippi during 1863 and 1864. Their most important actions came at Mansfield and Pleasant Hill during the Red River campaign in April 1864.[11]

The fourth, fifth, and sixth 1862 companies—numbers nine, ten, and eleven overall—were the Marshall Mechanics, Clough and Hill Avengers, and the Cypress Tigers. These three companies joined the Fourteenth Texas Infantry, commanded by Col. Edward Clark, the Marshall resident who had succeeded Sam Houston as governor in 1861. They served in Walker's Texas Division in Louisiana in 1863–64 and fought in the Red River campaign.[12]

The seventh and eighth 1862 companies were known simply as Hec McKay's Company and S. W. Webb's Company, named for their captains. They joined the First Cavalry Regiment of Partisan Rangers, commanded originally by W. P. Lane of Marshall and then by R. P. Crump, at which time the unit became known as Crump's Cavalry. They fought in the Trans-Mississippi in 1862–63 and saw their most important action at Mansfield and Pleasant Hill in April 1864.[13]

These thirteen companies included most but certainly not all of the men from Harrison County who served the Confederacy in a military capacity. In 1863 some of the county's men who had remained at home during the first two years of the war enlisted in the First Cavalry Battalion, State Troops. These men were generally older, only served six months, and did not engage in battle. Also, a significant number of Harrison County men served in units that are usually identified with other counties. For example, residents of the northern part of Harrison often joined the Eighteenth or the Nineteenth Texas Infantry regiments, both units raised primarily in neighboring Marion County. These regiments remained in the Trans-Mississippi as part of Walker's Texas Division and fought at Mansfield and Pleasant Hill. There were also Harrison County men in the Fourteenth and Thirty-Second Texas Cavalry regiments, both of which were in Ector's Brigade and fought at Chickamauga and in the Atlanta and Tennessee campaigns.[14]

This sketch of military activity easily establishes heavy participation in the Civil War by the white male population of Harrison County, but it does not provide the information necessary to answer key questions about the individuals who served. Determining exactly who those men were and what happened to them during and after the war required the compilation of a database that included every white male in Harrison County aged thirteen to forty-six in 1860. These age limits define the military-age population because by 1864, Confederate conscription laws applied to all men aged seventeen to fifty, meaning that a thirteen-year-old in 1860 would have reached draft age in 1864 and a forty-six-year-old in 1860 would have remained eligible four years later.[15]

The 1860 U.S. Census for Harrison County reported 1,728 white men and boys between the ages of thirteen and forty-six inclusive, that is 1,728 males who were of military age sometime between 1861 and 1865 (see table 1). Once this military-aged population had been identified, data were collected on the age, state of birth, marital status, and occupation of each individual and on the wealth and slaveholding status of their families. The next step was to search the compiled service records of Confederate veterans case by case through the companies raised primarily in Harrison County to determine which of these individuals served and what happened to them during their time in the military.[16] Confederate service records, however, are notoriously incomplete, especially for the later years of the war, and many names required confirmation beyond location in the service records. Thus five additional sources were searched for evidence on military service. First, the county's newspaper, the *Marshall Texas Republican,* printed the full rosters of some companies when they were organized and also published casualty lists throughout the war.[17] Second, by an act of the Texas legislature, muster rolls containing the names of all men aged eighteen to fifty in each county in the state were created in March 1862. These rolls, which were arranged precinct by precinct, indicate the men who were already in the military at that time as well as those who were eligible to serve.[18] Third, also by act of the legislature, county judges in early 1864 and 1865 made lists of servicemen whose families, widows, or dependents were eligible for relief payments from the state. These lists of "Confederate Indigent Families" proved a good source to determine who actually served.[19] Fourth, Confederate pension rolls, created after Texas began to pay benefits to disabled and indigent veterans or their widows in 1899, contain records on the service of many Harrison County residents, especially those who entered the military in 1863–64.[20] Finally, vertical files of family records in the Harrison County Historical Museum often provided direct evidence on service by family members as well as information—full name and precise ages, for example—useful in identifying individuals in other records.[21]

Because sizable numbers of men who lived in Harrison in 1860 served in companies recruited primarily in neighboring counties, the service records of those units also were searched carefully and with considerable success. For example, fifty-seven residents of Harrison County in 1860 served in the Eighteenth and Nineteenth Texas Infantry. Thirty-three 1860 residents enlisted in the Fourteenth and Thirty-Second Cavalry, and at least a few others were found in many of the other cavalry and artillery units raised in East Texas. In total, 215 of the 1,728 men in the database were identified as members of what can be called "non–Harrison County companies."

Once the database was completed, the Civil War experiences of Harrison County's 1860 population of military-age white men may be analyzed. The first point to consider is that almost half—844 (49 percent) of the 1,728 eligible men—entered military service at some time between 1861 and 1865 (see table 1).[22] As might be expected, the men who served were approximately five years younger than those who did not. Soldiers from the military-age group had a median age of twenty-three in 1860, whereas the median for nonsoldiers was

TABLE 1

Record of Military Service during the Civil War by Military-Age Men in Harrison County in 1860

Age and Number in 1860		Number and Percent Who Served	
13–46	1,728	844	49%
13–18 (Teens in 1861)	422	223	53%
19–28 (Twenties in 1861)	654	387	59%
9–38 (Thirties in 1861)	391	171	44%
39–46 (Forties in 1861)	261	63	24%

twenty-eight. Also as would be expected, unmarried men were more likely to serve than those who were married. Only 34 percent of the soldiers were married, whereas 45 percent of the nonsoldiers had wives (see table 2). Men who were slaveholders or members of slaveholding families entered military service at a notably higher proportion than did nonslaveholders. Of 770 slaveholders, 438 (57 percent) served as compared to 406 (42 percent) of 958 nonslaveholders (see table 3). For residents of Harrison County, the Civil War was a "rich man's war" and a "rich man's fight" and, considering that 406 nonslaveholders entered the service, it was a "poor man's fight" as well.

TABLE 2
Demographic Characteristics of Soldiers and Nonsoldiers in Harrison County in 1860

	Median Age	Native of Lower South	Native of Upper South	Native of Free State or Foreign Born	Married
Soldiers	23	63%	31%	6%	34%
Nonsoldiers	28	54%	31%	15%	45%

TABLE 3
Service According to Economic Class of Military-Age Men of Harrison County in 1860

Economic Class	Total Population	Number & Percent Who Served		Year Entered Confederate Service		
				1861	1862	1863
Slaveholder	770	438	57%	38%	47%	13%
Nonslaveholder	958	406	42%	32%	57%	9%
Slaveholder—$16,000 or More in Wealth	325	191	59%	46%	41%	11%
Slaveholder—Less than $16,000 in Wealth	445	247	56%	31%	52%	14%
Nonslaveholder—$1,500 or More in Wealth	239	119	50%	25%	62%	11%
Nonslaveholder—Less than $1,500 in Wealth	719	287	40%	35%	56%	8%

TABLE 4

Experience of Harrison County Soldiers during the Civil War

Type of Experience	Percentage
Served without Serious Illness or Wound	26%
Killed/Fatally Wounded in Action	6%
Died of Disease	11%
Died while Prisoner of War	4%
Suffered Serious Illness/Survived*	7%
Wounded/Survived*	7%
Prisoner of War/Survived*	13%
Discharged after Passage of Conscription Act	6%
Received Disability Discharge	5%
Deserted/AWOL	2%
Miscellaneous	2%
No Record of Military Experience Except that Served	11%

*A few individuals are counted twice in these categories because they both were wounded and prisoners or war or they both suffered illnesses and were prisoners of war.

Of course, the critically important issue that follows determining which men among Harrison County's military-age white male population entered military service is discovering what happened to those men between 1861 and 1865. Table 4 shows that only around one-quarter (26 percent) can be documented as having served much of the war without suffering serious illnesses or wounds. At least one-half lost their lives or had experiences involving serious physical or psychological suffering. A little more than one-fifth (21 percent) died in the army—6 percent in battle, 11 percent from disease, and 4 percent in prisoner-of-war camps. Another 14 percent suffered serious illnesses or wounds but survived and continued to serve, while 13 percent spent time as prisoners of war, some on two separate occasions. Five percent received disability discharges, most of which resulted from illness. Thus 53 percent died or faced serious physical or psychological suffering. The military experiences of 21 percent fell into miscellaneous categories such as transferring to a non-Texas regiment or could not be documented.

After the surrender in April 1865, 667 of Harrison County's 1860 military-age white men who had served the Confederate army in some capacity returned to civilian life, many of them in or near the homes they had left during the war.

They were not welcomed home with public celebrations of the sort that had marked their departure in 1861–62. Instead, returning veterans generally received respect as men who had done their duty and exhortations to return quietly to everyday life. For example, the *Marshall Texas Republican* in July 1865 commented on the arrival of three veterans from east of the Mississippi: "It is a heartfelt pleasure to welcome them home. They have made good soldiers, and will make good citizens."[23]

Fifteen years after Appomattox, 30 percent of the 667 military-age white men who lived in Harrison County in 1860 and then served in the Confederate army and survived the war remained as residents (see table 5). At first glance this geographical persistence rate may seem low, but it is comparable to the rates for population groups in other parts of the United States during the mid-nineteenth century.[24] Moreover, it is impressively higher than the rate for 1860 white male residents of Harrison County aged thirteen to forty-six who did not enter military service. Table 5 shows that only about 11 percent of that group could be identified as residents of the county fifteen years after the war. Veterans who returned to Harrison County and remained there in 1880 appear to have led lives typical of rural and small-town East Texas at the time. Three-quarters were married and supported their families as farmers. By 1900 only seventy-four veterans remained from the 1860 military-age white male population, but even at that, they greatly outnumbered those who did not serve (see table 6). Thus

TABLE 5

Status of Harrison County's 1860 Military-Age White Male Population as of 1880

	Men Who Served (844)	Men Who Did Not Serve (884)
Died during the War/Survived the War	177/667	18*/866
Known to Have Died between End of War in 1865 & 1880	57	40
Disappeared from County by 1880 (Moved, Died but No Record of Death, Unable to Identify in Census, etc.)	409	732
Number and % of Survivors in 1865 still Present in 1880	201 (30.1%)	94 (10.9%)

*Only eighteen of those who did not serve in the army can be identified as having died by 1865. The number may well have been larger.

TABLE 6

Status of Harrison County's 1860 Military-Age
White Male Population as of 1900

	Men Who Served (844)	Men Who Did Not Serve (884)
Died during the War/ Survived the War	177/667	18*/866
Known to Have Died between End of War in 1865 & 1900	147	93
Disappeared from County by 1900 (Moved, Died but No Record of Death, Unable to Identify in Census, etc.)	446	748
Number and % of Survivors in 1865 still Present in 1900	74 (11.1%)	25 (2.9%)

*Only eighteen of those who did not serve in the army can be identified as having died by 1865. The number may well have been larger.

Harrison County Confederate veterans tended to return home to lives that were at least as stable in terms of place of residence, marital status, and occupation as were those of the broader population.

Many veterans, though they survived the war, suffered constant physical pain as a result of wounds and the lingering effects of hardships such as serving in wet and cold weather without adequate clothing. The debilitating effect of wounds and hardships is suggested by comparing the death rates of veterans and nonveterans after 1865. Tables 5 and 6 show that 22 percent of veterans are known to have died between 1865 and 1900 as compared to 11 percent of nonveterans. Perhaps death dates for veterans were easier to locate than those for nonveterans, more of whom had left the county. Nevertheless, the difference is impressive, especially since veterans were five years younger on the average in 1860 than were nonveterans.

The best evidence concerning the physical devastation suffered by veterans is found, of course, in pension claims filed when Texas began to offer financial support for indigent or incapacitated soldiers and/or their wives in 1899. For example, Josiah Perry Alford, a young member of the Seventh Texas Infantry, suffered a thigh wound at the Battle of Chickamauga and had his left leg amputated on the field without benefit of anesthetic. He survived, came home, married in 1883, and lived productively, serving as the county clerk of Harrison County for more than ten years. Yet he died in 1897 at the relatively young age of fifty-three, having, in the words of his widow, "suffered from [the wound and amputation] as long as he lived."[25] Frederick S. Bass, the VMI graduate who left Marshall as captain of the Marshall Guards and ended the war as colonel of the First Texas Infantry, also died in 1897. Wounded three times during the war, Bass spent his last two years at a home for Confederate veterans in Austin, "crippled in body and broken in health."[26] John D. Hartley, a member of the Twenty-Eighth Texas Cavalry, suffered an ankle wound that, according to his 1899 application, left him unable to do manual labor for the rest of his life. Hartley received his pension but died in 1906 at the age of sixty.[27] Numerous pensioners, rather than suffering from wounds, reported health problems caused by "exposure in the war" or "exposure in the Confederate Army."[28]

The lasting psychological effect of war on veterans is far more difficult to document than the physical. In the last fifty years, the concept of post-traumatic stress disorder (PTSD) as a result of modern military combat has been accepted widely, but there is still some debate as to its existence among Civil War soldiers. Numerous cases of mental instability among veterans are easily documented, but it is impossible to prove conclusively that wartime experiences caused the problems. Almost certainly some percentage of veterans would have had mental difficulties regardless of their military service.[29] Among soldiers who returned to Harrison County, there is no evidence of widespread PTSD, but a few cases hint at its existence. First, the pension application filed by James R. Boisseau in 1899 listed "nervous prostration" as one basis for his disability claim.[30] Second, an 1897 account of the career of John Burke, a renowned scout for the Army of Northern Virginia who lived in Marshall for a few years after the war, includes the following statement: "Burke was rather backward about telling the story of his exploits, except to very intimate friends, and then only when . . . persons with whom he served or came in contact were present to verify the accuracy of his statements." This reaction, which is common among veterans, especially in the years immediately following their service, may have been a response to the stress of battle. Finally, a tragic incident, possibly involving PTSD, occurred in June 1869 when Sheriff L. C. DeLisle attempted to arrest a veteran named Stephen S. Lott at his home near Marshall on a peace warrant. Lott came out to the fence in front of his house, told the sheriff that he "would not" be arrested, and began to walk back across the yard. Sheriff DeLisle ordered Lott to stop, and when he did not, drew and fired his pistol, hitting Lott in the leg. Although wounded, Lott turned and shot the sheriff in the head, killing him on the spot. Lott's leg had to be amputated, and he died the next day. The *Marshall Texas Republican* completed its account of the incident by noting, "Lott was subject to fits of derangement, and it is supposed was crazy at the time."[31] These three cases may not have resulted from PTSD, and even if Boisseau, Burke, and Lott did suffer from combat trauma, they were only three of many Harrison County veterans. At least, however, their stories suggest the possibility of psychological scars on some of the soldiers who came home in 1865.

The physical and psychological wounds that many veterans brought with them from the war—and perhaps simply the shadow of defeat—may have deterred some from participation in political life after 1865. Several studies have found that lethargy and disinterest in public life was common among veterans.[32] In Harrison County, however, that was not the case, as former soldiers played a notable role in politics during Reconstruction and beyond. For example, John Burke, the veteran mentioned above for his reluctance to talk about wartime experiences, served as one of the two delegates elected in January 1866 to represent the county in the constitutional convention under Presidential Reconstruction. Burke indicated that he intended to make the fewest concessions possible to having lost the war, telling voters that he would acquiesce in the end of slavery but wanted the state constitution to bar Freedmen from voting or holding office. "It is impossible," he said, "for me to vote for any measure which makes the Negro the equal of the white man."[33]

Burke's stance on the rights of Freedmen strongly suggests that his only regret about secession was losing the war, an unrepentant attitude almost certainly shared by the great majority of Harrison County veterans who sought to vote and participate in politics during Reconstruction. Most ex-soldiers left no record of their sentiments toward the war because the amnesty requirements established by Pres. Abraham Lincoln and Andrew Johnson required only that they take an oath of future loyalty without saying anything about the past. But thirteen classes of ex-Confederates, including army officers above the rank of colonel or men who owned at least $20,000 worth of taxable property, fell outside the general-amnesty requirements and had to request presidential pardons on an individual basis. Three Harrison County veterans—Thomas W. Winston, Walter P. Lane, and Elkanah Greer—filed petitions in which they expressed their views of secession. Greer, who had held the rank of brigadier general in the Confederate army, explained that he had voted for secession, "believing as he did that any State had a constitutional right to secede from the Union when her grievances therein became intolerable." His service in the Confederate army, he wrote, came in the firm belief that "it was just, and that his course was not treason against the Government of the United States, and that his first allegiance was due to the State of which he was a citizen." Lane, who also had attained the rank of brigadier general, wrote, "at the time of secession it was not only not considered a crime, but a duty to support the State in the defense of [secession]." Greer and Lane both wrote that they accepted the result of the war and promised loyalty to the United States, but President Johnson rejected their petitions, probably because of the high rank held by both men. Winston, who had held only the rank of captain but had to request a pardon because he had more than

$20,000 in taxable property, admitted to having been in favor of the war but said nothing about the right of secession. Unlike Greer and Lane, he received a pardon, though that was probably due more to his not having held high military rank than to seemingly greater repentance on his part.[34]

Thus veterans demonstrated a notable desire to vote and possibly participate in politics almost immediately after the war. In the first county government elected under Presidential Reconstruction in June 1866, veterans served as county clerk (Josiah Perry Alford), a county commissioner (R. W. Blalock), and county treasurer (J. C. Harris). Also, John Burke became district attorney for the county. He killed a man in a personal dispute the next year and tried to resign, only to have Gov. James W. Throckmorton, also an ex-Confederate, refuse to accept his resignation.[35]

The political influence established by Harrison County veterans in 1866 lasted only a little more than a year before Congress took control of Reconstruction and authorized the removal of former Confederates from the offices to which they had been elected. Josiah Perry Alford, for example, lost his position as county clerk in November 1867. Then enfranchisement of the county's black majority meant that officeholders from the new Republican Party, virtually none of whom were veterans, controlled local government for the next ten years. Ex-Confederates fumed under Republican officials until the fall of 1878 and then played a major role in restoring conservative control of the county, a process known across the South as "Redemption." Conservatives "redeemed" Harrison County by creating a "Citizens Party" (essentially the Democratic Party under a name intended to appeal to anyone with a grievance against the local Republicans) and calling for all those interested in ridding the county of expensive and corrupt government to support their slate of candidates.[36] Jonathan D. Rudd, a former officer in the Fourteenth Texas Cavalry and chairman of the Harrison County Democratic Party, provided much of the leadership. Rudd's obituary, which appeared in the *Confederate Veteran* in 1920, contended, "No man in the county did more than Major Rudd to overthrow the infamous rule that burdened the people with debt and inflicted upon them the most humiliating form the curses of misgovernment, official graft, and corruption."[37]

Rudd and the Citizens Party eventually won the local elections of 1878, thanks perhaps in some part to intimidation and fraud but ultimately because of a technicality. The Republican-controlled Commissioners Court in preparing for the election ordered that for safety's sake the ballot box for one of their strongest precincts, Precinct 3, be placed within the limits of the town of Marshall. That location, however, happened to be outside the boundaries of Precinct 3. When the votes were counted, it became clear that with the Precinct 3 ballots, the Republicans had won and that without them, the Citizens Party had won. Conservatives appealed to the like-minded judge of the district court for Harrison County for an injunction against counting the votes in the Precinct 3 box. Then, armed with a court order, they declared victory and simply took over all county offices. The incumbent Republican county clerk refused to give up his office, whereupon the Citizens Party candidate, Josiah P. Alford, the veteran who had held the office previously in 1866–67, came with, in the incumbent's words, "as many men as could conveniently enter the room" and ordered him out. Amory R. Starr, a young man who had run away from home in an effort to join the Confederate army while still in his early teens and finally joined the Fourth Texas Cavalry in 1864, presided over the Commissioners Court as it directed the conservative takeover. "Politics have run high," Starr wrote a friend, "and we have beaten them out. . . . It's good fun, but I have had no rest."[38]

Once Harrison County was "redeemed," veterans occupied many of the key offices of county government during the remainder of the century. In 1882, for example, ex-Confederates won the positions of county clerk, district clerk, county treasurer, tax assessor, three of the four commissioners on the county court, and two justices of the peace. From 1893 to 1899 James W. Pope, a veteran of Hood's Texas Brigade, served as county judge, the most important office in local government.[39] Veterans also consistently represented Harrison County at the state level during the last two decades of the century. At least one ex-Confederate from the county served in every legislative session from 1881 to 1899. Jonathan D. Rudd, the Citizens Party leader, was a state representative in four legislatures from 1891 to 1897, and William H. Pope, a man who had entered the Confederate army in 1864 at the age of seventeen, held a seat in the state senate from 1883 through 1891. Pope's admirers praised him for his work as a primary author of the 1891 law requiring segregated coaches on Texas railroads, the state's first Jim Crow law.[40]

Politically aware Harrison County veterans supported state legislation in the interests of ex-Confederates such as the establishment of a pension system that began in 1899. Their spokesmen, however, drew the line at help from the national government. When a congressman from Arkansas proposed the establishment of federal pensions for Confederate veterans, Thomas A. Elgin of Marshall wrote to Sen. Charles A. Culberson of Texas, himself the son of a Confederate officer: "The Confederate soldier fought for principle, not as a hireling. Our noble slain died for a principle, and their comrades left behind cannot and will not accept a pension to dishonor their memories."[41] Reunion had its limits.

The political prominence of veterans in Harrison County was accompanied by increasing recognition of their special social standing in the community. Wives, daughters, and other female relatives of former soldiers formed a local chapter of the United Daughters of the Confederacy in 1900 and spearheaded efforts to memorialize the warriors of the Confederacy. Their greatest success came on January 19, 1906 (Robert E. Lee's birthday), when they dedicated a nineteen-foot-tall monument on the courthouse square in Marshall. Laura Elgin, president of the Marshall UDC (and wife of Sgt. Thomas A. Elgin of the Second Texas Cavalry), spoke at the dedication ceremony, as did several local veterans. Maj. Khleber M. Van Zandt of the Seventh Texas Infantry, a Harrison County native who had returned to Marshall at the close of the war and then moved to Fort Worth in late 1865, also spoke, recalling how his company had left for war from virtually the spot on which the monument stood. Poems of tribute were inscribed on two sides of the memorial. One began, "Take our love and our tears today; take them, all that we have to give." Smaller monuments to Harrison County's Confederate soldiers were erected in 1908 in the Marshall city cemetery and in 1922 in the cemetery in Scottsville, a small settlement east of Marshall.[42]

In summary, an examination of the experiences of Confederate veterans in postwar Harrison County, Texas, indicates that soldiers returning home in 1865 did not receive a hero's welcome, but neither were they greeted with indifference. Instead they met with the respect accorded men who have done their duty. Some left the county, but many settled into the lives of married men with families, supporting themselves by farming. Certainly far more veterans than non-veterans in the same age group remained in the county in 1880 and 1900. Many of the veterans, of course, continued to pay a physical price for the wounds and general hardships suffered during the war, and a few may have suffered from some form of post-traumatic stress disorder. Somewhat surprisingly, in light of recent interpretations that emphasize the tendency of Civil War veterans to withdraw from society immediately after their return home, Harrison County veterans participated in important ways in the politics of Reconstruction and Redemption. Then during the 1880s and 1890s, they provided much of the leadership in local government and dominated representation of the county at the state level. In the early twentieth century, the special status of veterans received recognition in numerous ways but above all in the form of a monument on the courthouse square in Marshall. Perhaps the position attained by veterans in Harrison County is best summarized by a statement in the Marshall newspaper about Archibald G. Adams, a veteran of the Seventh Texas Infantry and the county's tax assessor for fourteen years, at his death in September 1915: "His record as a Confederate soldier will always be an honor to his family, his country, and to that cause he loved so well and constantly."[43] It is remarkable—understandable in terms of the South's need for justification but remarkable nonetheless—that soldiers could exercise so much power and be remembered so positively after fighting on the losing side in a war for a "country" and a "cause" that disappeared with their defeat.

Maj. Gen. David S. Stanley.
Courtesy U.S. Army History Institute,
Carlisle, Pennsylvania

9

"I Seemed to Have No Thought of the Past, Present, or Future"

Texans React to Confederate Defeat

Carl H. Moneyhon

In mid-May 1865 Confederate general Sterling Price and others met at New Orleans with Maj. Gen. E. R. S. Canby to negotiate a surrender of Southern forces in the Trans-Mississippi Department. After agreeing on terms, Canby sent Brig. Gen. Edmund J. Davis, a former state judge who had joined Union forces in 1862, to Galveston so that Gen. E. Kirby Smith could sign the document. On June 2 Smith and Maj. Gen. John Bankhead Magruder met Davis on the *Fort Jackson,* flagship of the blockading squadron, and signed the document. This formal surrender completed a messy breakup that had begun at least two weeks before, with soldiers abandoning their regiments and pillaging Confederate ordnance and commissary stores as they left. Having failed to keep his army intact, Smith had opened the way for the war's end in a letter to the Federal commander at Shreveport that advised, "The citizen and soldier alike, weary of war, are ready to accept the authority and yield obedience to the laws of the United States."[1]

Within less than a year, Smith's assessment of the feelings of Texans was called into question by the commanders of the military forces that occupied the state after the surrender. They perceived Texans as particularly resistant to the efforts of both the army and the Freedmen's Bureau and willing to use violence to achieve their ends. Federal officers explained this perceived defiance to the fact that Texans had never felt the real ravages of war and were never subdued. In February 1866 Maj. Gen. David S. Stanley stated this overtly when he appeared before Congress's Joint Committee on Reconstruction to testify about to his experiences in Texas at the war's end. Focusing on the trouble he had encountered in securing the punishment of individuals who had murdered or otherwise abused freedmen, Stanley attributed the refusal to help federal officials to the fact that the "State had not been surrendered by Lee" and had not been "conquered by the United States." The general did believe that returning Rebel officers were more disposed to accept the condition of things, but "those who had remained at home—the greater portion of the rebel army in Texas—were insolent and overbearing where they dared to be." Ultimately Stanley concluded that he considered "Texas in a worse condition than any other State, for the reason that they were never whipped there." Brig. Gen. William E. Strong drew a similar picture of conditions in Texas that he encountered on an inspection of the condition of the freedmen in the state. He reported that residents there were more violent and cruel toward the freedmen and Yankees than elsewhere in the South, explaining the apparent feeling as resulting from the fact that Texans "know less about the war, and have seen less of our troops than any other people, and therefore cannot appreciate the power and strength of the government."[2]

To a considerable degree, scholars examining events at the time of the Confederacy's breakup have agreed with the assessment of these federals. Brad Clampitt touches on the issue in his 2005 article in the *Southwestern Historical Quarterly* contending that many soldiers in the West simply went home without experiencing defeat. In short, unlike Texas soldiers who had fought in the East, soldiers in the West went home "not because of defeat, but because they never had the chance to do anything to stave off defeat." These men rationally realized that if the armies in the East could not stop a Union juggernaut, then there was little point in sacrificing themselves to the cause. That did not mean that they felt they had been conquered, however, and they returned to their homes unwilling to accept the authority of the United States or to yield obedience.[3]

Clampitt's conclusion is significant particularly because of its implications for explaining Texas in the postwar era and has provided an underlying reason for the apparent reluctance of Texans to submit readily to Reconstruction and for the racial and political violence that exploded across the state. One of the foremost historians of Reconstruction, Barry Crouch, began his study of the

Freedmen's Bureau in Texas by pointing to the special problems that confronted its personnel. First of these was the fact that the state had been relatively untouched by the armies of the North. But he also saw Texans carrying into the postwar years the idea that "their state had never been subdued" and possessing minds "unscarred by the psychology of defeat."[4]

The conclusion that Texans did not feel defeated has relied to a considerable degree on the generalizations made by Federal officials. To a lesser degree they have been based on the memoirs written in the years after the war by Texas Confederates. Less attention has been paid to what happened at the time. What was Rebel Texans' assessment of the military situation as the war came to an end? How did they behave? What feelings did they express as Confederate armies surrendered and broke up? Answers to these questions offer a different picture of the majority of Texans at the surrender and suggest that rather than feeling unsubdued, they experienced a profound sense of defeat.

Understanding the significance of the actions and words of Texas veterans in the spring of 1865 begins with a comprehension of the goals these men had sought to achieve in their military service. Psychologically, to be subdued would mean to accept the fact that none of the goals for which they had devoted years of their lives, suffered personally, and seen friends die would be obtained. At the beginning probably many of the young men who went to war in 1861 and 1862 had little deep commitment but were moved by a martial spirit such as that which prompted William A. Fletcher to join the Fifth Infantry at Beaumont.[5] Quite simply, Fletcher remembered that the public "clamor had dethroned what little reason I had," and despite his father's advice to the contrary, he joined the army. Nonetheless, the army, military service, and battle, with all that these experiences entailed, gave men purposes that were reasonable and weighty. None could have been abandoned readily or without psychological ramifications.[6]

The ideas Texans embraced to explain and justify their military experiences probably were as numerous as the men who served in the army. Still, some reasons did emerge that many held in common. Protection of their rights and the liberty to exercise these rights probably was the most universally expressed goal. Alexander Cameron, with the Thirty-First Cavalry in the Indian Territory in 1862, provided a typical statement of this when he informed his wife of the extent to which he missed her. "Permelia I think of you often," he wrote, "and if it were not for our liberties I could not be hired to Stay from you in this campaign." Samuel A. Cooke, with the Seventeenth Cavalry, later recalled a similar purpose for joining the army, a desire to help the South defend its "principles." Likewise, John W. Hill of the Eighth Cavalry considered "southern Liberty" to be the cause for which he fought and unhesitatingly asked friends at home for prayers to help obtain that goal. Port Smythe with the First Mounted Rifles was another of the men who perceived the war as one for "rights and liberties." Their importance for him was made clear when he stated his belief that Southerners "should be called upon to suffer and bleed for them at least once in fifty or a hundred years; they must be re-baptized in blood that they may be hallowed in the memories of our children."[7]

What "rights and liberties" had been threatened that called for such sacrifice? Soldiers did not always agreed on what was at stake. Some saw the conflict in broad philosophical terms, perceiving it as a clash of two completely different cultures. In this mode Theophilus Perry of the Twenty-Eighth Cavalry believed that the war was being fought because the people of the North had strayed from their knowledge of "Law." Assuming that there was such a thing as an objective definition of the law, Perry went so far as to blame the spirit of democracy for having eroded the people's knowledge of the what that law was. He saw the inevitable possibility of a despot emerging to reassert the truth. Why? It was one of the necessities of government "when law is badly interpreted[;] law always and will always regain." John Hill of the Eighth Cavalry also defined the conflict as of one of law, though he clearly perceived the North and abolitionists as defying God's law. For him his opponents were "*God Defying enemies,*" and he wanted to keep them out of Texas, where their presence would pollute the soil. A private with the Fourth Infantry, J. H. Manahan perceived the conflict in slightly different terms, defining it as one between two unique societies. The spread of "Yankee laws morality philosophy and philanthropy" was unacceptable. Defeat was not acceptable, and Manahan viewed exile from the South as preferable to living in a land whose "social and political framework" would be destroyed if the Confederacy lost the war. It would be impossible for any Southerner to live as a slave to "those whom they scorn and execrate from the profoundest depths of their souls."[8]

Other soldiers, however, defined the principle for which they fought as a struggle for property rights—and by property that meant slavery. They believed that the North sought to destroy slavery, a result that was too horrible to accept. That they saw the war in this way is not surprising since resistance to abolitionism was part of the generally stated purpose of disunion. The Texas Ordinance of Secession was clear in its reasons for withdrawing from the Union: The non-slaveholding states had worked to exclude slavery from the nation's territories as a first step toward destroying the institution in Texas and other slaveholding states. The ordinance asserted that the actions of this hostile section was intent on abolishing the South's "beneficent and patriarchal system of African slavery, [and] proclaiming the debasing doctrine of the equality of all men, irrespective of race or color." Secession was necessary because the recent national elections finally had put in power men pledged to "the ruin of the slaveholding States." Their reasons could not have been made clearer. Some soldiers agreed that this was what the war was about. J. K. Polk Blackburn of the Eighth Cavalry later justified his service in essentially the same terms as those used by the convention. He fought for self-preservation and the defense of the South and her institutions, but he also made clear what he believed the North threatened. He pointed to that section's fugitive-slave laws, their war on slaveholders in Kansas, their lionizing of John Brown, and the subsequent election of a president and congressional majority from whom the South could expect only "humiliation and destruction of her institutions." Yet humiliation and destruction were only the beginning of what abolition meant. Rudolph Coreth of the Thirty-Sixth Cavalry explained the war slightly differently, seeing it as one that could free the slaves and must be resisted because that would precipitate "terrible events."[9]

Not all men considered themselves called to protect some principle. Many acted because they perceived it as a man's responsibility to family and community to fight when their people went to war. Edwin Becton, a Texas surgeon, explained his actions as part of his personal duty, his war service as a "debt" to his country. John Street of the Fourteenth Cavalry insisted that his place in the army was a part of his responsibility and that not acting accordingly would bring shame to himself and to his family. In offering this explanation, Street likened himself to one of the patriots of the 1770s and revealed in a letter to his wife that one of his primary motives was his desire that "toryism" never be "cast in the teeth of *our* off spring." Later in the war John Hill of the Eighth Cavalry observed that he continued to fight despite the fact that many men in his unit were ready to come home. He saw his action as an obligation. "Our First Duty is to the 'God' who made us," he explained to his sister. "Our next Duty is to Our Country & Our Country needs us now and here and we must stand at our post."[10]

As the war progressed and men saw the results of military action on the countryside and the civilians who occupied it, the idea that they were fighting to prevent specific wrongs from being visited on their own homes also became a part of the rationale for service. John Hill had expressed early on his ideological motives, but his experiences with the Eighth Cavalry in Georgia and South Carolina hardened his resolve to continue fighting all the more. For him defeat came to mean a terrible fate for the women of the South. Writing to his sister in Bastrop, Hill denounced those at home who welcomed deserters or in any other way interfered with the war effort. He advised her to insist that all Texans should learn from those who found themselves behind Yankee lines during Sherman's march to the sea. If they realized the destruction that had been wrought they would "know the fate that awaits them."[11]

The shared experiences of men in battle, experiences that linked them in a common bond, also served to reinforce the will to fight and to provide a meaning to defeat that made it completely unacceptable. Capt. Dee Hardeman Ridley of the Ninth Infantry typically displayed the ties created in a unit that had survived Shiloh and then four more years of war when he characterized his feelings toward his men. "My fortunes are cast with as gallant a Regiment as ever tread Confederate soil," he wrote, "and I have been with it until they all seem as brothers nearly." Volney Ellis of the Twelfth Infantry was also typical, rejecting his wife's request that he return home. Ellis noted that he was fighting for "*human rights* and *liberties*," but he also acknowledged that his experiences had created other reasons holding him to his post. Tens of thousands had died in the Confederate cause and endured suffering, hardship, and privation. This made it impossible for him ever to surrender. "No this will not do," he insisted. "We must battle on until the end for which we began is attained or we ourselves are broken and scattered." The ever-articulate John Hill showed similar motivation when he informed his sister that he could never surrender and that no one in the South should consider it. "We can never yield," he wrote, for "the bleaching bones of an hundred thousand gallant comrades as ever trod the soil would rise and shake their . . . fingers and cry shame upon us. Their tongues would be clothed in living fire to curse to eternal infamy the man who would whisper yield." He would go on to conclude, "There is honor in extermination."[12]

Combined, the reasons for fighting held by soldiers and the dire implications of failure meant that defeat was unacceptable and surrender certainly not an action to be taken lightly. Whether they viewed the war as one for principles, for slavery, for honor, to keep their homeland from destruction, or ultimately to honor those who already had sacrificed their lives for the cause, all believed that losing would inflict a slavery on all who had fought. Charles Trueheart, a young Texan fighting near Richmond in a Virginia artillery battery, predicted that in the event the Yankees won, the result would be the "most degrading and galling yoke of bondage; that ever any people were called upon to bear." Eldridge G. Littlejohn of the Twentieth Cavalry pictured a similar fate for a defeated South, which would have to surrender to "the cruel relentless yoke of Yankee Tyranny." As others also stated, the duty of the Texas soldier was to keep this from happening. The conclusion of Levi. L. Wright of the Second Cavalry was not untypical of Texans. As late as February 1865, he believed that the fight must continue. "We cannot submit to the tyranicle [*sic*] powers of the north," he wrote. "No, Death is preferable."[13]

Given what these men consider to be the seriousness of their purpose, surrender could hardly be justified on the grounds that the enemy might have more men, more arms, or even possess inevitable victory. As Hill and Wright made clear, a fight to the death clearly should have been preferable to surrender. Certainly there were some men who had not enlisted initially for any specific ideological purpose, but any man who continued to fight through the war inevitably must have felt the need to justify the deaths and sacrifices that had occurred. Discontinuing the struggle was therefore in itself a psychological act of abject surrender. It would have meant giving up all hope that a man's goals would be achieved and also admitting the unthinkable—all the privations and death in the end had been for nothing. But in the end their actions and thoughts indicate that most came to accept the reality of that unthinkable conclusion.

Through much of the war, morale among Texas Confederates ebbed and flowed. At times they believed their situation looked hopeless, but this usually was followed by times of great hope for their cause. Few men gave up all hope. But to a considerable degree this ability to regain optimism died in the winter of 1864–65. Confederate officials inevitably contributed to the perception that the South's plight was dire when they began to debate whether or not to arm slaves for the defense of the Confederacy. For some Texas soldiers the idea made sense, though their feelings probably depended on their own view of the war's purpose. If freedom was the only goal, then black troops were acceptable. At least one Texan, James Monroe Watson, writing from Mobile, Alabama, during the height of the discussion on arming blacks, noted that some of the men he knew favored the measure, though others opposed it. He personally supported it, writing, "I am in favor of anything before subjugation." Sam Watson, an enlisted man with the First Infantry in the Army of Northern Virginia, was equally positive, concluding that enlisting blacks would help end the war and volunteered to his friend back home that he was even willing to apply for a command of a unit of "buck Negroes."[14]

James and Sam Watson were not in the majority, however. Most Texans viewed arming blacks as wrong. For them emancipation represented a major change in the reason for war and made clear that they would be unable to achieve one of the most important goals for which they were fighting. Samuel F. Foster of the Twenty-Fourth Cavalry, writing from Georgia at the time of the debate, explained why he found the idea unacceptable. To free slaves and arm them, he lamented to his wife, "makes them our equals." Eldridge Littlejohn, who was still with the Twentieth Cavalry at the time, speculated on the discussions from his camp near Verona, Mississippi, in January 1865. Like Foster, he found the debate equally disturbing and could see no point in arming slaves. He reasoned that to do so changed the whole point of the war, which was to keep blacks as slaves and as inferiors, and he believed that many of his fellow soldiers would quit fighting if Congress approved the policy. Accepting blacks as soldiers was "to adopt a principal which they [the men] have been fighting against." He informed his wife, "Instead of fighting for the existence of slavery as at first, we are now fighting for the existence of the government." D. Boyd, a barely literate soldier with the Ninth Infantry, said much the same when he informed a friend that on the question of placing blacks in the service, "that is one thing that I cannot favr [sic] To be."[15]

Texans at home were not immune from the realization that the debate on arming blacks indicated that even a victory would bring a possible end to slavery, which meant the South could never achieve its goal of maintaining the institution. A vital war aim thus had been lost. Orange C. Connor of the Nineteenth Infantry proved particularly thoughtful in a letter to his wife written from Shreveport in February 1865. He confessed that he was as "*low spirited*" as at any time since the onset of the war and that he had little hope for the success of the Confederacy. "In fact," he wrote, "I have no hope of our *complete* success." Why had he changed his mind? In part it had happened because he had concluded that the war would bring an inevitable end to slavery. "I am convinced that the Institution of slavery is now virtually destroyed & with it we loose the great object for which the Confederacy was made, & without which there never would have been a Confederacy," he reasoned. Rudolf Coreth of the Thirty-Sixth Cavalry also recognized that the war was leading to what he now considered to be inevitable—abolition. He worried about what freeing the slaves meant, but he confessed himself willing to accept emancipation since that would "not be prevented anyway by a prolongation of the fight."[16]

The debate over arming black troops may have been an important factor in the destruction of Confederate morale, but inevitably the military situation played an even more critical role in confronting Texans with defeat. The events that had the most profound effect were Union general William T. Sherman's march to the sea that took place in the autumn of 1864 and Confederate general John Bell Hood's unsuccessful foray into Tennessee. The Texans who saw most clearly the meaning of these military actions were those directly involved, but the news and its implications was shared rapidly with those back home. In January 1865 John W. Rabb of the Eighth Cavalry informed his mother that Confederate lines were uncertain after Sherman had marched to the Atlantic. He shared his pessimism, portraying conditions as looking "dark over here at this time." Robert Hodges, a soldier with the Twenty-Fourth Cavalry (Dismounted), a survivor of Hood's campaign, was one of the men clearly shaken by events. Hood's failure and Sherman's movements greatly diminished his hope for success. He remained with his unit as it regrouped in North Carolina, but in March he advised his father to prepare for defeat. "I am beginning to believe he [Sherman] is sufficient for almost any emergency. He is in my opinion the best general of the age. Grant and Lee not excepted."[17]

Texans in the eastern theaters were more acutely aware of conditions than their counterparts to the west. Despite their distance from home, however, their growing awareness of failure would play an important role in shaping the minds of those who were back in Texas. Depressing letters steadily increased through the spring of 1865. The usually optimistic John Hill, whose Eighth Cavalry had fought Sherman through Georgia and into South Carolina, had expressed little hope by that January. He concluded that the Yankees still could be turned back, but that the "people and some of the Soldiers are Subjugated." Even though he wanted to fight on, he found that "when I see our cavalry whiped [sic] and driven back by the Enemy[,] . . . [i]t makes my heart sink and I am almost ready to give it up." Hill clearly detected a loss of will among his fellow soldiers and observed that many were always away from their commands, shirked details, and when the fighting began, found a reason to "go to the river." "How few," he asked, "are the numbers that can lay their hands on there Hearts and say that they done all they could for their Bleeding Country?" Another of those who saw the will of the armies deteriorating, but who personally remained hopeful even following Lee's surrender, was Texan Henry Trueheart, who confided to his mother that this hope was limited and that only foreign intervention might still save the Confederacy. Otherwise he saw few willing to try to keep fighting. He observed, "we are whipped completely."[18]

When full recognition of defeat finally came, Texas soldiers in the East reacted as might be expected of those who had given their lives for a cause now lost. The surrender of the Confederate armies made the disaster patent, and the despair expressed was almost universal. William Fletcher, serving with the Fifth Infantry in the Army of Northern Virginia, recalled the tremendous sense of loss that overwhelmed him after Lee's capitulation. He remembered that he spent several days of the "blankest part of my existence. I seemed to have no thought of the past, present or future." Capt. Samuel Foster of the Twenty-Fourth Cavalry (Dismounted) recalled the sense of loss that spread among the men in camp on the evening of Gen. Joseph Johnston's surrender. He recounted that the men "go over the war again, count up the killed and wounded, then the results obtained." He found that they tried to find some meaning in their sacrifice but could find little. They sought some reason for the tremendous "waste" of human life. J. W. Watkins of the Tenth Cavalry actually regretted having survived. "Far better to have fell on the Gory battle field than to witness what is now going on," he wrote. "Thrice happy are they whose bodies bleach on the plains of Shiloh, Manassas, Murfreesboro, and Chickamauga, and whose spirits now rest from strife." Another veteran of the Army of Tennessee, Charles Lesuchner of the Sixth Infantry, shared with his diary his own reaction to the war's end and defeat. On his return home to peace, he wrote: "I espectat to be happy, and I was for a little while; but it is not so now, my heart has a whegd [weight] thrown upon it which cannot so easily be taken off. It pains me. I may forget it a minute or two, but it will come in my mind."[19]

Texans serving west of the Mississippi River and those still within the state held on to hope longer than those in the East. Distance and the efforts of Confederate officials to control the news meant that accurate official information was difficult to obtain. Frequently rumor replaced fact, and inevitably the rumor pointed to continued Confederate successes. In December 1864, for example, Dunbar Affleck, with Terry's Scouts in Rusk County, wrote to his mother, informing her that the unit had heard that Lee had inflicted a whipping on Grant at Richmond, killing and capturing six thousand men, and that Sherman had surrendered to Hood. The following January James Black, with the First Heavy Artillery at Galveston, informed his wife that they had received nothing but good news: Sherman's army had been captured in Georgia, and Hood had taken Nashville. John Simmons, with the Twenty-Second Infantry in Louisiana, reported that his unit had received equally good news as late as May 1864. Their information was that Joseph E. Johnston was having his way with Sherman and still had an opportunity to stop the Yankee advance into North Carolina.[20]

Through the spring of 1865, Confederate authorities in Texas possibly believed that they had effectively contained news of the critical military situation in the East among their own soldiers and prevented the spread of defeatism. At least in their public statements, they often contended that the soldiers of the West had not lost their fighting spirit and were not ready to give up the fight. In his General Orders No. 20, issued on April 23, General Magruder urged his men to set an example of "devotion, bravery, and patriotism, worthy of the holy cause of liberty and independence"; reminded them that Dick Dowling and forty-two Irish soldiers had driven fifteen thousand Yankee soldiers into the sea; and asserted his belief that even defeat in the East would see men rally around the Confederate banner, "which will still float defiantly west of the Mississippi River." As late as April 28, Magruder informed the Trans-Mississippi commander, E. Kirby Smith, that he believed the men in Texas at least were still ready to fight. "As yet the disposition of the army, as far as I have been able to judge," he wrote, "is one of proud and patriotic defiance."[21]

In fact most Texas soldiers in the Trans-Mississippi had learned not to trust the news by this time. Volney Ellis of the Twelfth Infantry, in Louisiana at the time, was typical when he complained as early as the summer of 1863: "I hate news. I have become sick of rumors, reports, extras, and newspapers, all lies, lies from beginning to end." This perception became even more pervasive by the spring of 1865 and clearly infected soldiers in the Trans-Mississippi. Dunbar Affleck sounded little different from Ellis when he warned his mother that any good news he shared with her should be viewed with skepticism. As for himself, "I don't believe any thing I hear and only half I see, and then it has to have the signature of some big General to make it good." John Simmons, who had informed his wife of positive news regarding setbacks for the Union forces in the Carolinas, admitted that he did not believe the news and blamed Confederate authorities with trying to manipulate the information received by the troops. By March 1865 he had cynically come to see no news as bad news for Confederate arms. He observed, "If the news were in our favor, they would not be afraid to publish it." At Galveston James Black was forced to concede only two weeks after having informed his wife of the positive word coming from the East that none of it was true. He concluded that in fact everything was "very gloomy indeed for our cause."[22]

The inability of Confederate authorities to contain bad news is hardly surprising. Even though soldiers in the East often counseled the recipients of their letters not to share their despondency with people at home, word probably spread nonetheless. In addition, as the military situation there deteriorated, many soldiers simply started for home, bringing with them the news of Confederate disaster. In March John Simmons reported from Shreveport that the countryside was overrun with large number of soldiers, who all claimed to have furloughs, on the move through the area coming from the east. He confided to his wife, however, that he personally believed that many of the furloughs were "of their own making." Word of soldiers coming home also came from other sources. Several weeks after Simmons had written his letter, Elbridge Littlejohn, still with the Tenth Cavalry near Mobile, reported that many men were "going without papers." Littlejohn was not one of them, however, and his own desire to come home "honorably" led him to assert strongly, "I will never run away."[23]

The mood that spread through Confederate units in the West can hardly be described as defiant. Few expressed any willingness to fight to the death. Instead contemporaries described the pervasive spirit as one of hopelessness, one of having been defeated. The words used to explain these feelings varied, but all inevitably reflected an awareness that they had fought in vain and a sense of personal depression. As early as January James Black reported from Galveston that the gloomy news the men received left most "low-spirited." Caleb Forshey, a staff officer there, also indicated this early shift of morale. He believed that Sherman's march had a particular effect, not so much because it had been made but because he had met virtually no resistance. The result had been to "dishearten our troops." Simmons confided to his wife that he believed Confederate forces east of the Mississippi had been whipped and that once that happened the armies in the West would go home. In fact he personally was ready to accept the loss. To his wife he confided, "I begin to believe that our bad news is our best news, for the Feds are bound to out-do us, and the sooner the better is my opinion." William "Buck" Walton, a major in the Twenty-First Cavalry, recalled in later years the collapse of morale among his men and the complete loss of any fighting spirit. They knew the Confederacy had gone to pieces and turned timid and fearful. "They were afraid," he remembered, "after boldly breasting, in battle & exposure, every danger, that they might be killed, when there was no need to die—when it would do no good to the country for them to die. The war was over—they were going home."[24]

When not characterizing the feeling that spread among soldiers in the Trans-Mississippi in words that expressed the emotions of hopelessness or depression, contemporaries often used terms that best described physical defeat. The soldiers themselves often characterized the feelings of those around them as that of being "whipped," a word clearly implying physical punishment. Obviously some of the observers were personally ready to keep on fighting, but the problem they saw was the loss of hope among the mass of soldiers. At Hempstead General Magruder ran into this defeatist sentiment in April when he appeared before his men to encourage them to stand up to the enemy. In his speech Magruder insisted that they would meet the enemy at the water's edge and fight them every inch. These were not the sentiments of most of the soldiers, however. One soldier in the camp reported that he had attended meetings held by "brass buttons" urging the men to "fight on" and that local papers also published reports of meetings at which the troops expressed their loyalty and determination to fight, but these were not the sentiments of the men. He viewed the men as "whipped" and ready to go home. At one of the camp rallies about a third of the soldiers respectfully listened to speeches while the rest "stood off some hundred yards and kept up a yell to break it up." In May a soldier in John H. Forney's Texas Division, a formation that had proven its valor throughout the war under John Walker and known as "Walker's Greyhounds," provided an equally pessimistic view of his comrades' morale. He concluded that demoralization among the men in the unit had reached such a low level that he would be afraid to use them in a fight. Indeed, while he believed the cavalry remained firm, "the boasted infantry are the worst whipped, worst demoralized and in fact not worth a d—m—. I sometimes wish that I had the power over them. I would have the 1st one who refused to do his duty shot without even a court martial."[25]

The testimony of Confederate commanders further confirms the spirit that pervaded through the Texas units, perceiving their men as beaten. Brig. Gen. Hamilton Bee, describing the conditions of the men in his camp and the feelings of civilians near Liverpool, Texas, to Galveston lawyer Guy M. Bryan, painted a dismal scene of defeat. Bee believed that little fight remained in either the troops or the people. He personally desired to stay at the front and make a fight of it, a fight that would "complete the brilliant record of Texas in history, and if we must yield at last it will be with our honor saved." Yet he had concluded that it was "folly to try and convince ourselves that the people will stand." On May 16 Magruder informed General Smith that he had received reports from division commanders that convinced him the troops in Walker's Division and Maxey's command "will fight no longer." In an addendum General Walker concurred with this assessment of the infantry, though noting that the cavalry "are still firm and quiet." Brig. Gen. James E. Slaughter was direct in his May 19 report from Brownsville. Despite war meetings and speeches intended to bolster the morale of the men, he found that such efforts had not achieved the desired effect. They say, he wrote, "We are whipped."[26]

Of course the extent to which this sense of defeat had spread cannot be measured fully by the words of the soldiers. In the end a relatively modest number of men actually wrote letters sharing their thoughts, and even fewer pieces of such evidence survive. Ultimately the actions of the men give some indication of how widespread this despair was within the armies. Significant behavior indicating the state of Confederate morale was the steady increase in the number of men deserting the colors. The meaning of desertion has been a topic of some debate among scholars. The earliest student of the subject, Ella Lonn, believed that it often was an expression of a loss of support for the Confederate cause. Many recent scholars, however, have seen the motivation of individual soldiers as more benign, explaining desertion often as only a temporary thing, with men returning home to help harvest crops, take care of business, or simply visit family. Lonn's interpretation appears to be the more valid one when explaining the actions of Texans by the winter of 1864–65 and the subsequent spring. Going home at this stage of the war was abandoning the South at a critical point in its revolution. Soldiers may have concluded that their families needed them more than their country, but to desert even in such instances meant the surrender of all hope that the individual could do anything to achieve Southern independence. Desertion at this point necessarily meant accepting defeat.[27]

Desertion had always been a problem for both Confederate and Union armies, but across the South and then among soldiers in Texas, it reached epidemic proportions following the winter disasters of 1864–65. While the reasons Southerners left is not always clear, it is certain that they departed in great numbers. As early as January 1865, General Slaughter reported from Brownsville that the area had become overrun with bands of deserters and that his own force had to spend time keeping them in check. Some of these deserters organized and continued to operate like military companies, just not within the army. Clearly sensing a growing loss of faith in the Confederate cause, however, Slaughter encouraged headquarters to keep his force intact at Brownsville because he feared that if they were ordered east, at least a fourth of his remaining men would desert. On March 4 Julius Giesecke, a captain in the Fourth Cavalry, noted in his diary, without comment on the reason, that the regiment "revolted." As a result 127 men had gone home "without leave of absence," including 18 from his own company.[28]

As word concerning the military situation in the East spread, desertion increased further, and commanders found it difficult to keep their units together. W. W. Hurley of the First Reserve Corps wrote to his wife early in April that the men in camp were ready to go home. Brig. Gen. Jerome B. Robertson, commander of the Texas Reserves, managed to keep his men in the ranks, though only by promising them that the corps would be disbanded soon. Despite the general's pleas, Hurley indicated the growing distrust many felt for their officers; he concluded that they were only manipulating the men. "I think they both think more of their own interest and aggrandizement than they do of the general [view] of the country."[29]

After word reached Texas of Lee's surrender on April 9 and Johnston's on April 26, desertion rates indicate that the vast majority of Texas troops concluded that the war was lost. Men abandoned their units in camps across the state. Near Huntsville the Fifth Cavalry virtually disintegrated. An officer with that unit despaired of the future and reported that "desertions are occurring every day in all commands." Among the troops camped around Galveston, the situation was equally bleak. Magruder informed General Smith that on April 14 some four hundred troops had deserted the city. These men had walked away, clearly still capable of putting up a fight since they carried their arms with them, forcing Magruder to use the loyal men from Col. Bernard Timmon's Infantry Regiment and Hobby's Eighth Infantry to keep them from escaping. Conditions were equally grave along the Rio Grande, where General Slaughter reported that at least half of the men in the Western Sub-District of Texas had deserted or probably would abandon the colors soon.[30]

Some soldiers remained, but they were not motivated by any optimistic views about the future. John Simmons and the Twenty-Second Infantry in late April were at Hempstead, where he reported that many troops were getting restless and noted that "some talk of breaking up and going home." He was not one of those who advocated desertion, however, but this indicated no faith in the Confederate cause—instead his policy was to wait and see what happened. Simmons believed "that we will get to come home without running off." Rudolf Coreth, whose Thirty-Sixth Cavalry was stationed in the same area, admitted that many in his regiment had deserted by mid-May. Of those who remained, he believed that most stayed only so they could "go home openly."[31]

How did these men feel as all hope vanished and they faced the inevitability of defeat. Few shared their feelings, but those Texans in the West who did express their sentiments differed little from the Texans in the East. William Heartsill was one of the soldiers at home who did write about the war's end, and the feelings he observed appeared to have been widespread. He personally remained optimistic about the chances for victory practically to the end, but his view was shared by few. Several weeks before the collapse of the armies in Virginia and North Carolina, he had tried to get his comrades to approve resolutions expressing their undying support of the Confederacy. He failed, and his failure ultimately opened his own eyes to the situation. In seeing the lack of spirit among the men, Heartsill recognized that his country was subjugated and the cause lost. Reacting to this realization, he wrote with despair in his diary, "My heart swells, my lip quivers, my tongue refuse to give utterance, the very depths of my soul is stirred up; yes I could fall down in the dust and weep over our great misfortunes, our great calamities." An Arkansas surgeon with Walker's Texas Division observed much the same thing and was surprised as hundreds of men deserted. "Everyone," he informed his wife, "citizen and soldier, is completely demoralized."[32]

Many Texas soldiers considered what had happened in terms of personal humiliation. Joseph Blessington of the Sixteenth Texas, another veteran of Walker's Division, later tried to characterize the feelings of the men camped at Hempstead as they came to accept defeat. Their faces told a "fearful story of how bitter was the hopeless surrender of the cause for which they had fought, toiled, suffered for long years. The humiliation was unbearable." William P. Ballinger, a Galveston attorney and political official who had witnessed events in camp, testified that this sense of humiliation had also spread to civilians. Seriously upset by events, he found that defeat gave him a personal sense of "humiliation" and "dishonor" in his circumstances. His surrender was abject. Ballinger could see no reason for "vain writhings" or "self-inflicted blows" against the enemy. "If we *are* in his power," he reasoned, "nothing wld gratify him more."[33]

The implications of this despair were profound for some men, who saw in their defeat personal and social shortcomings. George Wythe Baylor, one-time commander of the Second Mounted Rifles and a man whose duel with Maj. Gen. John Wharton that April showed him hardly a man without spirit, recalled later that following Lee's surrender, he almost lost faith in God. "I began to doubt the power of prayer," he wrote. Only his later belief that defeat actually had been for the good, since success would have left the nation like Poland, unable to stand up against foreign powers, made it possible for him to regain his faith in "God's mercy and justice." J. W. Watkins of the Fifth Cavalry never doubted the existence of God, but he did conclude something had gone wrong. He believed that the South's fate ultimately had lain in its own hands and that as a people, Southerners had failed. He did not know the reason but concluded, "We are a God forsaken people and will be shut out from the blessings of the good being for some sin committed."[34]

None of these men appeared ready to continue the war, though their feelings about their future life in the Union varied from man to man. Some Confederate Texans clearly were not happy with the course that events had taken, and they certainly were not ready to be friends with the Yankees. The pain of defeat was apparent in the writings of J. W. Watkins, a cavalry officer who ultimately found that he was willing to submit but not necessarily forget. "I am willing to play the child's game with the yanks," he informed his wife. "If they let me alone I will let them alone. But if one crooks his finger at me I will be good for his *meat*. I intend to keep as far from them as possible and want them to keep away from me." At the same time, a few others quickly put aside such feelings. William Fletcher remembered much later that he "carried no hatred against the victorious foe." Indeed he came to see that his former enemies considered their participation as part of a sacred duty, just as he had. Fletcher also recalled that upon his return to his home, when U.S. troops were stationed at Beaumont, he and other former Confederates became acquainted with the Yankee soldiers and found them to be "nice, jovial young fellows." They particularly liked that they were equipped with cash, so it did not "hurt our pride to take a drink with the Yanks." Fletcher believed that he and his friends had seen "service enough to learn not to pine over the by-gone or carry hatred for a victorious foe."[35]

There is no way of knowing if either of these feelings dominated the thoughts of Texas' Confederate soldiers as they returned home. Most said nothing, but when they did recall what happened immediately after the war, it appears that their thoughts consisted more often of determining how they would survive in the postwar world. Instead of chewing over the past, they just went back to work. Many saw themselves facing a new, more critical challenge, whether or not they and their families would have anything to eat. "Buck" Walton found on his return to Austin that he had virtually nothing. His slaves had been freed, and they had even less than he. His home had an unpaid mortgage. He had no money and no clothes except for one pair of gray pants, two flannel shirts, and a black buckskin suit full of holes. Walton hunted, fished, copied court records, and "did everything that I could lay my hands to." Alfred M. Henderson of the Thirteenth Texas Cavalry described an equally abject surrender to the necessity of the moment. Discharged at Alto, Texas, he walked twenty miles to Columbus in Austin County. He spent the rest of his life farming. "The morning after I reached home," he recalled, "was plowing at 6 o'clock." Fletcher recalled that he "went home and gathered up father's old carpenter tools and went on a job at $1.50 per day, about one hundred feet from the place where I left off work."[36]

These Confederate veterans went back to work, and many also appeared to have accepted the war's results, particularly the end of slavery. They thus were "subjugated" ideologically as well. John Cochran, who had fought in the Eighth Cavalry, explained that he had returned to his family near Hempstead in the fall of 1865, immediately started farming, and had not hesitated to use freedmen as laborers. He noted that while everyone complained of the "worthlessness" of the workers, "[s]till they are in a great demand." A year after Lee's surrender, he concluded that most of the people he knew were "becoming somewhat reconciled to the new order of things." "Who would have imagined four years ago," he asked, "that the people of the South a harty [sic] race would have submitted to such proceedings." Former Confederate congressman Frank B. Sexton, writing from San Augustine in the spring of 1866, expressed similar surprise at Texans and Southerners as a whole. Recalling events the previous spring, he confessed: "I could not think that the Southern people would give up everything so tamely, so suddenly and so universally as they did. I thought they knew what *subjugation* meant and were prepared to face *extermination* rather. But I was mistaken." How far would they go? He admitted that even on the question of black equality, politically and socially, as to whether or not Southerners would submit, "*I say I do not know.* Once I would have answered distinctly & unhesitatingly, no! But I have been so surprised at what has happened that I will not allow myself to have any opinion as to what may happen."[37]

Despite the fact that the majority of soldiers appear to have accepted defeat and gone home to recover their fortunes, Texas would become a place of considerable violence and opposition to the Reconstruction policies. In looking for other sources of what ultimately would happen, one must consider the state's secessionist and Democratic leaders. Even at the war's end, they clearly had an eye not only to their own fortunes but also on retaining their power over the citizenry. Attorney and politician William Pitt Ballinger was one of these leaders and saw the potential for real upheaval in the status quo unless the loyalty of common Texans to their old leaders could be maintained. He believed that could be done. Texans had become attached to the just-ended revolution, and their having lost family in the service or having members who had served honorably would make them remain "*Southern* in their sympathies and feelings." The state's leaders had to ensure that northern men did not convince their constituents that secession had been the work of ambitious or designing leaders but was a defense against northern wrongs done solely to secure the honor and happiness of the southern people. Leaders continued this struggle as long as hope existed, but when hope fled, "no useless sacrifices were exacted, not one unnecessary drop of blood was shed, nor dollar expended."[38] Ultimately men like Ballinger would accomplish their goal and set the tone for how Texans viewed both the Civil War and Reconstruction for the next hundred years.

Ballinger's efforts at restoring faith in the Confederate cause and its leaders would take place later. In 1865 most Texas soldiers appeared to have accepted the advice William Fletcher took to heart as he marched through North Carolina alongside a regiment of cavalry. An infantryman from a North Carolina regiment marching ahead was talking with the cavalrymen when he "drawled out, in rather a long tone: 'Boys, have you got any bacon.'" The reply from the cavalrymen was, "Yes." The infantryman then said, "Grease and slide back into the Union." Fletcher recalled that he laughed but then rode on and made up his mind to "follow the lesson taught by the crude advice." From that point on, he began to think that there would be a future, and "the sunshine of my being grew brighter."[39]

The statue of Jefferson Davis, president of the Confederate States of America, on the grounds of the University of Texas at Austin. *Courtesy Alexander Mendoza*

The statue of Robert E. Lee, commanding general of the Army of Northern Virginia, on the grounds of the University of Texas at Austin. *Courtesy Alexander Mendoza*

10

Causes Lost but Not Forgotten

*George Washington Littlefield, Jefferson Davis, and
Confederate Memories at the University of Texas at Austin*

Alexander Mendoza

In April 1990 two incidents of racial strife shook the campus of approximately fifty thousand students at the University of Texas at Austin (UT-Austin). First, on Monday, April 9, students learned that a car used by the Zeta Tau Delta fraternity during the previous weekend's Sixtieth Annual Spring Round-Up Parade, an annual alumni celebration, had been painted with racial slurs such as "Fuck coons" and "Fuck you nigs die" and smashed with a sledgehammer in an apparent triumphant acclamation of the day's activities. Even though Darrel Armer, president of the Zeta Tau Deltas, denied responsibility for the racial epithets, the university community struggled to deal with the growing controversy as the Student Association and the university's Interfraternity Council debated punishment and possible sanctions. Students had barely begun to digest the news of the Tau Delta incident when Tuesday's edition of the school's student newspaper, *The Daily Texan,* revealed that a second fraternity, Phi Gamma Delta, also faced charges of racism for selling and distributing t-shirts with a "Sambo" caricature at a basketball tournament during the same Round-Up weekend. Marcus Brown, president of the Black Student Alliance, declared that the two incidents indicated "that there is racism on campus" and that Round-Up represented "an indication of white supremacy by going back to the vestige of Reconstruction."[1]

The racial strife of UT-Austin's Round-Up weekend galvanized protesters, according to *The Daily Texan*. For several years black students had already been organizing for the sake of promoting multiculturalism and protesting university investments in apartheid South Africa. Yet the racial incidents involving the two fraternities brought out approximately one thousand people to a rally on Wednesday afternoon, a figure observers recognized as abnormally high despite the short notice and lack of formal planning. The events in question even forced UT-Austin president William Cunningham to plan a speech addressing the incidents for Friday, April 13. In the swirling maelstrom of this racially tinged climate, the controversy surrounding what the Black Student Association called "institutionalized racism" at the school soon engulfed the placement and meaning of a group of statues honoring high-ranking generals and politicians of the Confederacy on the university's South Mall, where Wednesday's rally was held. In particular, student anger focused on the statue of former Confederate president Jefferson Davis, first installed on the university grounds in 1933, which held a prominent position near the south entrance of the university's main building and stood slightly to the west of to the statue of former U.S. president Woodrow Wilson. Tony Barrueta, a second-year law student, exemplified the students' frustration as he launched a hunger strike to implore university officials to remove the statue. According to Barrueta, he "had to do something" to beseech the administration's action to prevent the building racial tension stemming from the Round-Up activities from erupting into violence.[2]

The fact that Barrueta had focused his hunger strike on the Jefferson Davis statue should not have been surprising, especially considering that in the previous year, student angst over the monument had resulted in two significant cases of vandalism. The second incident actually occurred in the fall semester, on September 4, when the words "'Roots' (of KKK)" and "fight racism now!" were spray painted in red on its base. According to Lt. R. G. Thomas, a nineteen-year veteran of the UT-Austin Police Department, the South Mall statues have been frequent targets of vandalism. The 1989 incident was the second time that year that the Davis statue had been targeted by angry students. Earlier, in February, unknown assailants had defaced the bronze statue with bleach, resulting in permanent damage to it. And while Barrueta's hunger strike may have failed to move university officials into removing the statues from the South Mall, the attacks and their meanings continued well after the racially tinged events surrounding the 1990 Round-Up celebration. In September 1990, more than half a year after the fraternity incidents, the Davis statue was again defaced by vandals who wrote "Am I Your Hero?" on the front of the base. According to one student, the statue was a "disgrace to the campus and an insult to the people of color, and people defacing it is a reflection of the frustration that the people of color on this campus feel." In contrast, Lieutenant Thomas expressed anger against those who would turn their backs on history, disregarding the social message behind the defacement. "That's just plain old graffiti," he said. "People just don't give a damn about their heritage and about their country."[3]

As UT-Austin students grappled with the meanings and implications of an homage to the Confederate States of America on their campus, the truth of the matter remained that most of them had no idea how the Jefferson Davis statue and other Confederate monuments found their place on the South Mall. And while the Davis statue—along with the Wilson monument—holds a prominent location near the university main building's south entrance, an additional four statues to the purported heroes of Texas and the South—Robert E. Lee, Albert Sidney Johnston, James C. Hogg, and John Reagan—flanked the Davis and Wilson memorials amid the large oak trees lining the two pedestrian paths heading southward to the *pièce de résistance,* the Littlefield Memorial Fountain. Described as a war memorial by university officials established following U.S. participation in the First World War, the Littlefield Fountain ultimately came to encompass an important place in the structural design of the university. Yet the concept and ideas that spurred the late-twentieth-century debates over the judgment and meaning behind monuments that stood for a racist past were actually rooted in the vestiges of the Old South as symbols of reverence to what the memorial's main benefactor, George Washington Littlefield, considered imperative reminders of the state's heritage in the newly commercialized and politicized world in which Texans lived. To Littlefield and his supporters, the monuments represented a commemoration of their Confederate past and the South's proper place in the reunified nation. But more importantly, they would remind future generations about those "who suffered and died in defense of the righteous cause of the states," even if that cause included the protection of slavery.[4]

George Washington Littlefield was born the oldest of four children in Panola County, Mississippi, on June 21, 1842, before his family moved to Texas in 1850. Like many other children reared during Texas' early statehood, Littlefield enjoyed a vibrant life at his family's plantation near Belmont, about fifteen miles north of Gonzalez, before attending Gonzalez College and then later, for a short time, Baylor University. Littlefield cut short his education and returned to help his mother on the plantation, an estate that eventually grew to include more than eighty slaves. When Texas followed the path of her sister states during the secession crisis of 1860–61, Littlefield enlisted in Company I, Eighth Texas

Cavalry, better known as Terry's Texas Rangers, in August 1861. He fought in various engagements, including the Battle of Shiloh, and rose to the rank of major before receiving a wound that cut short his military career in 1864 at the age of twenty-three. After the war Littlefield returned to Texas, where he ventured into the very business he was most familiar with, farming and cattle. By the last decade of the nineteenth century, he had accumulated enough wealth through his ranching ventures that he moved to Austin and organized the American National Bank, of which he served as president until 1918, and acquired a fair stake of other businesses as well.[5]

While Littlefield prospered, his service to the Confederacy remained a vital aspect of his life. As Robert Vinson, a former president of UT-Austin and a friend of Littlefield, observed: "to a degree unsurpassed by any man I have ever known, Major Littlefield lived and died in the firm conviction of the righteousness of that [Confederate] cause." In post–Civil War Texas, Littlefield, like many of his fellow Confederate veterans throughout the South, found an abundance of outlets for soldiers who desired to remember their war experience. Mass-market periodicals like *The Land We Love* and *Southern Magazine* were some of the first publications to devote coverage to battle narratives written by former Confederate soldiers. By the 1870s the *Southern Historical Society Papers* had given these veterans the opportunity to rationalize their cause with thorough, legalistic discussions on the constitutionality of secession in response to northern aggression and analytical articles expounding on strategy and tactics during the war. The goal of the Southern Historical Society (SHS), as explained by former Confederate general Jubal Early in 1873, was to write the South's version of the war for future generations of southerners. Early and his supporters were among the foremost architects of the Lost Cause, a literary and social movement that sought to reconcile the Confederacy losing the war with self-serving justifications that the South was never truly defeated but instead merely overwhelmed by superior manpower and resources.[6]

Former Confederate soldiers inspired by the *Southern Historical Society Papers'* messianic message promoting the Lost Cause soon gave impetus to a different way of remembering the war, the creation of veterans' organizations and monument dedications. The death of Gen. Robert E. Lee on October 12, 1870, spurred them to organize and sponsor a monument to the departed southern icon. As the former soldiers mobilized to revere Lee and other individual heroes, these memorial associations, which existed at a local and regional level, soon helped inspire annual veteran reunions. A formal regionwide Confederate veterans' association emerged in 1889 in the form of the United Confederate Veterans (UCV). The UCV, which was similar in purpose to the Southern Historical Society, dedicated its efforts to preserving the South's version of the war. To accomplish this task, the organization produced the *Confederate Veteran* magazine, a monthly periodical first published in 1893, which publicized many of the club's activities. As historian Gaines Foster has noted, the *Veteran's* human-interest stories and devotion to various Confederate celebratory activities made it an immensely popular tool for inspiring southern audiences. As such, camp membership in the UCV increased significantly at the turn of the century, to 850 local camps by 1896 and 1,565 by 1904. The movement to preserve this Confederate heritage proved so popular in fact that organizations for female and male descendants of Confederate veterans, the United Daughters of the Confederacy (UDC) and the United Sons of Confederate Veterans (later known as the Sons of Confederate Veterans), were also formed during the final decade of the nineteenth century.[7]

Yet the Lost Cause activism of these organizations also masked a white-supremacist version of remembering the Civil War. The UCV's leadership denied the centrality of the role of slavery to the onset of the war and instead expended a disproportionate amount of energy advocating the imagery of the brave soldier, the faithful slave, and the suffering yet loyal southern woman. Amid the harsh realities of *Plessy v. Ferguson* and the Jim Crow South, the UCV's representation of the conflict grew to dominate the landscape of Civil War remembrance. James Conquest Cross Black, a former U.S. congressman from Georgia, epitomized this vision when he addressed the audience at a UCV reunion in Augusta, Georgia, in 1903, proclaiming, "We did not fight to perpetuate African slavery, but we fought to preserve and perpetuate for our posterity the God-given right of the freedom of the white man." Black, who had served in the Ninth Kentucky Cavalry, urged his fellow veterans to continue the struggle of recording the South's proper version of the war as he insisted that if any liberation had to be commemorated, it would be the "Anglo-Saxon emancipation" of southern whites from their postwar northern "oppressors." In essence the Confederate memory of the war, as promoted by the UCV and its dependant organizations, served as a bastion against perceived northern biases and distortions of their own idealized past.[8]

Class strife in the postwar South added to the maelstrom of nostalgia and race in the struggle to interpret and memorialize the Civil War. Southern elites, besieged by the social ferment created by the late-nineteenth-century reform movements of the Grange, the Farmers Alliance, and the Populist Party, grew uneasy with the agrarian protests that threatened their supremacy in the region. This oligarchy also felt threatened by perceived northern attacks upon their region. Consequently they used the Confederate historical societies to perpetuate the Old South's values as illustrated through the Lost Cause rhetoric to reassert their political and social influence over disgruntled white and black farmers. As Fred A. Bailey has argued, southern elites realized that to galvanize support, they had to make sure that all "southern whites must be taught to think correctly, to appreciate the virtue of elite rule, to fear the enfranchisement of blacks, and to revere the Confederate cause."[9]

In this highly charged atmosphere, George Washington Littlefield, called by his Civil War rank of major by his friends, moved to Austin in 1883 to continue his real estate and banking ventures while gradually becoming a politically influential person thanks to his growing wealth and interest in state affairs. Soon after arriving in the Texas capitol, Littlefield joined the John Bell Hood Camp of Confederate veterans. In the early 1890s the camp joined the UCV in concentrating on following the regional organization's goals of promoting the South's interpretation of the war through the preservation of history and the establishment of monuments celebrating the Confederate cause. As William Von Rosenberg, chairman of the UCV's Confederate Monument Committee of Texas, stated in 1895, Texans "had a special duty upon us caring for the memory of all the heroes of the 'Lost Cause.'"[10]

This proved to be a rallying cry for Texas veteran organizations as they led movements to build monuments throughout the Lone Star State. In 1896 Littlefield and his fellow members of the John Bell Hood Camp received a message from the chairman of the Ben E. McCulloch Camp urging them to forego the minutia of recounting battles for the sake of embracing the bravery and conviction of the Confederate cause. For Littlefield his membership in the UCV and his responsibility as an officer in the Terry's Texas Rangers Association meant that he played a prominent role in staking a claim to the public memory of the war. In June 1898 Littlefield and his fellow UCV veterans met with Texas governor Charles Allen Culberson and received approval to build a monument in front of the decade-old Texas Capitol to celebrate the bravery of Texans who fought in the Civil War. After a slight delay caused by a lack of resources for construction, Littlefield and his fellow veterans raised the necessary funds to build a monument featuring Jefferson Davis surrounded by figures honoring the four branches of the Confederate military: the infantry, artillery, cavalry, and navy. The monument committee awarded the contract to Frank Teich, a German immigrant sculptor and stonecutter living in San Antonio. Teich in turn advertised for a sculptor for the bronze statue of Davis and found Pompeo Coppini, an Italian immigrant living in New York, who was willing to move to Texas to take on the challenge. In 1901 the monument was unveiled on the south entrance of the capitol grounds. Coppini's initial work would launch a longstanding relationship between the Italian sculptor and Texas veterans' groups that would lead to the erection of dozens of additional memorials throughout the Lone Star State.[11]

Yet Coppini was not solely responsible for the Confederate memorial renaissance that proliferated throughout numerous county seats in Central, North, and East Texas at the turn of the twentieth century. From creating statues dedicated to the pantheon of Confederate leaders, Jefferson Davis, Robert E. Lee, Stonewall Jackson, and Albert Sidney Johnston, to creating monuments devoted to the common soldier of the Confederacy, veterans' organizations and their supporting descendants' groups rallied to preserve the southern memory of the war.[12] In the last decade of the nineteenth century, newspapers throughout the Lone Star State urged readers to unite behind these groups to remember and honor the sacrifices of the Lost Cause generation. As Von Rosenberg, chairman of the Texas monument committee, argued in his "appeal" to the people of Texas: "In the 'lost cause' the south has failed to establish a nation, but the deeds of her heroes who fought, suffered and died for the cause are as exalted . . . as any of which history tells us." He urged citizens to consider how important their state was to the preservation of the Confederate cause, pointing out that in the post-Reconstruction years, people from throughout the former Confederacy now chose to call Texas home. That alone, according to Von Rosenberg, imposed "a special duty upon us of caring for the memory of all the heroes of the 'lost cause' without distinction." From the 1890s to the World War I era, Confederate apologists proved formidable, intertwining monument construction with elaborate unveiling celebrations that sought to bring white citizens together for the sake of civic pride and regional nostalgia.[13]

While the monuments and the unveiling ritual served vital roles in presenting the proper memory of the South, the apostles of the Lost Cause in Texas had another equally important task at hand: the need to ensure that a correct and proper history of the Confederacy be preserved for future generations. In the late nineteenth century, Texas Confederate societies were appalled by the growing criticism of northern writers who condemned the southern aristocracy for launching the Civil War. Consequently the Texas Division of the UDC spearheaded a propaganda campaign to emphasize the central tenets of the Lost Cause. Allied with the UCV, the two organizations published lists of critical northern texts, urged libraries to eliminate disapproved books, and mobilized southerners to defend their ideological and social values. In June 1897 the efforts of these partisans resulted in the passage of Texas' uniform textbook law, which required all cities with populations of less than 10,000 to adopt state-mandated textbooks. Moreover, with the introduction of a board to review textbooks, hold hearings, and select proper academic works advocating the South's version of the war for subsequent generations, Texas legislators ensured that the state's youth would receive a sanitized version of the Civil War emphasizing the southern spirit and highlighting the state's patriotism. The Texas UCV and UDC even focused their wrath on colleges that used history texts with a purported northern bias. Through their efforts one highly criticized text, Henry William Elson's *History of the United States of America* (1904), which dared to describe the Civil War as a "Slaveholders' War" and praised Pres. Abraham Lincoln for the preservation of the Union, was removed from the curriculum at Sam Houston State Normal Institute and UT-Austin in the first decades of the twentieth century.[14]

George Washington Littlefield found himself directly involved in the UT-Austin's decision to drop Elson and the equally controversial Edward Channing book, *A Student's History of the United States* (1898). As the first decade of the twentieth century came to a close, Littlefield received an appointment to serve on the Texas Library and Historical Commission from Gov. Thomas M. Campbell. A few years later, in 1911, Gov. Oscar Colquitt appointed him to the Board of Regents of the University of Texas. Littlefield's selection to the board led the historian of the Texas Division of the UCV to write optimistically that the Austin banker was now "in a position to lay the ax to the root of this deadly Upas tree."[15] Littlefield's prominent role in Texas Confederate veterans' groups in the last two decades had clearly influenced his way of thinking about the South's legacy in regards to the Civil War and Reconstruction. As Texan native John H. Reagan, the former postmaster of the Confederacy, argued in an address to all veterans, the real causes of the war remained the South's constitutional prerogative in response to the revenue policies of the federal government. Reagan also defended the South's role in relation to slavery, pointing out that national leaders like George Washington and Andrew Jackson were also slaveowners, albeit without the taint of treason painted on the former Confederates by northern partisans.[16] Littlefield, like many of his fellow veterans, were thus privy to the Lost Cause rhetoric espousing the righteousness of secession and supporting the romantic image of the plantation culture, particularly to the innocence of the South regarding slavery.

Littlefield took his newfound responsibilities as an arbiter of southern history to heart. By the time he joined the Board of Regents, he had begun the gradual process of withdrawing himself from his business affairs and viewing his duties to influence future generations of Texans with a deep reverence. Accordingly Littlefield urged UT-Austin president Edward Mezes to seek a reason for why the History Department used the Elson book. The department chairman, Eugene C. Barker, conceded Elson's failings in regards to the views of southern slaveholders and President Lincoln, but he argued that the author's views of Reconstruction were in accordance with the South's general disdain for that era. Barker assured Mezes that he was loyal to the South. "I beg to remind you, sir, that I am a southern man," he wrote. "I was born, and have lived all of my life, in Texas." Even though Barker might have compromised his academic principles for the sake of appeasing his superiors and retaining his position as department chair, the Elson episode actually gave him an opportunity to petition Littlefield for a donation to develop a southern manuscript collection to provide an adequate basis for a southern interpretation of the past. Despite an added controversy brought on by the John Bell Hood Camp over the university's use of the Channing text, Barker eventually succeeded in winning over Littlefield. In March 1914 Littlefield called the professor to his downtown office. For the next month he negotiated the creation of a fund for southern history, culminating with a gift of $25,000 to secure adequate resources for a proper history of the South. In a letter to Clarence Ousley, the chairman of the Board of Regents, Littlefield announced his "desire to see a history written of the United States with the plain facts concerning the South, especially since 1860, fairly stated—that the children of the South may be truthfully taught, and persons matured since 1860 may be given opportunity to inform themselves correctly." On April 28 the board formally accepted Littlefield's gift to establish the Littlefield Fund for History.[17]

This donation to create a true history of the South drew statewide praise for Littlefield's efforts to curb a growing sense of perceived injustice at the hands of northerners. For southerners, many of whom still felt affronted by biased histories, the idea that an authentic history of the South would be promoted and emphasized was a godsend. Newspapers like the *Fort Worth Record* and the *Austin Statesman* heaped praise on the Austin philanthropist for his efforts to promote the notion that the "South's part in history should be known, not only for the justification of the South in seeking to dissolve the Union, but for the instruction of the nation in the causes which might again imperil the Union."[18] While the media organs trumpeted the virtues of a nonpartisan approach to studying the past, to "enable the world to learn the real facts . . . without prejudice," the truth of the matter was that the history Littlefield extolled sought to vindicate the Confederacy, defend southern culture, and preserve the social strata in the New South as defined by class and race.[19] As one newspaper boasted: "Major Littlefield's gift, to have a true history of the South written, proves that his southern sentiments are not lost in the vortex of commercialism. . . . [T]he white people love Major Littlefield because he is a great man, but the negroes love him because he is a good man. In all industrial affairs, God has interlaced the white man's brain with the negro's muscle, and both must be just, honest, and helpful to each other and when the history is written and published that Major Littlefield knows the world needs, this will be proven." Littlefield's financial support for a southern archival research depository thus touched upon the pro-southern issues that perpetuated in Texas during the Progressive period. These concepts drew widespread support from individuals, who heaped praise on the former Confederate officer.[20] Notably, Littlefield's donation also drew a tribute from Georgia native Mildred Lewis Rutherford, the UDC's official historian from 1911 to 1916, who happened to be in Texas on a speaking tour dealing with the South and history when she received word of Littlefield's bequest. Rutherford, whose views on "true" southern history condemned Reconstruction, praised the Ku Klux Klan as defenders of southern virtue, and offered a benevolent view of slavery, informed the major that his actions in Texas deserved to be replicated in Georgia.[21]

Littlefield's efforts to ensure a proper reinterpretation of the past involved areas other than textbooks. The monument-building wave that permeated the national landscape in the years following the Civil War showed few signs of abating during the early twentieth century.[22] In the decade following the dedication of the Confederate armed forces monument at the capitol, Littlefield had seen an additional three monuments built in his adopted hometown. In 1906 the UDC celebrated the dedication of a monument to Albert Sidney Johnston at the Texas State Cemetery, a celebration followed by the unveiling of a memorial to Terry's Texas Rangers on the capitol grounds the following year. Finally, in March 1910, members of Hood's Texas Brigade dedicated a monument to their unit on the increasingly crowded capitol grounds.[23] And while Littlefield was both directly and indirectly drawn to the monument building in Austin, he also ventured to areas outside the Lone Star State to help with the memorialization of his beloved South, particularly supporting the construction of a monument to Jefferson Davis in Fairview, Kentucky, the birthplace of the former Confederate president. During World War I, he donated $40,000 to "further honor the memory" of Davis and "the cause which he should personify to the American people" with the building of a 351-foot obelisk column.[24]

Despite the fact that Davis received a great deal of criticism during the war, including much of the blame for the Confederacy's failures, his postwar career and perceived suffering at the hands of northern Republicans had remade the former president into a powerfully symbolic figure in the postwar South. Davis's death on December 5, 1889, completed the transformation from scapegoat to southern icon. In 1807 more than 200,000 spectators came to witness the dedication of the Jefferson Davis monument in Richmond, Virginia. The following year the newly created Jefferson Davis Monument Association in New Orleans planned a memorial for the one hundredth anniversary of Davis's birth on June 3, 1908. Throughout the South, tributes to the former Confederate president emerged in various forms. Littlefield had been cognizant of the partisans' rhetoric regarding Davis. The UCV had long praised the former president and his interpretation of secession. In Texas the UCV chapters echoed the South's adoration of his leadership during the Civil War as they incorporated him in various monuments throughout the state. Yet Texans took the adulation of Davis a step further by tying him to the annexation of Texas. In one address delivered at a meeting of the Pat Cleburne Camp No. 22 on the anniversary of Davis's birth, the Reverend S. A. King pointed out that Davis was a member of the U.S. Congress when the subject of Texas annexation came up and that he "favored the measures leading to the expansion of the United States which took in Texas." As such Davis clearly meant a great deal to those who sought to maintain ties to the state's past and its birth.[25]

For Littlefield to revere the Confederate president was thus not out of the ordinary in the New South. Yet his desire to commemorate Davis and the heroes of the Confederacy needed some direction. After all, the major facets of the Texas Confederate experience were already memorialized on the capitol grounds and in the Texas State Cemetery. The major would find a new site for maintaining his vision of the South and the Confederacy on the campus of UT-Austin. Through his business ventures and political contacts, Littlefield had found himself drawn to the events on the Forty Acres campus. When he received the governor's appointment to the Board of Regents, he saw it as a responsibility to shape the minds and memories of future Texans. Even though he lived practically across the street from the campus and had contributed small gifts to the school prior to receiving his appointment to the board, the real catalyst and motivation for his utmost devotion to the university in his waning years would stem from his belief that it had been under the negative influence of a disloyal Texan, George Washington Brackenridge, a man who had left the state to avoid joining the Confederacy during the Civil War, for far too long.[26]

Brackenridge, a native of Indiana, had moved to Texas at the age of twenty-one in 1853 and eventually prospered in the cotton trade by the outbreak of the Civil War. Even though three of his brothers served in the Confederacy, Brackenridge held Unionist sympathies. In 1863 he left the Lone Star State to take a position in the U.S. Treasury Department in Union-occupied New Orleans. After the war he moved to San Antonio and became a wealthy banker and businessman with Republican leanings until he received his appointment to the UT-Austin Board of Regents. In his later years the Harvard-educated Brackenridge directed his philanthropy to educational pursuits, including donations to UT-Austin and Guadalupe College, a school for African Americans in Seguin, among others. His political and educational philosophies thus worked at cross-purposes to Littlefield's views on revering the Old South. This proved especially true in 1910, when Brackenridge remained the lone regent to vote against an offer from the UDC to provide a $25 award given to the student writing the best paper on southern history at the university. The mere fact that Brackenridge felt the university should not invest itself in discussions of the Civil War was tantamount to treason to Littlefield, who had devoted a significant portion of his time and money to that very purpose. As Littlefield's biographer, J. Evetts Haley, argues, Brackenridge's views against the pro-southern version of the Civil War only compounded the dissatisfaction the major felt regarding the man's disloyalty to the South during the war and Reconstruction years.[27]

Although Brackenridge resigned his place on the board the same year Littlefield assumed his duties as regent, the San Antonio residents' antipathy for all things Confederate would move the Austin banker to slowly chip away at the legacies he left behind. Foremost among these was Brackenridge's desire to move the university campus to a five-hundred-acre tract of land by the Guadalupe River and away from Austin's commercial district. Brackenridge had already donated money to establish the Brackenridge Loan Fund for Women Students in Architecture, Law, and Medicine and provided funding for the first dormitory for men on the university campus, Brackenridge Hall, or "B" Hall, before attempting to donate the riverfront property. Yet it was his overall imprint on university life that made Littlefield fume. As UT-Austin president Robert Vinson observed: "When Mr. Brackenridge spoke of the University of Texas he always emphasized the word University. Major Littlefield emphasized the word Texas." For Littlefield, anything that minimized or decried Texas and the views of the Old South that he and his Confederate partisans promoted had to be addressed.[28]

The idea of memorializing the Confederacy on the UT-Austin campus first surfaced during Littlefield's tenure as regent. According to Coppini, Littlefield had been pondering a way to build a Confederate monument on the university grounds for a few years. Yet it was not until 1916 when Coppini's dire financial circumstances forced him to take the initiative and urge Littlefield to contract him to build a "monument to the Confederate cause at the south entrance of the University Campus" and "keep me in Texas, and from selling my beautiful studio and home." During their negotiations Littlefield divulged his plans to memorialize the South with a monumental arch affixed with statues dedicated to Jefferson Davis, Texas governor James Hogg, Confederate postmaster general John H. Reagan, and Gens. Robert E. Lee and Albert Sidney Johnston. The problem, though, was that Littlefield planned to venerate the southern heroes for the sum of $50,000, a figure Coppini thought was extraordinarily low. Dejected, the sculptor left his meeting with Littlefield and proceeded to sell his home and studio in San Antonio before moving to Chicago shortly afterward. But the idea to revere the heroes of the South would germinate with Littlefield for the next few years.[29]

The fact that Coppini suggested to Littlefield the idea for a memorial to the Confederacy should not have been surprising. Coppini after all had established a reputation throughout the South, if not the nation, for his statues and monuments to Texas and the Confederacy during the early twentieth century. His work on Texas memorials, including a statue commemorating the survivors of the Galveston flood and a cenotaph of the Alamo, also brought praise and support from influential figures in the state. U.S. senator Morris Sheppard, in a reference letter supporting the Italian artist's work on a monument to Stonewall Jackson in Richmond, noted that Coppini "has chosen to identify himself particularly with the South and is so thoroughly in sympathy with southern tradition and ideals that I consider him peculiarly well-qualified for a work of this character." Coppini's sympathies for all things southern did not end with a special reverence for fallen heroes. He also took the New South's attitudes in regards to racial relations to heart. In his autobiography Coppini recounts how he was forced to sell his home once a "Negro" moved into his neighborhood, thereby "punishing" all the white residents. The sculptor supported segregation and questioned those willing to challenge "God's will" in regards to racial amalgamation. He thereby epitomized the white-supremacist views that characterized Texas and the South during the Jim Crow era.[30]

As Coppini moved to the Midwest, Littlefield prepared his legacy at the university. He retired from his position as president of American National Bank and began to consolidate his wealth and formulate his last will and testament. In those last years Littlefield set aside additional money for the Southern History Collection, purchasing the John Wrenn Library of rare literary works from Chicago, and provided $300,000 for the Alice Littlefield Dormitory for freshman girls. More importantly for the major, he set aside a considerable sum for a memorial to the South's heroes on the university campus, providing $200,000 "to erect a massive bronze arch over the south entrance to the campus of the University of Texas" upon his death. When Littlefield died on November 10, 1920, he left behind a detailed will that named fellow regent Will C. Hogg and American National Bank vice president H. A. Wroe as executors of the project, which would feature President Davis as the centerpiece atop the proposed arch, with Generals Lee and Johnston flanking the former chief executive and Texas heroes Reagan and Hogg supporting the venerated southern icons. The major provided specific instructions for the arch, leaving discretionary orders for his executors to "change" the "design as they wish." Yet he wanted control over choosing the sculptor who would forge the statues of his heroes. So in March 1920, just months before he passed away, Littlefield contacted Coppini and contracted him for the work. By the summer of that year, the sculptor had persuaded Littlefield to donate $250,000 for the monument, to be divided in two sums, half for the construction costs and half for sculptural work.[31]

Citing the rising costs of labor and material after the Great War, Coppini was never confident that a memorial arch across the southern entrance of the university could be built with the money Littlefield allotted. Accordingly he and the Littlefield Memorial Committee quickly set out to modify the plans Littlefield left behind. One of the first modifications was to touch on the spirit of national reunification in the post–World War I era by including an homage to the North. Within a few months additional changes came about. Specifically, in lieu of an arch, the committee came up with the concept of commemorating the fallen soldiers of the Great War by building a memorial fountain in front of the university's main building to be flanked with two tall pillars, representing the North and South, being united by a central statue representing the "Spirit of Columbia" in the act of crossing the ocean with her "army and navy" bringing the "inspiration" of "freedom." The memorial would stand on two elevations, according to these early plans: the first level would include the fountain and the Columbia centerpiece, while the second, higher level would consist of the two main columns and the additional statues to the South's heroes that Littlefield proposed. Atop the two pillars would stand figures of U.S. president Woodrow Wilson and Jefferson Davis, the Confederate president thus epitomizing "states rights" and Wilson standing for "world's rights," according to Coppini.[32]

Littlefield's will ensured that his vision for memorializing the southern heroes of the South would live on at the UT-Austin campus. Despite the few changes brought about by the monument committee, the fact remained that Littlefield's interpretation of the past and his reverence for his beloved region was meticulously planned. Not only did Littlefield secure the services of the particular sculptor to relate to the rest of the world the design he had envisioned years earlier but also established a strict completion schedule, which specified to his executors that the work must be finished no later than seven years after his death. With such stringent guidelines left behind, Coppini started to work on the first set of sculptures less than a year after Littlefield died. By the fall of 1921, he had finished the preliminary work on the statues of Davis and Johnston.[33]

Yet despite all the care and planning that went into Littlefield's last will and testament regarding the memorial, a mild resistance to his nostalgic view of the Confederacy and the Old South began to emerge during the 1920s. Texans were undergoing a gradual transformation in how they perceived themselves. The memories and celebrations of the Confederate past, which unified white Texans with their fellow white southerners at the turn of the century, slowly began to recede after World War I in favor of a Texas exceptionality that celebrated the state's history as uniquely American, more western than southern. As historian Walter Buenger has noted, Texans, who had already distorted their history to perpetuate the popular myth that the Civil War was fought for states' rights and that slavery was a benevolent institution, began to alter their past once more, this time to emphasize the notion that Texans had more in common with the American frontier spirit than the slave-ridden South. As Texas moved toward its

1936 centennial celebration, "Texans abandoned the limited possibilities and racist ideology implicit in the Lost Cause and adopted the mantle of progress of the Texas Revolution."[34] Accordingly the Lone Star State shifted from its Old South and Confederate traditions and reached toward a form of Texas nationalism that celebrated its unique past.

This shifting historical emphasis was not the only issue that threatened to minimize Littlefield's vision. More directly related to the monument, President Wilson, a longtime advocate of the Lost Cause and southern history, had refused to participate in Coppini's sculptural vision. President Vinson asked Postmaster General Albert Sidney Burleson (a Texan) to bring the matter to Wilson's attention, secure his support for the erection of his statue, and provide Coppini with articles of clothing for an accurate model. Wilson, however, refused to cooperate because he did not support the notion that the Littlefield project conveyed the spirit of national unity it proclaimed. "I am sorry to say I must express an entire unwillingness to have my effigy mounted as is suggested in association with the proposed memorial," the president wrote. "Moreover . . . I don't fancy the partner [Davis] they offer me." Despite this rebuff, university officials persevered. As Vinson reluctantly informed Coppini: "[I]t was impossible to interest him [Wilson] in the matter, or secure his permission to make use of him for the purpose of the Littlefield Memorial. I am sure that the work will have to be done without his permission."[35] Even though Wilson had long propagated insensitive racial views toward African Americans and sympathies with the South during Reconstruction, during the last decade of his life, he demonstrated a more ambivalent view regarding racial matters. In a 1923 letter to Senator Sheppard, Wilson described the recently revived Ku Klux Klan as an "obnoxious" and "harmful" organization.[36]

While the shifting importance on revering Texas's southern version of history might have proved a significant obstacle for Coppini, a truly formidable challenge for the artist's sculptures came in the form of university officials who grew uneasy with Littlefield's vision. Foremost among them was William James Battle, a professor of classics, a former university president, and member of the Board of Regents. Born in North Carolina and educated at the University of North Carolina and Harvard, Battle arrived on the Forty Acres campus in 1893 as an associate professor of Greek. In addition to his teaching duties, Battle had a certain artistic vision that allowed him to play a prominent role in the development of the university, going as far as designing the official university seal in 1901 and serving as the chairman of the Faculty Building Committee in 1920.[37]

In 1921 Professor Battle traveled to Coppini's art studio in Chicago to observe the Italian sculptor's progress and to determine how Littlefield's vision would be incorporated onto the university campus. Immediately he balked at the intended national memorial: "The conception of the Entrance Memorial seems to me open to serious objections. If I understand Mr. Coppini correctly, the monument is intended to commemorate the Reunion of the Nation after the Civil War. The conception is noble and defensible in itself, but a fatal objection is the fact that every single statue represents a southern man. How can a group composed of men from only one section stand for a united nation?"[38] Battle did not wholly object to the idea of a southern monument, rather he demurred from the disingenuous description of the memorial as a symbol of reunification. He mildly criticized the sculptor's work on the statues of Davis and Johnston but offered a more damning assessment by openly questioning how Littlefield's memorial would stand the test of time. "The Monument may be out of scale with or not stand in suitable relation to the future buildings on the campus," he reported to President Vinson. Shortly after receiving Battle's letter, Vinson wrote to Coppini and echoed many of the professor's concerns, arguing that the proportions of the monument need to be reconsidered in regards to the "environs of the University buildings."[39]

Coppini was incensed with Battle's evaluation. In a private letter to Vinson, he questioned Battle's credentials for critiquing his sculptural work and castigated the classics professor for not divulging his apprehensions while he visited with him in Chicago. More importantly Coppini argued that the direction and the vision Littlefield marked in his will remained incontrovertible: "Why should then this Prof. Battle alone in his condemnation approach you with such a contentable [*sic*] affront to my work, to my conception, to the Architects' work and studies, to your judgment in approving it, and to the judgment of Major George W. Littlefield in wanting what he wanted in that Monument and in selecting me and you for your ability, honesty, and integrity?" The day after he wrote Vinson, Coppini contacted Harry Hertzberg, a San Antonio lawyer, and asked him to examine his contract with the university to see how much artistic control he really had over the Littlefield monument. The sculptor also asked Hertzberg to "smooth the rough" waters between him and Vinson, who also happened to be a friend of the attorney. Hertzberg advised Coppini that he should not worry about Battle's letter and urged him to show a bit of restraint when communicating with Vinson. He even went as far as to compose a letter for Coppini that retreated from calling Battle a "snake rattler" in lieu of a more diplomatic but equally terse message suggesting that the professor misjudged Coppini's conception and pointed out how the "criticisms are not only injust [*sic*] but villainous." Coppini complained about the matter, but he followed Hertzberg's advice and continued to work on the memorial's statues throughout the winter of 1921–22.[40]

Battle's critique and the accompanying doubts expressed by Vinson served as the opening salvos in what would eventually be a decade-long struggle over Littlefield's vision to memorialize his southern heroes and university officials' concerns about the propriety of a massive shrine to the Confederacy on the campus grounds. Yet the aesthetic and architectural interpretations of the memorial were not the only problems at hand. Within a year after the Battle debacle, Coppini was writing to the Trustees of the Littlefield Memorial, President Vinson, and H. A. Wroe to complain about the litany of difficulties he faced, including rising costs of materials and the poor facilities in his Chicago studio. Adding to these woes, university officials and the monument committee threatened to reduce the opulence of the memorial due to budgetary shortfalls and its failure to harmonize with the university's architectural design. Coppini realized that it had been more than six years since Littlefield had passed away, and time was running short on the seven-year deadline. Conscious of time and his own dwindling resources, Coppini furiously wrote letters to his architects, James R. M. Morison and Frank Chase Walker, which outlined his frustrations working with the university and their failure to recognize Littlefield's vision. Not one to quell his anger, Coppini fired an angry letter to the Littlefield trustees at the end of 1926, charging the committee, which now included Dr. William R. M. Splawn, who had taken over for Vinson as university president in 1924, with "neglect in studying the contract." In essence he hinted that the Littlefield Memorial funds had been misappropriated by the committee. Coppini continued to campaign to preserve Littlefield's vision by writing letters to influential Texans, hoping to gain their support.[41]

For the next three years, as the deadline came and went, Coppini's battle with the university and the monument committee centered around school officials' resistance to the lavish southern memorial and the trustees' refusal to use the accrued interest of the $250,000 bequest to pay for the cost overruns caused by the ensuing delays. Undaunted by the challenge of facing the university and the committee, Coppini argued that he did not seek to become a wealthy man but wanted "the vision of Littlefield preserved." By 1928 he bragged that "[a]t last the fight has started and the battle from now on will be as furious as the Chicago Election." In a letter to newly appointed UT-Austin president Harry Y. Benedict, Coppini threatened that "there shall be no redesigning of the Littlefield Memorial" lest the university wants long litigation. Despite the sculptor's pleas for common sense and devotion to Littlefield's vision, the committee remained steadfast, informing him that the money just simply was not available and that the memorial had to be completed "within the limits of the sum provided." Even Coppini's complaints that the university architects contradicted Littlefield's intentions went unheeded. By 1929 an exasperated Wroe informed Coppini that his goal of fulfilling the major's bequest looked bleak.

Your contract was signed by Major Littlefield. Neither the courts nor the executors will recognize any alleged verbal agreement, and if you care to listen to your legal advisors, the courts are open for you. As to the trustees or executors of the Estate putting up additional funds to complete this memorial, that is impossible and will not be done. . . . You state in your letter that the design was accepted by Major Littlefield. That may be true, but the funds are not sufficient to erect it according to the plans and specifications furnished. As far as Mr. [Herbert M.] Greene is concerned, he is the architect for the University of Texas, and has something to say as to the location of the buildings, etc., on the grounds, and we conferred with Mr. Greene after we found that it was impossible to use the plans and specifications that had been submitted.

Even though Coppini fired off another letter to Hertzberg, he and his architects began to consider revised plans for the Littlefield Memorial by the fall.[42]

If money and design were the bane of Coppini's artistic vision during the last few years, an additional challenge surfaced in the last few weeks of 1929. On December 9 Wroe informed him that the Board of Regents did not want the memorial on the southern entrance to the university and preferred a more discrete location just east of the football stadium, approximately six hundred yards to the east. This latest development deeply exasperated Littlefield's widow, Alice, and the UDC, who still longed to see a memorial to the heroes of the South on campus. Mrs. Littlefield threatened to donate the completed monument, whose statues were still being held in storage, to the City of Austin if her husband's wishes in regards to the specific location were not observed. This latest challenge festered for several months while Mrs. Littlefield sought alternatives to fulfill her late husband's wishes. In the meantime Coppini's associates urged him to demonstrate a bit of restraint when communicating with university officials. Still, by January 1930 the board had made no decision regarding the monument.[43]

By the spring of 1930, the university had finally moved to resolve the issue of the Littlefield Memorial. On March 8 the Board of Regents hired Paul Phillipe Cret as UT-Austin's supervising architect and commissioned him to draw up a general development plan for the campus. Even though his master plan would not be submitted until 1933, Cret quickly offered the board a series of sketches that dealt with the Littlefield Memorial and how it would fit with the aesthetic quality of the overall campus design. He supported keeping the fountain as the centerpiece of the memorial on the south entrance of the school. But instead of the two-tiered design with the statues to the heroes of the South surrounding the fountain, Cret recommended that the six figures could go on each side of two different pedestrian sidewalks leading from the main building southward to the fountain amid separate rows of majestic oaks. He hoped the statues would serve as sentinels that would stand guard in front of six new buildings to be separated by a large lawn designed to inspire students to congregate. Cret argued that his design for what would eventually be known as the South Mall would bring about the best sense of symmetry and order to the campus. Battle, who first showed ambivalence about the Littlefield Memorial almost nine years earlier, had worked tirelessly behind the scenes as the chairman of the Faculty Building Committee to persuade the regents to hire Cret. It remains unclear if Battle's initial opposition to Littlefield's design made it into his discussions with the regents nine years later. Nevertheless, unexpected funding from the federal government's Public Works Administration during the Great Depression made Battle and Cret's vision a reality. On July 16, 1930, the Board of Regents officially approved the plans for the Littlefield Memorial within the confines of the campus master plan.[44]

With this approval secured, Coppini moved quickly. By late 1931 the figures of Davis and the other champions of the South had already been shipped to Texas. Coppini continued to work on the statue of Columbia, but rising construction costs and a general lack of funds continued to frustrate him. Over the next year the sculptor and the trustees exchanged letters that resonated with the same themes of the previous decade: Coppini asked for more money; the trustees refused.[45] Finally, on March 3, 1932, Coppini instructed Hertzberg to threaten a lawsuit against the trustees and the Board of Regents for failing to fulfill Littlefield's gift, which should have been completed five years earlier. With the school's fiftieth-anniversary celebration looming on the horizon and the potential public-relations nightmare that accusations of malfeasance might have caused, the board approved the additional funds needed to complete the project by dipping into the university's general fund. In a letter marked "personal" to Coppini's attorney, UT-Austin president H. Y. Benedict offered a prognostication on the board's decision just days before the regents met. As soon as the board made it official, Hertzberg sent Coppini a telegram offering his congratulations on fulfilling Littlefield's project. By the fall of 1932, the *San Antonio Express* reported that the remaining figures for the Littlefield Memorial had been shipped from New York City.[46]

While the university's challenges to Littlefield's original design and the budgetary struggles over his bequest served as the main points of conflict between Coppini and school officials, a new source of friction stemmed from the final placement of the statues and a miscommunication regarding the monument unveiling. Even though he was aware that the spirit of Littlefield's design was not going to be incorporated into the university's general plan, he was still angry that he had no control over the final stages of construction. Coppini was disconcerted with Cret's sentinel design.[47] Particularly Coppini felt that the figures should have faced south, like many Confederate statues throughout the region.

"My memorial has been crippled by those in charge of that institution," he complained to Hertzberg, "but the truth will come out and their name will be despised if not forgotten."[48] Also troubling the sculptor was his belief that the university would not celebrate Littlefield's Memorial with an elaborate unveiling alongside the school's dedication of several new buildings. It irked him that he would not be visibly recognized for his artwork. In a bold move Coppini asked a few newspaper reporters to expose the failure of university officials to publicly acknowledge Littlefield's grand memorial and his artistic contribution to the project. Ironically, the same day that Coppini was attempting to sabotage the celebration, Read Granberry, an officer in the Ex-Students Association, invited Coppini and Hertzberg to attend the memorial unveiling ceremony during the university's Round-Up festivities, scheduled for April 29, which would also coincide with the school's dedication of several new buildings on the Forty Acres campus. As soon as he received this official notification, Coppini sent telegrams to his newspaper contacts and asked them to stop the publicity highlighting his erroneous belief that he was to be ostracized from the unveiling.[49]

On April 29, 1933, the date of the commemoration, *The Daily Texan* declared that the Littlefield Memorial would be among the "Most Magnificent in World." The newspaper merely repeated what Coppini told them. The dignitaries, the alumni, and the invited guests for Round-Up viewed an elaborate dedication that not only included the tribute to the Littlefield Memorial but also the dedication of nine new school buildings. President Benedict and Professor Battle proudly proclaimed a historic benchmark for the university, one that would herald UT-Austin, in Benedict's words, "becoming the greatest institution of its kind in the world in the next fifty years." This camaraderie and spirit of generosity soon dissipated, however. Despite Coppini's positive outlook at the unveiling, he reminded Benedict that the university narrowly averted a lawsuit for forsaking Littlefield's vision. Within two years Coppini had no qualms charging that university officials had ruined the monument. In a speaking engagement with the Texas-Exes in October 1935, the sculptor reminded his audience that university officials had betrayed Littlefield's vision. The *San Antonio Express* heralded the news: "Maj. Littlefield Memorial Ruined Sculptor Asserts." In his autobiography, written more than fifteen years after the unveiling, Coppini maintained many of his previous points, asserting that although he carried out his contract to the letter, there were forces at work beyond his control that prohibited the erection of the memorial as originally planned. On that point he cannot be disputed. Key university officials saw through the charade of the Littlefield Memorial standing as a symbol of national reunification when it actually represented an homage to the southern Confederacy and supported a certain nostalgic vision of the South. Littlefield's vision was so strong that he tied it to more than a million dollars he bequeathed to the university. School officials had little recourse but to accept his monument or risk offending the school's largest donor during its first fifty years.[50]

When the Littlefield Memorial was completed during the Great Depression, the Lone Star State was in the midst of a general movement commemorating the Confederacy. Just two years prior to the unveiling, legislators passed a resolution to celebrate Robert E. Lee's birthday, January 19, as a state holiday. This measure coincided with a general mood throughout the state. For the remainder of the decade, cities and towns throughout Texas celebrated their Confederate past by venerating an icon of that period. Newspapers carried pleas for donations to build shrines; restore the Lee home in Stratford, Virginia; and to restore Camp Cooper (in present Shackelford County), where the future Confederate general was stationed during the 1850s. Texans were particularly interested in tying Lee to the Lone Star State despite his brief service as part of the U.S. Second Cavalry. Yet by the centennial celebration in 1936, Texans slowly began to distance themselves from their Confederate past in order to embrace the spirit of exceptionality and maintain a stronger tie to the American frontier. As such, by the mid-twentieth century they began to identify more with the symbols of cattle and oil than with the images of the Lost Cause and Confederate heroes.[51]

As Texans moved away from their Old South past to embrace the spirit of modernization, the statues on the South Mall and the nostalgia they were designed to inspire were largely ignored for two decades—that is until civil-rights activists began to chip away at UT-Austin's segregationist policies during the 1940s and 1950s. Like many schools throughout the South, UT-Austin practiced segregation. But on June 5, 1950, the U.S. Supreme Court ruled unanimously in *Sweatt v. Painter* that the separate-but-equal concept was inherently flawed and ordered the university to admit Heman Sweatt and several other African American students to various graduate school programs. Within six years UT-Austin became the first major university in the South to admit blacks as undergraduates. The following decade, as civil-rights forces galvanized, university students and those from Huston-Tillitson College (a historically black college in eastern Austin) staged demonstrations urging integration throughout the university and the capital. The Civil Rights Act of 1964, which outlawed racial discrimination in public accommodations, accelerated this process.[52]

By the late 1960s the student body furthered the cause of civil rights by militant student organizations like the Afro-Americans for Black Liberation (ABL) and Mexican American Student Organization (MASO), which championed the plight of ethnic minorities. The ABL and MASO demanded affirmative action, dismissal of racist faculty, and a sensitivity to the history and study of ethnic minorities. Begrudgingly, the administration gave in to some demands, creating an ethnic-studies program in 1970 and frowning upon the racist caricatures and stereotypes that continued to pervade some student groups at the school. In one case the Texas Cowboys, a university male-student organization, discontinued the use of blackface in its annual minstrel show.[53]

Civil-rights activists spurred a counter-reaction from pro-segregationist forces that resisted the integration of schools and facilities. Many of these conservative advocates of the status quo rallied behind the images of the Confederacy and the states' rights philosophy it upheld. To many of these white southerners, the civil-rights movement stood as a second war of "northern aggression." Accordingly, in the mid-1960s organizations such as Society for the Prevention of Negroes Getting Everything (SPONGE) and other counter-protesters waved the Confederate flag and sang "Dixie" to counter the "We Shall Overcome" spirit of integrationist forces at UT-Austin. Yet as the struggle for civil rights continued at the university, the anti-segregationists also attacked the images of the Old South around which white students rallied. *The Daily Texan* noted the parallels to the Confederacy during April 1965, the centennial of the South's surrender in the Civil War. Stories and editorials discussed how the South was undergoing a "Second Reconstruction Era" on the hundredth anniversary of Appomattox. Students criticized the university's perpetuation of the "racist tradition of the South" and urged others to unite against the "myopic Confederate pomposity" of white supremacy.[54]

By the American bicentennial celebration, the activist movement of the sixties, which included aspects of the counterculture and antiwar protests, waned significantly, a trend that was only exacerbated by the "Reagan Revolution" of the 1980s. During this decade the conservative backlash against left-leaning students, their organizations, and their agendas polarized the student body at UT-Austin as organizations like the White Students' Association challenged the legacy of the counterculture. New student organizations like the Mexican American Youth Organization (MAYO) and the Black Student Alliance (BSA) struggled to overcome what they perceived were decades of established racism at the school. These groups—and others—advocated women's rights, gay rights, and multicultural studies at UT-Austin and protested South African apartheid and university-sponsored celebrations like Texas Independence Day because it glorified the abuse of Mexican Americans.[55]

This was the highly charged environment in which the Zeta Tau Delta and Phi Gamma Delta incidents in the spring of 1990 occurred and forced the university to deal with its legacy of insensitivity to ethnic-minority students. As the stories of fraternities using outdated and insensitive negative stereotypes circulated, additional students organized to counter these remaining relics of the South's racist past. Candlelight vigils and marches marked some of the student activism following the events at Round-Up. Yet conservative white students resisted what they perceived was an attack on their history and their heritage. In one instance Greg Smith, a student at the university and member of the Chi Phi Fraternity, caused an uproar at a BSA march when he held a sign that read "Keep Sambo." Even though Smith eventually quit Chi Phi to avoid drawing additional ire to the fraternity, his unwanted notoriety led him and others to charge that too much was "already given" to minorities. Smith argued that he and others were "tired of hearing a small, vocal group of blacks . . . complain about the supposed inequalities" in America. Later that year university officials suspended the two fraternities, but student angst continued. Especially troubling to minority students was the meaning of the Confederate statues that lurked amid the large oak trees on South Mall. Students at UT-Austin, which was now more diverse than ever, openly questioned the legitimacy of statues of men who were not directly tied to the university, who supported slavery, and who championed the segregation of blacks and other minorities. This antiracism movement proved so great that Dr. Tom Philpott, a history professor at the university since the early 1970s, claimed that he had "never seen as much life in the students" in his nearly twenty years on campus.[56]

University students continued to protest the Confederate statues well after the spring of 1990, the discourse carrying over to the following year when Democratic representative Sam Hudson from Dallas sponsored a bill urging their immediate removal from campus. Hudson, who had joined students on their April 1990 protest march against racism, believed the Davis statue in particular "could be recognized in other places rather than on that campus." But after more than an hour of testimony from students and Texas citizens, the legislature buried the bill in subcommittee. The whirlwind over the six statues did not die with the stalled bill, though, and minority students continued to agitate for greater sensitivity to their heritage and their past.[57]

But university officials soon seemed to have found a safety valve. Ever since September 1989, a group of students had sought support for erecting a statue for civil rights leader Martin Luther King on campus. Becky Helton, the group's founder, criticized the university for not giving its full-fledged support despite two years of lobbying efforts. But in the wake of the April 1990 incidents, plans for a King statue were approved on December 7, and construction commenced the following spring. Financial shortfalls and other problems delayed the unveiling until September 1999. But if university officials hoped this would finally ease the student angst that had marked the early nineties, they were mistaken. Soon after the statue was unveiled on the East Mall, vandals attacked the monument on several occasions. This proved so troublesome that Dr. Larry R. Faulkner, president of UT-Austin, created the Task Force on Racial Respect and

Fairness to investigate the situation. Among their recommendations, which were released on January 2004, the committee urged the relocation of Littlefield's Confederate statues in order to include more racially diverse figures on the South Mall. Incoming president Larry Faulkner responded to this report in May. Faulkner questioned whether any committee could challenge the artistic value of the statues and demurred from outright removal because it resembled "censorship." Among the ideas he had under consideration was putting the statues back at the originally planned site, near the Littlefield Fountain, in order to provide a broader historical significance to each piece. As students, professors, and other citizens continued to clamor for their removal, Confederate heritage groups galvanized in support of the statues.[58]

By January 2007 the issue of what to do with those Littlefield statues was still unresolved as groups from both sides continued to debate the matter. Adding fuel to the fire was Texas land commissioner Jerry Patterson, who argued for a more "balanced" view of history and accepted a donation from the Descendants of Confederate Veterans for an archive-preservation project on Confederate Heroes Day. Patterson, himself a descendant of a Rebel soldier, argued that opponents of Confederate memorials were unfamiliar with southern heritage. "All too often," he said, "the introduction of a young black man in the South [to the Confederacy and its history] is when a pickup truck blows by and a beer bottle comes flying out and on the back of the bumper is a Confederate battle flag."[59]

As students and other observers await a resolution to the debate, lost is the original purpose of the Littlefield Memorial and its controversial aspects during the 1920s and 1930s. While university officials considered returning the statues to the original position as Coppini intended, they have paid little heed to Littlefield's actual goals. Littlefield remained a southern nationalist who wielded the Lost Cause as a weapon against any dissenting opinions. While his supporters praised his generosity to the university and his benevolence to African Americans, the Austin banker remained rooted to the Old South ideology of racial superiority. Contrary to what Coppini later wrote in his autobiography, the original intent for the memorial was not to show the unity between North and South after World War I, rather Littlefield used his wealth and influence to impose his cultural and social views on a financially needy university by tying his artistic vision to more than a million dollars worth of donations. Professor Battle and university officials altered Littlefield's original design because they recognized the inherently pro-South message the memorial implied. At present UT-Austin campus has the country's largest homage to the Confederacy in a major public institution. What those statues stand for is a reminder of what Littlefield had always wanted: a positive interpretation of the Old South and its social values. As neo-Confederate groups and other advocates argue that the statues stand as symbols of the South's heritage of states' rights and individual sovereignty, they fail to note that the revered heroes themselves would have had no qualms about admitting that they supported the subjugation of African Americans.

The 1863 Exhibit, Pearce Civil War Museum,
Navarro College, Corsicana, Texas.
Courtesy Julie Holcomb

11

"Tell It Like It Was"

Texas, the Civil War, and Public History

Julie Holcomb

"We are not here to visit upon the children the sins of the fathers, but we are here to remember the causes, the incidents, and the results of the late rebellion."

—*Frederick Douglass*

"If you don't tell it like it was, it can never be as it ought to be."

—*Fred Shuttlesworth*

In April 2000 the Center for American History at the University of Texas at Austin brought together a group of experts to discuss the memoirs of José Enrique de la Peña, a Mexican army lieutenant who fought with Santa Anna at the Alamo. In his account Peña described the surrender and execution of Davy Crockett. That one passage in the nearly seven-hundred-page document generated a firestorm of controversy. Even before university alumni Thomas O. Hicks and Charles W. Tate purchased the Peña manuscript at auction for $350,000 in

1998, the manuscript's authenticity and the author's veracity were called into question. Indeed Bill Groneman, author of *Death of a Legend: The Myth and Mystery Surrounding the Death of Davy Crockett* and *Defense of a Legend: Crockett and the De La Peña Diary,* declared the Peña manuscript a forgery. The question "How did Davy die?" shaped the direction of the center's day-long symposium on the memoir.[1]

Why did it matter how Crockett died? One need only look at Robert Jenkins Onderdonk's famous painting *Fall of the Alamo* to answer that question. Or listen to "The Ballad of Davy Crockett," which sold more than ten million copies in the mid-1950s. One of the strongest images of the Alamo story is that of Crockett fighting to the death using his rifle as a club. This legend, as journalist Gregory Curtis noted in 2000, "was part of the state's sacred legend. After December 1954, the Texas version and the Disney version coalesced and became the only version for those who believe in Davy." Thus to say that Crockett surrendered and was later executed at Santa Anna's order is to challenge a fundamental element of Texas history.[2]

Like the Alamo, the Civil War is part of Texas's "sacred legend." A Google search using the terms "Texas" and "Civil War" reveals hundreds of sites—some by non-Texans—all containing a range of historical accuracy and celebrating the state's role in the Civil War. The mere mention of Terry's Texas Rangers, Hood's Texas Brigade, or Granbury's Texas Brigade conjures up images of larger-than-life heroism on the battlefield and stories that straddle the border between history and legend. Slavery, if mentioned at all in these interpretations, is generally portrayed as relatively unimportant. Moreover, the Lost Cause interpretation of the Civil War—the idea that "slavery was a benign institution, that secession had been a last resort occasioned by fanatical abolitionist attacks on southern constitutional rights, and that Confederates had struggled bravely for four years to sustain those rights but finally had been beaten by a materially superior foe"—dominated interpretation at Civil War–related sites in Texas and throughout the country well into the 1970s. The centennial celebration (and it was a celebration) of the Civil War as well as the civil-rights movement failed to dislodge this perspective. Indeed, the Lost Cause interpretation has had such an influence that often it still unwittingly slips into the historical narrative at public-history sites.[3]

In the years since the Civil War centennial, the breadth and depth of historical research on the conflict has grown exponentially. Slavery has figured prominently in much of this scholarship.[4] Significantly, historians like David W. Blight and James Oliver Horton have examined not only the history of that period but also the subsequent public memory of the Civil War.[5] Unfortunately, public historians have been late to join their academic colleagues in challenging the dominance of the Lost Cause.[6] Until the 1990s most public historians avoided any discussion of the causes and consequences of the war in their institution's exhibits and program. Yet there are signs that this attitude is beginning to shift. Change is being driven by the growing body of scholarship about slavery and the Civil War, the growing number of African American history museums, the increasing emphasis on education and professionalism for public historians, and the continuing work of the American Association of Museums and other public and academic professional organizations in addressing diversity issues at museums.

Still, much remains to be done. The approaching sesquicentennial of the Civil War offers the current generation of public historians a chance to reflect on their professional practice as it relates to interpretation and public memory of the war. In doing so, however, they must not shy away from the challenge of a more inclusive historical interpretation at their Civil War–related sites. The past fifty years has seen a dramatic change in the interpretation of slavery as a cause and motivation. The next fifty years are critical to the continuing discussion of race relations in contemporary society. Those discussions will begin, for most people, at museums and historic sites. Because public historians practice their scholarship outside the confines of the classroom, they more than their academic colleagues have the opportunity to engage a broad range of citizens in discussions about the Civil War, its meaning, and its aftermath. This is particularly true for those in Texas and other former Confederate states because they daily confront the contested nature of Civil War history.

The National Park Service (NPS) has already begun the process of developing a more inclusive interpretive strategy. In 1998, at the landmark "Holding the High Ground" meeting in Nashville, Tennessee, NPS superintendents initiated a systemwide assessment of interpretation at Civil War–related national-park sites. Prior to that meeting, interpretation at such sites had focused on descriptive narration of battles and avoided any substantive analysis of the causes and consequences of the war. As a result of this conference, superintendents concluded that "battlefield interpretation must establish the site's particular place in the continuum of the war; illuminate the social, economic, and cultural issues that caused or were affected by the war; illustrate the breadth of human experience during the period; and establish the relevance of the war to people today." Congressional approval followed in 1999 along with the charge to "encourage Civil War battle sites to recognize and include in all of their public displays and multi-media presentations the unique role that the institution of slavery played in causing the Civil War and its role, if any, at the individual battle sites." In the words of retired NPS chief historian Dwight Pitcaithley, the new interpretive program "fundamentally altered" interpretation at these sites.[7]

The "Holding the High Ground" meeting developed from a partnership between the NPS and the Organization of American Historians (OAH). Beginning in the early 1990s, NPS staff worked with historians from the OAH to evaluate the park service's Civil War interpretation. Those historians determined that interpretation to that time was too narrowly focused on the military history of the war. Moreover, they suggested that the NPS expand site interpretation to "place more emphasis . . . on causes and consequences, on civilians and slaves, on meaning and significance."[8] In 2000, two years after the "Holding the High Ground" meeting, the NPS along with the National Park Foundation and Eastern National Park and Monument Association sponsored a landmark two-day symposium at Ford's Theater in Washington, D.C. "Rally on the High Ground" brought together leading scholars, park managers, interpreters, and educators to discuss new research and analysis of the Civil War period. This culminated nearly a decade of fruitful partnership between the OAH and the NPS and marked a watershed moment in NPS interpretation of the Civil War. According to Secretary of the Interior Bruce Babbitt, the NPS plan and the related congressional mandate was about "challenging [us] to find a larger view, lifting our eyes up from the din of battle, and seeing if we can enter into the lives of the participants in order to comprehend and reflect upon the causes and consequences of that struggle."[9]

But the emotional public outcry against that plan reveals the degree to which public discussion of the Civil War and its memory even today remains framed by questions of honor and heritage. Jerry Russell of HERITAGEPAC, a "lobbying group" interested in the preservation of Civil War battlefields, charged Pitcaithley and the NPS with "mov[ing] away from the 'military interpretation' of battlefields, toward a 'broader scope' of interpretation, completely ignoring the Congressional actions which established these national battlefield parks to commemorate battles." Russell described the NPS plan as a "cosmic threat to *all* battlefields in this country." The causes and consequences, he declared, "should not—*must not*—supplant the interpretation of the military actions that were the battle."[10] An article in the *Confederate Veteran,* published by the Sons of Confederate Veterans (SCV), encouraged its supporters to send preprinted postcards to the secretary of the interior protesting the NPS plan. This campaign generated nearly 2,200 cards and letters of complaint. In addition to these efforts, opponents of the plan wrote hundreds of letters to the NPS condemning the new interpretive strategy:

> It is not one of the functions of NPS to change history so that it is politically correct. When we do that, we ape the Soviet government of the 1930s through the 1960s. . . .
> Now, what I don't come to a National Battlefield Park for—to be subjected to yet another "piss-on-my-leg" story about slavery, having a not-so-thinly veiled purpose of disparaging, insulting and slandering

approximately half of the soldiers the park was built and staffed to honor.[11]

Pitcaithley draws three relevant generalizations from the outcry against the NPS plan. First, any mention of slavery in relation to the Civil War is seen as "disparaging, insulting, slandering, South-bashing propaganda." One SCV member described the proposal as an "attempt to discredit and dishonor our ancestors." Second, opponents conflated attempts to incorporate current scholarship into site interpretation with ideological objectives. According to John Coski, director of the Museum of the Confederacy, "a large segment of the American population believes that politically correct or 'revisionist' historians have hijacked history and have distorted the truth with 'context.'" Third, opponents of the NPS plan believed national battlefield parks should focus solely on the military aspects of the war: "These Great Battlefields are the only means by which we true lovers of American History can get a full understanding and complete account of what actually took place in regard to the battle and the men who fought it. Why and how these two armies got to that battlefield is irrelevant at the point of the battle. The only thing that matters at that point is WHAT happened and not why. Allow the NPS to deal only with the facts about the battle and leave the why to the educators." According to Pitcaithley, the protest against the NPS plan demonstrates an "especially striking" commitment to the "Lost Cause" interpretation of the American Civil War, noting the continued popularity of books like *The South Was Right!; Was Jefferson Davis Right?;* and *Facts the Historians Leave Out: A Confederate Primer* as evidence of a persistent selective memory of the war and its causes.[12]

In Texas similar cries of "South bashing" and "political correctness" have been heard in the debates surrounding Confederate iconography on state property. In January 2000 the Texas chapter of the National Association for the Advancement of Colored People (NAACP) began pressing Texas governor and presidential candidate George W. Bush to remove two Confederate memorial plaques from the state-supreme-court building. Gary Bledsoe, state NAACP president, called them "an unnecessary stain on our judiciary." Initially Bush disagreed, stating that the plaques should remain because the building had been paid for with funds from the Confederate pension fund. When the governor changed his mind, the SCV, the Texas Heritage Coalition, and the United Daughters of the Confederacy (UDC) mounted a public campaign against their removal. Despite an eleventh-hour lawsuit by the SCV, the plaques were removed and replaced by a new sign reading, "The courts of Texas are entrusted with providing equal justice under the law to all personas regardless of race, creed or color."[13]

This public debate initiated a simultaneous dispute about the Confederate statues on the campus of the University of Texas at Austin. Yet to date, after more than six years of study and discussion by the public, university administration, and the state legislature, the fate of those statues remains undecided. In May 2004 university president Larry Faulkner recommended a dual solution to the controversy: "1) bringing the statues together around Littlefield Fountain so as to realize the original intent of artist [Pompeo] Coppini, which was to show unity between North and South in the context of America's involvement in World War I, and 2) the creation of plaques explaining the artist's intent and putting the historical figures in context." As Faulkner explained: "There is no question that many from all races interpret some of our statues as displaying a kind of institutional nostalgia for the Confederacy and its values. Most who receive that message are repelled." But he waffled between relocation and maintaining the status quo. In a response to the University's Task Force on Racial Respect and Fairness, the president stated: "I do not believe the status quo serves the University well, nor do I see a need to maintain it. At the same time, I cannot judge that simple removal is a sound action for us. There is, for me, a tone of censorship that seems fundamentally unhealthy. Surely we can find a wiser path." In the end Faulkner did nothing, and the statues remained in place.[14]

Three years later State Rep. Sid Miller introduced House Bill 459 to expand the definition of public monuments or memorials and the protection they received. Two years earlier Miller had tried and failed to pass a similar measure, HB 946, which died in the Senate Administration Committee. According to supporters of his new measure, "HB 459 would ensure that all monuments on any type of state property, including public universities, that honor citizens of the United States be protected from arbitrary or capricious removal, relocation, or alteration in order to conform to changing conceptions of the propriety or value of those monuments." Moreover supporters of the bill noted the June 2000 removal of two Confederate plaques from the Texas Supreme Court Building as evidence that the policies of the Texas Historical Commission (THC) were inadequate and in need of strengthening. Opponents noted that HB 459 took direct aim at efforts to remove the Confederate bronzes from the Austin campus: "As inclusive institutions that serve diverse populations, universities should be able to remove or relocate monuments to reflect changing needs."[15]

Supporters and opponents of HB 459 reacted strongly. During the House debate, Rep. Beverley Wooley, who brought the measure to the floor, and Rep. Senfronia Thompson, who opposed the bill, had to be forcefully separated by other members of the House when the two women started shaking fingers and raising their voices. "I'm insulted by your bill. And I feel offended by the speaker letting this bill come to the floor," Thompson declared. Rep. David Swinford later apologized to the House for sending the measure forward. His committee had believed the bill would protect public memorials from being renamed for "big buck" givers. In the end Miller withdrew the measure and postponed further consideration of the bill until July 4, well after the end of the legislative session on May 28.[16]

The SCV, the Texas Heritage Coalition, and the UDC interpreted the removal of the plaques and the threat to the statues as yet another assault on their ancestors' honor. As SCV member Bruce Marshall said, "We are here to stop the molestation of monuments and memorials . . . we need to commemorate the courage and devotion of the fighting Confederate man." In an ironic and typical Lost Cause statement, Steve Van Roeder, a lieutenant commander in the SCV, declared, "None of those gentlemen of the statues would have said they were fighting for slavery." According to Kevin Levin, author of the blog Civil War Memory, the debate over Confederate iconography hinges on privileging one interpretation of the past over another: "The removal of the statues from the grounds to a museum sends the message that their preferred interpretation of the past is no longer valid or relevant. The defensiveness that accompanies this typically brings out the rants about liberals and political correctness rather than a more serious consideration of how public objects are now being interpreted by parties that traditionally have had little or no say in how the past is remembered." Levin supports moving the statues to a museum, "where they can be interpreted properly. There visitors can learn when and under what circumstances the statues were commissioned and dedicated, which fits perfectly into a school's mission to educate. This one it seems to me is a no-brainer."[17] Historian Sanford Levinson makes a similar argument. In a discussion of the Confederate memorial on the Texas Capitol grounds, Levinson calls for the removal of all Confederate monuments and flags on state property. Placing such racially and politically charged symbols in museums and appropriate historic sites removes any tacit or perceived approval by the state of past historical interpretations.[18] Along similar lines, John Coski argues in his landmark study of the Confederate battle flag:

> The battle over the battle flag represents one of the most intensive and extensive ongoing public dialogues about U.S. history. The debate over the proper place of the Confederate battle flag in American life is an important means by which citizens engage with the meaning of the Civil War and its legacies. More specifically, the flag debates offer a barometer of modern popular perceptions of the Confederate States of America. The Confederacy was the most important organized and armed dissent in American history since the Revolution. The conflicting attitudes

toward it reflect accurately the divergent views on constitutional and racial issues that have persisted from the nineteenth century to our own day, despite the Civil War and despite the civil rights movement.[19]

Because those issues persist today, debates about Confederate symbols offer public historians an opportunity to enter the forum and create an opportunity to discuss the contentious nature of history. Certainly Levin's suggestion to use the statues as a teaching moment is not without precedent. In 1988 the University of Oklahoma placed a marker on former DeBarr Hall, named for Ku Klux Klan leader Edwin C. DeBarr, explaining who DeBarr was and why the building was renamed. The University of Southern Mississippi renamed a building to honor Clyde Kennard, an African American who had sought admission to the all-white university during the civil rights era. While tending to business in the admissions office, someone placed illegal whiskey in Kennard's car (Mississippi was a dry state at the time). Kennard was arrested, tried, and sentenced on numerous trumped-up charges. He later developed stomach cancer while in the state penitentiary, was denied medical attention until it was too late, and released to die in a Chicago hospital in 1963. At the 1993 dedication, university president Aubrey Lucas said: "By placing [Kennard's] name on this landmark building, we're saying to the world we apologize for the indignities he suffered." James Loewen notes that when universities confront their history "fully and honestly," they "exemplify good historical practice for their students." Moreover such institutions "provide a much-needed lesson about the contentious, sometimes unpleasant, nature of truth." Cities can also create such teaching moments. For example, Waco, Texas, is attempting to redress its history of racial violence by creating the Lynching Issue Task Force, which will seek ways to publicly remember the 1916 lynching of Jesse Washington. The task force holds out hope that "by healing the wounds of our shameful legacy through acknowledgment and apology, Waco and McLennan County can end our documented history of silence."[20]

In addition, several states have issued or are considering apologies for their role in supporting slavery. At present Virginia and Maryland have already passed such legislation, while Georgia, Delaware, New York, Massachusetts, Missouri, and Vermont are considering measures. In Texas in the wake of the statue debate, Sen. Rodney Ellis and Representative Thompson began building consensus for a state apology for slavery. Moreover they want to create a commission to study the consequences of slavery. As Kristen Mack of the *Houston Chronicle* noted, "The potential cost of such an undertaking, which eventually could include the creation of museums and textbook revisions, has yet to be determined." Apology measures have generated emotion on both sides of the debate. An editorial in the *Dallas Morning News* called on the legislature to act "in good faith and inscribe a statement of regret in the public record." Speaking of her great uncle's lynching in 1905, Nona Baker of Waco said simply: "I would like to have had a little memorial service down at that bridge and maybe a plaque. But most of all, I would like an apology." King Salim Khalfani, head of the NAACP in Virginia, said of his state's measure: "You're damned right they owe an apology. They need to repair the damage." Still, not everyone agrees on the need for an apology for slavery or other past events of racial violence. Mychal Massie with the National Leadership Network of Black Conservatives believes an apology will not heal the social wounds of slavery. Virginia SCV member Frank Earnest concurs, saying: "Not every black person in this country is a descendent of slaves. Not every white person in this country is a descendent of people who owned slaves. It worsens the tensions between blacks and whites."[21]

For those on both sides of the debate, objects like memorials to Confederate leaders or the Confederate battle flag have lost their historical context. For opponents, those symbols are emblems of racism and hatred. For supporters, however, they are symbols of heritage and ancestral honor. As Coski notes in his study of the battle flag, Confederate sympathizers "are proud of their Confederate ancestors, conservative in their politics, and increasingly sensitive to what they believe are unfair attacks upon their ancestors and their values." For both Confederate and Union sympathizers, ancestry is often intimately related to honor and the reputation of not only past generations but also current and future one. Part of the problem, as Robert Penn Warren noted during the war's centennial, is that southerners and northerners have conflated causes and consequences with personal identity. The war gave the South the "Great Alibi": "Even now, any common lyncher becomes a defender of the Southern tradition, and any rabble-rouser the gallant leader of a thin gray line of heroes. . . . He turns defeat into victory, defects into virtue." In contrast the war gave the North the "Treasury of Virtue": "[T]he Republicans were ready, in 1861, to guarantee slavery in the South, as bait for a return to the Union. It is forgotten that in July, 1861, both houses of Congress, by an almost unanimous vote, affirmed that the War was waged not to interfere with the institutions of any state but only to maintain the Union."[22]

Indeed personal identity is often the basis for interest in the past. In their 1998 study of the popular uses of history, Roy Rosenzweig and David Thelen found that most Americans care about the past and are engaged in some form of hobby or collection related to history.[23] Moreover their survey reveals that people felt most connected to the past when visiting historic sites and believed museums and historic sites were among the most reliable sources of information about the past other than family members, who ranked slightly higher. For

Americans the past and ancestry are intimately linked. And that ancestry can be problematic if it includes Civil War participants, be they Confederate, Union, or African American. Ira Berlin sums up the dilemma quite well: "What makes slavery so difficult for Americans, both black and white, to come to terms with is that slavery encompasses two conflicting ideas—both with equal validity and with equal truth, but with radically different implications. One says that slavery is one of the great crimes in human history; the other says that men and women dealt with the crime and survived it and even grew strong because of it. One says slavery is our great nightmare; the other says slavery left a valuable legacy. One says death, the other life."[24]

Public historians seem to be in a "damned if you do, damned if you don't" position when it comes to Civil War–related exhibit planning. And as if that were not stressful enough, add the fiscal reality that museums must address as attendance in many institutions continues to decline. In January 2007 *America's Civil War* reported that the Museum of the Confederacy faced an uncertain future. Funding shortfalls and declining attendance had led the museum to decrease its hours of operation, suspend new exhibits, cut staff, and reduce its publication schedule. In a 2005 discussion of rural Massachusetts museums, Bruce Courson reported that many institutions had seen annual attendance drop by as much as 50 percent over the previous three decades. At his own museum, the Sandwich Glass Museum, annual attendance in the early 1980s was nearly 84,000; in 2000 the museum reported only 42,000 visitors. Urban museums have faced similar declines in recent years, according to Terry Teachout. Courson, Teachout, and others attribute a number of factors for this decline: weather, 9/11, cheap airline travel, middle-class urban emigration, and exhibit design and museum programming that have not kept up with visitor's demands.[25]

Visitor demographics and expectations have also changed in recent decades. Our society has become more racially and culturally diverse than at any time in the past. As Rosenzweig and Thelen concluded in their 1998 study, visitors seek an active and collaborative engagement with the past: "the most powerful meanings of the past come out of the dialogue between the past and the present, out of the ways the past can be used to answer pressing current-day questions about relationships, identity, immortality, and agency." The museum public insists on the opportunity to participate in the creation of the meaning of the past. Moreover, by seeking an increasingly interactive experience, visitors have eroded the curatorial authority that at one time promoted an elitist and celebratory view of the past. As David E. Kyvig notes: "Museums are the community's attic, the storage site for artifacts once created there or brought to that place for one reason or another. We may seldom visit the attic and, when we do, may find it difficult to sort through what has been preserved there, but nevertheless that is where we know to look for tangible evidence of our past." While Kyvig is describing local museums, the analogy is appropriate for Civil War museums regardless of their geographical focus or location. These institutions "allow us to connect somehow to a time, a place, or a phenomenon we desire to revisit in our mind or visit for the first time."[26]

Moreover visitors are coming to museums and historic sites with more information than ever. As one visitor noted, with the availability of information online, "I can do more pre-travel research than ever before, and pick and choose the most interesting sights." They are likely to have watched popular history programming like *History Detectives, Antiques Roadshow,* or Ken Burns's *Civil War* series. Museum visitors also have often read historical novels like *The Killer Angels* by Michael Shaara, scholarly works like *Battle Cry of Freedom* by James McPherson, or popular polemical works like *Facts the Historians Leave Out: A Confederate Primer.* At the Pearce Museum docents frequently encounter visitors who can recite encyclopedic knowledge about a battle, a regiment, a soldier, or some other aspect of the war. And as historian Ira Berlin has noted, "Slavery now has a greater presence in American life than anytime since 1865." Certainly this is reflected in the popularity of movies like *Glory, Amistad,* and *Beloved* as well as the recent PBS series *Slavery and the Making of America.* In addition, countless books like Berlin's *Many Thousands Gone: The First Two Centuries of Slavery in North America* have shaped visitors' views of slavery and the Civil War beforehand. And public historians should not discount the ongoing influence of *Gone with the Wind,* both the movie and the novel. Public historians are confronted by a literate, politically savvy visitor base, and often they find that it is easier to shrink from the challenge of addressing such a public than it is to confront the ambiguity of history.[27]

Changing demographics and increased competition for leisure time are particularly difficult challenges for public historians. As interpretation expands and evolves to enable a more diverse group of visitors to connect to "a time, a place, or a phenomenon," public historians risk losing visitors. As the debate over public Confederate memorials in Texas makes clear, Confederate sympathizers are sensitive to changes in interpretation at Civil War–related sites. They will vote with their feet, so to speak, and refuse to visit museums they feel dishonor their heritage. Moreover, inclusion does not guarantee an increase in African American attendance. As Kevin Levin has observed, despite all that historians have done to bring slavery and African Americans into the history of the Civil War, there is still a sense that the war is not part of African American history. Part of the problem is that for far too long whites have interpreted Civil War history for blacks.[28] As the Pearce Civil War Museum has learned, expanding interpretation to include African Americans and adding black-history-month programming does not automatically translate into higher numbers of African American visitors.

And the insidiousness of the Lost Cause interpretation continues to plague public historians' efforts to broaden the interpretation of the war. Despite an exhibit on slavery, the subject is still woefully underdiscussed at the Pearce Civil War Museum. Moreover, docents often unwittingly present Lost Cause messages in their tours. The state's newest Civil War–related museum, the Texas Civil War Museum in Fort Worth, presents a northern-southern account of the conflict. Yet slavery is still noticeably absent. More significantly, its motto—"Our State. Our Rights."—sends a clear message to potential visitors. In Hillsboro the well-established Confederate Research Center and Texas Heritage Museum at Hill College remains firmly and unabashedly entrenched in the Lost Cause, referring to the war as the "War between the States." And even when museums are successful in presenting a more inclusive narrative, visitors are not always receptive. As historian James Oliver Horton notes, visitors to our museums and historic sites are often "unprepared and reluctant to deal with a history that, at times, can seem very personal." Identifying slavery as the central cause of the Civil War is discomfiting for many museum visitors and public historians. Ira Berlin perceptively states: "While slavery may provide an entry point for a dialogue—a dialogue we so desperately need—on the question of race, it carries with it deep anger, resentment, indignation, and bitterness for some, along with embarrassment, humiliation, and shame for others. And here I speak of both black and white, for everyone is touched by this complex legacy of slavery." Clearly it is far easier to debate military strategy, troop movements, or brigade actions at particular battles than it is to debate the cause of the Civil War, the recruitment of black soldiers, or the reasons for the Emancipation Proclamation.[29]

Certainly that seems to be the message of the THC. The commission continues to focus on the military history of the Civil War in its literature and programs. The THC's History Programs Division is charged with "identify[ing], evaluat[ing], and interpret[ing] the historic and cultural resources of Texas." Within the division's organization, Civil War history falls under the Military Sites program, while African American history, including slavery, is managed as part of the African American Heritage program. This bifurcation of (African American) slavery and (white) Civil War (military) history only contributes to the dilemma facing public historians in Texas. More significantly, the THC's 2002 brochure *Texas in the Civil War* does not directly address slavery as the cause of the war or really even as part of Texas history: "The United States was rife with conflict and controversy in the years leading to the Civil War. Perhaps nowhere was this struggle more complex than in Texas. Some Texans supported

the Union, but were concerned about political attacks on Southern institutions."
Moreover the twenty-four-page brochure mentions slaves or slavery only seven
times. Slave life is described once in an entry about Armstead Roderick Barker,
who was owned by the Larkin family: "Armstead Roderick Barker came to Texas
as a slave of the Larkin Family in 1859. Barker was one of several enslaved
Africans who constructed the Larkins' farm and homestead." Barker's postslav-
ery life is described in redemptive terms: "Freed in 1865, he married and
became a sharecropper for his former master. By 1870, hard work enabled him
to purchase 160 acres of land." In the community listing of Civil War sites, only
one, Varner-Hogg Plantation in West Columbia, specifically identifies slavery as
part of its story.[30]

How should public historians deal with the "tough stuff of American memory"? If, as James Oliver Horton and Lois Horton tell us in *Slavery and Public
History*, so much remains to be done to overcome our historical amnesia, where
do public historians begin? Two strategies are apparent. First, public historians
need to redefine what makes a "Civil War site." Whether museum, national park,
or historic house, what narrative does that particular site tell? If, as Levin has
suggested on his blog Civil War Memory, people only visit one or two Civil War
sites in their lives, what "lessons" do public historians want those visitors to take
with them?[31] What is the greater lesson here—military strategy or a more complex understanding about the war? This step begins with public historians
taking a hard look at those core policy documents that guide museums and
archives: collecting policies, interpretive plans, and programming plans. Those
policy documents translate into a selected historical memory and ultimately
form the historical narrative that visitors encounter. Archivists and curators are
responsible for selecting, arranging, and describing the primary source materials of the past. Educators and curators use those materials to craft a particular
narrative, and docents disseminate that narrative to museum visitors. While
broadening the context of their Civil War–related sites to include slavery, public historians must remain mindful of their institutions' power to disseminate a
particular perspective. Through collection development and interpretive decisions, they hold society's power either to remember or to forget the past. The
SCV and other heritage organizations are concerned about respect for their
ancestors; however, as historian Edward T. Linenthal argues, respect comes from
complexity:

It is not my purpose, nor would it be appropriate for me to tell people
how to make sense of the sacrifice of their ancestors in the Civil War.
What I do believe is that we honor Civil War ancestors most profoundly
when we present them not as stick figures in a comforting morality play,

but as complex human beings capable of all the heroism, folly, violence, and contradictory impulses that continue to define the human condition. Restoring a richer context in which these battles are described and interpreted transforms the war into more than a bloodbath. Visitors then are allowed to reflect on participants as fully human beings with convictions that might attract us, repel us, confuse us, anger us, but ultimately leave us with an appreciation for the many reasons why they fought.[32]

Additionally these policy decisions need to be guided by the "long view," as Barbara Franco suggested at the 2006 meeting of the American Association for State and Local History, because public historians "have a responsibility to reconnect history to the concept of citizenship and to reintroduce historical literacy into education. Without a long view and an understanding of what has come before, it is almost impossible to make good decisions about the present let alone the future."[33]

Next public historians need to develop thoughtful, creative partnerships. The success of the partnership between the NPS and the OAH is a prominent example. Yet museum professionals need to look beyond their comfort zone and find other, possibly nontraditional partners. For example, the Pearce Civil War Museum has had an excellent relationship with the local SCV camp. This connection is based on both personal and professional relationships developed over the course of several years. This has led to the camp and the museum collaborating on a project to erect a state historical marker in front of the museum to commemorate the Navarro Rifles, a local regiment that served in Hood's Texas Brigade. By focusing on interpreting the history of that unit, both have been able to find a point of agreement and engagement despite their ideological differences.

Likewise, Museum of the Confederacy director John Coski has had to find such points of engagement with diverse groups. As he notes, he and his staff have "had to find and maintain balance between sensitivity to the views of a core pro-Confederate constituency and scrupulous attention to scholarship and inclusiveness." Nevertheless, the museum has become "caught up in a strong backlash among white southerners and white Americans in general against a perceived political correctness running amok in America today." Coski believes historians are guilty of maintaining a double standard and of "hold[ing] Confederate Americans and their brand of history in great contempt." Such attitudes, he argues, may be perpetuated out of fear of offending African Americans or encouraging neo-Confederates. Moreover, historians have difficulty "acknowledging fundamental agreement with some of the neo-Confederate points about Lincoln's equivocation over emancipation and his abuses of power. Failure to acknowledge this lends credibility to the neo-Confederate's argument that these are suppressed truths. The case of the watershed importance of slavery to the Confederacy and the Civil War can be made while avoiding the perception that it is a condemnation of Confederate ancestors or the promotion of a neo-Reconstructionist agenda."[34] Constructive engagement, while often limited by political passions, may hold some promise of bringing the two sides of the debate closer together.

Public historians also need to look beyond the boundaries of their profession. Too often they become caught up in their own professional organizations (such as the Society of Southwest Archivists or the Texas Association of Museums) rather than participating in organizations like the Texas State Historical Association, the Southern Historical Association, the OAH, or the American Historical Association, all of which attract academic historians. Moreover, bridging the divide between academic and public historians needs to begin with the graduate programs that train these professionals. Academic-public historical partnerships should be the norm here rather than the exception.

Historians—public and academic—may not be able to fully bridge the divide that separates Americans in their relationship to the story and continued meaning of the Civil War. But they must try because, as Kevin Levin points out, "the Civil War still matters": "as a nation we have yet to take it seriously. We've turned the war into a celebration of our collective imagination that emphasizes values that are deemed safe by white Americans. We choose to celebrate military leaders without coming to terms with the fundamental social changes that their actions wrought. And we reflect on the minutia of the battlefield completely divorced from their causes and their consequences. As the story goes, battlefields are places where white Americans sacrificed for values of equal worth—no blame, no guilt, no right or wrong."[35]

I am optimistic that some common ground can be found and believe our museums are the place to start. As former civil-rights leader Fred Shuttlesworth has said, "If you don't tell it like it was, it can never be as it ought to be."[36] Historians need to maintain their commitment to "tell it like it was" because the stakes are high. But doing so will make public historians uncomfortable, as Levin notes on Civil War Memory:

> If we are going to take the Civil War seriously we have to learn to put aside what we have traditionally been comfortable examining; in short, we have to be willing to get a little dirty. Battles were not simply slugfests between mindless pawns manipulated by disinterested generals. The evolution of the war brought about an end to slavery and the recruitment of black soldiers into the Union army. Soldiers argued about slavery and

race and many came to see on both sides of the Potomac that the war would eventually bring an end to the nation's "peculiar institution." We do a disservice to history if we do not acknowledge the centrality of race in our Civil War.

As Texas and the nation prepares for 2011 and the sesquicentennial of the Civil War, I hope my colleagues are willing to make a mess. The sesquicentennial is our chance to achieve that which eluded us in 1961. Like Levin, I hope "we take the opportunity to use our battlefields as well as scholarship to craft a more inclusive history that honors all who fought and how the founding principles that we hold so dear were brought closer to fruition."[37] Only then can we truly "tell it like it was."

Notes

Abbreviations

CAH   Center for American History, University of Texas at Austin
CCCC   County Clerk of Colorado County, Columbus, Tex.
CCDC   Colorado County District Clerk, Columbus, Tex.
NA   National Archives, Washington, D.C.
OR   U.S. War Department, *The War of the Rebellion: Official Records of the Union and Confederate Armies,* 128 vols. (Washington, D.C.: War Department, 1880–1901). All citations to series 1 unless otherwise stated.
THM   Texas Heritage Museum, Hill College, Hillsboro, Tex.
TSLAC Texas State Library and Archives Commission, Austin.

Introduction

1. *The (Corsicana, Tex.) Navarro Express,* July 18, 1861.

2. Bell I. Wiley, *The Life of Johnny Reb: The Common Solider of the Confederacy* (1943; reprint, Baton Rouge: Louisiana State University Press, 1994), and *The Life of Billy Yank: The Common Solider of the Union* (1952; reprint, Baton Rouge: Louisiana State University Press, 1994). The first significant wave of edited diaries, letters, and memoirs have included Richard Lowe, ed., *A Texas Cavalry Officer's Civil War: The Diary and Letters of James C. Bates* (Baton Rouge: Louisiana State University Press, 1999); Spurlin, *Civil War Diary of Charles Leuschner;* Jerry D. Thompson, ed., *Westward the Texans: The Civil War Journal of Private William Randolph Howell* (El Paso: University of Texas at El Paso Press, 1990), and *From Desert to Bayou: The Civil War Journal and Sketches of Morgan Wolfe Merrick* (El Paso: University of Texas at El Paso Press, 1991); E. B. Williams, *Rebel Brothers;* and Thomas Cutrer, ed., *Longstreet's Aide : The Civil War Letters of Major Thomas J. Goree* (Charlottesville: University of Virginia Press, 1995).

3. There are other works that examine the Great Hanging at Gainesville and similar topics, including McCaslin, *Tainted Breeze;* L. D. Clark, ed., *Civil War Recollections of James Lemuel Clark and the Great Hanging at Gainesville, Texas* (Plano: Republic of Texas Press, 1997); and David Pickering and Judy Falls, *Brushmen and Vigilantes: Civil War Dissent in Texas* (College Station: Texas A&M University Press, 1998).

4. No recent book examines exclusively the lives of women in Texas during the Civil War, but the closest is Rutie Winegarten, *Black Texas Women: 150 Years of Trial and Triumph* (Austin: University of Texas Press, 1995).

5. Slavery in Texas is a topic that has received a great amount of attention. The most noted examinations are Randolph B. Campbell, *An Empire for Slavery: The Peculiar Institution in Texas, 1821–1865* (Baton Rouge: Louisiana State University Press, 1989); and Alwyn Barr, *Black Texans: A History of Negroes in Texas, 1528–1971* (Austin, Tex.: Jenkins, 1973).

6. Numerous books have been written about German immigrants in Texas. The most noted are Jordan, *German Seed;* Biesele, *German Settlements in Texas;* Theodore Gish and Richard Spuler, eds., *Eagle in the New World: German Immigration to Texas and America* (College Station: Texas A&M University Press, 1986); and Goyne, *Lone Star and Double Eagle.*

7. Some works that have examined the lives of Civil War soldiers after the war include Maris A. Vinovskis, "Have Social Historians Lost the Civil War? Some Preliminary Demographic Speculations," *Journal of American History* 76 (June 1989): 34–58; Foster, *Ghosts of the Confederacy;* Gerald F. Linderman, *Embattled Courage: The Experience of Combat in the American Civil War* (New York: Macmillan, 1987); Larry M. Logue, *To Appomattox and Beyond: The Civil War Soldier in War and Peace* (Chicago: Ivan R. Dee, 1996); and Eric T. Dean Jr., *Shook over Hell: Post-Traumatic Stress, Vietnam, and the Civil War* (Cambridge, Mass.: Harvard University Press, 1997).

8. For excellent overviews of Reconstruction in Texas, see Crouch, *Freedmen's Bureau and Black Texans;* Carl H. Moneyhon, *Republicanism and Reconstruction in Texas* (Austin: University of Texas Press, 1979); and Moneyhon, *Texas after the Civil War.*

9. Some of the more notable works on history and memory include David W. Blight, *Race and Reunion: The Civil War in American Memory* (Cambridge, Mass.: Harvard University Press, 2001); James Oliver Horton and Lois Horton, eds., *Slavery and Public History: The Tough Stuff of American Memory* (New York: New Press, 2006); Robert J. Cook, *Troubled Commemoration: The American Civil War Centennial, 1961–1965* (Baton Rouge: Louisiana State University Press, 2007); Foster, *Ghosts of the Confederacy;* Gary Gallagher and Alan T. Nolan, eds., *The Lost Cause and Civil War History* (Bloomington: Indiana University Press, 2000); Thomas L. Connelly and Barbara Bellows, *God and General Longstreet: The Lost Cause and the Southern Mind* (Baton Rouge: Louisiana State University, 1982); Karen L. Cox, *Daughters of Dixie: The United Daughters of the Confederacy and the Preservation of Confederate Culture* (Gainesville: University Press of Florida, 2002); Michael Kammen, *Mystic Chords of Memory: The Transformation of Tradition in American Culture* (New York: Knopf, 1991); W. Scott Poole, *Never Surrender: Confederate Memory and Conservatism in the South Carolina Upcountry* (Athens: University of Georgia Press, 2004); Timothy B. Smith, *This Great Battlefield of Shiloh: History, Memory, and the Establishment of a Civil War National Military Park* (Knoxville: University of Tennessee Press, 2004); and John Coski, *The Confederate Battle Flag: America's Most Embattled Emblem* (Cambridge, Mass.: Harvard University Press, 2005). Some noted works that exclusively examine Texas include

Buenger, "Texas and the South"; F. A. Bailey, "Free Speech and the 'Lost Cause' in Texas"; Buenger, *Path to a Modern South;* Buenger, "'Story of Texas'?"; and Gregg Cantrell and Elizabeth Hayes Turner, eds., *Lone Star Pasts: Memory and History in Texas* (College Station: Texas A&M University, 2007).

10. Although the statues have been a topic of debate in Austin newspapers; the campus newspaper of the University of Texas at Austin, *The Daily Texan;* and *Texas Monthly* (July 2007), it has never received any scholarly analysis.

1. Texas, Jefferson Davis, and Confederate National Strategy

1. See Wooster, *Texas and Texans in the Civil War,* 257–90; and Bell, "Civil War Texas," 205–32.

2. Major studies include Archer Jones, *Civil War Command and Strategy* (New York: Free Press, 1992); Thomas L. Connelly and Archer Jones, *The Politics of Command: Factions and Ideas in Confederate Strategy* (Baton Rouge: Louisiana State University Press, 1973); Archer Jones, *Confederate Strategy from Shiloh to Vicksburg* (Baton Rouge: Louisiana State University Press, 1961); and Frank E. Vandiver, *Rebel Brass: The Confederate Command System* (Baton Rouge: Louisiana State University Press, 1956). Robert G. Tanner, *Retreat to Victory? Confederate Strategy Reconsidered* (Wilmington, Del.: SR Books, 2001), 25, briefly comments on Texas. See also Steven E. Woodworth, *Davis and Lee at War* (Lawrence: University Press of Kansas, 1995), esp. 327–33; Richard E. Beringer et al., *Why the South Lost the Civil War* (Athens: University of Georgia Press, 1986); and Herman Hattaway and Archer Jones, *How the North Won the Civil War* (Urbana: University of Illinois Press, 1983). Cogent analysis is in Woodworth, "Dismembering the Confederacy," 1–2. See also A. J. Bailey, "Abandoned Western Theater," 35–54.

3. Texas led the CSA in total livestock (combined numbers of horses, mules, cattle, and hogs) with 5,295,000 animals; Missouri was second with 3,900,000. See Lewis C. Gray, *History of Agriculture in the Southern United States to 1860,* 2 vols. (New York: Carnegie Institution, 1933), 2:1042.

4. Vandiver, "Texas and the Confederate Army's Meat Problem," 225–33; Alwyn Barr, "Texas," in *Encyclopedia of the Confederacy,* ed. Richard N. Current, 4 vols. (New York: Simon and Schuster, 1993), 4:1583–87; Barr, "Galveston," in ibid., 2:655 and passim for other states.

5. Davis inaugural, Feb. 18, 1861, in *The Papers of Jefferson Davis,* ed. Haskell M. Monroe, Lynda L. Crist, et al., 11 vols. (Baton Rouge: Louisiana State University Press, 1971–2003), 7:46–50 (quote, 47, emphasis added). The Confederate provisional constitution (art. 1, sec. 6, para. 18) simply states, "The Congress shall have power to admit other States." See Charles R. Lee Jr., *Confederate Constitutions* (Chapel Hill: University of North Carolina Press, 1963), 162.

6. Davis to the Confederate Congress, Apr. 29, 1861, in James D. Richardson, ed., *A Compilation of the Messages and Papers of the Confederacy,* 2 vols. (Nashville: United States Publishing, 1905), 1:63.

7. Editorial, Jan. 8, 16, 1862, in John M. Daniel, *The Richmond Examiner during the War* (New York: by the author, 1868), 34.

8. Richardson, *Messages and Papers,* 1:82. William J. Cooper Jr., *Jefferson Davis, American* (New York: Knopf, 2000), 353. Major biographies fail to mention Texas in relation to the development of Confederate strategy and expansion, including Cooper, *Jefferson Davis, American;* Hudson Strode, *Jefferson Davis,* 3 vols. (New York: Harcourt, Brace, & World, 1955–64); and William C. Davis, *Jefferson Davis: The Man and His Hour* (New York: HarperCollins, 1991). William C. Davis, though, is critical of the CSA for admitting *any* states west of the Mississippi River. *Jefferson Davis,* 699. The expedition into New Mexico is briefly mentioned in Herman Hattaway and Richard Beringer, *Jefferson Davis, Confederate President* (Lawrence: University Press of Kansas, 2002), 150. An exception among the biographers is Clement Eaton, who contends that Davis hoped to push Confederate boundaries into the West and therefore authorized an expedition to achieve that goal. See Eaton, *Jefferson Davis* (New York: Free Press, 1977), 187–88.

9. Jefferson Davis to Joseph Davis, June 18, 1861, in Monroe, Crist, et al., *Papers of Jefferson Davis,* 7:203; Davis, address to the Confederate Congress, Nov. 18, 1861, in ibid., 7:412–13, 414.

10. Selected historians also indicate Davis's defensive strategy. See Robert S. Henry, *The Story of Confederacy* (Indianapolis: Bobbs-Merrill, 1931), 49–50, 63, 76; E. Merton Coulter, *The Confederate States of America, 1861–1865* (Baton Rouge: Louisiana State University Press, 1950), 342–43, 346; Clement Eaton, *A History of the Southern Confederacy* (New York: Macmillan, 1954), 124–28; and Charles Roland, *The Confederacy* (Chicago: University of Chicago Press, 1960), 39–40. Departing from the consensus of Davis's strategy being only defensive but rather the "offensive-defensive" concept are Frank E. Vandiver, *Their Tattered Flags: The Epic of the Confederacy* (New York: Harper's, 1970), 88–89, 94; Vandiver, "Jefferson Davis and Confederate Strategy," in *The American Tragedy: The Civil War in Retrospect,* ed. Avery O. Craven and Frank E. Vandiver (Hampden-Sydney, Va.: Hampden-Sydney College Press, 1959), 19–32; and Emory M. Thomas, *The Confederate Nation, 1861–1865* (New York: Harper & Row, 1979), 105–8, 157–58. See also William C. Davis, *Jefferson Davis,* 373.

11. James I. Robertson Jr., *Civil War Virginia* (Charlottesville: University Press of Virginia, 1991); Emory M. Thomas, *The Confederate State of Richmond: A Biography of the Capital* (Austin: University of Texas Press, 1971); Thomas L. Connelly, *Civil War Tennessee* (Knoxville: University of Tennessee Press, 1979); John G. Barrett, *The Civil War in North Carolina* (Chapel Hill: University of North Carolina Press, 1963).

12. Davis, speech to the Senate (mentioning slave labor), Feb. 14, 1850, in *Jefferson Davis, Constitutionalist,* ed. Dunbar Rowland, 10 vols. (Jackson: Mississippi Department of Archives and History, 1923), 1:289. Davis, speeches and remarks to Senate (advocating railroad), 1858–59, in ibid., 3:363–460. On Secretary of War Davis and his keen antebellum interest in the West, see Cooper, *Jefferson Davis, American,* 244–76 (esp. 256).

13. See, for example, T. Harry Williams, "The Military Leadership of North and South," in *Why the North Won the Civil War,* ed. David Donald (Baton Rouge: Louisiana State University Press, 1960), 29–31, 35, 37; Connelly and Jones, *Politics of Command,* 24–30; Hattaway and Jones, *How the North Won,* 21–24; and Beringer et al., *Why the South Lost,* 16–20. By contrast, concluding that Jomini's works had little influence on cadets is James Morrison, *The Best School in the World: West Point, the Pre–Civil War Years* (Kent, Ohio: Kent State University Press).

14. The first American edition in English is Antoine Henri Jomini, *Summary of the Art of War,* trans. O. F. Winship and E. E. McLean (New York: Putnam, 1854), 80, 84 (quote, emphasis added), 85. Translators in an edition published during the war reversed the phrase to become *"defensive-offensive."* Jomini, *The Art of War,* trans. G. H. Mendell and W. P. Craighill (Philadelphia: J. B. Lippincott, 1862), 74.

15. For Davis's study of French, see Walter L. Fleming, "Jefferson Davis at West Point," *Publications of the Mississippi Historical Society* 10 (1909): 253; and Jefferson Davis, *The Rise and Fall of the Confederate Government,* 2 vols. (New York: D. Appleton, 1881), 1:361, 2:132–33 (emphasis added). I am grateful to William C. Davis for providing the page references to Davis's memoir.

16. R. S. Alexander, *Napoleon* (London: Arnold, 2001), 148, 162–64; Henry W. Halleck, *Elements of Military Art and Science* (New York: Appleton, 1846; reprint, Westport, Conn.: Greenwood, 1971), 46–60; Davis, speech (briefly mentioning Napoleon), Jan. 20, 1859, in Rowland, *Davis, Constitutionalist,* 3:416; Sec. of War Davis, *Annual Report,* Dec. 1, 1856, 34th Cong., 3rd sess., H. Exec. Doc. 1, serial 894, 8, 15, 16; Davis, *Annual Report,* Dec. 1, 1853, 33rd Cong., 1st sess., H. Exec. Doc. 1, serial 711, 6, 22. For Davis as general or president, see Davis to Alexander Clayton, Jan. 30, 1861, in Monroe, Crist, et al., *Papers of Jefferson Davis,* 7:28; Davis, *Rise and Fall of the Confederate Government,* 1:230; and William C. Davis, *Jefferson Davis,* 297.

17. A wide-ranging discussion of American expansion is Fred Anderson and Andrew Cayton, *The Dominion of War: Empire and Liberty in North America, 1500–2000* (New York: Viking, 2005). They do not link the concepts of expansion and "empire" to the Confederacy, as does Frazier, *Blood and Treasure.*

18. In the future Davis authorized or condoned major departures from defense. In 1862 the Confederate army moved into Maryland, a slave state that had not seceded, and in 1863 made a similar offensive movement into Pennsylvania. An offensive into Kentucky in 1862 intended to reattach the state to the CSA, not invade it.

19. Adj. Gen. Samuel Cooper to Henry H. Sibley, July 8, 1861, in U.S. War Department, *The War of the Rebellion: Official Records of the Union and Confederate Armies,* 128 vols. (Washington, D.C.: War Department, 1880–1901), ser. 1, 4:93 [hereafter cited as *OR,* with citations to series 1, unless indicated]; L. Boyd Finch, *Confederate Pathway to the Pacific: Major Sherod Hunter and Arizona Territory, C.S.A.* (Tucson: Arizona Historical Society 1996), 28–49; Ezra J. Warner, *Generals in Gray: Lives of the Confederate Commanders* (Baton Rouge: Louisiana State University Press, 1959), 276.

20. Thompson, *Henry Hopkins Sibley,* 216–18 and passim; Hall, *Sibley's New Mexico Campaign,* 3–32; Frazier, *Blood and Treasure,* 18–22, 75. See also Shelby Foote, *The Civil War: A Narrative,* 3 vols. (New York: Random House, 1958–74), 1:293–305; James W. Bellah, "The Desert Campaign," *Civil War Times Illustrated* 3 (Apr. 1961): 4–6, 24; and Stanley S. Graham, "Campaign for New Mexico, 1861–1862," *Military History of Texas and the Southwest* 10, no. 1 (1972): 5–28.

21. Sec. of War Leroy P. Walker to Davis, Apr. 27, 1861, in *OR,* ser. 4, 1:250. For pro-CSA activities in Arizona, see Attorney M. H. McWillie (also spelled Macwillie), June 30, 1861, enclosure quoted in A. T. Bledsoe, CSA War Department, to Ben McCulloch, Aug. 1, 1861, in ibid., 4:96; and Gov. Edward Clark to Philemon T. Herbert, May 16, 1861, Executive Record Book, TSLAC, microfilm reel 5.

22. Bertram Wyatt-Brown, *Southern Honor: Ethics and Behavior in the Old South* (New York: Oxford University Press, 1982).

23. William C. Davis, *Look Away! A History of the Confederate Sates of America* (New York: Free Press, 2002), 163–64. Davis clearly labels Sibley's actions an "invasion" and "imperialism." Clement Eaton also uses "invasion." *Southern Confederacy,* 40. If the offensive was not an "invasion," it was a way to get to California.

24. Joseph G. Dawson III, *Doniphan's Epic March: The 1st Missouri Volunteers in the Mexican War* (Lawrence: University Press of Kansas, 1999).

25. On the railroad see Hall, *Sibley's New Mexico Campaign,* 9; and Alberts, *Battle of Glorieta,* 8. On sympathy with the Confederacy in Colorado, see Francis J. Marshall to Davis, May 20, 1861, *OR,* 3:578–79. The strength of those Confederate sympathies was questionable. See Duane A. Smith, *The Birth of Colorado: A Civil War Perspective* (Norman: University of Oklahoma Press, 1989), 12, 18, 20, 27. For other western territories see Howard R. Lamar, *The Far Southwest, 1846–1912: A Territorial History* (New Haven, Conn.: Yale University Press, 1966), esp. 338 (for Mormons' concern over the Republican Party's anti-polygamy attitude); and Ray C. Colton, *The Civil War in the Western Territories: Arizona, Colorado, New Mexico, and Utah* (Norman: University of Oklahoma Press, 1959).

26. Trevanion T. Teel, "Sibley's New Mexico Campaign: Its Objects and the Causes of Its Failures," in *Battles and Leaders of the Civil War,* ed. Robert U. Johnson and Clarence C. Buel, 4 vols. (reprint, New York: Thomas Yoseloff, 1956), 2:700; Latham Anderson, "Canby's Services in the New Mexican Campaign," in ibid., 697–98.

27. Frazier, *Blood and Treasure,* 21.

28. Teel, "Sibley's New Mexico Campaign," 2:700. Lincoln's Inaugural, Mar. 4, 1861, in *Collected Works of Abraham Lincoln,* ed. Roy P. Basler et al., 8 vols. (New Brunswick, N.J.: Rutgers University Press, 1953–55), 4: 267–68; Gen. Edwin Sumner to Col. E. D. Townsend, Apr. 28, 1861, *OR,* 50(1):472; Sumner to Townsend, Sept. 7, 1861, ibid., 610. For the uncertainty of the situation in California, see Carl P. Schlicke, *General George Wright, Guardian of the Pacific Coast* (Norman: University of Oklahoma Press, 1988), 213–30; Ward M. McAffee,

"California's House Divided," *Civil War History* 33 (June 1987): 115–30; and Ronald C. Woolsey, "The Politics of a Lost Cause," *California History* 69 (Winter 1991): 372–83.

29. Baylor's proclamation, Aug. 1, 1861, *OR,* 4:20–23; Baylor to Brig. Gen. Earl Van Dorn, San Antonio, Aug. 14, 1861, ibid., 25; Thompson, *John Robert Baylor,* 24–34; Finch, *Confederate Pathway,* 103; Davis's proclamation, Feb. 14, 1862, in Richardson, *Messages and Papers,* 1:167. Baylor later represented Texas in the Confederate Congress. See Ezra J. Warner and W. Buck Yearns, eds., *Biographical Register of the Confederate Congress* (Baton Rouge: Louisiana State University, 1975), 19–20.

30. Drew Gilpin Faust, *The Creation of Confederate Nationalism* (Baton Rouge: Louisiana State University Press, 1988), 6, 16. See also Paul D. Escott, *After Secession: Jefferson Davis and the Failure of Confederate Nationalism* (Baton Rouge: Louisiana State University Press, 1978). Neither Faust nor Escott discuss Davis's actions regarding New Mexico or how territorial expansion might have affected Confederate nationalism. See also Beringer et al., *Why the South Lost,* 64, 66–67, 74–77; Gary W. Gallagher, *The Confederate War* (Cambridge, Mass.: Harvard University Press, 1997), 17–19, 63–111; and Harry P. Owens and James J. Cooke, eds., *The Old South in the Crucible of War* (Jackson: University Press of Mississippi, 1983).

31. Capt. Gurden Chapin to Maj. Gen. Henry W. Halleck, Feb. 28, 1862, *OR,* 9:634–35; Thompson, *Henry Hopkins Sibley,* 217. For a valuable survey of engagements in the West and a well-illustrated supplement, see Josephy, *Civil War in the American West;* and Josephy, *War on the Frontier.*

32. William E. Parrish, *Turbulent Partnership: Missouri and the Union, 1861–1865* (Columbia: University of Missouri Press, 1963); Parrish, "Missouri," in *The Confederate Governors,* ed. W. Buck Yearns (Athens: University of Georgia Press, 1985), 130–39. On the bitter guerrilla warfare that developed in Missouri, see Michael Fellman, *Inside War: The Guerrilla Conflict in Missouri during the American Civil War* (New York: Oxford University Press, 1989. Missouri and Texas were linked in an unusual way: Missouri's government in exile was located at Marshall, Texas, from November 1863 to the end of the war.

33. Abraham Lincoln to Orville H. Browning, Sept. 22, 1861, in Basler, *Collected Works of Abraham Lincoln,* 4:532; Lowell H. Harrison, *The Civil War in Kentucky* (Lexington: University of Kentucky Press, 1975); Harrison, "Kentucky," in Yearns, *Confederate Governors,* 83–90. Lincoln rejected all methods of secession and in his First Inaugural Address asserted that the Union was "perpetual." Basler, *Collected Works of Abraham Lincoln,* 4:264–65.

34. Walter L. Brown, *A Life of Albert Pike* (Fayetteville: University of Arkansas Press, 1997), 353–81. See also Lary C. Rampp and Donald L. Rampp, *The Civil War in Indian Territory* (Austin, Tex.: Presidial, 1975).

35. See the intriguing map of 1862 by George Johnson, reproduced in Finch, *Confederate Pathway,* 66.

36. The most complete cartographic representations of the Confederacy are in Kerby, *Kirby Smith's Confederacy,* 3; and D. W. Meinig, *Continental America, 1800–1867,* vol. 2 of *The Shaping of America: A Geographical Perspective on 500 Years of History,* 4 vols. (New Haven, Conn.: Yale University Press, 1986–2000), 485. These maps also show Kentucky, Missouri, and Indian Territory in the CSA. Effective representations of the Confederate West are in Frazier, *Blood and Treasure,* 35; Finch, *Confederate Pathway,* 66, end papers; Hall, *Sibley's New Mexico Campaign,* 5; Campbell, *Gone to Texas,* 251; and Jay J. Wagoner, *Arizona Territory 1863–1912: A Political History* (Tucson: University of Arizona Press, 1970), 3.

37. For examples of works with maps representing a circumscribed Confederacy, see Henry, *Story of the Confederacy,* end papers (stops western boundary near San Antonio); Clifford Dowdey, *Experiment in Rebellion* (Garden City, N.Y.: Doubleday, 1947), end papers (stops western boundary near Galveston); Coulter, *Confederate States,* foldout map following 354 (stops western boundary near Austin, Texas); Clifford Dowdey, *The Land They Fought For: The Story of the South as the Confederacy, 1832–1865* (Garden City, N.Y.: Doubleday, 1955), end papers (stops western boundary near Galveston, Texas); Roland, *Confederacy,* xiv (stops western boundary near Austin, Texas); Vandiver, *Their Tattered Flags,* end papers (stops western boundary at border of Texas and New Mexico); Thomas, *Confederate Nation,* 96–97 (stops western boundary at border of Texas and New Mexico); and Josephy, *War on the Frontier,* 2–3 (stops western boundary at border of Texas and New Mexico). Eaton, *Southern Confederacy,* and William C. Davis, *Look Away,* contain no map of the Confederate States. Maps in Roland, Vandiver, Thomas, and Josephy do not include Missouri, Kentucky, and Indian Territory in the CSA, whereas maps in Dowdey (*Land They Fought For*) and Coulter are ambiguous regarding those places.

38. Thompson, *Henry Hopkins Sibley,* 89–92, 132–33; Frazier, *Blood and Treasure,* 140, 152; Hall, *Sibley's New Mexico Campaign,* 54; Jack D. Welsh, *Medical Histories of Confederate Generals* (Kent, Ohio: Kent State University Press, 1995), 196–97. Alternatives to Sibley included West Pointers Earl Van Dorn and Paul O. Hébert.

39. Adj. Gen. Cooper to Sibley, July 8, 1861, *OR,* 4:93 (emphasis added); Sibley to Cooper, Jan. 3, 1862, ibid., 167; Thompson, *Henry Hopkins Sibley,* 216; Frazier, *Blood and Treasure,* 21, 75.

40. Sec. of War Judah P. Benjamin to Davis, Dec. [14?], 1861, *OR,* ser. 4, 1:791; Sibley to Cooper, Jan. 27, 1862, ibid., 4:169–70.

41. Williamson S. Oldham, *Rise and Fall of the Confederacy: The Memoir of Senator Williamson S. Oldham, CSA,* ed. Clayton E. Jewett (Columbia: University of Missouri Press, 2006), 147, 241.

42. Thompson, *Henry Hopkins Sibley,* 224–26; Frazier, *Blood and Treasure,* 78, 94–96.

43. Col. Henry McCulloch to Gen. Paul O. Hébert, Sept. 20, 1861, *OR,* 4:107–8.

44. Lincoln, First Inaugural, Mar. 4, 1861, in Basler, *Collected Works of Abraham Lincoln,* 4:264–66, 271.

45. Max L. Heyman Jr., *Prudent Soldier: A Biography of Major General E. R. S. Canby, 1817–1873* (Glendale, Calif.: Arthur H. Clark, 1959); Flint Whitlock, *Distant Bugles, Distant Drums: The Union Response to the Confederate Invasion of New Mexico* (Boulder: University Press of Colorado, 2006).

46. Frazier, *Blood and Treasure*, 157–80; Thompson, *Henry Hopkins Sibley*, 253–72, 305–6; Hall, *Sibley's New Mexico Campaign*, 83–108, 115–19, 225–26; John Taylor, *Bloody Valverde: A Civil War Battle on the Rio Grande* (Albuquerque: University of New Mexico Press, 1995).

47. Heyman, *Prudent Soldier*, 165–82; Capt. George H. Pettis, "The Confederate Invasion of New Mexico and Arizona," in Johnson and Buel, *Battles and Leaders*, 2:103–11; Frazier, *Blood and Treasure*, 181, 188.

48. Frazier, *Blood and Treasure*, 208–30; Thompson, *Henry Hopkins Sibley*, 279–93; Hall, *Sibley's New Mexico Campaign*, 146–63; Alberts, *Battle of Glorieta;* Taylor, *Battle of Glorieta Pass.*

49. Sibley to Cooper, Jan. 27, 1862, *OR*, 4:169–70; Hall, *Sibley's New Mexico Campaign*, 180–201; Finch, *Confederate Pathway*, 198, 221–22.

50. Aurora Hunt, *Major General James Henry Carleton, 1814–1873, Western Frontier Dragoon* (Glendale, Calif.: Arthur H. Clark, 1958), 202–5, 217, 229–33; Frazier, *Blood and Treasure*, 268; Sibley to Cooper, May 4, 1862, *OR*, 9:511–12. Thompson delivers thoughtful criticism of Sibley in *Henry Hopkins Sibley*, 301–6.

51. For example, in *Land They Fought For*, Dowdey does not mention New Mexico. Robert S. Henry includes one cryptic sentence that Sibley led a "disastrous expedition" without elaborating. *Story of the Confederacy*, 105. Briefly Charles Roland encapsulates Sibley's defeat to mean "Confederate hopes of expansion in the Southwest were gone." *Confederacy*, 54.

Single-volume histories provide varying coverage. E. Merton Coulter describes Davis's hopes for the West and provides strategic analysis that explains how New Mexico "was a prize which if secured would place the Confederacy almost on the Pacific." He concludes that Sibley's defeat "snuffed out the Territory of Arizona." *Confederate States*, 52–53. Clement Eaton offers that "[t]he Confederacy temporarily acquired two territories in the Southwest: New Mexico by force of arms, and Arizona with the cooperation of the leading inhabitants." He characterizes the Sibley expedition as "an invasion of New Mexico that resulted in the hoisting of the Confederate flag over Albuquerque and the capital, Santa Fe." Then Canby's Federals defeated Sibley and sent him in retreat to Texas. *Southern Confederacy*, 40–41. Frank Vandiver's succinct summary is one of the best: "Davis approved a bold plan of veteran General Henry H. Sibley to carry the war to the enemy in New Mexico and Arizona in February. A successful expedition from Texas might well add a vast western domain to the Confederacy and hence win diplomatic as well as military advantage," but it turned out to be "fruitless." *Their Tattered Flags*, 121, 190. Emory Thomas describes how Baylor "invaded New Mexico and claimed it for the Confederacy." Trying to support the Texan, Sibley suffered defeat and "abandoned New Mexico." *Confederate Nation*, 123–24.

The massive text that long dominated the field, James G. Randall and David H. Donald, *The Civil War and Reconstruction* (Lexington, Mass.: D. C. Heath, 1969) completely neglects Confederate military action in New Mexico. The revised edition also includes nothing on CSA expansion: David H. Donald et al., *Civil War and Reconstruction* (New York: W. W. Norton, 2001). Both William L. Barney's *Battleground for the Union* (Englewood Cliffs, N.J.: Prentice Hall, 1990) and James M. McPherson's *Ordeal by Fire* (New York: McGraw-Hill, 1982, 1992) contain no discussion of Arizona or Sibley. Likewise McPherson's *Battle Cry of Freedom* (New York: Oxford University Press, 1988) presents nothing on actions in New Mexico after secession. Among British authors, neither Peter Parish, *The American Civil War* (New York: Holmes & Meier, 1975), nor Robert Cook, *Civil War America* (New York: Longman, 2003), mentions Confederate expansion or forces in New Mexico. Allen C. Guelzo, *The Crisis of the American Republic: A History of the Civil War and Reconstruction* (New York: St. Martin's, 1995), briefly mentions the expedition. Charles Roland allocates a few sentences in *American Iliad: The Story of the Civil War,* 2nd ed. (New York: McGraw-Hill, 2002), 65. Page Smith covers events in the Southwest on one page in *Trial by Fire: A People's History of the Civil War and Reconstruction* (New York: McGraw-Hill, 1982), 29. Several strong paragraphs on Sibley, Canby, and their battles are provided in Michael Fellman et al., *This Terrible War: The Civil War and Its Aftermath* (New York: Longman, 2003), 118–20. Herman Hattaway concludes that "[t]he Confederate presence in the Far Western territory had come to naught," in *Shades of Blue and Gray* (Columbia: University of Missouri Press, 1997), 62. Insightful is Robert H. Jones, *Disputed Decades: The Civil War and Reconstruction Years* (New York: Scribner, 1973), 324–26.

Specialized, detailed works include Frazier, *Blood and Treasure;* Thompson, *Henry Hopkins Sibley;* Hall, *Sibley's New Mexico Campaign;* and Finch, *Confederate Pathway.* See also Silverman, "Confederate Ambitions for the Southwest"; and Seymour V. Connor, *Texas: A History* (Arlington Heights, Ill.: AHM Publishing, 1971), 197.

52. For a contrasting view, that Davis was not imaginative enough as president, see William Marvel, *Mr. Lincoln Goes to War* (Boston: Houghton Mifflin, 2006), xvii.

53. Davis, Second Inaugural Address, Feb. 22, 1862, in *Jefferson Davis: The Essential Writings,* ed. William C. Cooper Jr. (New York: Modern Library, 2003), 224–29 (quotes, 226, 228).

54. See art. 4, sec. 3, para. 1, in Lee, *Confederate Constitutions,* 195.

55. On plans to recapture New Orleans, possibly involving General Sibley, see George G. Shackelford, *George Wythe Randolph and the Confederate Elite* (Athens: University of Georgia Press, 1988), 128–42.

56. Rick Halperin, "Leroy Pope Walker and the Problems of the Confederate War Department, February–September 1861" (Ph.D. diss., Auburn University, 1978), 42–75; Gov. Clark to Walker, May 11, 1861, Edward Clark Papers, CAH. Barr, "Texas Coastal Defense," provides sound coverage.

57. Clark to Davis, Apr. 17, 1861, *OR,* 1:626; Clark to Texas Legislature, Nov. 1, 1861, ibid., ser. 4, 1:715; Clark to Davis, May 12, 1861, Executive Record Book, TSLAC, microfilm reel 5. Clark's actions are reflected in the communications of two aides: X. B. Debray to Sec. of War Walker, Aug. 28, 1861, *OR,* 4:98–100; and Adj. Gen. William Byrd to Henry McCulloch, Sept. 9, 1861, ibid., 104.

58. An excellent survey of Texas governors is Ralph A. Wooster, "Texas," in Yearns, *Confederate Governors,* 195–215. See also Fredericka A. Meiners, "The Texas Governorship, 1861–1865: Biography of an Office" (Ph.D. diss., Rice University, 1975).

59. Clark to legislature, Nov. 1, 1861, *OR,* ser. 4, 1:720. In 1862 the CSA also lost control of Roanoke Island, North Carolina; New Orleans; and Fernandina and Pensacola, Florida. Bern Anderson, *By Sea and By River: The Naval History of the Civil War* (New York: Knopf, 1962), 26, 34–38, 48–58, 61–64, 79–80, 124–27.

60. Thomas Waul urged Clark to "do everything to forward the great object we have in view" for Sibley's expedition. T. N. Waul to Clark, July 10, 1861, folder 22, Box 301-37, Clark Papers, Records of the Governors, TSLAC; C. W. Raines, ed., *Six Decades in Texas, or Memoirs of Francis Richard Lubbock: Governor of Texas in War-Time, 1861–1863* (Austin, Tex.: Ben C. Jones, 1900), 325–26, 329.

61. Lubbock to Davis, Jan. 27, 1862, folder 12, Box 301-39, Francis Lubbock Papers, Records of the Governors, TSLAC. Hébert's laments are found in Hébert to Sec. of War, Sept. 27, Oct. 24, 31, Nov. 15, 1861, *OR,* 4:112–13, 126–27, 130–31, 139. Lubbock indicated his concerns about protecting the coast and disappointment with the general's defensive measures. Raines, *Six Decades,* 344, 346. See also Barr, "Texas Coastal Defense."

62. Benjamin to Hébert, Feb. 23, 1862, *OR,* 15:871 (emphasis added regarding the railroad); Gov. John Gill Shorter (Alabama) to Benjamin, Mar. 4, 1862, ibid., 52(2):281–82; Benjamin to Lubbock, Mar. 17, 1862, Box 301-40, folder 21, Lubbock Papers, Records of the Governors, TSLAC. It is worth noting that Benjamin specified that troops were not to be withdrawn from the Rio Grande or western frontiers.

63. Cotham, *Battle on the Bay;* Frazier, *Cottonclads!*

64. Paul D. Casdorph, *Prince John Magruder* (New York: John Wiley, 1996), 223–35; Alwyn Barr, "The 'Queen City of the Gulf' Held Hostage," *Military History of the West* 27 (Fall 1997): 119–38 (esp. 126–27); Kerby, *Kirby Smith's Confederacy,* 165. See also Rodman L. Underwood, *Waters of Discord: The Union Blockade of Texas during the Civil War* (Jefferson, N.C.: McFarland, 2003).

65. Lubbock to Davis, Nov. 13, 1862, *OR,* 53:834; Sec. of War James A. Seddon to Lubbock, Dec. 13, 1862, ibid., 53:838.

66. A thorough account is Cotham, *Sabine Pass.* See also Muir, "Dick Dowling and the Battle of Sabine Pass," 399–428; Tolbert, *Dick Dowling at Sabine Pass;* and Wooster, *Texas and Texans in the Civil War,* 87–92.

67. John French, president of San Antonio & Mexican Railroad, to Murrah, Dec. 19, 1863, folder 9, Box 301-44, Murrah Papers, Records of the Governors, TSLAC;

Kerby, *Kirby Smith's Confederacy,* 192, 283–311; Townsend, *Yankee Invasion of Texas;* L. H. Johnson, *Red River Campaign;* Joiner, *One Damn Blunder;* J. W. Hunt, *Last Battle of the Civil War.*

68. A comprehensive treatment is Smith, *Frontier Defense in the Civil War.* See also Wooster, *Texas and Texans in the Civil War,* 32–33, 97, 105–6, 133, 170–71.

69. W. S. Oldham and John Hemphill to Walker, Mar. 30, 1861, *OR,* 1:619; Lubbock to Postmaster General John Reagan, Dec. 27, 1861, ibid., 4:161; Lubbock to Davis, Nov. 13, 1862, Mar. 27, 1863, ibid., 53:834, 852–54. Lubbock described his attention to the frontier in Raines, *Six Decades,* 463–84.

70. Smith, "Conscription and Conflict," 250–61; Roth, "Frontier Defense Challenges in Northwest Texas," 21–44.

71. Ralph A. Wooster, "Pendleton Murrah," in *Portable Handbook of Texas,* ed. Roy R. Barkely (Austin: Texas State Historical Association, 2000), 602.

72. On trade difficulties see Tyler, "Cotton on the Border," 456–77 (esp. 460–68). See also Irby, *Backdoor to Bagdad.*

73. Daddysman, *Matamoros Trade,* 35–36, 107, 121, 160, 167–68.

74. Gen. Edmund Kirby Smith to Murrah, July 5, 1864, *OR,* 53:1010–15; John Moretta, "Pendleton Murrah and States Rights in Civil War Texas," *Civil War History* 45 (June 1999): 126–46.

75. For an article covering several aspects of social and economic history beyond its title, including matters pertaining to transportation, see David C. Humphrey, "A 'Very Muddy and Conflicting' View: The Civil War as Seen from Austin, Texas," *Southwestern Historical Quarterly* 94 (Jan. 1991): 369–414.

76. Seddon to Smith, Aug. 30, 1863, *OR,* 53:894–95; Seddon to Davis, Nov. 26, 1863, ibid., ser. 4, 2:991; Governors of Louisiana, Texas, Arkansas, Missouri, and the Indian Nations to the People, Aug. 18, 1863, ibid., 53:892. See also Prushankin, *Crisis in Confederate Command,* 49–51.

77. Governors of Louisiana, Texas, Arkansas, Missouri, and the Indian Nations to the People, Aug. 18, 1863, *OR,* 53:893, 894 (emphasis added); Kerby, *Kirby Smith's Confederacy,* 198–207, 402–10; Joseph A. Parks, *General Edmund Kirby Smith, C.S.A.* (Baton Rouge: Louisiana State University Press, 1954), 311–36, 465–66. Raines, *Six Decades,* 485, 497–98; Clampitt, "The Breakup," 499–534.

78. Robert C. Black III, *Railroads of the Confederacy* (Chapel Hill: University of North Carolina Press, 1952), 4, 7, 76, 160–61, 299; Allan C. Ashcraft, "Texas, 1860–1866: The Lone Star State in the Civil War" (Ph.D. diss., Columbia University, 1960), 22–27; Coulter, *Confederate States,* 246, 270–73, 280, map following 354, 400; Sen. W. S. Oldham to Gov. Clark, Apr. 16, 1861, folder 4, Box 301-35, Edward Clark Papers, Records of the Governors, TSLAC.

79. John E. Clark, *Railroads in the Civil War* (Baton Rouge: Louisiana State University Press, 2001), 45, 90 (map); Judah Benjamin to A. L. Rives (Engineer Bureau), Feb. 22, 1862, *OR,* ser. 4, 1:947; Angus J. Johnston, *Virginia Railroads in the Civil War* (Chapel Hill: University of North Carolina Press, 1961), 183.

80. Charles P. Zlatkovich, *Texas Railroads* (Austin: University of Texas Bureau of Business Research, 1981), 5, 107.

81. Lawrence E. Estaville, *Confederate Neckties: Louisiana Railroads in the Civil War* (Ruston, La.: McGinty Publications, 1989), 5–7, 39–41, 76–80.

82. The Confederate Congress approved the construction bonds on April 19, 1862. *OR,* ser. 4, 1:1073–74; Sec. of War George W. Randolph to Jacob W. Payne, May 1, 1862; Randolph to Gen. Paul Hébert, May 5, 1862, ibid., 1:1108–9, 1113.

83. Estaville, *Confederate Neckties,* 5, 7, 76–80; Campbell, *Southern Community in Crisis,* 92–95, 213, 260.

84. The first bridge across the Mississippi came in 1874 at St. Louis, Missouri. For the lower river, Louisiana governor Huey Long planned a bridge in the 1930s.

85. Humphrey, "'Very Muddy and Conflicting' View," discusses Texans' transportation and telegraph difficulties. See also Kerby, *Kirby Smith's Confederacy,* 22, 27, 81–83, 85, 101–4.

2. Warriors, Husbands, and Fathers

1. *Annual Report of the American Historical Association for the Year 1912* (Washington, D.C.: American Historical Association, 1914), 190; Bell I. Wiley, *The Life of Johnny Reb: The Common Soldier of the Confederacy* (Indianapolis: Bobbs-Merrill, 1943). In the 1980s and 1990s, military historians called for more attention to the social aspects of the war. For examples see Edward M. Coffman, "The New American Military History," *Military Affairs* 48 (Jan. 1984): 1–5; and John A. Lynn, "The Embattled Future of Academic Military History," *Journal of Military History* 61 (Oct. 1997): 777–89. Approaching the same goal from the opposite direction, one scholar, Maris Vinovskis, has called for more research by social historians on military topics. See "Have Social Historians Lost the Civil War? Some Preliminary Demographic Speculations," *Journal of American History* 76 (June 1989): 34–58.

2. The patriarchal view is outlined in Bertram Wyatt-Brown, *Southern Honor: Ethics and Behavior in the Old South* (New York: Oxford University Press, 1982); and Catherine Clinton, *The Plantation Mistress: Women's World in the Old South* (New York: Pantheon Books, 1982). The other interpretation is in Jane Turner Censer, *North Carolina Planters and Their Children, 1800–1860* (Baton Rouge: Louisiana State University Press, 1984); Jan Lewis, *The Pursuit of Happiness: Family and Values in Jefferson's Virginia* (New York: Cambridge University Press, 1983); and Melinda S. Buza, "'Pledges of Our Love': Friendship, Love, and Marriage among the Virginia Gentry, 1800–1825," in *The Edge of the South: Life in Nineteenth-Century Virginia,* ed. Edward L. Ayers and John C. Willis (Charlottesville: University Press of Virginia, 1991), 9–36. Other noteworthy works on Southern families include Carolyn Earle Billingsley, *Communities of Kinship: Antebellum Families and the Settlement of the Cotton Frontier* (Athens: University of Georgia Press, 2004); and Joan E. Cashin, "The Structure of Antebellum Planter Families: 'The Ties that Bound us Was Strong,'" *Journal of Southern History* 56 (Feb. 1990): 55–70.

3. Robert W. Glover, ed., "The War Letters of a Texas Conscript in Arkansas," *Arkansas Historical Quarterly* 20 (Winter 1961): 356, 359–60, 364. Original

spellings and punctuation in soldiers' letters have been retained except where the original versions might cause confusion.

4. E. H. Ross to [his wife], Oct. 6, 1861, Edward Hampton Ross Letters, Wharton County Historical Museum, Wharton, Tex., available online at The Online Archive of Terry's Texas Rangers, http://www.terrystexasrangers.org/letters/ross_eh/ (accessed Mar. 23, 2007); E. H. Ross to Dear Wife, Nov. 10, 1861, Edward H. Ross File, Eighth Texas Cavalry Collection, THM; E. H. Ross to Dear wife, Nov. 23, 1861, Ross Letters.

5. S. W. Farrow to Dear Josephine, July 28, Aug. 9, 1862, Samuel Farrow Papers, CAH; A. T. Rainey to My Sweetest Little Wife, July 5, 1861, A. T. Rainey, First Texas Infantry File, THM.

6. H. A. Wallace to My Dear Wife, Sept. 16, 1862, Harvey Alexander Wallace Papers, Southwest Arkansas Regional Archives, Washington, Ark.; John M. Holcombe to Mandy, Sept. 12, Oct. 1, 1862, Mar. 15, 1862 [1863], John and Amanda Holcombe Letters, private collection of John Wilson, Playa del Rey, Calif. For similar realizations of the importance of family, see James Marten, "Fatherhood in the Confederacy: Southern Soldiers and Their Children," *Journal of Southern History* 63 (May 1997): 292.

7. Rugeley, *Batchelor-Turner Letters,* 80; W. L. Edwards to My affectionate companion, June 2, 1862, William L. Edwards, Fourth Texas Infantry File, THM. Edwards was wounded in the Battle of Gaines's Mill a few weeks later and died in a military hospital near Richmond on July 18, 1862, consoled no doubt by the expectation that he would meet his Roxie in heaven one day.

8. E. P. Becton to My Dear Mary, Aug. 12, 1862, Edwin Pinckney Becton Papers, CAH; J. S. Bryan to My Dear wife, Dec. 10, 1862, John Samuel Bryan Papers, Indiana Historical Society Library, Indianapolis; Glover, "War Letters of a Texas Conscript," 381.

9. Rugeley, *Batchelor-Turner Letters,* 24; H. A. Wallace to My Dear Wife, Sept. 16, 1862, Feb. 7, 1863, Wallace Papers.

10. Glover, "War Letters of a Texas Conscript," 364.

11. Theophilus Perry to Dear Harriet, Feb. 2, 1863, Theophilus Perry Letters, Presley Carter Person Papers, Duke University Library, Durham, N. C. An excellent annotated edition of the Perry letters is in Johansson, *Widows by the Thousand.*

12. Brown, *Journey to Pleasant Hill,* 145, 163.

13. H. A. Wallace to My Dear Wife, Feb. 22, 1863, Wallace Papers; Glover, "War Letters of a Texas Conscript," 357.

14. Granville L. Gage to Dear Wife little Children uncle & Grandmother, July 25, 1862, Grenville L. Gage, First Texas Infantry File, THM; Connor, *Dear America.*

15. John M. Holcombe to Mandy, Dec. 1, 1862, Holcombe Letters.

16. Brown, *Journey to Pleasant Hill,* 104.

17. Brown, *Journey to Pleasant Hill,* 104; E. P. Becton to My dear Mary, Feb. 24, 1863, Becton Papers.

18. Josephine Farrow to Dear Husband, June 3, 1862, Farrow Papers; Cutrer, "'Experience in Soldier's Life,'" 125; J. R. Loughridge to Mrs. Mary F. Loughridge, June 17, 1862, James Rogers Loughridge Family Papers, 1838–1972, Pearce Civil War Collection, Navarro College, Corsicana, Tex.

19. Harriet Perry to Theophilus Perry, Sept. 5, 24, Oct. 26, Dec. 3, 13, 1862, Perry Letters.

20. Harriet Perry to Theophilus Perry, Jan. 18, 1863, Dec. 23, 1862, Perry Letters.

21. E. W. Cade to Dear Wife, June 29, 1862, Edward W. and Allie Cade Correspondence, John Q. Anderson Collection, TSLAC; Allie Cade to My own loved Husband, Aug. 5, 1862, ibid.; E. P. Becton to My dear Mary, Oct. 10, Dec. 14, 1862, Becton Papers.

22. Mary [Becton] to My dear Edwin, Feb. 27, 1863, Becton Papers.

23. A convenient summary of the literature is in Marten, "Fatherhood in the Confederacy," 269–70 (quote, 270). Marten's findings also conflict directly with the older interpretation.

24. J. R. Loughridge to My dearest [wife], Aug. 12, 1861, Loughridge Family Papers; J. R. Loughridge to Little Miss Ella Loughridge, Mar. 15, 1862, ibid.; J. S. Bryan to Dear Nancy, July 13, 1862, Bryan Papers; Brown, *Journey to Pleasant Hill,* 89; R. Waterhouse to [wife], Dec. 23, 1862, Waterhouse Letters.

25. Pat H. Martin to Mrs. S. E. Truitt, Sept. 22, 1862, James W. Truitt Papers, CAH; J. R. Loughridge to Little Miss Ella Loughridge, Mar. 15, 1862, Loughridge Family Papers.

26. John M. Holcombe to Amandy, Oct. 1, Nov. 4, 1862, Holcombe Letters; D. E. Young to Dear Wife and Children, Mar. 6, 1863, D. E. Young, Seventeenth Texas Infantry File, THM; A. T. Rainey to My Dearest and Sweetest Little Wife, July 11, 1861, A. T. Rainey, First Texas Infantry File, ibid.; Glover, "War Letters of a Texas Conscript," 65.

27. T. T. Clay to Mrs. Betty Clay, Nov. 17, 1861, "The War Letters of Tacitus C. Clay," Pearce Civil War Collection, typescript; A. T. Rainey to My Own Sweet Little Wife, Aug. 8, 1861, A. T. Rainey, First Texas Infantry File, THM; E. Steele to My Dear Wife, Feb. ?, Mar. 16, 1862, E. Steele Papers, private collection of Wanda Cuniff, Nacogdoches, Tex.; E. W. Cade to Dear Wife, June 8, 18, 1862, Cade Correspondence. The dread that their children might forget them was common among Confederate soldiers. Marten, "Fatherhood in the Confederacy," 276.

28. S. W. Farrow to Dear Josephine, July 5, 1862, Farrow Papers; Glover, "War Letters of a Texas Conscript," 361, 383; John M. Holcombe to Mandy, Sept. 12, 1862, Holcombe Letters.

3. "If We Should Succeed in Driving the Enemy Back out of My Native State"

1. The purpose of this chapter is not to examine every motivation that influenced every Texan who fought east of the Mississippi River. Instead it will examine the influence of local attachments on the men's decision to enlist and fight in the

Cis-Mississippi. Obviously this influence, as with most others, does not apply to every Texan in the East. Other motivations motivated the men who enlisted, including but not limited to youthful ambitions, slavery, nationalism, adventure, honor, continuance of a profession, and religion. Not intended to supplant these ideas, this study uses Texas, the most removed state from the major battles of the Civil War, to clearly demonstrate the importance of local attachments on Southerners' decision to fight for the Confederacy. Chuck Carlock and V. M. Owens, *History of the Tenth Texas Cavalry (Dismounted) Regiment* (North Richland Hills, Tex.: Smithfield, 2001), 6; Allan C. Ashcraft, *Texas in the Civil War: A Resume History* (Austin: Texas Civil War Centennial Commission, 1962), 10; James I. Robertson, *Soldiers Blue and Gray* (Columbia: University of South Carolina, 1988), 5; James M. McPherson, *For Cause and Comrades: Why Men Fought in the Civil War* (New York: Oxford University Press, 1998), 21, 30–31, 80, 95–96; Larry J. Daniel, *Soldiering in the Army of Tennessee: A Portrait of Life in a Confederate Army* (Chapel Hill: University of North Carolina, 1991), 14; James M. McPherson, *Drawn with the Sword: Reflections on the American Civil War* (New York: Oxford University Press, 1996), 15.

　　2. Wooster, *Lone Star Regiments,* 4–6; Rainey to Wife, Aug. 8, 1861, A. T. Rainey, First Texas Infantry File, THM.

　　3. Warren Wilkinson and Steven E. Woodworth, *A Scythe of Fire: A Civil War Story of the Eighth Georgia Infantry Regiment* (New York: HarperCollins, 2002), 301–3; "Red River" Company Agreement, 1862 Collection, CAH; *Louisville Weekly Courier,* Apr. 30, 1862.

　　4. Roy R. Grinker and John P. Speigel, *Men under Stress* (Philadelphia: Blakiston, 1945), 39.

　　5. T. R. Fehrenbach, *Lone Star: A History of Texas and the Texans* (New York: Macmillan, 1968), 287, 288; Frank Owsley, *Plain Folk of the Old South* (Baton Rouge: Louisiana State University Press, 1949), 55; Llerena B. Friend, "The Texan of 1860," *Southwestern Historical Quarterly* 62 (July 1958): 2; Jordan, *German Seed,* 9, 19, 20, 29; Randolph B. Campbell and Richard G. Lowe, *Wealth and Power in Antebellum Texas* (College Station: Texas A&M University Press, 1972), 15; Buenger, *Secession and the Union in Texas,* 11.

　　6. Mark E. Nackman, *A Nation within a Nation: The Rise of Texas Nationalism* (Port Washington, N.Y.: Kennikat, 1975), 49; Allen C. Ashcraft, "Texas, 1860–1866: The Lone Star State in the Civil War" (Ph.D. diss., Columbia University, 1960), 1; Buenger, *Secession and the Union in Texas,* 8; Joseph C. G. Kennedy, *Population of the United States in 1860: Compiled Returns of the Eighth Census* (Washington, D.C.: Government Printing Office, 1864), iv, xiii, xvii, xxix, xxxiii, 616–19.

　　7. Buenger, *Secession and the Union in Texas,* 8.

　　8. *Marshall Texas Republican,* June 22, 1861. The advertisement can also be found in Davis Blake Carter, *Two Stars in the Southern Sky: General John Gregg C.S.A and Mollie* (Spartanburg, S.C.: Reprint Co., 2001), 70.

9. Randolph B. Campbell, "Fighting for the Confederacy: The White Male Population of Harrison County in the Civil War," *Southwestern Historical Quarterly* 104 (July 2000): 25.

10. Campbell, *Gone to Texas,* 247; Harold B. Simpson, ed., *Soldiers of Texas* (Waco, Tex.: Texian, 1973), 51; Harold B. Simpson, *Hood's Texas Brigade: Lee's Grenadier Guard* (Waco, Tex.: Texian, 1970), 12; Barnes F. Lathrop, *Migration into East Texas, 1835–1860: A Study from the United States Census* (Austin: Texas State Historical Association, 1949), 51; Harold B. Simpson, *Gaines' Mill to Appomattox: Waco & McLennan County in Hood's Texas Brigade* (Waco, Tex.: Texian, 1963), 32; Kathryn Hooper Davis, Linda Ericson Devereaux, and Carolyn Reeves Ericson, comps., *Texas Confederate Home Roster* (Nacogdoches, Tex.: Ericson Books, 2003). The figures provided in the paragraph came from examining Davis, Devereaux, and Ericson, *Texas Confederate Home Roster,* a source that provides details to the history of the Confederate men and women that visited for medical care.

11. George T. Todd, *First Texas Regiment* (Waco, Tex.: Texian, 1963), ix–xi; Julia L. Vivian, "Todd, George T." in *New Handbook of Texas,* ed. Ron Tyler et al., 6 vols. (Austin: Texas State Historical Association, 1996), 6:514.

12. Asa Roberts Reminiscences, Fourth Texas Infantry File, THM; Campbell, *Southern Community in Crisis,* 226; William H. Hamman, Fourth Texas Infantry, THM; James D. Roberdeau, Fifth Texas Infantry File, THM; "Captain J. D. Roberdeau," *Confederate Veteran* 18 (1910): 439; John Robert Keeling, First Texas Infantry File, THM.

13. Simpson, *Gaines' Mill to Appomattox,* 31; Donald E. Everett, ed., *Chaplain Davis and Hood's Texas Brigade* (Baton Rouge: Louisiana State University Press, 1999), 172; Civil War Diary, 1864–65, Edward Richardson Crockett Collection, CAH; Robert W. Glover, ed., *"Tyler to Sharpsburg," Robert H. and William H. Gaston: Their War Letters, 1861–1862* (Waco, Tex.: W. M. Morrison, 1960), 1.

14. Harold B. Simpson, ed., *Touched with Valor: Civil War Papers and Casualty Reports of Hood's Texas Brigade* (Hillsboro, Tex.: Hill Junior College Press, 1964), 2–4, 7, 8, 10, 11, 15.

15. B. P. Gallaway, ed., *Texas the Dark Corner of the Confederacy: Contemporary Accounts of the Lone Star State in the Civil War* (Lincoln: University of Nebraska Press, 1994), 25; Rainey to wife, Aug. 8, 1861, A. T. Rainey, First Texas Infantry File, THM; John W. Stevens, *Reminiscences of the Civil War: A Soldier in Hood's Texas Brigade, Army of Northern Virginia* (Hillsboro, Tex.: Hillsboro Mirror Print, 1902), 9; John W. Spencer, *The Confederate Guns of Navarro County* (Corsicana: Texas Press, 1986), 2; Richard E. Beringer et al., *Why the South Lost the Civil War* (Athens: University of Georgia Press, 1986), 108; Fehrenbach, *Lone Star,* 354; Simpson, *Touched with Valor,* 17.

16. Eddy R. Parker, ed., *Touched by Fire: Letters from Company D, 5th Texas Infantry, Hood's Brigade, Army of Northern Virginia, 1862–1865* (Hillsboro, Tex.: Hill College Press, 2000), 39.

17. Harold B. Simpson, "Hood's Texas Brigade," in Simpson, *Soldiers of Texas,* 52; Simpson, *Gaines' Mill to Appomattox,* 32; McPherson, *For Cause and Comrades,* 30–31, 44.

18. Parker, *Touched by Fire,* 89.

19. Hunter to Mrs. Dulcenia Pain Harrison Roman, Dec. 17, 1864, James T. Hunter, Fourth Texas Infantry File, THM.

20. Worsham to Mother, Sept. 24, 1863, C. S. Worsham, Fourth Texas Infantry File, THM.

21. Stephen Chicoine, "'Willing Never to Go in Another Fight': The Civil War Correspondence of Rufus King Felder of Chappell Hill," *Southwestern History Quarterly* 106 (Apr. 2003): 575–76, 587.

22. Chicoine, "'Willing Never to Go in Another Fight,'" 592.

23. Lester Newton Fitzhugh, "Terry's Texas Rangers," in Simpson, *Soldiers of Texas,* 75; Jeffrey D. Murrah, *None but Texians: A History of Terry's Texas Rangers* (Austin, Tex.: Eakin, 2001), 5, 6; "John Austin Wharton," Online Archive of Terry's Texas Rangers, http://www.terrystexasrangers.org/biographical_notes/w/wharton_ja.html (accessed Oct. 9, 2004); Kenneth W. Hobbs Jr., "Benjamin Franklin Terry," in *Ten More Texans in Gray,* ed. W. C. Dunn (Hillsboro, Tex.: Hill Junior College Press, 1980), 153; Blackburn, Giles, and Dodd, *Terry Texas Ranger Trilogy,* xi.

24. *OR,* 50(2):156; Hobbs, "Benjamin Franklin Terry," 153, 156; Simpson, *Soldiers of Texas,* 77.

25. *Dallas Herald,* May 8, 1861; Murrah, *None but Texians,* 18, 21.

26. Blackburn, Giles, and Dodd, *Terry Texas Ranger Trilogy,* 12, 100; Simpson, *Soldiers of Texas,* 79.

27. "John W. Hill to Mary Scott Hill—Sept. 30, 1861, New Orleans, La.," Online Archive of Terry's Texas Rangers, http://www.terrystexasrangers.org/letters/hill_jw/1861_09_30.htm (accessed Oct. 9, 2004).

28. Simpson, *Soldiers of Texas,* 79; Steven E. Woodworth, *Jefferson Davis and his Generals: The Failure of Confederate Command of the West* (Lawrence: University Press of Kansas, 1990) 39, 51; Davis, Devereaux, and Ericson, *Texas Confederate Home Roster.*

29. "Thomas Harrison," Online Archive of Terry's Texas Rangers, http://www.terrystexasrangers.org/biographical_notes/h/harrison_t.html (accessed Oct. 9, 2004); Blackburn, Giles, and Dodd, *Terry Texas Ranger Trilogy,* xii.

30. Blackburn, Giles, and Dodd, *Terry Texas Ranger Trilogy,* xxix, 199, 212, 215.

31. Wooster, *Lone Star Generals,* 154–55; Anne J. Bailey, "Richard Montgomery Gano," in *The Confederate General,* ed. William C. Davis, 6 vols. (N.p.: National Historical Society, 1991), 2:154–55; Jerry B. Rushford, "Apollos of the West: The Life of John Allen Gano" (M.A. thesis, Abilene Christian College, 1972), 212–13; John C. Waugh, *Sam Bell Maxey and the Confederate Indians* (Fort Worth: Ryan Place Publishers, 1995), 72; S. M. Fields, "Texas Heroes of the Confederacy," *Dallas Times Herald,* May 10, 1925; Margret Hancock Pearce, "The Gano Cabin History

and a Story from Narratives," *The Dallas Journal: Dallas Genealogical Society* 42 (Dec. 1996): 31–32; *Biographical Souvenir of the State of Texas* (Chicago: F. A. Battery, 1889), 315; *Memorial and Biographical History of Dallas County, Texas, Illus.* (Chicago: Lewis Publishing, 1892), 999; Clement A. Evans, ed., *Confederate Military History: A Library of Confederate States History . . . ,* 12 vols. (Atlanta: Confederate Publishing, 1899), 11:407; *Louisville Courier Journal,* Aug. 8, 9, 1869. All material on the Grapevine Volunteers can be found in Charles D. Grear, "For Land and Family: The Affects of Multiple Local Attachments in the Organization and Service of the Grapevine Volunteers in the Early Months of the Civil War," *Military History of the West* 33 (2003); and C. W. Raines, ed., *Six Decades in Texas, or Memoirs of Francis Richard Lubbock: Governor of Texas in War-Time, 1861–1863* (Austin, Tex.: Ben C. Jones, 1900), 341.

32. Julia K. Garrett, *Fort Worth: A Frontier Triumph* (Austin, Tex.: Encino, 1972), 197; Douglas Hale, *The Third Texas Cavalry in the Civil War* (Norman: University of Oklahoma Press, 1993), 24; Robertson, *Soldiers Blue and Gray,* 4; Fields, "Texas Heroes of the Confederacy"; Bell I. Wiley, *The Life of Johnny Reb: The Common Soldier of the Confederacy* (New York: Bobbs-Merrill, 1943), 19; muster roll of Capt. R. M. Gano's Company of Mounted Riflemen, TSLAC. Previous brief accounts about the Grapevine Volunteers state that they did not organize as a unit in the regular Confederate army until 1862.

33. Bureau of the Census, *Population Schedules of the Eighth Census of the United States, 1860,* M653 (Washington, D.C.: NA, 1967). A complete list of the states and countries that the men came from are Alabama, Arkansas, Iowa, Kentucky, Louisiana, Massachusetts, Mississippi, Missouri, Pennsylvania, Tennessee, Texas, and Germany.

34. "Personal War Record of Brigadier-General Richard Montgomery Gano," Richard Montgomery Gano Collection, Brown Special Collections Library, Abilene Christian University, Abilene, 38; *Dallas Herald,* Jan. 28, 1862.

35. Gano to Breckenridge, Apr. 8, 1862, NA Microfilm Publications, *Compiled Service Records of Confederate Soldiers Who Served in Organizations from the State of Texas* (Washington, D.C.: NA, 1960), microcopy 323, roll 192.

36. Gano to Jordon, May 9, 1862, *Compiled Service Records,* microcopy 323, roll 192.

37. As the war progressed and the Texans' homes appeared threatened after the Union victory at Pea Ridge, the temporary capture of Galveston Island, and the siege of Vicksburg, Gano and some of the remnants of the Grapevine Volunteers left the Cis-Mississippi to fight for their state. Gano assumed command of the Fifth Texas Cavalry Brigade, with the men serving as the Gano Guards, his bodyguards. In the Trans-Mississippi they fought alongside Confederate Indians and captured and destroyed $1.5 million worth of Union supplies at the Second Battle of Cabin Creek, Indian Territory. Col. R. M. Gano to Col. G. W. Brent A.A.F. and Chief of Staff of the Army of Tennessee, B. Marshall, Chief Surgeon 2nd Brigade Morgan's Division, and D. W. Mandell Surgeon Hardee's Corps Civil War, n.d., Service

Records of Confederate General and Staff Officers, M331-101, NA; Wooster, *Lone Star Generals*, 124; Cunningham to Magruder, Oct. 21, 1863, *OR*, 26(2):342.

38. E. B. Williams, *Rebel Brothers*, xii, 5, 9, 24–25, 27, 69, 80.

39. Singleton B. Bedinger, *Texas and the Southern Confederacy* (Taylor, Tex.: Merchants, 1970), 29–30; Adam Rankin Johnson, *The Partisan Rangers of the Confederate States Army* (Louisville: George G. Fetter, 1904), 1, 2, 9, 38; Wooster, *Lone Star Generals*, 195–97.

40. Johnson, *Partisan Rangers*, 38.

41. Two companies of Texans were temporarily attached to Forrest's unit. Johnson, *Partisan Rangers*, 39; Bedinger, *Texas and the Southern Confederacy*, 30; John Allen Wyeth, *That Devil Forrest: Life of General Nathan Bedford Forrest* (Baton Rouge: Louisiana State University Press, 1989), 64; Blackburn, Giles, and Dodd, *Terry Texas Ranger Trilogy*, 26; Brian Steel Wills, *The Confederacy's Greatest Cavalryman: Nathan Bedford Forrest* (Lawrence: University Press of Kansas, 1992), 53–55; Jack Hurst, *Nathan Bedford Forrest: A Biography* (New York: Alfred A. Knopf, 1993), 78–80.

42. Johnson, *Partisan Rangers*, 47, 48–49.

43. Johnson, *Partisan Rangers*, 52; Wills, *Confederacy's Greatest Cavalryman*, 63–64; Hurst, *Nathan Bedford Forrest*, 85.

44. Johnson, *Partisan Rangers*, 96, 97.

45. Johnson, *Partisan Rangers*, 103, 109, 118, 129; *The Austin State Gazette*, Dec. 10, 1862.

46. Johnson, *Partisan Rangers*, 133.

47. Johnson, *Partisan Rangers*, 134.

48. Johnson, *Partisan Rangers*, 32.

4. The Price of Liberty

1. This article is a condensation of McCaslin, *Tainted Breeze*. Because that volume is heavily annotated and space here is limited, only sources for quotations are provided for this chapter. It should be noted that there is an important difference in this account of the Great Hanging. In the book primary responsibility for the event was attributed to local officials. The use of new sources, specifically the letterbook of Jeremiah Y. Dashiell cited below, shifts the roles of state officials from passive observers to active participants, and so they bear more of the responsibility.

2. David J. Eddleman, "Autobiography of the [?]," Archives Division, University of North Texas Library, Denton, typescript, 24.

3. William B. Parker, *Unexplored Texas: Notes Taken during the Expedition Commanded by Capt. R. B. Marcy, U.S.A.* (Philadelphia, 1856), 84, 86–87; *Clarksville Standard*, Apr. 30, 1859; *The Texas Almanac for 1861* (New Orleans, 1860), 188.

4. *Austin Texas State Gazette*, July 28, 1860.

5. *Austin Texas State Gazette*, Feb. 2, 1861.

6. *McKinney Messenger,* Mar. 1, 1861; *Austin Texas State Gazette,* Jan. 26, 1861.

7. Hugh F. Young to Jeremiah Y. Dashiell, Mar. 10, 1862, Adjutant General's Records, TSLAC.

8. Sarah I. S. Rogers, "Memoirs," Feb. 8, 1937, Morton Museum, Gainesville, Tex., typescript, 56.

9. *Clarksville Standard,* July 7, 1862; Hugh F. Young to Dashiell, Mar. 31, 1862, Adjutant General's Records, TSLAC; Dashiell to Young, Apr. 8, 1862, ibid.; Dashiell to William R. Hudson, June 10, 1862, ibid.; Young to Francis R. Lubbock, Mar. 2, 1862, Governor's Records, TSLAC.

10. Dashiell to Hudson, Sept. 22, 30, Oct. 21, Nov. 1, 1862, Jeremiah Y. Dashiell Letterpress, 1862, Rosenberg Library, Galveston. See also Dashiell to Hudson, Sept. 22, 30, 1862, Adjutant General's Records, TSLAC; Lubbock to Paul O. Hebert, Sept. 13, 25, 1862, Governor's Records, TSLAC; Lubbock to Hudson, Sept. 25, 1862, ibid.; and James Paul to Dashiell, Sept. 30, 1862, ibid.

11. Acheson and O'Connell, *George Washington Diamond's Account of the Great Hanging,* 36–38, 40.

12. Barrett, *Great Hanging,* 8–9.

13. War Department, Compiled Service Records, Confederate States of America: 5th Texas Partisan Rangers, RG 109, NA.

14. *Clarksville Standard,* Nov. 1, 1862; *Marshall Texas Republican,* Nov. 1, 1862; *Little Rock True Democrat,* Nov. 5, 1862.

15. Dashiell to Hudson, Oct. 21, 1862, Adjutant General's Records, TSLAC; Dashiell to Hudson, Nov. 1, 1862, Governor's Records, TSLAC. Both of these letters are also in the Dashiell Letterpress at the Rosenberg Library.

16. Smith P. Bankhead to John B. Magruder, Aug. 9, 1863, *OR,* 53:888; Henry E. McCulloch to James E. Slaughter, May 28, 1864, ibid., 34(4):635.

5. The Civil War and the Lives of Texas Women

1. This chapter is a slightly edited version of Boswell, *Her Act and Deed,* chap. 5.

2. Colorado County, Texas, Seventh and Eighth Census of the United States (1850 and 1860); Lowe and Campbell, *Planters and Plain Folk,* 44, 179, 209, 258; Bill Stein, "Consider the Lily: The Ungilded History of Colorado County, Texas, Part 5," *Nesbitt Memorial Library Journal* 7 (Jan. 1997): 45; *Colorado Citizen,* Apr. 10, 1858, Oct. 27, 1859 (among others). Even though the vast majority of whites were not slaveholders, their commitment to the institution has been documented in many ways. See for instance Randolph B. Campbell, "The Slave Hire System in Texas," *American Historical Review* 93 (1988): 107–14; and Boswell, *Her Act and Deed,* chap. 3.

3. R. V. Cook in *Colorado Citizen,* Oct. 12, 1861; *Colorado Citizen,* Mar. 2, 1861. The editors' response to the representative's story was "Pretty good." See also *Colorado Citizen,* July 6, Aug. 3, 10, Sept. 14, 1861. For a discussion of the meanings of women's support and the reasons for glorifying women's sacrifices, see

Catherine Clinton, *Tara Revisited: Women, War, and the Plantation Legend* (New York: Abbeville, 1995), 139–59; and Drew Faust, "Altars of Sacrifice: Confederate Women and the Narratives of War," in *Divided Houses: Gender and the Civil War,* ed. Catherine Clinton and Nina Silber (New York: Oxford University Press, 1992), 174.

    4. *Colorado Citizen,* July 6, Aug. 3, 24, Oct. 12, 1861. For examples in other parts of the South, see Drew Gilpin Faust, *Mothers of Invention: Women of the Slaveholding South in the American Civil War* (Chapel Hill: University of North Carolina Press, 1996), 11–27; LeeAnn Whites, *The Civil War as a Crisis in Gender: August, Georgia, 1860–1890* (Athens: University of Georgia Press, 1995), 30–31, 40, 47–49; Clinton, *Tara Revisited,* 79–82; and George C. Rable, *Civil Wars: Women and the Crisis of Southern Nationalism* (Urbana: University of Illinois Press, 1989), 32.

    5. *Colorado Citizen,* Sept. 7, 1861; John Samuel Shropshire to Caroline Tait Shropshire, Sept. 28, 1861, in "Civil War Letters of John Samuel Shropshire," *Nesbitt Memorial Library Journal* 7 (Jan. 1997): 62. See also Clinton, *Tara Revisited,* 57.

    6. *Colorado Citizen,* Sept. 21, 1861; Whites, *Civil War as a Crisis in Gender,* 10–24; Rable, *Civil Wars,* 46–51, 139–142. Women were expected to repress their concern for relatives and kin for the good of the South and not only to allow them but also to encourage them to go to war. Faust, *Mothers of Invention,* 17–18; Faust, "Altars of Sacrifice," 172, 178; Clinton, *Tara Revisited,* 59.

    7. John Samuel Shropshire to Caroline Tait Shropshire, Jan. 26, 1862, in "Civil War Letters," 69. See also Joan Cashin, "'Since the War Broke Out': The Marriage of Kate and William McLure," in Clinton and Silber, *Divided Houses,* 208–12. At least in the beginning, the Civil War made very clear to women their helplessness and dependence when (at that point) they felt they had no role to play. Faust, *Mothers of Invention,* 22; Whites, *Civil War as a Crisis in Gender,* 31–37. But they knew more about running plantations than they admitted because the war was not the first time individual women had been left in charge of the plantations. Rable, *Civil Wars,* 32, 113.

    8. Rable, *Civil Wars,* 113–15; Whites, *Civil War as a Crisis in Gender,* 38; Cashin, "Since the War Broke Out," 201–12. As men were removed to battlefields, husbands and wives were made strangers to each other and to each other's lives. Faust, *Mothers of Invention,* 10.

    9. Faust, *Mothers of Invention,* 10; Cashin, "Since the War Broke Out," 200–212; Campbell, *Grass-Roots Reconstruction in Texas,* 8, 30–31; Randolph B. Campbell, *An Empire for Slavery: The Peculiar Institution in Texas, 1821–1865* (Baton Rouge: Louisiana State University Press, 1989), 231; Clinton, *Tara Revisited,* 109–14, 149–52; Whites, *Civil War as a Crisis in Gender,* 5, 62; Rable, *Civil Wars,* 91–111; Faust, "Altars of Sacrifice," 182–83.

    10. Petition, B. T. Ingram vs. E. K. Turner, Aug. 31, 1865, Docket 1810, CCDC (quote); Clinton, *Tara Revisited,* 114; Cashin, "Since the War Broke Out," 204, 208–12. Evidence exists for other soldiers from many different sources. For instance,

Beverly M. Lacy is described as having been a soldier at home on furlough in his wife's divorce petition, but he was not one of the soldiers in the four Colorado County volunteer companies. Petition, Ellen Lacy vs. Beverly M. Lacy, Sept. 7, 1865, Docket 1813, CCDC. Forty-one more soldiers from Colorado County not listed in these companies can be found in the Widow's Confederate Pension Records. These were men who served in the army and had widows who survived until at least 1899 but never remarried, remained in Colorado County, and were in destitute enough circumstances to warrant a pension. Undoubtedly there were many more who served but did not meet all of those criteria. Confederate Pensions, Colorado County, Texas, TSLAC. One-hundred and fifty-six of the men buried in existing Colorado County cemeteries were Confederate veterans, and at least four others fought in the Union army.

11. *Colorado Citizen,* Oct 12, 1861; *Colorado County Chronicles,* 79, 904; District Court Minutes, 1861–65, CCDC.

12. Clinton, *Tara Revisited,* 109; Whites, *Civil War as a Crisis in Gender,* 5.

13. Women elsewhere in the South also moved into business management or working for wages during the war. "Ladies keep the stores here now . . . their husband having joined the army." Faust, *Mothers of Invention,* 80–90.

14. Deposition, J. G. Walker vs. James A. Darby et al., Apr. 17, 1866, Docket 2032, CCDC.

15. J. G. Walker vs. James A. Darby et al., Apr. 17, 1866–Mar. 2, 1869, Docket 2032, CCDC. Although originally named as defendants, the plaintiff dismissed the case "as to V. D. Le Tulle and endorsers" before proceeding to a jury. District Court Minutes, Mar. 2, 1869, Book D, CCDC, 212.

16. Bond and Mortgage Records, Book E, Apr. 3, 1862, CCCC, 622. For seven cases see Nov. 5, 1856, Docket 1173; Apr. 18, 1857, Docket 1224; Feb. 18, 1858, Docket 1307; Apr. 19, 1858, Docket 1356; Mar. 14, 1861, Docket 1645; May 6, 1859, Docket 1425; and Jan. 28, 1860, Docket 1493, CCDC.

17. Bond and Mortgage Records, Book E, Mar. 1, 1863, CCCC, 658.

18. Deed Records Transcribed, Book L, Mar. 20, 1865, CCCC, 518.

19. Petition, Robert E. Stafford vs. Martha Pankey et al., Oct. 19, 1866, Docket 2099, CCDC.

20. Indictment, State of Texas vs. William Thompson et al., May 5, 1866, Docket 594, CCDC; Petition and Deposition, C. W. Nelson vs. William Alley, Apr. 2, 1866, Feb. 25, 1867, Docket 2040, CCDC; Williamson Simpson Oldham and George W. White, *A Digest of General Statute Laws of the State of Texas: To Which Are Subjoined the Repealed Laws of the Republic and State of Texas, by, through, under which Rights Have Accrued: Also, the Colonization Laws . . . Which Were in Force before the Declaration of Independence by Texas,* (Austin, Tex.: J. Marshall, 1859), 313.

21. Estate of Eliza Grace, Probate Final Record, Book F, Apr. 28, 1862, CCCC, 550. See also Estate of Elvy Ann Carson, Probate Final Record, Book G, Aug. 27, 1866, CCCC, 41–45.

22. Estate of Eliza Grace, Probate Final Record, Book F, April, 28, 1862, CCCC, 550.

23. Estate of C. Windrow, Probate Minutes, Book E, Aug. 25, 1862–Oct. 30, 1865, CCCC, 11, 244, 263, 264, 276, 334, 342, 348; Petition, H. F. Dunson et al. vs. Josiah F. Payne, Sept. 16, 1872, Docket 2882, CCDC; Estate of James W. Carson, Probate Minutes, Book E, Jan. 27, 1862–Oct. 20, 1865, CCCC, 220, 239, 316, 317, 343–46.

24. Estate of Jesse W. Tanner, Probate Minutes, Book E, Apr. 28, 1862, CCCC, 231; Estate of Allen Kuykendall, Probate Minutes, Book E, Apr. 27, 1863, CCCC, 277.

25. Rable, *Civil Wars,* 83–85; Clinton, *Tara Revisited,* 114–15; Petition, Maria Dungan, admx. of Frank Dungan, decd., vs. Conrad Shupp, June 4, 1867, Docket 2151, CCDC.

26. The average age of those who chose to administer (thirty-five) was higher than those who chose not to administer (twenty-eight), with the largest difference coming from those who chose to coadminister versus any other option (average age forty-eight for coadministrators, thirty-two for administrators, and twenty-eight for no administrators).

27. *Colorado Citizen,* Sept. 7, 1861; Marriage Record Index, Book D, 1861–65, CCCC. Although 1861 witnessed a record number of marriages, the number was not significantly higher than during the antebellum years. Between 1853 and 1860, the number of marriages per year averaged 42: 1853 (44), 1854 (39), 1855 (42), 1856 (32), 1857 (45), 1858 (50), 1859 (38), 1860 (43). See Marriage Record Index, Books B, C, and D, 1853–60, CCCC.

28. Petition, S. T. and J. Harbert vs. Mary Toland, May 4, 1865, Docket 1803, CCDC; Petition, M. Reichmann and Co. vs. H. L. Lackey and Louisa Odom, Sept. 22, 1865, Docket 1821, CCDC; Petition, Julia A. Curry vs. A. Cryer et al., Sept. 22, 1865, Docket 1819, CCDC; Petition, Elizabeth McAshan vs. J. S. Hancock, Mar. 19, 1866, Docket 1978, CCDC; S. E. Kuykendall vs. T. G. Schultz, July 22, 1870, Justice of the Peace Docket Book, CCDC, 104; Petition, Noah Bonds and wife vs. J. W. E. Wallace, Oct. 12, 1865, Docket 1846, CCDC; Petition, Lucy Byars vs. B. M. Lacey et al., Oct. 17, 1865, Docket 1862, CCDC; Petition, Mary A. Taylor vs. Jno C. Slaton et al., Oct. 8, 1866, Docket 2081, CCDC; Estate of Sarah A. Mason, decd., Probate Minutes, Book E, Mar. 31, 1862, CCCC, 230.

29. Petition, Leonora Miller vs. John D. Taylor, Aug. 22, 1865, Docket 1808, CCDC.

30. Petition, B. T. Ingram vs. E. K. Turner, Aug. 31, 1865, Docket 1810, CCDC.

31. Petition, B. T. Ingram vs. E. K. Turner, Aug. 31, 1865, Docket 1810, CCDC; Faust, *Mothers of Invention,* 51–71; Faust, "Altars of Sacrifice," 182–84; Drew Gilpin Faust, "Trying to Do a Man's Business: Gender, Violence, and Slave Management in Civil War Texas," *Gender and History* 4 (Summer 1992): 197–214; Jacqueline Jones, *Labor of Love, Labor of Sorrow: Black Women, Work, and the Family from Slavery to the Present* (New York: Basic Books, 1985), 48.

32. Rable, *Civil Wars,* 63–111; Faust, *Mothers of Invention,* 32; Whites, *Civil War as a Crisis in Gender,* 65–75, 89; Clinton, *Tara Revisited,* 79, 144–45; Faust, "Altars of Sacrifice," 193–99; Bynum, *Unruly Women,* 121, 130–50.

33. Colorado County Court Minutes, Book 2, CCCC, 424–25; Police Court Minutes Book, 1862–76, CCCC, 3–22.

34. Rable, *Civil Wars,* 51, 193–95.

35. Petition, Martha A. Conner vs. Stephen Conner, Sept. 30, 1864, Docket 1788, CCDC; Copy of marriage certificate, Martha A. Conner vs. Stephen Conner, Apr. 30, 1866, Docket 1788, CCDC. Drew Faust also found examples of conflict between the mothers and wives of absent soldiers as families combined without the presence of the one person that held them in common. Faust, *Mothers of Invention,* 37.

36. Petition, George Metz vs. Sarah Metz, Aug. 29, 1865, Docket 1807, CCDC. The couple had married in 1849. In 1865 George was sixty years old, Sarah was thirty-two. Marriage Records, Book B, CCCC; Schedule 1 (Free Inhabitants), Colorado County, Texas, Eighth Census of the United States (1860).

37. Deposition of Peninah Daniel, wife of Wm. Daniel, Oct. 24, 1865, Docket 1807, CCDC.

38. Petition, George Metz vs. Sarah Metz, Aug. 19, 1865, Docket 1807, CCDC; Bond and Mortgage Records, Book E, Dec. 8, 1856, CCCC, 96. Rumors abounded in the South about illicit affairs. See Faust, *Mothers of Invention,* 126.

39. Petition, E. H. Blum vs. Emma Blum, Mar. 12, 1862, Docket 1764, CCDC. Victoria Bynum, "Reshaping the Bonds of Womanhood: Divorce in Reconstruction North Carolina," in Clinton and Silber, *Divided Houses;* Clinton, *Tara Revisited,* 79; Bynum, *Unruly Women,* 119–20.

40. Petition, H. A. Tatum vs. Jane Tatum, Oct. 7, 1864, Docket 1790, CCDC.

41. Answer, H. A. Tatum vs. Jane Tatum, May 3, 1865, Docket 1790, CCDC.

42. Ellen Lacy sued for divorce three times before finally pursuing the case to a jury. The first two cases were dismissed when Ellen chose to believe Beverly's protestations of reform.

43. Petition, Sylvania Olds vs. Jno T. Olds, Oct. 4, 1860, Docket 1563, CCDC; Petition, Martha Richardson vs. Benjamin F. Richardson, Apr. 5, 1861, Docket 1710, CCDC; Petition, Martha Conner vs. Stephen Conner, Sept. 30, 1864, Docket 1788, CCDC; Petition, H. A. Tatum vs. Jane Tatum, Oct. 7, 1864, Docket 1790, CCDC.

44. A "breakdown in expectations about men's and women's roles" within marriage occurred during the war. When men were no longer there to perform their function of protection, relationships were often strained as women and men sought new foundations for their marriages. Faust, *Mothers of Invention,* 136; Rable, *Civil Wars,* 59–61; Cashin, "Since the War Broke Out," 206.

45. Whites, *Civil War as a Crisis in Gender,* 5; Rable, *Civil Wars,* 157–58; Faust, "Altars of Sacrifice," 198.

6. Slaves Taken to Texas for Safekeeping during the Civil War

1. Van Moore quoted in Tyler and Murphy, *Slave Narratives of Texas,* 13; "The Lone Star Flag," *Dallas Herald,* Nov. 21, 1860, 1; Baum, *Shattering of Texas Unionism,* 120.

2. Robert Delaney, "Matamoros, Port for Texas during the Civil War," *Southwestern Historical Quarterly* 58 (Apr. 1955): 473–87; Wallace, *Texas in Turmoil,* 125–27, 301; Wooster, *Texas and Texans in the Civil War,* 106–7; *Message of Gov. F. R. Lubbock to the Tenth Legislature* (Austin, Tex.: State Gazette Book and Job Office, 1863), 12–13; *Marshall Texas Republican,* June 16, 1865; Randolph B. Campbell, *An Empire for Slavery: The Peculiar Institution in Texas, 1821–1865* (Baton Rouge: Louisiana State University Press, 1989), 241.

3. Campbell, *Empire for Slavery,* 94–95, 244.

4. Records of the Comptroller of Public Accounts, Ad Valorem Tax Division, County Real and Personal Property Tax Rolls 1858, TSLAC, microfilm; Campbell, *Empire for Slavery,* app. 2, 264–67.

5. James M. McPherson, *Battle Cry of Freedom: The Civil War Era* (New York: Oxford University Press, 1988), 292; *Clarksville (Tex.) Standard,* June 22, 1861, 2; *Dallas Herald,* Oct. 16, 1861, 2.

6. Records of the Comptroller of Public Accounts, Ad Valorem Tax Division, County Real and Personal Property Tax Rolls, 1858, 1860, 1862, and 1864, TSLAC; Bureau of the Census, *Population Schedules of the Eighth Census of the United States, 1860,* Texas (Slave Schedules), microcopy 653, 1,438 rolls (Washington, D.C.: NA, 1967), roll 1312.

7. David Williams, *A People's History of the Civil War: Struggles for the Meaning of Freedom* (New York: New Press, 2005), 337; Marten, *Texas Divided,* 110; *San Antonio Weekly Herald,* Aug. 22, 1863, 2; *Houston Telegraph,* Dec. 29, 1864.

8. Luke Gournay, *Texas Boundaries: Evolution of the State's Counties* (College Station: Texas A&M University Press, 1995), 33; Samuel Augustus Mitchell, *County Map of Texas* (Philadelphia, Penn.: S. Augustus Mitchell, 1860); Williams, *People's History,* 394–410; Marten, *Texas Divided,* 112–13.

9. *Austin State Gazette,* Apr. 6, 1864, 1; and Feb. 22, 1865, 1; Elvira Boles quoted in Marten, *Texas Divided,* 113.

10. Gournay, *Texas Boundaries,* 33; James Madison Hall, "A Journal of the Civil War Period by James Madison Hall, 1860–1866," May 29, 1865, James Madison Hall Papers, CAH; Campbell, *Empire for Slavery,* 246; Carl H. Moneyhon, *The Impact of the Civil War and Reconstruction on Arkansas: Persistence in the Midst of Ruin* (Baton Rouge: Louisiana State University Press, 1994), 134–40.

11. Charles Christopher Jackson, "Grimes County," in *The New Handbook of Texas,* ed. Ron Tyler et al., 6 vols. (Austin: Texas State Historical Association, 1996), 3:344.

12. Mary Elizabeth Massey, *Refugee Life in the Confederacy* (Baton Rouge: Louisiana State University Press, 1964), 93; *Houston Tri-Weekly Telegraph,* Jan. 23,

1862; *Galveston Weekly News,* Nov. 26, 1862, 1; Dec. 17, 1862, 2; and Aug. 19, 1863, 2.

13. Col. C. J. [*sic*] Forshey, "The Exodus," *Galveston Weekly News,* Aug. 19, 1863, 2; "Caleb Goldsmith Forshey," in Tyler et al., *New Handbook of Texas,* 2:1084.

14. Forshey, "The Exodus," 2; *Galveston Weekly News,* May 27, 1863, 1; Smith Austin quoted in Campbell, *Empire for Slavery,* 243–44, 246.

15. Marten, *Texas Divided,* 112; Campbell, *Empire for Slavery,* 247–48; Hans Peter Nielson Gammel, comp., *The Laws of Texas, 1822–1897,* 10 vols. (Austin, Tex.: Gammel Book, 1898–1902), 5:484; Forshey, "The Exodus," 2; *Galveston Weekly News,* Jan. 7, 1863, 1; Massey, *Refugee Life in the Confederacy,* 232; and *Marshall Texas Republican,* Sept. 16, 1864, 2.

16. *Galveston Weekly News,* Sept. 9, 1863, 1; Hunt County Commissioners Court Minutes, Book A-2, quoted in Campbell, *Empire for Slavery,* 245.

17. Campbell, *Empire for Slavery,* 254; John Gardner McNemar to his wife "Neicy," Lafayette County, Miss., Sept. 15, 1863, and Panola County, Miss., Aug. 12, 1863, Waul's Texas Legion File, Paul Click, THM.

18. Mary Collie-Cooper, comp., "Robertson County, Texas, 1860 Census," Carnegie Center of Brazos Valley History, Bryan, Tex., typescript (July 4, 1985), 65; Bureau of the Census, *Population Schedules of the Eighth Census of the United States,* 1860, roll 1312, Texas (slave schedules), vol. 2 (307–628), Robertson County, 22, 25; "Muster Roll of State Troops of Beat No. 2, 3, & 6 of Robertson County, Tex. for July 1863," Box 3S167, Josephus Cavitt Papers, CAH; "A List of Names Liable to the Draft Beats No. 2, 3, & 6," n.d., Box 2J98, ibid.; Harvey Mitchell to Andrew J. Hamilton, Aug. 21, 1865, folder 14, box 49, Governor's Papers: Hamilton, RG 301, TSLAC.

19. "Robertson County Tax Rolls, 1836–1882," 1863, reel 1198-01, County Clerk's Office, Robertson County, Tex.; Joseph Allen Myers, "Life of Joseph Allen Myers: Written in the Month of Nov. 1927" (transcribed by William Allen Myers, Nov. 20, 2001), Bryan Public Library, Bryan, Tex., typescript, 6–8; State of Texas vs. Telephus A. Johnson, Case 401, Spring Term 1864, Book "J [452–922]," Minutes of the District Court, Robertson County, Tex., 491; Gammel, *Laws of Texas,* 5:484; Harvey Mitchell to Andrew J. Hamilton, Aug. 21, 1865, folder 14, box 49, Governor's Papers: Hamilton; Telemachus Louis Augustus Albertus Johnson, "Off the Beaten Path in Waco, Texas," http://www.barbaramartin.com/offbeatnepath.html (accessed May 30, 2005); Glenna Fourman Brundidge, *Brazos County History: Rich Past—Bright Future* (Bryan, Tex.: Family History Foundation, 1986), 98.

20. Ruth J. Hary and Janis J. Hunt, comp., "Abstract Book, 1863–1866, Brazos County Tax Assessor-Collector, Brazos County, Texas," Carnegie Center of Brazos Valley History, Bryan, Tex., typescript (n.d.) [hereafter cited as "Abstract Book"]. The 128 slaveholders enumerated in the 1860 federal slave census for Brazos County contain at least six duplications. See "1860 U.S. Census—Slave Schedules," database online at Ancestry.com (Provo, Utah: MyFamily.com, 2004) [hereafter cited as *Ancestry.com 1860*]. The original data for 1860 are from Bureau of the

Census, *Population Schedules of the Eighth Census of the United States, 1860,* M653, 1,438 rolls (Washington, D.C.: NA, 1860).

21. Section A: For Daniel E. Batte see "Danl Batt" [26 slaves owned in 1860], *Ancestry.com 1860,* Beat 2, Harrison County, Tex., M653, roll 1296, p. 451, image 343; "Daniel E. Batt by J. H. Batt (Guard.)," in "Abstract Book," 1864, 61–62; and "Daniel E. Batt by J. H. Batt, Guard.," in ibid., 1865, 126 (found online at "Daniel E. Batte," Civil War Soldiers & Sailors System, http://www.itd.nps.gov/cwss/soldiers.cfm [hereafter cited as *Soldiers & Sailors*], M227, roll 2). For William A. Bell see "Wm A. Bill [*sic*]" [9 slaves owned in 1860], *Ancestry.com 1860,* Franklin Township, Union County, Ark., M653, roll 51, p. 271, image 274; "W. A. Bell," in "Abstract Book," 1864, 59; and "List of Franklin Township Home Guard," Union County [Ark.] Court Record Book E, July 8–Oct. 23, 1861, Union County Courthouse, El Dorado, Ark, 632–43. For Louis B. Benefield see "Louis B Benefield" [1 slave owned in 1860], *Ancestry.com 1860,* Avoyelles Parish, La., M653, roll 407, image 331; and "L. B. Benefiel," in "Abstract Book," 1864, 59. For Thomas Boone see "Thomas Boone" [14 slaves owned in 1860], *Ancestry.com 1860,* Police District 4, Carroll County, Miss., M653, roll 578, p. 29, image 266; "Thomas Boone," in "Abstract Book," 1864, 59; and "Dr. Thos. Boone, agent for Sarah A. Knox," in ibid., 1864, 83. For James B. Durant see "J A Durant" [42 slaves owned in 1860], *Ancestry.com 1860,* Brazoria County, Tex., M653, roll 1289, p. 64, image 130; "J. B. Durant," "G. W. & J. B. Durant," and "Estate of J. A. Durant," in "Abstract Book," 1863, 9; and "J. B. Durant," *Soldiers & Sailors,* M227, roll 10. For Joel Evans see "Joel Evans" [58 slaves owned in 1860 in Chickasaw County, Miss.], *Ancestry.com 1860,* Columbus, Lowndes County, Miss. [notation by the enumerator in the Slave Schedules states "West Point, Miss.," indicating that Evans lived in Clay County, located between Chickasaw and Lowndes counties], M653, roll 586, p. 0, image 255; and "Joel Evans," in "Abstract Book," 1863, 12, and 1864, 71. For William H. Farner see Libbie Nolan, "The Great Civil War: Opposite Sides," *Landmark* 26 (Spring 1983): 24; Leona Postell, "Father and Son, Confederate and Federal Soldiers," *Landmark* 13 (Summer 1970): 4; "W. H. Foriner by E. C. Knox, (agt.)," in "Abstract Book," 1864, 73; and "W. H. Farner," *Soldiers & Sailors,* M227, roll 11. For Malcolm Gandy see "Malcolm Gandy" [0 slaves owned in 1860, but his father, Daniel Gandy, owned 6 slaves, and Alfred Gandy, living next door, owned 5 slaves], *Ancestry.com 1860,* Lavaca, Lavaca County, Tex., M653, roll 1299, p. 227, image 462; "M. Gandy," in "Abstract Book," 1864, 74; and "M. Gandy," *Soldiers & Sailors,* M227, roll 13. For A. C. L. Hill see "A. C. L. Hill" [11 slaves owned in 1860], *Ancestry.com 1860,* Franklin Township, Union County, Ark., M653, roll 51, p. 268, image 271; "A. C. L. Hill," in "1850 U.S. Census—Slave Schedules," database online at Ancestry.com (Provo, Utah: Generations Network, 2005) [hereafter cited as *Ancestry.com 1850*], M432, roll 30, p. 284, image 562 [the original data for 1850 are from Bureau of the Census, *Seventh Census of the United States, 1850,* M423, 1,009 rolls (Washington, D.C.: NA, 1850)]; "A. C. L. Hill," in "Abstract Book," 1864, 81; and "A. C. L. Hill," in "List of Franklin Township Home Guard,"

Union County (Ark.) Court Record Book E, July 8–Oct. 23, 1861, Union County Courthouse, El Dorado, Ark., 632–43. For the Lovett brothers, Richard W., Thomas F., and William C., see "Wm C Lovett," "Richard Lovett," and "Thos. Lovett" [13, 9, and 9 slaves owned in 1860], *Ancestry.com 1860,* Franklin Township, Union County, Ark., M653, roll 51, p. 278, image 281; "R. W. Lovett," "T. F. Lovett by R. W. Lovett," and "W. A. Lovett," in "Abstract Book," 1864, 87; "W. C. Lovett," *Soldiers & Sailors,* M376, roll 14; "Thos. F. Lovett," in "List of Franklin Township Home Guard," Union County (Ark.) Court Record Book E, July 8– Oct. 23, 1861, Union County Courthouse, El Dorado, Ark., 632–43 (available online at http://www.couchgenweb.com/civilwar/ unionco.html), and "Richard Lovett," Brazos County Commissioners' Minutes Book A, Feb. 15, 1864, Brazos County Commissioners' Court, Brazos County, Tex., 124. For Thomas M. Neal see "Thomas Neal" [not found in 1860 Slave Schedules but owning more than $15,000 worth of personal property and $80,000 in real estate], *Ancestry.com 1860,* Rapides Parish, La., M653, roll 423, p. 0, image 220; and "Thos. M. Neill by B. A. Christie, agt.," in "Abstract Book," 1864, 99. For Willis C. Pollard see "Willis Pollard" [4 slaves owned in 1860], *Ancestry.com 1860,* Caddo Parish, La., M653, roll 409, p. 0, image 38; and "W. C. Pollard by T. R. Mosel[e]y," in "Abstract Book," 1864, 102. For Watson Reed see "W Reed" [24 slaves owned in 1860], *Ancestry.com 1860,* Ward 2, Claiborne Parish, La., M653, roll 410, p. 0, image 224; and "Watson Reed," in "Abstract Book," 1864, 105. For James M. Turner see "James M. Turner" [28 slaves owned in 1860], *Ancestry.com 1860,* Northern Division, Lowndes County, Ala., M653, roll 14, p. 503, image 18; "James M. Turner," in "Abstract Book," 112–13; and multiple listings for "James M. Turner" in *Soldiers & Sailors.*
Section B: For Andrew J. Allen see "A J Allen" [7 slaves owned in 1860], *Ancestry.com 1860,* Bethel, Anderson County, Tex., M653, roll 1287, p. 68, image 141; "A. J. Allen," in "Abstract Book," 1863, 1, and 1864, 57; and "Andrew J. Allen," *Soldiers & Sailors,* M227, roll 1. For John Burrows see "John Burris" [18 slaves owned in 1860], *Ancestry.com 1860,* [near Berwick Bay], St. Mary's Parish, La. [Slave Schedules]; "John Burras by R. P. McMichael, adm." in "Abstract Book," 1864, 58; and "John Burrows" (obituary), *Galveston Tri-Weekly News,* Oct. 1 1863, 1; Dec. 30, 1863, 1. For John Collins see "John Collins" [5 slaves owned in 1860], *Ancestry.com 1860,* Athens, Henderson County, Tex., M653, roll 1297, p. 17, image 36; and "John Collins," in "Abstract Book," 1863, 7, and 1864, 64. For K. David Stevens see "David Stephans" [13 slaves owned in 1860], *Ancestry.com 1860,* Franklin Township, Union County, Ark., M653, roll 51, p. 278, image 281; "K. D. Stevens by R. W. Lovett," in "Abstract Book," 1864, 107–8; and "David Stevens," *Soldiers & Sailors,* M227, roll 35.
22. Note 21, sec. A; "Malcolm Gandy," *Ancestry.com 1850,* Somerville, Morgan County, Ala., M432, roll 12, p. 275, image 410; "M. Gandy," Voter Registration Certificate 980, Lavaca County, in *An Index to the 1867 Voter Registration of Texas,* by Donaly E. Brice and John C. A. Barron, CD-ROM 1354 (Bowie, Md.: Heritage Books, 2000), 806; "Malcolm Gandy," "1870 U.S. Census—Slave Schedules,"

database online at Ancestry.com (Provo, Utah: Generations Network, 2003) [here-
after cited as *Ancestry.com 1870*], Lavaca County, Tex., M593, roll 1595, p. 504,
image 237. The original data for 1870 are from Bureau of the Census, *Ninth Census
of the United States, 1870,* M593, 1,761 rolls (Washington, D.C.: NA, 1870).

   23. Note 21, sec. A; "J. B. Durant," Registration Certificate 352, Brazos County,
in Brice and Barron, *Index to the 1867 Voter Registration,* 654; *Galveston Daily News,*
June 7, 1867, 2; Warranty Deed, James B. Durant to James Wilkerson, Dec. 3,
1869, Brazos County Deed Book N, Record of Deeds, Brazos County, Tex., 7b;
"Emma Durant" (buried Aug. 25, 1869) and "J. B. Durant" (buried June 20, 1875),
St. Andrew's Cemetery, Register 1, St. Andrew's Episcopal Church, Bryan, Tex., 118,
120; Ervin & Carr vs. J. B. Durant, Case 1353, Brazos County District Court Civil
Minutes, vol. F, Sept. 16, 1876, Office of the District Clerk, Brazos County, Tex.,
334; [James H. Batte obituary], *Bryan Weekly Eagle,* Oct. 9, 1890, 1; "Abstract
Book," 1866, 235, 236; Mary Collie-Cooper, transcriber, "Bryan City Cemetery,
Brazos County, Texas, Books 1, 2, 3, & 4" (Bryan, Tex.: Collie-Cooper Enterprises,
1987), bk. 4:21, 27; "James H. Batte," Registration Certificate 39, Brazos County,
in Brice and Barron, *Index to the 1867 Voter Registration,* 139; "Dan E. Batte,"
Registration Certificate 1172, Brazos County, in ibid.; "Local Confederate Graves,
Brazos County, Texas," http://www.geocities.com/sulrosscamp/localburied.html
(accessed May 28, 2006); James H. Batte of Brazos County, case filed on May 28,
1868, by his attorneys Hancock & West, and Daniel E. Batte of Brazos County, case
filed on Dec. 21, 1868, by his attorney W. L. Robards, in "Some Brazos County
Bankruptcy Cases: 1867–68, 1871–73" [filed in U.S. District Court for the Western
District of Texas, Austin], comp. Bill Page (2002), http://user.txcyber. com/~bga/
data/ bankruptcys.txt (accessed Mar. 17, 2007); and *Austin Weekly Republican,* June
24, 1868, 3. The three wealthiest families in Brazos County in 1864 were the
Wilson, Edrington, and Beall families. See "Abstract Book," 1864, 62, 63, 70, 117.

   24. Note 21, sec. A; Gary Duke, "Eleazer A. Jeter 1821 Panola Co. Texas," Sept.
29, 2004, http://www.ladytexian.com/TXPanola/bios/ family/ jeter1821.htm;
Libbie Nolan, "The Great Civil War: Opposite Sides," *Landmark* 26 (Spring 1983):
24; Leona Postell, "Father and Son, Confederate and Federal Soldiers," *Landmark*
13 (Summer 1970): 4; "W. C. Moseley," "T. R. Moseley," and "Daniel Moseley," in
"Abstract Book," 1864, 94–95; "S. [*sic*] B. Benefield," listed in "Oath Is a 'Must'
after War," *Bryan Daily Eagle,* June 24, 1962, Centennial Section, 9; Brazos County
District Court Civil Minutes, vol. C, Petit Jurors Spring Term, 1866, Office of the
District Clerk, Brazos County, Tex., 270; Deed, Watson Reed Sr. to Watson Reed
Jr., Walker County Deed Book, vol. "F," Apr. 19, 1966, Records of Deeds, Walker
County, Tex., 450–51; "W. H. Foriner [*sic*] by E. C. Knox, (Agent)," in "Abstract
Book," 1864, 73; "William H. Farner" and "Sallie Swindler," Nov. 5, 1863, Book B,
Vital Statistics, Marriage Records, County Clerk's Office, Brazos County, Tex., 49;
"William H. Farner" and "Sallie A. Farner" in *Brazos County 1870 Census,* comp.
Mary Collie-Cooper (Bryan, Tex.: Collie-Cooper Enterprises, 1987), no. 60 [Post
Office, Bryan], printed 30A; Richter, *Overreached on All Sides,* 51–52, 289; *San
Antonio Express,* Aug. 10, 1869, 2; *Houston Daily Times,* Aug. 5, 1869, 2.

25. Note 21, sec. A; *Bryan Weekly Eagle,* Mar. 13, 1890, 1; Mar. 20, 1890, 4; *Bryan Daily Eagle,* Apr. 8, 1897, 4; "William Augustus King" (b. Mar. 1, 1818, and d. June 28, 1858, Union County, Ark.), Descendants of Samuel Wilds, http://www.southern-style.com/wilds.htm; A. C. L. Hill of Brazos County, case filed on Apr. 1, 1868, by his attorneys Bowers and Walker, *Austin Daily Republican,* Nov. 11, 1868, 4, cited in Page, "Some Brazos County Bankruptcy Cases"; "Tom Lovett" [biographical entry] in Parker, *Historical Recollections of Robertson County,* 170; "A. C. L. Hill," *Ancestry.com 1870,* Brazos County, Tex., M593, roll 1577, p. 23; "Col A. C. L. Hill," Bryan City Cemetery, Book 4, 114; *Galveston Daily News,* Mar. 19, 1869, 3; and Aug. 16, 1881, 1; "Wm C Lavit [*sic*]" and "Thst [*sic*] F Lavit [*sic*]," *Ancestry.com 1870,* Precinct 1, Robertson County, Tex., M593, roll 1602, 189.

26. Note 21, sec. A; "Joel Evans," in "Abstract Book," 1865, 132; "Joel Evans Decd," in ibid., [after slavery abolished], 219; "Estate of Joel Evans," in ibid., 1866, 297; "Sarah Knox," *Ancestry.com 1870,* Current River, Randolph County, Ark., M593, roll 63, p. 425, image 21; "Thomas Boon," in Collie-Cooper, *Brazos County 1870 Census,* no. 128 [Post Office, Bryan], printed 64A.

27. Note 21, sec. A; "James Turner," *Ancestry.com 1870,* Crockett Township, Arkansas County, Ark., M593, roll 47, p. 27, image 55; J. M. Turner," in "Abstract Book," 1865, 171.

28. Campbell, *Southern Community in Crisis,* 393; "Notice" [by William H. Hardy], *Galveston Tri-Weekly News,* June 18, 1862, 1.

29. Note 21, sec. B; "K. D. Stevens," in "Abstract Book," 1866, 247; "John Collins," Registration Certificate 152, Henderson County, in Brice and Barron, *Index to the 1867 Voter Registration,* 471; "K. D. Stevens," Registration Certificate 58, Brazos County, in ibid., 2212; "John Burrows," Case 21A, filed on Sept. 30, 1863, Brazos County Probate Record Book E, County Clerk's Office, Brazos County, Tex., 341–42; "A. J. Allen," *Ancestry.com 1870,* Clinton, DeWitt County, Tex., M593, roll 1582, p. 227; F. W. Johnson, *History of Texas and Texans,* 3:1290.

30. Campbell, *Empire for Slavery,* 245.

31. John Gardner McNemar to his wife "Neicy," Panola County, Miss., Aug. 12, 1863, Waul's Texas Legion File, John Gardner McNemar, THM; Baum, *Shattering of Texas Unionism,* 114. In addition to the Civil War Soldiers & Sailors System, online at http://www.itd.nps.gov/cwss/soldiers.cfm, the following sources were also searched: Texas Confederate Military Service Records, compiled from muster rolls in the Texas State Archives, 1999, TSLAC, microform; and Janet B. Hewett, ed., *The Roster of Confederate Soldiers, 1861–1865,* 16 vols. (Wilmington, N.C.: Broadfoot, 1995). When the age limit for the draft was expanded to forty-five in the fall of 1862, only Joel Evans, A. C. L. Hill, Thomas Lovett, and Richard Lovett would have eligible, having been, upon their arrival in Texas in 1863, between the ages of forty-one and forty-four. By February 1864, when the age limit was extended to fifty, Louis Benefield, Richard Lovett, and Hill, being then close to or over forty-five, would have been held back for state defense in the Texas Home Guard or county militia groups.

32. Voter registration boards set up by the U.S. Army routinely barred from voting any freedman who had not yet chosen a surname. See Baum, *Shattering of Texas Unionism,* 173–74.

33. Recollection of W. A. Adair in "Early Days in Brazos Bottoms," *The Bryan Daily Eagle,* Mar. 29, 1926, 4; "J T Mills," *Ancestry.com 1860,* Beat 5, Harrison County, Tex., M653, roll 1296, p. 478, image 397; "John T. Mills," Tax Roll for 1864, "Robertson County Tax Rolls, 1836–1882," County Clerk's Office, Robertson County, Tex., microfilm, reel 1198-01.

34. "Statement of Wash Wilson," in *The American Slave: A Composite Autobiography,* ed. George P. Rawick, vol. 5, pt. 4 (Westport, Conn.: Greenwood, 1972), 195–97.

35. Crouch, *Freedmen's Bureau and Black Texans,* 57–58; Campbell, *Empire for Slavery,* 246; *New Orleans Advocate,* May 25, 1867.

36. U.S. Army, Fifth Military District, State of Texas, General Order 73, "Tabular Statement of Voters (White and Colored) Registered in Texas at Registration in 1867, and at Revision of the Lists in 1867–'68–'69; Showing also the Number (White and Colored) Stricken off the Lists. Tabular Statement of Votes (white and colored) cast at Election Held in the State of Texas, under the Authority of the Reconstruction Acts of Congress," Apr. 16, 1870, 2–5; Bureau of the Census, *Ninth Census, 1870: Population* (Washington, D.C.: Government Printing Office, 1872), table 23.

7. New Perspectives on Texas Germans and the Confederacy

1. This is a lightly revised version of an article first published in the *Southwestern Historical Quarterly* (102 [1999]: 441–55). Portions were also used in the introduction to Walter D. Kamphoefner and Wolfgang Helbich, eds., *Germans in the Civil War: The Letters They Wrote Home* (Chapel Hill: University of North Carolina Press, 2006), 15–19. The editors devote several pages (394–476) of their book to letters by Texas Germans.

2. "True to the Union," *Houston Chronicle,* Aug. 20, 1989, 4E.

3. Jordan, *German Seed.* Jordan's later work is simply a more systematic restatement of his earlier interpretations without any additional evidence. See Terry Jordan, "Germans and Blacks in Texas," in *States of Progress: Germans and Blacks in America over 300 Years,* ed. Randall Miller (Philadelphia: German Society of Pennsylvania, 1989), 89–97 (quote, 96). The beginnings of a reinterpretation were already signaled by Biesele, *German Settlements in Texas.* See also Rudolph L. Biesele, "German Attitudes toward the Civil War," in *New Handbook of Texas,* ed. Ron Tyler et al., 6 vols. (Austin: Texas State Historical Association, 1996), 3:138–39 (apparently reprinted posthumously and unrevised).

4. Jordan, *German Seed,* 106–11, 180–85; Jordan, "Germans and Blacks," 89–97; Cornelia Küffner, "Texas-Germans' Attitudes toward Slavery: Biedermeier Sentiments and Class Consciousness in Austin, Colorado, and Fayette Counties" (M.A. thesis, University of Houston, 1994), 17–20, 46–68, 110–14, 123–26. The

interpretations of Küffner's data are largely my own based on further calculations from her table 2 to more clearly reveal German-Anglo contrasts. On Texas landholdings see Jordan, *German Seed,* 115–17. For parallels in Missouri, see Walter D. Kamphoefner, *The Westfalians: From Germany to Missouri* (Princeton, N.J.: Princeton University Press, 1987), 116–17.

5. Buenger, *Secession and the Union in Texas,* 84. For Missouri parallels, see Kamphoefner, *The Westfalians,* 116–17.

6. Buenger, *Secession and the Union in Texas,* 26–33, 91–94.

7. Buenger, *Secession and the Union in Texas,* 67, 151, 174–75. Biesele's statement that Comfort had voted 42–15 and neighboring Boerne 85–6 against secession appears erroneous and exceeds the total number of votes cast in the county. *German Settlements in Texas,* 206. Cf. Bob Bennett, *Kerr County, Texas, 1856–1956* (San Antonio: Naylor, 1956), 136. Biesele may be referring to a preliminary vote held on December 22, 1860.

8. Lawrence P. Knight, "Becoming a City and Becoming American: San Antonio, Texas, 1848–1861" (Ph.D. diss., Texas A&M University, 1997), 189–200, 267–81. The rural areas of the county had a slightly lower foreign-born percentage than the city and probably more Anglos and fewer Hispanics as well.

9. *La Grange (Tex.) State Rights Democrat,* Mar. 7, 21, 1861. According to a report of November 13, 1863, in the *Neu Braunfelser Zeitung,* Grassmeyer was arrested as a traitor and taken to Houston along with four Fayette County Anglos.

10. *Bellville Countryman,* Feb. 27, Mar. 17, 1861. The issue of January 16, 1861, shows that New Ulm, which voted 36–30 for secession in February, had gone 52–1 against in a preliminary election on December 22, 1860, to elect state delegates, in which German slaveholder and secessionist Knolle came in last among six candidates, further evidence of Anglo suspicions. Despite the name, Shelby's (also known as Roeder's) Mill was a largely German settlement in the extreme northwest corner of Austin County. Biesele, *German Settlements in Texas,* 52–53.

11. Buenger, "Secession and the Texas German Community," 395–96; Selma Metzenthin-Raunick, "One Hundred Years [of the] *Neu Braunfelser Zeitung,"* *American-German Review* 19 (1953): 15–16; Karl J. R. Arndt and May E. Olson, *German-American Newspapers and Periodicals, 1732–1955,* 2nd rev. ed. (New York: Johnson Reprint, 1965), 628.

12. Buenger, *Secession and the Union in Texas,* 12, 164.

13. Arndt and Olson, *German-American Newspapers,* 628; Metzenthin-Raunick, "One Hundred Years," 15–16; *Neu Braunfelser Zeitung* [hereafter *NBZ*], June 6, July 3, 1863, and elsewhere.

14. Similar patterns show up in a statewide quantitative analysis of the secession referendum. Lutherans, the denomination most unambiguously German, were estimated to have given no votes for secession and at least 80 percent against. Catholics, ethnically mixed with a considerable German component, showed the highest proportion of stay-at-homes, at least two-thirds. The largest Anglo-Protestant denominations, Methodist, Baptist, and Presbyterian, all gave around 50 percent support to secession and only 6–12 percent opposition, the other 40 percent or so not voting.

Robin E. Baker and Dale Baum, "The Texas Voter and the Crisis of the Union, 1859–1862," *Journal of Southern History* 53 (1987): 395–420, esp. table 10.

15. Marten, *Texas Divided,* 26, 76–77.

16. See for example Buenger, *Secession and the Union in Texas,* 83. In one instance of a family spanning the Mason-Dixon line, the brother living in St. Louis volunteered for the Union and rose to the rank of captain; the brother in Fayette County, Texas, appears to have avoided service altogether. With another family, however, a married brother in Fort Worth served the Confederacy, though no war letters have survived to indicate whether he volunteered; of his Illinois relatives, none of the married men served, but two single brothers in law did. Kamphoefner and Helbich, *Germans in the Civil War,* 120–30, 387–94.

17. Muster rolls of Voigt's, Wickland's, and Nathusius's companies, Waul's Legion, TSLAC; William Hander, diary, Feb. 7 (quote), 28, 1863 C.W. Hander Papers, CAH; Robert Voigt, letters, Dec. 18, 1862, Feb. 11 (quote), Mar. 31, 1863, in Kamphoefner and Helbich, *Germans in the Civil War,* 412–13, 417, 418. The complete muster roll of Capt. J. W. McDade's Austin County company was published by the *Bellville Countryman,* Mar. 8, 1862.

18. Carl Bauer Letters [translations], 1862–64, TSLAC.

19. Jordan, "Germans and Blacks," 92; Claude Elliott, "Union Sentiment in Texas, 1861–1865," *Southwestern Historical Quarterly* 50 (1947): 472–74. Contemporary accounts are given in the *Bellville Countryman,* Jan. 10, Mar. 28, 1863; and *NBZ,* Jan. 2, Mar. 13, 1863.

20. Richard N. Current, *Lincoln's Loyalists: Union Soldiers from the Confederacy* (Boston: Northeastern University Press, 1992), 136–37. The most complete compilations of accounts of the Battle of Nueces is contained in Guido E. Ransleben, *A Hundred Years of Comfort in Texas: A Centennial History* (San Antonio: Naylor, 1954), 79–126. For more details, particularly protagonists' routes and battle locations, see Underwood, *Death on the Nueces.*

21. Spurlin, *Civil War Diary of Charles A. Leuschner,* 12–14, 60, 93–96.

22. The importance of viewing the period from 1846 through 1876 as a whole rather than as three separate eras is emphasized in Randolph B. Campbell, "Statehood, Civil War, and Reconstruction, 1846–1876," in *Texas through Time: Evolving Interpretations,* ed. Walter L. Buenger and Robert A. Calvert (College Station: Texas A&M University Press, 1991), 165–66.

23. Chesley A. Mosman, *The Rough Side of War* (Garden City: Basin Publishing, 1987), 399–401. See also Oscar Haas, *History of New Braunfels and Comal County, Texas, 1844–1946* (Austin, Tex.: Steck, 1968), 196–7; and *NBZ,* July 14, 1865 (reporting a piece from the *San Antonio News,* July 7). The fact that even San Antonio, with its considerable Unionist element, did not risk an official celebration shows how unusual the New Braunfels festivities were. In Vicksburg, admittedly somewhat of a special case, the first time the Fourth of July was celebrated after the Civil War was 1942.

24. Cat Spring Agricultural Society, *A Century of Agricultural Progress, 1856–1956* (Cat Spring, Tex., 1956), 31–32.

25. *House Journal of the 12th Legislature of the State of Texas, First Session* (Austin, 1870), 803. On Zapp's Republican political career in Fayette County, see Theodora Vanderwerth Boehm, "Robert Zapp, German Texan Politician" (M.A. thesis, Texas A&M University, 2001).

26. Campbell, *Grass-Roots Reconstruction in Texas,* 27–62, 220, 222, 229.

27. Donald G. Niemann, "Black Political Power and Criminal Justice: Washington County, Texas, 1868–1884," *Journal of Southern History* 55 (1989): 391–420.

28. Letters, June 22, Aug. 22, 1888, Lehmann Collection, CAH.

29. Jeanette H. Flachmeier, "Wurzbach, Harry McLeary," in Tyler et al., *New Handbook of Texas,* 6:1095; "Wurzbach, Harry McLeary," Biographical Dictionary of the United States Congress, http://bioguide.congress.gov/scripts/biodisplay.pl?index=W000775 (accessed May 12, 2008). First elected to the 67th Congress, Wurzbach apparently lost his seat for the 71st Congress but successfully contested the election. He was again elected for the following term and died in office on November 6, 1931.

30. Gene B. Preuss, "Within those Walls: The African American School and Community in Lubbock and New Braunfels, Texas," *Sound Historian* (1998): 36–43; *U.S. History Transparency Set,* vol. 2 (Lexington, Mass.: D. C. Heath, 1996), table 43.

31. Edgar E. Robinson, *The Presidential Vote, 1896–1932* (Stanford: Stanford University Press, 1947), 117; Richard M. Scammon, ed., *Americans at the Polls, 1920–64* (New York: Arno, 1976), 437–52.

32. Bennett, *Kerr County,* 136; Meinrad Pichler, *Auswanderer: Von Vorarlberg in die USA, 1800–1938* (Voralberger Autoren Gesellschaft: Bregenz, 1993), 224–29.

33. For evidence on a nationwide level, see Walter D. Kamphoefner, "*'Auch unser Deutschland muss einmal frei werden'*: The Immigrant Civil War Experience as a Mirror on Political Conditions in Germany," in *Transatlantic Images and Perceptions: Germany and America since 1776,* ed. David Barclay and Elisabeth Glaser-Schmidt (Cambridge: Cambridge University Press, 1997), 87–107.

34. For an example of the kind of German most likely to "go native" in the antebellum South, see Struve, *Germans and Texans,* 76–78, 92–98; and Küffner, "Texas-Germans' Attitudes."

35. Machann and Mendl, *Krásná Amerika,* 35–38, 216–18; Baker, *First Polish Americans,* 64–77; George R. Nielsen, *In Search of a Home: Nineteenth-Century Wendish Immigration* (College Station: Texas A&M University Press, 1989), 94–96; Caldwell, *Texas Wends,* 62–63, 110. The *NBZ* reported on August 29, 1862, that Medina County elected as its officials by a 4-to-1 margin men who had been held prisoner for disloyalty. On June 19, 1863, it reported that cavalry surrounded Castroville, trying to capture the 160 conscripts in the county. Most were warned

and escaped, but of the 20 captured, 18 deserted and disappeared. Institute of Texas Cultures, *The Norwegian Texans* (San Antonio: University of Texas, 1970), unpaginated sections "1860" and "1865." Apparently the handful of antebellum Danish immigrants were of higher social status, came as isolated individuals, and were thus more integrated into Southern society. John L. Davis, *Danish Texans*, 12–14, 21–23, 32, 38–39.

36. The controversy involving Adolph Douai and the *San Antonio Zeitung* is well known (cf. Biesele, "German Attitudes toward the Civil War"), but for a Czech parallel, see Machann and Mendl, *Krásná Amerika*, 181; and *Bellville Countryman*, Aug. 4, 1860.

37. Baker, *First Polish Americans*, 68–73. On the experience of Germans, see Kamphoefner and Helbich, *Germans in the Civil War*, 447.

38. Nielsen, *In Search of a Home*, 96; Baker, *First Polish Americans*, 76–77; Machann and Mendl, *Krásná Amerika*, 37.

39. Deserter list published in *Bellville Countryman*, Dec. 27, 1862; Sean M. Kelley, "Plantation Frontiers: Race, Ethnicity, and Family along the Brazos River of Texas, 1821–1886" (Ph.D. diss., University of Texas at Austin, 2000), 391. Kelley covers some of the same ground as this article.

40. Baker, *First Polish Americans*, 84–96.

41. Civil War–era censuses have the drawback that they are primarily based on country of birth rather than ethnicity and tend to overlook groups such as Poles and Czechs. A more accurate reflection of the relative size of ethnic groups (including the second generation) is the 1887 enumeration made along with the agricultural census. Besides 33,807 British and Irish, it shows nearly 130,000 Germans, 100,000 more than all other Continental Europeans together. The latter excludes Czechs, who were not consistently enumerated. But five of their top six counties listed by Machann and Mendl (*Krásná Amerika*, 157–61) show nearly 13,000 Czechs and Moravians, and the other seven among the top twelve show about 3,000 of "all other" ethnicities, suggesting that there were fewer than 20,000 Czechs statewide (where "all other" came to 38,337). Nearly three hundred Wends were enumerated in Fayette County, but none in their main settlement of Lee County, where they probably constitute the majority of the 3,045 "Germans." L. L. Foster, commissioner, *First Annual Report of the Agricultural Bureau, 1887–88* (Austin, Tex., 1889), xlvi and passim.

42. Jordan, "Germans and Blacks," 96.

8. After the Surrender

1. Maris A. Vinovskis, "Have Social Historians Lost the Civil War? Some Preliminary Demographic Speculations," *Journal of American History* 76 (June 1989): 50.

2. Foster, *Ghosts of the Confederacy;* Gerald F. Linderman, *Embattled Courage: The Experience of Combat in the American Civil War* (New York: Macmillan, 1987);

Larry M. Logue, *To Appomattox and Beyond: The Civil War Soldier in War and Peace* (Chicago: Ivan R. Dee, 1996); Eric T. Dean Jr., *Shook over Hell: Post-Traumatic Stress, Vietnam, and the Civil War* (Cambridge, Mass.: Harvard University Press, 1997).

3. Campbell, *Southern Community in Crisis*, 24–27, 52, 190–91; Bureau of the Census, *Agriculture of the United States in 1860, Compiled from the Original Returns of the Eighth Census* (Washington, D.C.: GPO, 1864), 140–51, 240–42. (The cotton crop produced in San Augustine County in 1859 appears to have been the second largest in the state because it was reported incorrectly at 31,342 bales. The actual crop was 3,142 bales, far fewer than Harrison County produced.) Walter Buenger shows that it was not uncommon for Texas counties to support secession by 95 percent or more of the total vote cast. *Secession and the Union in Texas*, 164.

4. Campbell, *Southern Community in Crisis*, 200.

5. Campbell, *Southern Community in Crisis*, 200, 211–12, 216; Heartsill, *Fourteen Hundred and 91 Days in the Confederate Army*, xv–xviii, 2–14; Sifakis, *Compendium*, 99; A. J. Bailey, *Between the Enemy and Texas*, xv, 43–44. Walter P. Lane, though involved in the war from the outset, never served with the Lane Rangers. Ron Tyler et al., eds., *The New Handbook of Texas*, 6 vols. (Austin: Texas State Historical Association, 1996), 4:62–63.

6. Harold B. Simpson, *The Marshall Guards: Harrison County's Contribution to Hood's Texas Brigade* (Marshall, Tex.: Port Caddo, 1967); Campbell, *Southern Community in Crisis*, 201, 210, 216–17; Sifakis, *Compendium*, 106–8.

7. Campbell, *Southern Community in Crisis*, 201–2, 205–6, 210–11, 217; Sifakis, *Compendium*, 47–48; Douglas Hale, *The Third Texas Cavalry in the Civil War* (Norman: University of Oklahoma Press, 1993).

8. Campbell, *Southern Community in Crisis*, 204–2, 216–17; Sifakis, *Compendium*, 117–18; James L. Newsom, "Intrepid Gray Warriors: The 7th Texas Infantry, 1861–1865" (Ph.D. diss., Texas Christian University, 1995).

9. Albert Burton Moore, *Conscription and Conflict in the Confederacy* (New York: Macmillan, 1924), 13–15, 140–41, 308; *Marshall Texas Republican*, May 3, 1862. Word of the draft generally did not reach Texas until early May. See Francelle Pruitt, "'We've Got to Fight or Die': Early Texas Reaction to the Confederate Draft," *East Texas Historical Journal* 26 (Spring 1998): 7–8.

10. Campbell, *Southern Community in Crisis*, 206, 211–12, 216–17; Sifakis, *Compendium*, 74–75; McCaffrey, *This Band of Heroes*.

11. Campbell, *Southern Community in Crisis*, 206, 214; Sifakis, *Compendium*, 85–86.

12. Campbell, *Southern Community in Crisis*, 206, 214; Sifakis, *Compendium*, 125–26; Scott Dennis Parker, "'The Best Stuff which the State Affords': A Portrait of the Fourteenth Texas Infantry in the Civil War, 1862–1865" (M.A. thesis, University of North Texas, 1998).

13. Campbell, *Southern Community in Crisis*, 206–7, 214; Sifakis, *Compendium*, 40–41; Lane, *Adventures and Recollections*.

14. Sifakis, *Compendium,* 70–72, 88–90, 128–30; Tyler et al., *New Handbook of Texas,* 2:782, 6:802–3; Lowe, *Walker's Texas Division.*

15. Moore, *Conscription and Conflict,* is the basic work on draft laws in the Confederate States of America.

16. Index to the Compiled Service Records of Confederate Soldiers Who Served in Organizations from the State of Texas, Records of the Department of War, RG 109, NA; Compiled Service Records of Confederate Soldiers Who Served in Organizations from the State of Texas, Records of the Department of War, RG 109, NA. The search for Harrison County soldiers was aided greatly by a privately printed source, Jimmy and Patsy Oliphant, *Confederate Soldiers That Served in Units Formed in Harrison County, Texas* (Shreveport, La., n.d.). Also, Janet B. Hewett, ed., *Texas Confederate Soldiers, 1861–1865,* 2 vols. (Wilmington, N.C.: Broadfoot, 1997), the most extensive listing of Civil War soldiers from Texas available, proved extremely useful in identifying men from Harrison County by unit.

17. *Marshall Texas Republican,* 1861–65. For example, the issue of Apr. 27, 1861, carried the names of volunteers in the W. P. Lane Rangers, and the issue of June 8, 1861, carried the names of the Marshall Guards. The issue of September 9, 1862, carried a report on those killed, wounded, discharged, etc. from the Texas Hunters (Company A, Third Texas Cavalry).

18. Hans Peter Nielson Gammel, comp., *The Laws of Texas, 1822–1897,* 10 vols. (Austin, Tex.: Gammel Book, 1898–1902), 5:455–65; Muster Roll of the Harrison County Regiment, 1862, TSLAC.

19. Gammel, *Laws of Texas,* 5:675–76; Confederate Indigent Families List, 1863–65, TSLAC.

20. Hans Peter Nielson Gammel, comp., *The Laws of Texas, Supplementary Volume to the Original Ten Volumes, 1822–1897* (Austin, Tex.: Gammel Book, 1902), 182–85; Confederate Pension Application Files, 1899–1975, TSLAC.

21. Vertical Files on Harrison County Families, Harrison County Historical Museum Library, Old Courthouse, Marshall, Tex. Files with varying amounts of information exist for hundreds of families from the antebellum era.

22. The great majority of Harrison County soldiers served in what might be termed "regular" Confederate army units, but some, mostly older men, enlisted in Texas State Troop outfits that were organized in late 1863 and disbanded six months later without ever leaving the state. Harrison County men were found in three companies of one of these units, the First Cavalry Battalion, State Troops. It may be stretching the point to say that these men served in the Confederate army, but in an effort to be as inclusive as possible, they were counted as such. Sifakis, *Compendium,* 38.

23. *Marshall Texas Republican,* July 21, 1865.

24. For a summary of studies dealing with geographical persistence rates among populations in the mid-nineteenth century, see Campbell, *Southern Community in Crisis,* 380–82.

25. Application of Mrs. Addie Alford, 1926, Confederate Pension Application Files, TSLAC.

26. *Confederate Veteran* 5 (Aug. 1897): 427.

27. Application of John D. Hartley, 1899, Confederate Pension Application Files, TSLAC.

28. For examples of applications based on ailments related to "exposure," see Applications of W. R. Hargrove, 1899; Joseph Taylor, 1899; and David F. Hamilton, 1906, Confederate Pension Application Files, TSLAC.

29. Gaines Foster did not find significant evidence of post-traumatic stress disorder among Civil War veterans. "Coming to Grips with Defeat: Post-Vietnam America and the Post–Civil War South," *Virginia Quarterly Review* 66 (Winter 1990): 17–35. But Eric Dean found considerable evidence of a connection between military service and later mental problems. *Shook over Hell,* 91–114. John E. Talbott also has argued that the conflict created lasting mental stress for soldiers. "Combat Trauma in the American Civil War," *History Today* 46 (Mar. 1996): 41–47.

30. Application of James Rivers Boisseau, 1899, Confederate Pension Application Files, TSLAC.

31. *Marshall Texas Republican,* June 4, 1869.

32. Logue, *To Appomattox and Beyond,* 105–7; Foster, *Ghosts of the Confederacy,* 18.

33. *Marshall Texas Republican,* Dec. 25, 1865.

34. Case Files of Applications from Former Confederates for Presidential Pardons, 1865–67, U.S. Department of War, Records of the Adjutant General's Office, 1780s–1917, RG 94, NA. For an excellent description and analysis of the pardoning process after the war, see Brad R. Clampitt, "Two Degrees of Rebellion, Amnesty, and Texans after the Civil War," *Civil War History* 52 (Sept. 2006): 255–81.

35. Campbell, *Southern Community in Crisis,* 253–59; *Confederate Veteran* 5 (1897): 224.

36. Campbell, *Southern Community in Crisis,* 273–93, 337–43.

37. *Confederate Veteran* 28 (1920): 346.

38. Campbell, *Southern Community in Crisis,* 343–55; Tyler et al., *New Handbook of Texas,* 6:65. Republicans filed election appeals with the Texas Supreme Court, but the justices refused to hear their case on the grounds that it was a political rather than civil suit and as such could not be appealed to the highest court.

39. Election Registers, 1880–1900, Records of the Secretary of State, TSLAC.

40. *Members of the Texas Legislature, 1836–1939* (Austin: 1939), 17th–26th Legislatures; *Confederate Veteran* 21 (1913): 241.

41. *Confederate Veteran* 16 (1908): 112.

42. *Confederate Veteran* 14 (1906): 204–5; 30 (1922): 351.

43. Quoted in *Confederate Veteran* 23 (1915): 511.

9. "I Seemed to Have no Thought of the Past, Present, or Future"

1. *OR,* 48(1):193–94; E. J. Davis to William P. Doran, Aug. 3, 1876, E. J. Davis Letters, Rosenberg Library, Galveston, Tex.; E. J. Davis to Doran, Aug. 26, 1876, ibid.; *Galveston Daily News,* June 2, 1865.

2. Stanley Testimony, Feb. 7, 1866, in *Report of the Joint Committee on Reconstruction,* 39th Cong. 1st sess., H. Rpt. 30, pt. 4, 38 (Strong quote), 40 (Stanley quote).

3. Clampitt, "The Breakup," 533. See also White, "Disintegration of an Army," 40–47.

4. Crouch, *Freedmen's Bureau and Black Texans,* 12.

5. Since all of the units referred to in his chapter are Texas units, the state will not be used and the branch of service referenced instead.

6. Fletcher, *Rebel Private,* 3.

7. A. Cameron to Permelia Cameron, Apr. 28, 1862, in "A Soldiers Fare is Rough: Letters from A. Cameron in the Indian Territory, Arkansas Campaign, 1862–1864," ed. J. S. Duncan, *Military History of Texas and the Southwest* 12 (1975–76): 43; Bill O'Neal, ed., "The Civil War Memoirs of Samuel Alonza Cooke," *Southwestern Historical Quarterly* 74 (Apr. 1971): 536; John W. Hill to My Dear Sister, June 21, 1863, John W. Hill Papers, CAH, typescript; D. Port Smythe to My Dear Lou, July 19, 1861, in "Some Civil War Letters of D. Port Smythe," ed. John T. Duncan, *West Texas Historical Association Year Book* 37 (Oct. 1961): 163.

8. T. Holmes to Dear Harriet, Nov. 4, 1862, in Johansson, *Widows by the Thousand,* 9; John H. Hill to My Dear Sister, June 21, 1863, John W. Hill Papers, CAH, typescript; J. H. Manahan to Dear Friend, Apr. 4, 1862, James H. Manahan Letters, CAH.

9. Ernest W. Winkler, ed., *Journal of the Secession Convention of Texas, 1861* (Austin, Tex.: Austin Printing, 1912), 61–65 (quotes, 63, 64); Blackburn, Giles, and Dodd, *Terry Texas Ranger Trilogy,* 180–81; Rudolph to Family, Apr. 28, 1865, in Goyne, *Lone Star and Double Eagle,* 169.

10. E. P. Becton to My Dear Mary, Dec. 14, 1862, Edwin P. Becton Letters, CAH; J. K. Street to My Dear Ninnie, Mar. 3, 1862, John K. Street and Melinda East (Pace) Papers, Southern Historical Collection, University of North Carolina at Chapel Hill; John H. Hill to My Dear Sister, Jan. 8, 1865, John W. Hill Papers, CAH, typescript.

11. John H. Hill to My Dear Sister, Jan. 8, 1865.

12. Dee Ridley to My Very Dear Sisters, Jan. 19, 1865, Gee Library Archives, Texas A&M University at Commerce, transcriptions online at http://gen.1starnet.com/civilwar/deeridly.htm (accessed July 10, 2007); V. Ellis to My Dear Wife, Feb. 19, 1863, in Cutrer, "'Experience in Soldier's Life,'" 127; Bob Hill to My Dear Sister, Apr. 29, 1864, John W. Hill Papers, CAH, typescript.

13. C. W. Trueheart to Dear Father, Dec. 31, 1864, in E. B. Williams, *Rebel Brothers,* 135; E. G. Littlejohn to My dear Wife and Friends, Apr. 8, 1865, addition of May 4, 1865, in "The Civil War Letters of Eldbridge Littlejohn," ed. Vicki Betts, *Chronicles of Smith County, Texas* 18 (Summer 1979): 37; L. L. Wright to Dear Wife, Feb. 19, 1865, in Bitton, *Reminiscences and Civil War Letters of Levi Lamoni Wright,* 174.

14. Judy Watson McClure, ed., *The Civil War Letters of James Monroe Watson*

(Quannah, Tex.: Nortex, 1976), 32; Sam Watson to H. C. Lewis, Feb. 26, 1865, Harriet C. Lewis Papers, Special Collections, Duke University.

15. S. F. Foster to Dear May, Feb. 24, 1865, S. F. Foster Papers, CAH; E. G. Littlejohn to My dear Wife and Friends, Jan. 22, 1865, in Betts, "Civil War Letters of Eldbridge Littlejohn," 34; D. Boyd to Robert Boyd, Mar. 29, 1865, Robert Boyd Papers, Special Collections, Duke University Library, Durham, N.C.

16. O. C. Connor to Mary America Connor, Feb. 19, 1865, in Connor, *Dear America,* 106–7; Rudolph to Family, Apr. 28, 1865, in Goyne, *Lone Star and Double Eagle,* 169.

17. J. W. Rabb to Dear Ma, Jan. 11, 1865, in Cutrer, "'We Are Stern and Resolved,'" 223; Robt. Hodges to My Dear Father, Mar. 25, 1865, in Darst, "Robert Hodges Jr.," 39.

18. John H. Hill to Dear Sister, Jan. 7, 1865, John W. Hill Papers, CAH, type-script; [H. Trueheart] to My darling Mother, Apr. 24, 1865, in E. B. Williams, *Rebel Brothers,* 217.

19. Fletcher, *Rebel Private,* 145; Brown, *One of Cleburne's Command,* 170; J. W. Watkins to My Dear Irene, May 12, 1865, J. W. Watkins, Tenth Texas Cavalry File, THM; Spurlin, *Civil War Diary of Charles A. Leuschner,* 54.

20. Dunbar Affleck to Mrs. Thomas Affleck, Dec. 3, 1864, in Williams and Wooster, "Confederate Cavalry in East Texas," 18; James Black to Dearest Patience, Jan. 1, 1865, James Black, First Texas Heavy Artillery File, THM; John Simmons to Dear Companion and children, Mar. 14, May 4, 1865, in "The Confederate Letters of John Simmons," ed. John Harrison, *Chronicles of Smith County, Texas* 14 (Summer 1975): 48, 53.

21. General Orders 20, Apr. 23, 1865, *OR,* 48(2):1285; Magruder to Kirby Smith, Apr. 28, 1865, ibid., 1294.

22. V. Ellis to My Dear Wife, Aug. 17, 1863, in Cutrer, "'Experience in Soldier's Life,'" 140; Dunbar Affleck to Mrs. Thomas Affleck, Dec. 3, 1864, in Williams and Wooster, "Confederate Cavalry in East Texas," 18; John Simmons to Dear Companion and children, Mar. 14 (quote), May 4, 1865, in Harrison, "Confederate Letters of John Simmons," 48, 53; James Black to Dearest Patience, Jan. 1, 1865, James Black, First Texas Heavy Artillery File, THM.

23. John Simons to Dear Companion and children, Mar. 15, 1865, in Harrison, "Confederate Letters of John Simmons," 48; E. G. Littlejohn to My dear Wife and Friends, Apr. 18, 1865, in Betts, "Civil War Letters of Eldbridge Littlejohn," 36.

24. James Black to Patience Black, Jan. 13, 1865, James Black, First Texas Heavy Artillery File, THM; Forshey Diary, Jan. 2, 1865, Caleb Forshey Papers, Mississippi Valley Collection, University of Memphis; John Simmons to Dear Companion and children, May 4, 1865, in Harrison, "Confederate Letters of John Simmons," 53; Walton, *Major Buck Walton,* 92

25. John Simmons to Dear Companion and children, Apr. 25, 1865, in Harrison, "Confederate Letters of John Simmons," 52; J. W. Watkins to My Dear Irene, May 12, 1865, J. W. Watkins, Tenth Texas Cavalry File, THM.

26. H. P. Bee to G. M. Bee, May 15, 1865, Hamilton P. Bee Papers, CAH; J. B. Magruder to E. Kirby Smith, May 16, 1865, *OR*, 48(2):1308; J. B. Magruder to E. Kirby Smith, May 16, 1865, p.s. Walker, ibid., 1309; James E. Slaughter to J. B. Magruder, May 19, 1865, ibid., 1313–14.

27. Ella Lonn, *Desertion during the Civil War* (New York: Century, 1928). For examples of more recent scholarship on the issue, see Richard Bardolph, "Confederate Dilemma: North Carolina Troops and the Deserter Problem," pts. 1 & 2, *North Carolina Historical Review* 66 (Jan. 1989): 61–86, (Apr. 1989): 179–210; and William E. Emerson, "Leadership and Civil War Desertion in the Twenty-fourth and Twenty-fifth Regiments North Carolina Troops," *Southern Historian* 17 (1996): 17–33. Charles Grear touches on the movement of Texans in 1864 and 1865 and concludes that soldiers in the eastern theaters who considered coming home had no intention of returning to the fray in the East. "Texans to the Home Front," 22–23.

28. Jas. E. Slaughter to S. D. Yancey, Jan. 2, 1865, *OR*, 48(1):1311–13; Jas. E. Slaughter to A. H May, Jan. 30, 1865, ibid., 1353–55; Haas, "Diary of Julius Giesecke," *Texas Military History* 3 (Winter 1963): 54.

29. W. W. Hurley to Dear May, Apr. 3, 1865, W. W. Hurley Papers, CAH.

30. J. W. Watkins to My Own Dear Irene, May 16, 1865, J. W. Watkins, Tenth Texas Cavalry File, THM; J. B. Magruder to E. Kirby Smith, May 16, 1865, *OR*, 48(2):1308; James E. Slaughter to J. B. Magruder, May 19, 1865, ibid., 1313.

31. John Simmons to Dear Companion and children, Apr. 25, 1865, in Harrison, "Confederate Letters of John Simmons," 52; Rudolph Coreth to Family, May 19, 1865, in Goyne, *Lone Star and Double Eagle*, 174.

32. Heartsill, *Fourteen Hundred and 91 Days in the Confederate Army*, 244; J. N. Bragg to My Dear Wife, May 20, 1865, in Gaughan, *Letters of a Confederate Surgeon*, 276.

33. Blessington, *Campaigns of Walker's Texas Division*, 307; W. P. Ballinger Diary, May 13, 1865, W. P. Ballinger Papers, CAH.

34. *Confederate Veteran* 6, no. 11 (Nov. 1898): 526; J. W. Watkins to My Own Dear Irene, May 16, 1865, J. W. Watkins, Tenth Texas Cavalry File, THM. Baylor's comments on Poland reflected the general view of that nation's history at the time. After having been an independent nation into the eighteenth century, it was torn apart by its stronger nations a few decades later. By the time of Baylor's comments, Poland had been partitioned among Russia, Prussia, and Austria and had come to represent a classic example of failed nationalism.

35. J. W. Watkins to My Own Dear Irene, May 16, 1865, J. W. Watkins, Tenth Texas Cavalry File, THM; Fletcher, *Rebel Private*, 194 (first quote), 212 (second quote).

36. Walton, *Major Buck Walton*, 94; Gustavus W. Dyer and John Trotwood Moore, comps., *The Tennessee Civil War Veterans Questionnaires*, vol. 3 (Easley, S.C.: Southern Historical Press, 1985), 1070; Fletcher, *Rebel Private*, 213.

37. John Cochran to Matthew Gault, Feb. 27, 1866, Matthew Gault Papers,

Special Collections, Duke University Library, Durham, N.C.; F. B. Sexton to A. B. Springs, Mar. 10, 1866, Springs Family Papers, Southern History Collection, University of North Carolina at Chapel Hill.

38. William P. Ballinger Diary, May 13, 1865, in William P. Ballinger Papers, CAH.

39. Fletcher, *Rebel Private*, 195.

10. Causes Lost, But Not Forgotten

1. *Daily Texan*, Apr. 9, 10, 1990; "Program from the First Annual University of Texas Round-Up, Apr. 12, 1930," UT Ephemera Collection, CAH.

2. *Daily Texan*, Apr. 12, 13, 1990.

3. *Daily Texan*, Sept. 5, 6, 1989.

4. Mrs. W. M. Imboden to Maj. George W. Littlefield, May 5, 1914, George Washington Littlefield Papers, 1860–1942, CAH. For the concept of the South's place in the reunified nation, see Nina Silber, *The Romance of Reunion: Northerners and Southerners, 1865–1900* (Chapel Hill: University of North Carolina Press, 1993).

5. Haley, *George Littlefield*, chap. 1; David B. Gracy, "George Washington Littlefield: A Biography in Business" (Ph.D. diss., Texas Tech University, 1971); Lewis E. Daniell, *Types of Successful Men of Texas* (Austin, Tex.: Von Boeckmann, 1890).

6. Robert E. Vinson, "The University Crosses the Bar," *Southwestern Historical Quarterly* 43, no. 3 (Jan. 1940): 290; David Blight, *Race and Reunion: The Civil War in American Memory* (Cambridge, Mass.: Harvard University Press, 2001), 157–58; Foster, *Ghosts of the Confederacy*, 106; Gary Gallagher, "Jubal Early, the Lost Cause, and Civil War History," in *The Lost Cause and Civil War History*, ed. Gary Gallagher and Alan T. Nolan (Bloomington: Indiana University Press, 2000), 43; Foster, *Ghosts of the Confederacy*, 50–51; Thomas L. Connelly and Barbara Bellows, *God and General Longstreet: The Lost Cause and the Southern Mind* (Baton Rouge: Louisiana State University, 1982). On Early and his role, see Gallagher and Nolan, *Lost Cause*, chap. 1.

7. Foster, *Ghosts of the Confederacy*, 106; Karen L. Cox, *Daughters of Dixie: The United Daughters of the Confederacy and the Preservation of Confederate Culture* (Gainesville: University Press of Florida, 2002), 10–19; Thomas Fletcher Harwell, *Eighty Years under the Stars and Bars, Including Biographical Sketches of "100 Confederate Soldiers I Have Known": Information Concerning the Organization of the United Confederate Veterans Organization and History of Camp Ben McCulloch, United Confederate Veterans* (Kyle, Tex.: W. Turner Harwell, 1947), 10–15; Michael Kammen, *Mystic Chords of Memory: The Transformation of Tradition in American Culture* (New York: Knopf, 1991), 110–11. To avoid confusion with the U.S. Colored Volunteers, the United Sons of Confederate Veterans dropped the word "United" from their organization in 1908.

8. Blight, *Race and Reunion,* 273–74, 290–91 (quotations).

9. F. A. Bailey, "Free Speech and the 'Lost Cause' in Texas," 456–57.

10. *Confederate Veteran* 3 (1895): 355.

11. Ben E. McCulloch Chairman to John B. Hood Camp, Dec. 31, 1896, Littlefield Papers, CAH; *Confederate Veteran* 6 (1898): 372–73; *Galveston Daily News,* May 18, 1895, Jan. 28, 1887; Coppini, *From Dawn to Sunset,* 70, 72–80; Henry E. Shelly to William von Rosenberg [President, Board of Trustees, John Bell Hood Camp, UCV], Apr. 20, 1897, Littlefield Papers, CAH.

12. According to a 1985 study by the Texas Veterans Commission, by the mid-twentieth century, forty-eight Texas counties had erected a statue, monument, or memorial to the Confederacy. See *Directory of Memorials, Statues, and Monuments for Veterans* (Austin: Texas Veterans Commission, 1985). The counties were Bell, Bowie, Brazos, Brewster, Caldwell, Cherokee, Collin, Comal, Comanche, Cooke, Dallas, Denton, Ellis, Fannin, Franklin, Foard, Galveston, Gonzalez, Grayson, Gregg, Harrison, Hemphill, Hill, Hood, Hunt, Jasper, Kaufman, Lamar, Madison, Marion, Matagorda, McLennan, Navarro, Parker, Polk, Red River, Smith, Terry, Throckmorton, Titus, Travis, Upton, Victoria, Walker, Wilbarger, Williamson, Winkler, and Wise.

13. *Galveston Daily News,* Oct. 13, 1895; Buenger, *Path to a Modern South,* 123–28; Cox, *Dixie's Daughters,* 72; *Galveston Daily News,* Apr. 25, 1897. On Van Rosenberg's efforts, see also *Confederate Veteran* 3 (1895): 355.

14. F. A. Bailey, "Free Speech and the 'Lost Cause' in Texas," 456, 462, 464–67; F. A. Bailey, "Best History Money Can Buy," 36–39, 41–42; *Confederate Veteran* 22 (1914): 390.

15. John B. Hood Camp History Committee to G. W. Littlefield, May 3, 1913, Littlefield Papers, CAH; *Confederate Veteran* 22 (1914): 390 (quote). See also F. A. Bailey, "Free Speech and the 'Lost Cause' in Texas," 467. The Hood Camp of the UCV regarded the Channing text as displaying a northern bias against the South. The letter reads: "We are in the possession of Channing's Student's History (so-called) of the United States and are reading it through carefully, marking pages, with the view of writing a specific criticism of it in the near future. . . . [I]t was written from a narrow, contracted, bigoted New England Stand point."

16. *Confederate Veteran* 10 (1902): 209–11.

17. Eugene C. Barker to Edward Mezes, Apr. 12, 1911, enclosed in Eugene C. Barker to George Washington Littlefield, Apr. 17, 1911, Littlefield Papers, CAH; "University Attacked on History Version," *Fort Worth Tar Telegram,* Mar. 23, 1914; F. A. Bailey, "Best History Money Can Buy," 39–42; John B. Hood Camp History Committee to G. W. Littlefield, May 3, 1913, Littlefield Papers, CAH; George Littlefield to Clarence Ousley, Apr. 24, 1914, ibid.; Minutes of the Board of Regents, The University of Texas at Austin, Apr. 28, 1914, Office of the Board of Regents, Austin, Tex., 377–80. For discussions of the power of Confederate partisan groups over academic historians, see Foster, *Ghosts of the Confederacy,* 180–91; and Fred A. Bailey, "The Textbooks of the 'Lost Cause': Censorship and the Creation of State Histories," *Georgia Historical Quarterly* 75 (Fall 1991): 507–33.

18. *Fort Worth Record,* May 1, 1914. For additional newspaper accounts heaping praise on Littlefield for his donation to create a southern history collection, see *Austin Statesman,* May 10, 1914; *San Antonio Express,* June 4, 1914; *Corsicana Daily Sun,* May 16, 1914; and *Cameron Herald,* June 25, 1914. Fred Bailey traces additional newspaper support for Littlefield's donation. "Best History Money Can Buy," 30. Praise for Littlefield's financial support cannot be confined to Texas, for copies of positive newspaper articles from South Carolina and Missouri are also found in Littlefield's personal papers.

19. *Laredo Daily Times,* May 17, 1914. See also F. A. Bailey, "Best History Money Can Buy," 29–49; and Buenger, *Path to a Modern South,* 127.

20. Undated newspaper clipping in Littlefield Papers, CAH. The newspaper continues: "God intends to use the Southerners race pride and the negro's religious faith and meekness and evolve a Christianity that will save universal humanity." For a sample of the congratulatory letters sent by individuals to Littlefield, see Mrs. W. M. Imboden to Maj. George W. Littlefield, May 5, 1914, Littlefield Papers, CAH; Manelda Le Grand Barker to G. W. Littlefield, May 1, 1914, ibid.; C. N. Avery to Dear Major, Apr. 28, 1914, ibid.; E. J. Mathews to Honorable George W. Littlefield, May 6, 1914, ibid.; Mrs. Mabel Mussey Bates to Maj. G. W. Littlefield, June 26, 1914, ibid.; and Ike Pryor to Maj. G. W. Littlefield, Mar. 4, 1918, ibid.

21. Mildred Lewis Rutherford to Dear Major Littlefield, Apr. 28, 1914, Littlefield Papers, CAH. For an itinerary of Mrs. Rutherford's tour of Texas, see also Mrs. Emma H. Townsend to Dear Sir, May 1, 1914, ibid. For Rutherford's background, see Fred A. Bailey, "Mildred Lewis Rutherford and the Patrician Cult of the Old South," *Georgia Historical Quarterly* 78 (Fall 1994): 509–35; and Grace Elizabeth Hale, *Making Whiteness: The Culture of Segregation in the South, 1890–1940* (New York: Vintage, 1998), 61–62.

22. J. Michael Martinez and Robert M. Harris, "Graves, Worms, and Epitaphs: Confederate Monuments in the Southern Landscape," in *Confederate Symbols in the Contemporary South,* ed. J. Michael Martinez, William Richardson, and Ron McNinch-Su, (Gainesville: University Press of Florida, 2000), 154–57. See also Hale, *Making Whiteness,* 252–53; and Kirk Savage, *Standing Soldiers, Kneeling Slaves: Race, War, and Monument in Nineteenth-Century America* (Princeton, N.J.: Princeton University Press, 1991), 209–13.

23. See Thompson, "When Albert Sidney Johnston Came Home to Texas," 476–78; "Extract from the Proceedings of the 'Terry Texas Ranger Association' at a Meeting Held in the Driskill Parlors on Nov. 16, 1904," Littlefield Papers, CAH; and "Monument to Hood's Texas Brigade on Capitol Grounds," ibid. Littlefield was the chairman of the Terry Texas Rangers Association Monument Committee.

24. *Dallas Morning News,* Mar. 3, 1918; Decca Lamar West to G. W. Littlefield, Sept. 8, 1919, Littlefield Papers, CAH.

25. Gaines, *Ghosts of the Confederacy,* 72–74, 95–98; Kammen, *Mystic Chords of Memory,* 125–26; Rev. S. A. King, "Birthday Anniversary of Jefferson Davis," Littlefield Papers, CAH.

26. Haley, *George Littlefield,* 214–15, 253.

27. Sibley, *George W. Brackenridge,* 52–53; Frantz, *Forty-Acre Follies,* 44–48; Haley, *George Littlefield,* 214–15.

28. Sibley, *George W. Brackenridge,* 242–45; Frantz, *Forty-Acre Follies,* 44–45; Vinson, "University Crosses the Bar," 284.

29. Coppini, *From Dawn to Sunset,* 208 (quote), 209. According to Coppini, Littlefield first broached the idea of building a campus memorial to the Confederacy as early as 1910, when he and the major first discussed the feasibility of creating an art school on the UT-Austin campus. See ibid., 181.

30. Morris Sheppard to Dr. Jas. P. Smith, Mar. 1, 1915, Coppini-Tauch Papers (hereafter cited as CTP), CAH; Coppini, *From Dawn to Sunset,* 256–57.

31. Haley, *George Littlefield,* 270; "Will and Codicils of G. W. Littlefield," Littlefield Papers, CAH; George Washington Littlefield to Robert Vinson, Dec. 22, 1919, ibid.; Coppini, *From Dawn to Sunset,* 261–62; "Contract, State of Texas, County of Travis, Apr. 20, 1920 [Read and Signed by George Washington Littlefield on June 9, 1920]," CTP, CAH. The will reads:

> I give and direct my executors hereinafter named to pay to Will C. Hogg of Houston, Texas, H. A. Wroe of Austin and the person who occupies the position of president of the University of Texas as trustees the sum of two hundred thousand dollars (200,000), said committee to use said sum or so much thereof as may be necessary to erect a massive bronze arch over the south entrance to the campus of the University of Texas in Austin, Texas. One the top of the arch, I wish them to place a life size statue of Jefferson Davis, the president of the Southern Confederacy, to his right and below him I wish them to place a life size statue of Robert E. Lee, commander of the Army of Northern Virginia, to the left of President Davis and below him and opposite the statue of Robert E. Lee, I wish them to place a life size statue of Albert Sidney Johnston, Commander of the Army of Tennessee. Under General Lee I wish them to place a statue of John H. Reagan, Postmaster General of the Confederacy, and below the statue of General Johnston, a statue of James S. Hogg, the peoples' governor of Texas. The space in the center between the two driveways can be filled as the committee deems best. I desire the arch lettered as follows: under the statue of Jefferson Davis, the following: "President of the Confederate States of America"; under the statue of Robert E. Lee: "Commander o the Army of Virginia"; under the statue of General Johnston "Commander of the Army of Tennessee"; under the statue of Mr. Reagan: "Postmaster of the Confederacy"; under the statue of Governor Hogg: "The Peoples' Governor of Texas" and at some prominent place the following: "This arch built and donated to the University of Texas by George W. Littlefield."

32. "Remarkable Memorial for Austin, Texas," CTP, CAH; Pompeo Coppini to Robert Vinson, July 3, 1920, ibid.

33. Robert Vinson to Pompeo Coppini, Apr. 11, 1921, CTP, CAH; Pompeo Coppini to H. A. Wroe, Nov. 10, 1921, ibid.; Pompeo Coppini to Robert Vinson, Sept. 28, 1921, ibid.

34. Buenger, "Texas and the South," 323–24.

35. Woodrow Wilson to Albert Sidney Burleson, Nov. 15, 1920, in *The Papers of*

Woodrow Wilson, ed. Arthur Link, 69 vols. (Princeton, N.J.: Princeton University Press, 1966–94), 66:369; Robert Vinson to Pompeo Coppini, Apr. 25, 1921, CTP, CAH. Coppini noted this in his autobiography and suggested that the real reason Wilson did not like Jefferson Davis was "[p]ossibly because they had so much in common." See Coppini, *From Dawn to Sunset,* 266.

36. Woodrow Wilson to Morris Sheppard, Mar. 22, 1923, in Link, *Papers of Woodrow Wilson,* 68:298. For Wilson's racial views, see Kendrick Clements, *The Presidency of Woodrow Wilson* (Lawrence: University Press of Kansas, 1993), 44–46; and John Milton Cooper, *The Warrior and the Priest: Woodrow Wilson and Theodore Roosevelt* (Cambridge, Mass.: Harvard University Press, 1983), 210–11.

37. Eugene C. Barker, *Two Gentlemen of the University of Texas: An Appreciation of Henry Winston Harper and William James Battle* (Houston: Rein, 1941).

38. W. J. Battle to Robert E. Vinson, Sept. 22, 1921, CTP, CAH. The fact that the Monument Committee attempted to portray the Littlefield Memorial as a symbol of national unity contradicted some of the contemporary newspaper accounts, which described the endeavor as a "Memorial to the Confederacy." In June 1924 the *San Antonio Light* reported that the first four figures to form the "George W. Littlefield Memorial to the southern Confederacy" were already completed. See *San Antonio Light,* June 8, 1924.

39. W. J. Battle to Robert E. Vinson, Sept. 22, 1921, CTP, CAH; Robert Vinson to Pompeo Coppini, Sept. 24, 1921, ibid.

40. Pompeo Coppini to Robert Vinson, Sept. 28, 1921, CTP, CAH; Pompeo Coppini to Harry Hertzberg, Sept. 29, 1921, ibid.; Harry Hertzberg to Pompeo Coppini, Oct. 7, 1921, ibid.

41. H. A. Wroe to Pompeo Coppini, Apr. 11, 1922, CTP, CAH; Pompeo Coppini to Robert Vinson, Sept. 28, 1922, ibid.; Robert Vinson to Pompeo Coppini, Jan. 31, 1923, ibid.; Pompeo Coppini to H. A. Wroe, Jan. 25, 1923, ibid.; Pompeo Coppini to James R. M. Morison, July 17, 1925, ibid.; Pompeo Coppini to J. R. M. Morison, Jan. 30, 1926, ibid.; J. R. M. Morison to Pompeo Coppini, Dec. 23, 1926, ibid.; Pompeo Coppini to Dr. William R. Splawn, Will Hogg, H. A. Wroe, Trustees of the Major Littlefield Memorial for the University of Texas, Dec. 21, 1923, ibid.; Pompeo Coppini to Lutcher Stark, Feb. 19, 1927, ibid; Pompeo Coppini to Will Hogg, Mar. 3, 1927, ibid. See also J. R. M. Morison to Pompeo Coppini, Dec. 23, 1926, ibid.

42. Pompeo Coppini to Dr. William Splawn, Dec. 29, 1927, CTP, CAH; Pompeo Coppini to James R. M. Morison, Apr. 20, 1928, ibid.; Pompeo Coppini to H. Y. Benedict, May 21, 1928, ibid.; H. A. Wroe to Pompeo Coppini, Apr. 5, 1928, ibid.; H. Y. Benedict to Pompeo Coppini, May 17, 1928, ibid.; Pompeo Coppini to H. A. Wroe, Mar. 26, 1929, ibid.; Pompeo Coppini to Harry Hertzberg, May 7, 1929, ibid.; J. R. M. Morison to Pompeo Coppini, Sept. 19, 1929, ibid.; J. R. M. Morison to Pompeo Coppini, Nov. 29, 1929, ibid.

43. H. A. Wroe to Pompeo Coppini, Dec. 9, 1929, CTP, CAH; Pompeo Coppini to Harry Hertzberg, Jan. 30, 1930, ibid. In the meantime Coppini fired off various

letters theorizing why the delays to the memorial had been so difficult to overcome. At one point he even assumed that the Ku Klux Klan had exerted additional pressure on the Board of Regents to refuse working with the Italian sculptor due to his ethnicity. Coppini also speculated that the delays stemmed from a personal affront from the university architect, who wanted sole control over the memorial's design. In another theory Coppini thought that the university officials simply did not "love the cause for which the state fought in 1861–1865." See Pompeo Coppini to J. R. M. Morison and F. Walker, Apr. 14, 1930, ibid.; Pompeo Coppini to H. A. Wroe, Jan. 30, 1930, ibid.; and Pompeo Coppini to J. R. M. Morison, Feb. 4, 1930 (quote), ibid.

44. Minutes of the Board of Regents, The University of Texas at Austin, Mar. 8, 1930, Office of the Board of Regents, Austin, Tex., 80–81; *San Antonio Express,* May 31, 1930; Leo C. Haynes to Harry Hertzberg, May 28, 1930, CTP, CAH; R. L. Batts to Harry Hertzberg, June 10, 1930, ibid.; Paul Cret to J. R. M. Morison and Frank Walker, June 30, 1930, ibid.; Pompeo Coppini to Caro Bartelli, July 9, 1930, ibid.; "Paul Cret at Texas," *Daily Texan,* Apr. 4, 1983; Minutes of the Board of Regents, The University of Texas at Austin, July 16, 1930, Office of the Board of Regents, Austin, Tex., 198–99.

45. See Pompeo Coppini to H. A. Wroe, Nov. 10, 1931, CTP, CAH; H. A. Wroe to Pompeo Coppini, Dec. 3, 1931, ibid.; Harry Hertzberg to Pompeo Coppini, Dec. 12, 1931, ibid.; and H. A. Wroe to Gentlemen, Jan. 6, 1932, ibid.

46. Harry Hertzberg to Judge Batts, Mar. 1, 1932, CTP, CAH; H. Y. Benedict to Harry Hertzberg, Mar. 17, 1932, ibid.; Harry Hertzberg to Pompeo Coppini, Mar. 22, 1932, ibid.; H. Y. Benedict to Harry Hertzberg, Apr. 2, 1932, ibid.; *San Antonio Express,* Oct. 2, 1932; *Daily Texan,* Aug. 21, 1932.

47. Harry Hertzberg to H. Y. Benedict, Jan. 3, 1933, CTP, CAH. It is unclear how much information Coppini had as to the final placement of the statues since Professor Battle and board member Lutcher Stark had reported that they had met with the sculptor and his architects in the weeks leading up to the finalized plan submitted by Cret. "Stark reported that in accordance with the Board's instructions he had visited Philadelphia and New York and held conferences with the Consulting Architect of the University and with the sculptor of the Littlefield Memorial Gateway, Doctor Battle being present at these conferences. Mr. Stark stated in substance that Mr. Coppini was in agreement with the new plan for the Memorial Gateway prepared by Mr. Cret and approved by the Board of Regents at an earlier meeting." See Minutes of the Board of Regents, The University of Texas at Austin, July 16, 1930, Office of the Board of Regents, Austin, Tex., 162–63.

48. Pompeo Coppini to Harry Hertzberg, Mar. 13, 1933, CTP, CAH. See also Pompeo Coppini to Harry Hertzberg, Mar. 21, 1933, ibid. Coppini wrote: "Cret the architect has acted like a snake that bites and poisons you after you warmed him." In his autobiography, written fifteen years after the monument unveiling, Coppini claims he attempted to talk Littlefield out of his plans to build a Confederate memorial because it would be resented by future generations. Coppini, *From Dawn to Sunset,* 255.

49. *Daily Texan,* Apr. 11, 15, 1933; Read Granberry to Harry Hertzberg, Apr. 7, 1933, CTP, CAH; Pompeo Coppini to Frank Huntress, Apr. 7, 1933, ibid.; Pompeo Coppini to L. E. Adin, Apr. 7, 1933, ibid.; Pompeo Coppini to Frank Huntress, Apr. 10, 1933, ibid.; Pompeo Coppini to L. E. Adin, Apr. 10, 1933, ibid.

50. *Austin American,* Apr. 29, 1933; *Daily Texan,* Apr. 29, 30, 1933; Pompeo Coppini to H. Y. Benedict, May 14, 1933, CTP, CAH; *San Antonio Express,* Oct. 16, 1935; Coppini, *From Dawn to Sunset,* 373–75. Marilyn Sibley notes that Littlefield's donations, in addition to the $200,000 left for the memorial and the $250,000 for the Southern Historical Collection, included $500,000 for the construction of a new main building, a $300,000 girls' dormitory, and his mansion. *George W. Brackenridge,* 244–45.

51. Texas House Bill 126, 42nd Legislature, Regular Session, chap. 8; "When Robert E. Lee Came to Austin," *Austin American Statesman,* July 5, 1925; *San Antonio Express News,* Jan. 18, 1931; *Fort Worth Press,* Nov. 6, 1934; *Greenville Banner,* Jan. 1, 1935; *Nacogdoches Sentinel,* Nov. 7, 1934; "South Honors Robert E. Lee," *Galveston Tribune,* Jan. 19, 1932; "Stay of Robert E. Lee in this Section is Recalled on Birthday," *San Angelo Standard,* Jan. 19, 1932; "Robert E. Lee Birthday Recalls His Days in Hill Country," *Austin American,* Jan. 19, 1932; *Brownsville Herald,* Jan. 20, 1932; *Alpine Avalanche,* Jan. 28, 1932; "Plan to Restore Robert E. Lee's Fort Completed," *American Statesman,* July 26, 1931; "General Lee Statue to be Erected Here," *Dallas Morning News,* Jan. 20, 1935; "Dollars Asked for Restoring Robert E. Lee Home," ibid., Oct. 11, 1931; "Texans Sought in Preparing Shrine to Lee," *Lubbock Avalanche Journal,* Oct. 11, 1931; "Model Completed for $50,000 Dallas Statue of Lee," *Dallas Morning News,* Jan. 27, 1935; Buenger, "Texas and the South," 323–24. For a study that ties Lee to Texas, see Carl Coke Rister, *Robert E. Lee in Texas* (Norman: University of Oklahoma Press, 1946). Rister, a native Texan, argues that Lee left the Lone Star State unaware of how the region helped forge his character. Thus the ties to Texas were strengthened in the post-depression era.

52. "Sweatt Signed at Law School," *Austin Statesman,* Sept. 19, 1950; "UT CO-OP Council Votes Integration: Negroes Acceptable in Housing," ibid., Mar. 7, 1956; "Stand-ins Continue on Drag," ibid., Dec. 14, 1960; *Daily Texan,* Mar. 13, 15, 1960, Dec. 20, 1963; Tim Taliaffero, "Oscar Leonard Thompson: UT's First Black Graduate," *Alcalde* 95 (May–June 2007): 30; Shabazz, *Advancing Democracy,* 95–117, 196–200.

53. Durden, *Overcoming,* 4–7; Gould and Sneed, "Without Pride or Apology," 67–70.

54. *Daily Texan,* Apr. 4, 20, 28, 29, 30, 1965. For a study on white southerners' reactions to the civil-rights movement and its parallels with the Civil War, see Jason Sokol, *There Goes My Everything: White Southerners in the Age of Civil Rights, 1945–1975* (New York: Knopf, 2007), 153, 159, 200, 202.

55. Beverly Burr, "A History of Student Activism at the University of Texas at Austin," 1988 (unpublished paper in the author's possession), 55–59, 61–63 ; *Daily Texan,* Mar. 2, May 2, 1989, Mar. 2, Apr. 27, 1990, Mar. 1, 1991, Mar. 3, 1992. The White Students' Association was created in 1986.

56. *Daily Texan,* Apr. 12, 13, 18, 24, 30, 1990. The battle over the statues is epitomized by opinion pieces during September 1990. On behalf of proponents of the statues, the arguments called Davis a "great man" and maintained that the former Confederate president did not fight for slavery but for "self-determination." This was countered by others who pointed that the Confederacy's conception of states' rights held slavery central to their beliefs. *Daily Texan,* Sept. 14, 18, 1990. Black enrollment at UT-Austin actually decreased by 1990, dipping to 5,573 students that year, down from 6,361 the previous year. But enrollment of Hispanics, Asians, and Native Americans increased during that same time. Ibid., Sept. 20, 1990.

57. *Daily Texan,* Apr. 18, 1991. The Native American Student Organization and Jewish student groups have urged the idea of multiculturalism at UT-Austin. See ibid., Aug. 16, 1990, Mar. 4, 25, 1991, Apr. 6, 1992.

58. *Daily Texan,* Sept. 11, 1989, Mar. 18, 1991, Apr. 16, 2001; *Report of the Task Force on Racial Respect and Fairness* (University of Texas at Austin, Jan. 2004), 4, 14; Avrel Seale, "Southern Living: How to Start to End the Confederate Statues Controversy," *Alcalde* 95, no. 4 (Mar.–Apr. 2007): 18–19; Rachel Proctor May, "Confederacy of Love," *Austin Chronicle,* Nov. 19, 2004. The groups that supported the statues include the SCV, the Texas Heritage Coalition, and the UDC. See *Daily Texan,* Jan. 24, 2001.

59. *Dallas Morning News,* Jan. 17, 2007.

11. "Tell It Like It Was"

1. "Experts Gather at UT Austin to Examine Controversial Alamo Memoir," Office of Public Affairs, University of Texas at Austin, available online at http://www.utexas.edu/opa/news/00newsreleases/nr_200001/nr_memoir000412.html/ (accessed Sept. 12, 2007). See also David B. Gracy, "'Just as I Have Written It': A Study of the Authenticity of José Enrique de la Peña's Account of the Texas Campaign," *Southwestern Historical Quarterly* 105 (Oct. 2001): 255–91; Carmina Danini and Laura Tolley, "Alamo Diary Owners Donate Historic Buy to UT-Austin," *San Antonio Express-News,* Dec. 16, 1998; Gregory Curtis, "Should We Care?" *Texas Monthly* 28 (Mar. 2000): 9–12; Art Chapman, "Debate Rages on over Davy Crockett," *Fort Worth Star-Telegram,* Apr. 27, 2000; and Candy Moulton, "Did Davy Crockett Die Fighting, or Was He Captured and Then Executed at the Alamo?" *Wild West* 11 (Feb. 1999): 62–65.

2. Curtis, "Should We Care," 12. See also Richard R. Flores, "Memory-Place, Meaning, and the Alamo," *American Literary History* 10 (Autumn 1998): 428–45; Richard R. Flores, "The Alamo: Myth, Public History, and the Politics of Inclusion," *Radical History Review* 77 (2000): 91–103; Edward Rothstein, "Remembering the Alamo Is Easier When You Know Its Many-Sided History," *New York Times,* Apr. 30, 2007.

3. Robert J. Cook, "(Un)furl that Banner: The Response of White Southerners to the Civil War Centennial of 1961–1965," *Journal of Southern History* 68 (Nov.

2002): 881. See also James Oliver Horton and Spencer R. Crew, "Afro-Americans and Museums: Toward a Policy of Inclusion," in *History Museums in the United States: A Critical Assessment,* ed. Warren Leon and Roy Rosenzweig (Urbana: University of Illinois Press, 1989), 213–36; and Robert J. Cook, *Troubled Commemoration: The American Civil War Centennial, 1961–1965* (Baton Rouge: Louisiana State University Press, 2007). For the mixed messages of some Civil War–era exhibits, see Buenger, "'Story of Texas'?" 481–93. In this review of the Texas State History Museum, Buenger notes that while the "creators of the museum carefully included prominent Tejanos, blacks, and women . . . , their approach to the Texas past is just as much from the top down and just as simplistic and celebratory as fifty years ago" (485).

4. See Ira Berlin, *Many Thousands Gone: The First Two Centuries of Slavery in North America* (Cambridge, Mass.: Harvard University Press, 1998); John Blassingame, *The Slave Community: Plantation Life in the Antebellum South* (New York: Oxford University Press, 1979); Eugene D. Genovese, *Roll, Jordan, Roll: The World the Slaves Made* (New York: Random House, 1976); Herbert G. Gutman, *The Black Family in Slavery and Freedom, 1750–1925* (Random House, 1977); Peter Kolchin, *American Slavery, 1619–1877* (New York: Hill and Wang, 1994); Philip D. Morgan, *Slave Counterpoint: Black Culture in the Eighteenth Century Chesapeake and Lowcountry* (Chapel Hill: University of North Carolina Press, 1998); Kenneth M. Stampp, *The Peculiar Institution: Slavery in the Antebellum South* (New York: Vintage Books, 1989); Chandra Manning, *What This Cruel War Was Over: Soldiers, Slavery, and the Civil War* (New York: Alfred A. Knopf, 2007); and David W. Blight, *Beyond the Battlefield: Race, Memory, and the American Civil War* (Amherst: University of Massachusetts Press, 2002). For the relationship between slavery and public history, see Jennifer L. Eichstedt and Stephen Small, eds., *Representations of Slavery: Race and Ideology in Southern Plantation Museums* (Washington, D.C.: Smithsonian Institution Press, 2002); and James Oliver Horton and Lois Horton, eds., *Slavery and Public History: The Tough Stuff of American Memory* (New York: New Press, 2006).

5. See David W. Blight, *Race and Reunion: The Civil War in American Memory* (Cambridge, Mass.: Harvard University Press, 2001); Susan-Mary Grant and Peter J. Parish, eds. *Legacy of Disunion: The Enduring Significance of the American Civil War* (Baton Rouge: Louisiana State University Press, 2003); W. Scott Poole, *Never Surrender: Confederate Memory and Conservatism in the South Carolina Upcountry* (Athens: University of Georgia Press, 2004); Timothy B. Smith, *This Great Battlefield of Shiloh: History, Memory, and the Establishment of a Civil War National Military Park* (Knoxville: University of Tennessee Press, 2004); Jim Cullen, *The Civil War in Popular Culture: A Reusable Past* (Washington, D.C.: Smithsonian Institution Press, 1995); David R. Goldfield, *Still Fighting the Civil War: The American South and Southern History* (Baton Rouge: Louisiana State University Press, 2002); Thomas A. Desjardin, *These Honored Dead: How the Story of Gettysburg Shaped American Memory* (New York: DaCapo, 2003); Karen L. Cox,

Dixie's Daughters: The United Daughters of the Confederacy and the Preservation of Confederate Culture (Gainesville: University Press of Florida, 2003); William Alan Blair, *Cities of the Dead: Contesting the Memory of the Civil War in the South, 1865–1914* (Chapel Hill: University of North Carolina Press, 2004); Christopher Waldrep, *Vicksburg's Long Shadow: The Civil War Legacy of Race and Remembrance* (Lanham, Md.: Rowman & Littlefield, 2005); Blight, *Beyond the Battlefield*; and Cynthia Mills and Pamela H. Simpson, *Monuments to the Lost Cause: Women, Art, and the Landscapes of Southern Memory* (Knoxville: University of Tennessee Press, 2003).

6. Historians typically rely on a definition of public history that is based in vocation—public historians are historians who do not teach in universities. In a recent discussion on H-Public, Kathy Corbett and Dick Miller proposed the following as a working definition for "public history": "Public history practice is a multidimensional effort by historians and their publics, collaborating in settings beyond the traditional classroom, to make the past useful in the present." See Debbie Ann Doyle, "Public History Defined?" available online at http://blog.historians.org/profession/236/public-history-defined/ (accessed July 9, 2007). Throughout my essay, when I refer to public historians, I am referring to those who work outside the traditional classroom, while I refer to academic historians as those who work within the traditional classroom regardless of location (i.e., middle school, high school, or university).

7. Dwight T. Pitcaithley, "'A Cosmic Threat': The National Park Service Addresses the Causes of the American Civil War," in Horton and Horton, *Slavery and Public History,* 169–186 (quotes, 173). See also John Hennessy, "Interpreting the Civil War: Moving Beyond Battlefields," *Cultural Resource Management* 4 (2002): 10–12.

8. Hennessy, "Interpreting the Civil War," 10.

9. Robert Kent Sutton, ed., *Rally on the High Ground: The National Park Service Symposium on the Civil War* (Fort Washington, Penn.: Eastern National, 2000), available online at http://www.nps.gov/history/history/online_books/rthg/ (accessed May 7, 2007). See also Kevin Levin, "Looking Beyond the 'Rally on the High Ground' Initiative," Civil War Memory, http://civilwarmemory.typepad.com/civil_war_memory/2007/07/looking-beyond-.html/ (accessed May 7, 2007).

10. Quoted in Pitcaithley, "'Cosmic Threat,'" 175 (emphasis in original).

11. Quoted in Pitcaithley, "'Cosmic Threat,'" 174–76.

12. Pitcaithley, "'Cosmic Threat,'" 176–177, 180; John Coski, "Historians under Fire: The Public and the Memory of the Civil War," *Cultural Resource Management* 4 (2002): 13.

13. Paul Duggan, "Texas Removes Confederate Symbols from Court," *Washington Post,* June 13, 2000; Steve Miller, "Bush Not All Texans' Favorite Son: Protesters Want Return of Symbol," *Washington Times,* July 8, 2000; *Daily Texan,* Apr. 16, 2001. See also "A Change of Mind in Austin," *The Economist,* June 3, 2000.

14. Avrel Seale, "Southern Living: How to Start to End the Confederate Statues Controversy," *Alcalde* (Mar.–Apr. 2007), http://www.texasexes.org/alcalde/featureptr.asp?p=2056 (accessed May 23, 2007); Howard Witt, "War Icons Conjure Up Bitter Past: From the Confederate Battle Flag to Statues, Texas Tries to Come to Terms with Legacy That Hasn't Much Gray Area," *Chicago Tribune,* Feb. 11, 2007.

15. "Bill Analysis, HB 459," House Research Organization, Texas House of Representatives, Mar. 21, 2007, http://www.hro.house.state.tx.us/PDF/ba80r/HB0459.PDF.

16. W. Gardner Selby, "Monumental Tiff Goes Poof," *Austin American-Statesman,* Mar. 21, 2007, http://www.statesman.com//blogscontent/shared-gen/blogs/austin/legislature/entries/ (accessed May 23, 2007). See also *Daily Texan,* Mar. 22, 2007.

17. *Daily Texan,* Jan. 16, Apr. 16, 2001; Kevin Levin, "Is a Museum the Right Place for Confederate Statues?" Civil War Memory, http://www.civilwarmemory.typepad.com/civil_war_memory/2006/12/is_a_museum_the.html/ (accessed May 23, 2007).

18. Sanford Levinson, *Written in Stone: Public Monuments in Changing Societies* (Durham, N.C.: Duke University Press, 1998).

19. John Coski, *The Confederate Battle Flag: America's Most Embattled Emblem* (Cambridge, Mass.: Harvard University Press, 2005), x–xi.

20. James W. Lowen, "The Shrouded History of College Campuses," *Chronicle of Higher Education,* Jan. 28, 2000, http://chronicle.com/weekly/v46/i21/21b00601.htm/ (accessed June 11, 2007); Sylvia Moreno, "In Waco, a Push to Atone for the Region's Lynch-Mob Past," *Washington Post,* Apr. 26, 2006.

21. Kristen Mack, "Texas Pressed to Apologize for Slavery," *Houston Chronicle,* Mar. 24, 2007; "A Symbol We Need: Austin, Put Apology for Slavery in Public Record," *Dallas Morning News,* Apr. 7, 2007; Moreno, "In Waco, a Push to Atone for the Region's Lynch-Mob Past"; "Black Leaders Waiting for Virginia's Apology," *Dallas Morning News,* Feb. 4, 2007.

22. Robert Penn Warren, *The Legacy of the Civil War* (Lincoln: University of Nebraska Press, 1998), 53–66.

23. Roy Rosenzweig and David Thelen, *The Presence of the Past: Popular Uses of History in American Life* (New York: Columbia University Press, 2000). See also the related Web site, http://chnm.gmu.edu/survey/.

24. Ira Berlin, "Coming to Terms with Slavery in Twenty-First-Century-America," in Horton and Horton, *Slavery and Public History,* 7.

25. Kim A. O'Connell, "Cash-Strapped Museum of the Confederacy," *America's Civil War* 19 (2007): 10; Bruce Courson, "In the Fray: Why Rural Museums Are Becoming Ancient History," *Wall Street Journal,* Dec. 27, 2005; Terry Teachout, "Sightings: Visit to an Empty Museum—What Happens When the Audience Leaves Town?" *Wall Street Journal,* Feb. 4, 2006; Susan Applegate Krouse, "Anthropology and the New Museology," *Reviews in Anthropology* 35 (2006): 169–82; "Visitors Slowly Returning," *New York Times,* Mar. 22, 2006; Sophie Forgan, "Building the

Museum," *ISIS,* 96 (2005): 572–85; Stuart Davies, "Still Popular: Museums and Their Visitors, 1994–2004," *Cultural Trends* 14 (2005): 67–105.

26. Roy Rosenzweig, "Everyone a Historian," http://chnm.gmu.edu/survey/afterroy.html/ (accessed May 3, 2007); David E. Kyvig, "Foreword," in *Defining Memory: Local Museums and the Construction of History in America's Changing Communities,* ed. Amy K. Levin (Lanham, Md.: AltaMira, 2007).

27. Carol May, "Those Little Museums by the Side of the Road," *Wall Street Journal,* Dec. 30, 2005; Ira Berlin, "Slavery in American Life," in Sutton, *Rally on the High Ground.*

28. Interview with Kevin Levin, Aug. 7, 2007.

29. James Oliver Horton, "Slavery in American History: An Uncomfortable National Dialogue," in Horton and Horton, *Slavery and Public History,* 37; Berlin, "Slavery in American Life."

30. Texas Historical Commission, http://www.thc.state.tx.us/ (accessed Sept. 14, 2007); Texas Historical Commission, *Texas in the Civil War: Stories of Sacrifice, Valor, and Hope* (Austin: Texas Historical Commission, 2002). *Texas in the Civil War* does not list the Texas State History Museum in Austin, which does include slavery in its interpretation.

31. Levin, "Is It a Rising or Setting Sun?" Civil War Memory, http://civilwarmemory.typepad.com/civil_war_memory/2007/04/confederate_her_1.html/ (accessed May 23, 2007).

32. Edward T. Linenthal, "Healing and History: The Dilemmas of Interpretation," in Sutton, *Rally on the High Ground.*

33. Barbara Franco, "History and the Long Now: Remarks at 2006 AASLH Annual Meeting," reprinted in *History News* 62 (2007): 19.

34. Coski, "Historians under Fire," 13–14.

35. Kevin Levin, "Why the Civil War Still Matters," Civil War Memory, http://civilwarmemory.typepad.com/civil_war_memory/2006/03/why_the_civil_w.html/ (accessed May 23, 2007).

36. Quoted in David W. Blight, "If You Don't Tell It Like It Was, It Can Never Be as It Ought to Be," in Horton and Horton, *Slavery and Public History,* 34.

37. Levin, "Why the Civil War Still Matters."

Selected Bibliography

Books

Acheson, Sam, and Julia Ann Hudson O'Connell, eds. *George Washington Diamond's Account of the Great Hanging at Gainesville, 1862.* Austin: Texas State Historical Association, 1963.

Alberts, Don E. *The Battle of Glorieta: Union Victory in the West.* College Station: Texas A&M University Press, 1998.

Bailey, Anne J. *Between the Enemy and Texas: Parsons's Texas Cavalry Brigade in the Civil War.* Fort Worth: Texas Christian University, 1989.

Baker, T. Lindsay. *The First Polish Americans: Silesian Settlements in Texas.* College Station: Texas A&M University Press, 1979.

Barker, Eugene C. *Two Gentlemen of the University of Texas: An Appreciation of Henry Winston Harper and William James Battle.* Houston: Rein, 1941.

Barrett, Thomas. *The Great Hanging at Gainesville.* Austin: Texas State Historical Association, 1961.

Baum, Dale. *The Shattering of Texas Unionism: Politics in the Lone Star State during the Civil War Era.* Baton Rouge: Louisiana State University Press, 1998.

Biesele, Rudolph L. *The History of the German Settlements in Texas, 1831–1861.* Austin: Von Boeckmann–Jones, 1930.

Bitton, Davis ed. *The Reminiscences and Civil War Letters of Levi Lamoni Wright: Life in a Mormon Splinter Colony on the Texas Frontier.* Salt Lake City: University of Utah Press, 1970.

Blackburn, J. K. P, L. B. Giles, and E. S. Dodd. *Terry Texas Ranger Trilogy.* Austin, Tex.: State House Press, 1996.

Blessington, Joseph P. *The Campaigns of Walker's Texas Division.* New York: Lange, Little, 1875.

Boswell, Angela. *Her Act and Deed: Women's Lives in a Rural Southern County, 1837–1873.* College Station: Texas A&M University Press, 2001.

Brown, Norman D. ed. *Journey to Pleasant Hill: The Civil War Letters of Captain Elijah P. Petty, Walker's Texas Division, C.S.A.* San Antonio: Institute of Texan Cultures, 1982.

———, ed. *One of Cleburne's Command: The Reminiscences and Diary of Capt. Samuel T. Foster, Granbury's Texas Brigade.* Austin: University of Texas Press, 1980.

Brundidge, Glenna Fourman. *Brazos County History: Rich Past—Bright Future.* Bryan, Tex.: Family History Foundation, 1986.

Buenger, Walter L. *The Path to a Modern South: Northeast Texas between Reconstruction and the Great Depression.* Austin: University of Texas Press, 2001.

———. *Secession and the Union in Texas.* Austin: University of Texas Press, 1984.

Caldwell, Lillie Moerbe. *Texas Wends: Their First Half Century.* Salado, Tex.: Anson Jones, 1961.

Campbell, Randolph B. *Gone to Texas: A History of the Lone Star State.* New York: Oxford University Press, 2003.

———. *Grass-Roots Reconstruction in Texas, 1865–1880.* Baton Rouge: Louisiana State University Press, 1997.

———. *A Southern Community in Crisis: Harrison County, Texas, 1850–1880.* Austin: Texas State Historical Association, 1983.

Connor, Seymour V., ed. *Dear America: Some Letters of Orange Cicero and Mary America (Aikin) Connor.* Austin, Tex.: Jenkins, 1971.

Coppini, Pompeo. *From Dawn to Sunset.* San Antonio: Naylor, 1949.

Cotham, Edward T., Jr. *Battle on the Bay: The Civil War Struggle for Galveston.* Austin: University of Texas Press, 1998.

———. *Sabine Pass: The Confederacy's Thermopylae.* Austin: University of Texas Press, 2004.

Crouch, Barry A. *The Freedmen's Bureau and Black Texans.* Austin: University of Texas Press, 1992.

Daddysman, James W. *The Matamoros Trade: Confederate Commerce, Diplomacy, and Intrigue.* Newark: University of Delaware Press, 1984.

Davis, John L. *The Danish Texans.* San Antonio: Institute of Texas Cultures, 1979.

Durden, Almetris Marsh. *Overcoming: A History of Black Integration at the University of Texas at Austin.* Austin: University of Texas at Austin, 1979.

Fletcher, W. A. *Rebel Private, Front and Rear: Memoirs of a Confederate Soldier.* New York: Dutton Books, 1995.

Foster, Gaines M. *Ghosts of the Confederacy: Defeat, the Lost Cause, and the Emergence of the New South, 1865 to 1913.* New York: Oxford University Press, 1987.

Frantz, Joe B. *The Forty-Acre Follies.* Austin: Texas Monthly, 1983.

Frazier, Donald S. *Blood and Treasure: Confederate Empire in the Southwest.* College Station: Texas A&M University Press, 1995.

———. *Cottonclads! The Battle of Galveston and the Defense of the Texas Coast.* Fort Worth: Ryan Place, 1996.

Gaughan, Mrs. T. J., ed. *Letters of a Confederate Surgeon, 1865–1865.* Camden, Ark.: Hurley, 1960.

Goyne, Minetta, ed. *Lone Star and Double Eagle: The Civil War Letters of a German-Texas Family.* Fort Worth: Texas Christian University Press, 1982.

Haas, Oscar. *History of New Braunfels and Comal County, Texas, 1844–1946.* Austin, Tex.: Steck, 1968.

Haley, J. Evetts. *George Littlefield, Texan.* Norman: University of Oklahoma Press, 1943.

Hall, Martin H. *Sibley's New Mexico Campaign.* Austin: University of Texas Press, 1960.

Heartsill, William W. *Fourteen Hundred and 91 Days in the Confederate Army: A Journal Kept by W. W. Heartsill. . . .* Edited by Bell I. Wiley. Jackson, Tenn.: McCowat-Mercer, 1953.

Hunt, Jeffrey W. *The Last Battle of the Civil War: Palmetto Ranch.* Austin: University of Texas Press, 2002.

Irby, James A. *Backdoor to Bagdad: The Civil War on the Rio Grande.* El Paso: Texas Western Press, 1977.

Johansson, M. Jane ed. *Widows by the Thousand: The Civil War Letters of Theophilus and Harriet Perry, 1862–1864.* Fayetteville: University of Arkansas Press, 2000.

Johnson, Frank W. *A History of Texas and Texans.* 5 vols. Chicago: American Historical Society, 1914.

Johnson, Ludwell H. *Red River Campaign: Politics and Cotton in the Civil War.* Baltimore: Johns Hopkins University Press, 1958.

Joiner, Gary D. *One Damn Blunder from Beginning to End: The Red River Campaign of 1864.* Wilmington, Del.: Scholarly Resources, 2003.

Jordan, Terry G. *German Seed in Texas Soil: Immigrant Farmers in Nineteenth-Century Texas.* Austin: University of Texas Press, 1966.

Josephy, Alvin M., Jr. *The Civil War in the American West.* New York: Knopf, 1991.

———. *The War on the Frontier: The Trans-Mississippi West.* Alexandria, Va.: Time-Life Books, 1986.

Kerby, Robert L. *Kirby Smith's Confederacy: The Trans-Mississippi South, 1863–1865.* New York: Columbia University Press, 1972.

Lane, Walter P. *The Adventures and Recollections of General Walter P. Lane, a San Jacinto Veteran, Containing Sketches of the Texan, Mexican, and Late Wars, with Several Indian Fights Thrown In.* Reprint, Austin, Tex.: Pemberton, 1970.

Lowe, Richard G. *Walker's Texas Division, C.S.A.: Greyhounds of the Trans-Mississippi.* Baton Rouge: Louisiana State University Press, 2004.

Lowe, Richard G., and Randolph B. Campbell. *Planters and Plain Folk.* Dallas: Southern Methodist University, 1987.

Machann, Clinton, and James W. Mendl. *Krásná Amerika: A Study of the Texas Czechs, 1851–1939.* Austin, Tex.: Eakin, 1983.

Marten, James A. *Texas Divided: Loyalty and Dissent in the Lone Star State, 1856–1874.* Lexington: University Press of Kentucky, 1990.

McCaffrey, James M. *This Band of Heroes: Granbury's Texas Brigade, C.S.A.* Austin, Tex.: Eakin, 1985.

McCaslin, Richard B. *Tainted Breeze: The Great Hanging at Gainesville, Texas, 1862.* Baton Rouge: Louisiana State University Press, 1994.

Moneyhan, Carl H. *Texas after the Civil War: The Struggle of Reconstruction.* College Station: Texas A&M University Press, 2004.

Parker, Richard Denny. *Historical Recollections of Robertson County, Texas, with Biographical & Genealogical Notes on the Pioneers & Their Families.* Salado, Tex.: Anson Jones, 1955.

Prushankin, Jeffery S. *A Crisis in Confederate Command: Edmund Kirby Smith,*

Richard Taylor, and the Army of the Trans-Mississippi. Baton Rouge: Louisiana State University Press, 2005.

Ransleben, Guido E. *A Hundred Years of Comfort in Texas: A Centennial History.* San Antonio: Naylor, 1954.

Richter, William L. *Overreached on All Sides: The Freedmen's Bureau Administrators in Texas, 1865–1868.* College Station: Texas A&M University Press, 1991.

Rugeley, H. J. H., ed. *Batchelor-Turner Letters, 1861–1864: Written by Two of Terry's Texas Rangers.* Austin, Tex.: Steck, 1961.

Shabazz, Amilcar. *Advancing Democracy: African Americans and the Struggle for Access and Equity in Higher Education in Texas.* Chapel Hill: University of North Carolina Press, 2004.

Sibley, Marilyn McAdams. *George W. Brackenridge: Maverick Philanthropist.* Austin: University of Texas Press, 1973.

Sifakis, Stewart. *Compendium of the Confederate Armies, Texas.* New York: Facts on File, 1995.

Smith, David Paul. *Frontier Defense in the Civil War: Texas' Rangers and Rebels.* College Station: Texas A&M University Press, 1992.

Spurlin, Charles D. ed. *The Civil War Diary of Charles A. Leuschner.* Austin, Tex.: Eakin, 1992.

Struve, Walter. *Germans and Texans: Commerce, Migration, and Culture in the Days of the Lone Star Republic.* Austin: University of Texas Press, 1996.

Taylor, John. *The Battle of Glorieta Pass: A Gettysburg in the West.* Albuquerque: University of New Mexico Press, 1998.

Texas Historical Commission. *Texas in the Civil War: Stories of Sacrifice, Valor, and Hope.* Austin: Texas Historical Commission, 2002.

Thompson, Jerry. *Colonel John Robert Baylor.* Hillsboro, Tex.: Hill Junior College, 1971.

———. *Henry Hopkins Sibley, Confederate General of the West.* 1987. Reprint, College Station: Texas A&M University Press, 1996.

———. *Vaqueros in Blue and Gray.* Reprint, Austin, Tex.: State House, 2000.

Tolbert, Frank X. *Dick Dowling at Sabine Pass: A Texas Incident in the War between the States.* New York: McGraw-Hill, 1962.

Townsend, Stephen A. *The Yankee Invasion of Texas.* College Station: Texas A&M University Press, 2006.

Tyler, Ron, and Lawrence R. Murphy. *The Slave Narratives of Texas.* Abilene, Tex.: State House, 1974.

Underwood, Rodman L. *Death on the Nueces: German Texans "Treue der Union."* Austin, Tex.: Eakin, 2000.

Wallace, Ernest. *Texas in Turmoil, 1849–1875.* Austin, Tex.: Steck-Vaughn,1965.

Walton, William M. *Major Buck Walton: An Epitome of My Life, Civil War Reminiscences.* Austin, Tex.: Waterloo, 1965.

Williams, Edward B., ed. *Rebel Brothers: The Civil War Letters of the Truehearts.* College Station: Texas A&M University Press, 1995.

Wooster, Ralph A. *Lone Star Blue and Gray: Essays on Texas in the Civil War.* Austin: Texas Historical Association, 1995.
———. *Lone Star Generals in Gray.* Austin, Tex.: Eakin, 2000.
———. *Lone Star Regiments in Gray.* Austin, Tex.: Eakin, 2002.
———. *Texas and Texans in the Civil War.* Austin, Tex.: Eakin, 1995.

Articles

Bailey, Anne J. "The Abandoned Western Theater: Confederate National Policy toward the Trans-Mississippi Region." *Journal of Confederate History* 5 (1990): 35–54.
Bailey, Fred Arthur. "Free Speech and the 'Lost Cause' in Texas: A Study of Social Control in the New South." *Southwestern Historical Quarterly* 97 (January 1994): 453–78.
———. "The Best History Money Can Buy: Eugene Campbell Barker, George Washington Littlefield, and the Quest for a Suitable Past." *Gulf South Historical Review* 20 (Fall 2004): 28–48.
Baker, Robin E., and Dale Baum. "The Texas Voter and the Crisis of the Union, 1859–1862." *Journal of Southern History* 53 (1987): 395–420.
Barr, Alwyn. "The 'Queen City of the Gulf' Held Hostage." *Military History of the West* 27 (Fall 1997): 119–38.
———. "Texas Coastal Defense, 1861–1865." *Southwestern Historical Quarterly* 65 (July 1961): 1–31.
Bell, Walter F. "Civil War Texas: A Review of the Historical Literature." *Southwestern Historical Quarterly* 109 (October 2005): 205–32.
Buenger, Walter L. "Secession and the Texas German Community: Editor Lindheimer vs. Editor Flake." *Southwestern Historical Quarterly* 82 (April 1979): 379–402.
———. "'The Story of Texas'? The Texas State History Museum and Forgetting and Remembering the Past." *Southwestern Historical Quarterly* 105 (January 2002): 481–93.
———. "Texas and the South." *Southwestern Historical Quarterly* 103 (January 2000): 309–26.
Clampitt, Brad R. "The Breakup: The Collapse of the Confederate Trans-Mississippi Army in Texas." *Southwestern Historical Quarterly* 108 (April 2005): 499–534.
Cutrer, Thomas W. ed. "'An Experience in Soldier's Life': The Civil War Letters of Volney Ellis, Adjutant, Twelfth Texas Infantry, Walker's Texas Division, C.S.A." *Military History of the Southwest* 22 (Fall 1992): 109–72.
———, ed. "'We Are Stern and Resolved': The Civil War Letters of John Wesley Rabb, Terry's Texas Rangers." *Southwestern Historical Quarterly* 91 (October 1987): 185–226.
Darst, Maury, ed. "Robert Hodges Jr.: Confederate Soldier." *East Texas Historical Journal* 9 (March 1971): 20–49.

Elliott, Claude. "Union Sentiment in Texas, 1861–1865." *Southwestern Historical Quarterly* 50 (April 1947): 449–77.

Gould, Lewis L., and Melissa R. Sneed. "Without Pride or Apology: The University of Texas at Austin, Racial Integration, and the Barbara Smith Case." *Southwestern Historical Quarterly* 103 (July 1999): 67–90.

Grear, Charles D. "Texans to the Home Front: Why Lone Star Soldiers Returned to Texas during the Civil War," *East Texas Historical Journal* 45 (September 2007): 14–25.

Haas, Oscar, trans. "The Diary of Julius Giesecke, 1863–1865." *Texas Military History* 3 (Winter 1963): 49–92.

Muir, Andrew F. "Dick Dowling and the Battle of Sabine Pass." *Civil War History* 4 (December 1958): 394–428.

Niemann, Donald G. "Black Political Power and Criminal Justice: Washington County, Texas, 1868–1884." *Journal of Southern History* 55 (1989): 391–420.

Preuss, Gene B. "Within those Walls: The African American School and Community in Lubbock and New Braunfels, Texas." *Sound Historian* (1998): 36–43.

Pruitt, Francelle. "'We've Got to Fight or Die': Early Texas Reaction to the Confederate Draft." *East Texas Historical Journal* 36 (Spring 1998): 3–17.

Roth, Jeffery M. "Civil War Frontier Defense Challenges in Northwest Texas." *Military History of the West* 30 (Spring 2000): 21–44.

Silverman, Jason H. "Confederate Ambitions for the Southwest: A New Perspective." *Red River Valley Historical Review* 4 (Winter 1979): 62–71

Smith, David Paul. "Conscription and Conflict on the Texas Frontier, 1863–1865." *Civil War History* 36 (September 1990): 250–61.

Stein, Bill. "Consider the Lily: The Ungilded History of Colorado County, Texas, Part 5." *Nesbitt Memorial Library Journal* 7 (January 1997): 3–59.

Thompson, Jerry Don. "When Albert Sidney Johnston Came Home to Texas: Reconstruction Politics and the Reburial of a Hero." *Southwestern Historical Quarterly* 103 (April 2000): 453–80.

Tyler, Ronnie C. "Cotton on the Border, 1861–1865." *Southwestern Historical Quarterly* 73 (April 1970): 456–77.

Vandiver, Frank E. "Texas and the Confederate Army's Meat Problem." *Southwestern Historical Quarterly* 47 (January 1944): 225–33.

Vinson, Robert E. "The University Crosses the Bar." *Southwestern Historical Quarterly* 43 (January 1940): 281–94.

White, William W. "The Disintegration of an Army: Confederate Forces in Texas, April–June 1865." *East Texas Historical Association* 26 (1988): 40–47.

Williams, Robert, Jr., and Ralph A. Wooster. "With the Confederate Cavalry in East Texas: The Civil War Letters of Pvt. Isaac Dunbar Affleck." *East Texas Historical Journal* 6 (March 1963): 16–28.

Woodworth, Steven E. "Dismembering the Confederacy: Jefferson Davis and the Trans-Mississippi West." *Military History of the Southwest* 20, no. 1 (1990): 1–22.

List of Contributors

Dale Baum is professor of history at Texas A&M University and is the author of *Counterfeit Justice: A Texas Freedwoman's Story*, *The Shattering of Texas Unionism: Politics of the Lone Star State during the Civil War Era*, and *The Civil War Party System: The Case of Massachusetts, 1848–1876*.

Angela Boswell is professor of history at Henderson State University and the author of *Her Act and Deed: Women's Lives in a Rural Southern County, 1837–73*.

Randolph B. Campbell is Regents Professor of History at the University of North Texas and has had numerous books published on Texas history, including *Gone to Texas: A History of the Lone Star State*; *An Empire for Slavery: The Peculiar Institution in Texas, 1821–1865*; and *A Southern Community in Crisis: Harrison County, Texas, 1850–1880*.

Joseph G. Dawson III is professor of history at Texas A&M University and is the author of several books on military history, including *Doniphan's Epic March: The First Missouri Volunteers in the Mexican War*, and edited *The Texas Military Experience: From the Texas Revolution through World War II*.

Charles D. Grear is assistant professor of history at Prairie View A&M University and has published three articles on Texas in the Civil War.

Julie Holcomb is lecturer of museum studies at Baylor University and form director of the Pearce Collections Museum. Currently she is currently completing her Ph.D. at the University of Texas at Arlington. She has edited *Southern Sons, Northern Soldiers: The Remley Brothers and the 22nd Iowa Infantry*.

Walter D. Kamphoefner is professor of history at Texas A&M University and author or coeditor of many books about German immigrants, including *Germans in the Civil War: The Letters They Wrote Home*, *The Westfalians: From Germany to Missouri*, and *News from the Land of Freedom: German Immigrants Write Home*.

Richard Lowe is Regents Professor of History at the University of North Texas and has published numerous books on Texas in the Civil War, including *Walker's

Texas Division, C.S.A.: Greyhounds of the Trans-Mississippi, A Texas Cavalry Officer's Civil War: The Diary and Letters of James C. Bates, and *The Texas Overland Expedition of 1863.*

Richard B. McCaslin is associate professor of history at the University of North Texas and is the author of numerous works on the Civil War and Texas history, including *The Last Stronghold: The Campaign for Fort Fisher, Lee in the Shadow of Washington,* and *Tainted Breeze: The Great Hanging at Gainesville, Texas, October 1862.*

Alexander Mendoza is assistant professor of history at the University of Texas at Tyler and author of *A Struggle for Command: General James Longstreet and the First Corps in the West, 1863–1864,* and several articles.

Carl H. Moneyhon is professor of history at the University of Arkansas at Little Rock and has published numerous books on the Civil War and Reconstruction, including *Texas after the Civil War: The Struggle of Reconstruction; Arkansas and the New South, 1874–1929; The Impact of the Civil War and Reconstruction on Arkansas, 1850–1874: Persistence in the Midst of Ruin;* and *Republicanism in Reconstruction Texas.*

Index

259

Charles D. Grear is assistant professor of history at Prairie View A&M University. He serves as book review editor for H-CivWar, and he has received the Lawrence T. Jones III Research Fellowship in Civil War Texas History for the Texas State Historical Association. He is also a recipient of the fellowship to the 2007 West Point Summer Seminar in Military History.

976.405 F252   INFCW
The fate of Texas :the Civil War and
 the Lone Star State /

CENTRAL LIBRARY
05/10